Graphing Technology Guide
Calculus

Benjamin N. Levy

with contributions by

George W. Best

D. C. Heath and Company
Lexington, Massachusetts   Toronto

Address editorial correspondence to:

D. C. Heath and Company
125 Spring Street
Lexington, MA 02173

Trademark Acknowledgments: TI is a registered trademark of Texas Instruments, Inc. Casio is a registered trademark of Casio, Inc. Sharp is a registered trademark of Sharp Electronics Corp. Hewlett-Packard is a registered trademark.

Published simultaneously in Canada.

Printed in the United States of America.

International Standard Book Number: 0-669-35379-5

10 9 8 7 6 5 4 3 2

Graphing Technology Guide
Calculus

Contents

Part I. Graphics Calculators

Detailed contents for these calculator chapters begin on page iv.

Part II. Computer Graphing Utility: BestGrapher

Detailed contents for these computer chapters begin on page vi.

Part I of this Guide *contains parallel topics for each calculator model.*

Locate the discussion for your calculator in the appropriate column of page numbers.

x = *1* Texas Instruments TI-81
x = *2* Texas Instruments TI-82
x = *3* Texas Instruments TI-85
x = *4* Hewlett-Packard HP 48G
x = *5* Casio *fx*-7700GB
x = *6* Sharp EL-9200/9300

Part II of this Guide *contains parallel topics for each version of the BestGrapher software.*

Locate the discussion for your computer in the appropriate column of page numbers.

x = *7* BestGrapher for the IBM
x = *8* BestGrapher for the Macintosh

Graphing Technology Guide

Calculus

Introduction to Part I

This Guide provides keystroke-level calculator commands and instructions for working through the exercises in your textbook through the first semester of calculus. It does not replace the instruction manual that comes with the calculator. Refer to that manual to learn how to use additional capabilities that your calculator may have.

In Part I, we use different typefaces to distinguish *keystrokes* that you press from the *text* of this guide. Thus MATH and ENTER will represent the *labels* on your calculator's keys.

Calculators have function keys that assume different behavior in different contexts. To clarify the effect expected from depressing a function key, we sometimes write F1 *[COMMAND]*, where F1 names the key and *[COMMAND]* represents its corresponding function in the current menu. In Chapter 4, since the HP-48G calculator has six white function keys, we write *[COMMAND]* to represent the function key below the menu item COMMAND.

For convenience, when you are asked to type a *number*, say 345.67, we shall express the keystrokes as 345.67, without any spaces between the individual keys, instead of writing 3 4 5 . 6 7.

The calculator manufacturers - Casio, Hewlett-Packard, Sharp, and Texas Instruments - have all been cooperative through the writing of this guide, and the author gratefully acknowledges their helpfulness.

CHAPTER 1

Texas Instruments TI-81 Graphics Calculator

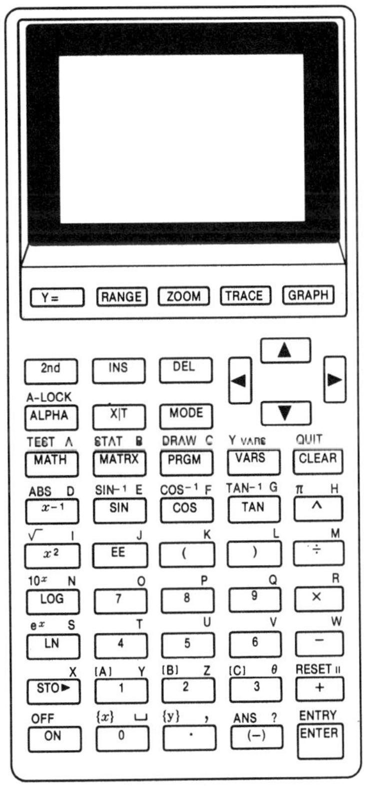

1.1 Getting started with the TI-81

1.1.1 Basics: Press the ON key to begin using your TI-81 calculator. If you need to adjust the display contrast, first press 2nd, then press and hold ▲ (the *up* arrow key) to increase the contrast or ▼ (the *down* arrow key) to decrease the contrast. As you press and hold ▲ or ▼, an integer between 0 (lightest) and 9 (darkest) appears in the upper right corner of the display. When you have finished with the calculator, turn it off to conserve battery power by pressing 2nd and then OFF.

Check the TI-81's settings by pressing MODE. If necessary, use the arrow keys to move the blinking cursor to a setting you want to change. Press ENTER to select a new setting. To start with, select the options along the left side of the MODE menu as illustrated in Figure 1.1: normal display, floating decimals, radian measure, function graphs, connected lines, sequential plotting, grid off, and rectangular coordinates. Details on alternative options will be given later in this guide. For now, leave the MODE menu by pressing CLEAR.

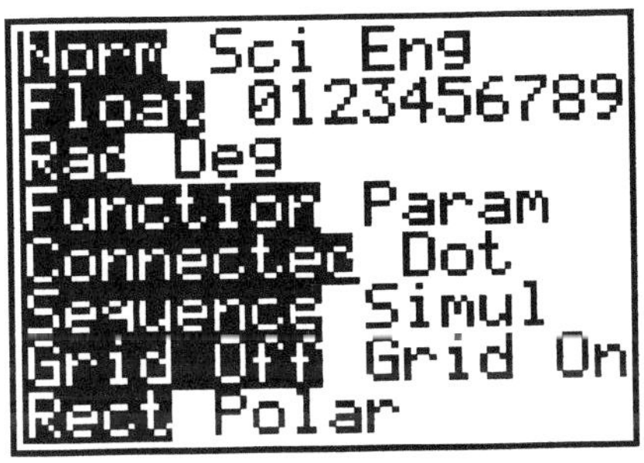

Figure 1.1: MODE menu

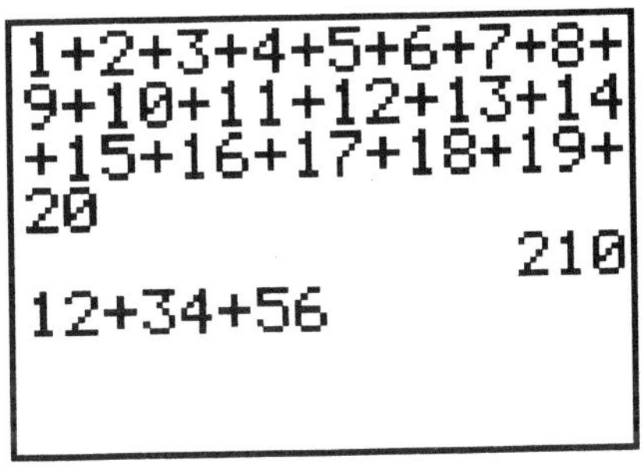

Figure 1.2: Home screen

1.1.2 Editing: One advantage of the TI-81 is that up to 8 lines are visible at one time, so you can *see* a long calculation. For example, type this sum (see Figure 1.2):

$$1 + 2 + 3 + 4 + 5 + 6 + 7 + 8 + 9 + 10 + 11 + 12 + 13 + 14 + 15 + 16 + 17 + 18 + 19 + 20$$

Then press ENTER to see the answer, too.

Often we do not notice a mistake until we see how unreasonable an answer is. The TI-81 permits you to re-display an entire calculation, edit it easily, then execute the *corrected* calculation.

Suppose you had typed 12 + 34 + 56 as in Figure 1.2 but had *not* yet pressed ENTER, when you realize that 34 should have been 74. Simply press ◄ (the *left* arrow key) as many times as necessary to move the blinking cursor left to 3, then type 7 to write over it. On the other hand, if 34 should have been 384, move the cursor back to 4, press INS (the cursor changes to a blinking underline) and then type 8 (inserts at the cursor position and other characters are pushed to the right). If the 34 should have been 3 only, move the cursor to 4 and press DEL to delete it.

Even if you had pressed ENTER, you may still edit the previous expression. Press 2nd and then ENTRY to *recall* the last expression that was entered. Now you can change it. If you have not pressed any key since the last ENTER, you can recall the previous expression by pressing ▲.

Technology Tip: When you need to evaluate a formula for different values of a variable, use the editing feature to simplify the process. For example, suppose you want to find the balance in an investment account if there is now \$5000 in the account and interest is compounded annually at the rate of 8.5%. The formula for the balance is $P(1+\frac{r}{n})^{nt}$, where P = principal, r = rate of interest (expressed as a decimal), n = number of times interest is compounded each year, and t = number of years. In our example, this becomes $5000(1+.085)^t$. Here are the keystrokes for finding the balance after t = 3, 5, and 10 years.

Years	*Keystrokes*	*Balance*
3	5000 (1 + .085) ^ 3 ENTER	\$6386.45
5	▲ ◄ 5 ENTER	\$7518.28
10	▲ ◄ 10 ENTER	\$11,304.92

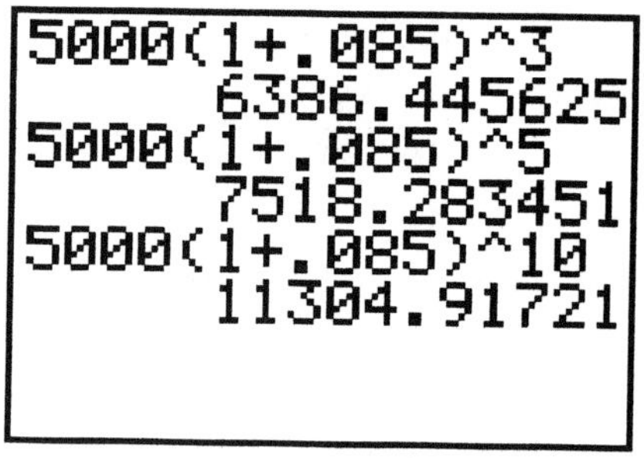

Figure 1.3: Editing expressions

Then to find the balance from the same initial investment but after 5 years when the annual interest rate is 7.5%, press these keys to change the last calculation above: ▲ ◄ DEL ◄ 5 ◄ ◄ ◄ ◄ ◄ 7 ENTER.

1.1.3 Key Functions: Most keys on the TI-81 offer access to more than one function, just as the keys on a computer keyboard can produce more than one letter ("g" and "G") or even quite different characters ("5" and "%"). The primary function of a key is indicated on the key itself, and you access that function by a simple press on the key.

To access the *second* function indicated to the *left* above a key, first press 2nd (the cursor changes to a blinking ↑) and *then* press the key. For example, to calculate $\sqrt{25}$, press 2nd √ 25 ENTER.

When you want to use a letter or other character printed to the *right* above a key, first press ALPHA (the cursor changes to a blinking **A**) and then the key. For example, to use the letter K in a formula, press ALPHA K. If you need several letters in a row, press 2nd A-LOCK, which is like **CAPS LOCK** on a computer keyboard, and then press all the letters you want. Remember to press ALPHA when you are finished and want to restore the keys to their primary functions.

1.1.4 Order of Operations: The TI-81 performs calculations according to the standard algebraic rules. Working outwards from inner parentheses, calculations are performed from left to right. Powers and roots are evaluated first, followed by multiplications and divisions, and then additions and subtractions.

Note that the TI-81 distinguishes between *subtraction* and the *negative sign*. If you wish to enter a negative number, it is necessary to use the (-) key. For example, you would evaluate $-5-(4\cdot-3)$ by pressing (-) 5 - (4 × (-) 3) ENTER to get 7.

Enter these expressions to practice using your TI-81.

Expression	*Keystrokes*	*Display*
$7-5\cdot3$	7 - 5 × 3 ENTER	-8
$(7-5)\cdot3$	(7 - 5) × 3 ENTER	6
$120-10^2$	120 - 10 x² ENTER	20
$(120-10)^2$	(120 - 10) x² ENTER	12100
$\frac{24}{2^3}$	24 ÷ 2 ^ 3 ENTER	3
$\left(\frac{24}{2}\right)^3$	(24 ÷ 2) ^ 3 ENTER	1728
$(7--5)\cdot-3$	(7 - (-) 5) × (-) 3 ENTER	-36

1.1.5 Algebraic Expressions and Memory: Your calculator can evaluate expressions such as $\frac{N(N+1)}{2}$ *after* you have entered a value for N. Suppose you want $N = 200$. Press 200 STO ▸ N ENTER to store the value 200 in memory location N. (The STO ▸ key prepares the TI-81 for an alphabetical entry, so it is *not* necessary to press ALPHA also.) Whenever you use N in an expression, the calculator will substitute the value 200 until you make a change by storing *another* number in N. Next enter the expression $\frac{N(N+1)}{2}$ by typing ALPHA N (ALPHA N + 1) ÷ 2 ENTER. For $N = 200$, you will find that $\frac{N(N+1)}{2} = 20100$.

The contents of any memory location may be revealed by typing just its letter name and then ENTER. And the TI-81 retains memorized values even when it is turned off, so long as its batteries are good.

1.1.6 Repeated Operations with ***ANS:*** The result of your *last* calculation is always stored in memory location ANS and replaces any previous result. This makes it easy to use the answer from one computation in another computation. For example, press 30 + 15 ENTER so that 45 is the last result displayed. Then press 2nd ANS ÷ 9 ENTER and get 5 because $\frac{45}{9} = 5$.

With a function like division, you press the ÷ key *after* you enter an argument. For such functions, whenever you would start a new calculation with the previous answer followed by pressing the function key, you may press just the function key. So instead of 2nd ANS ÷ 9 in the previous example, you could have pressed simply ÷ 9 to achieve the same result. This technique also works for these functions: + - × x^2 ^ x^{-1}.

Here is a situation where this is especially useful. Suppose a person makes $5.85 per hour and you are asked to calculate earnings for a day, a week, and a year. Execute the given keystrokes to find the person's incomes during these periods (results are shown in Figure 1.4):

Pay period	*Keystrokes*	*Earnings*
8-hour day	5.85 × 8 ENTER	$46.80
5-day week	× 5 ENTER	$234
52-week year	× 52 ENTER	$12,168

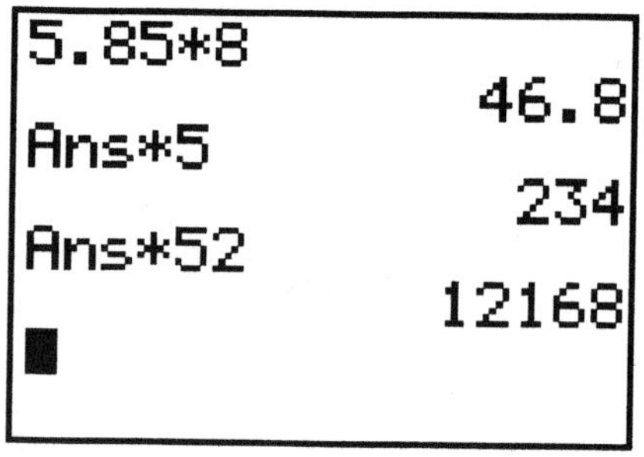

Figure 1.4: ANS variable

1.1.7 The ***MATH*** *Menu:* Operators and functions associated with a scientific calculator are available either immediately from the keys of the TI-81 or by 2nd keys. You have direct key access to common arithmetic operations (x^2, 2nd $\sqrt{\ }$, x^{-1}, ^, 2nd ABS), trigonometric functions (SIN, COS, TAN) and their inverses (2nd SIN^{-1}, 2nd COS^{-1}, 2nd TAN^{-1}), exponential and logarithmic functions (LOG, 2nd 10^x, LN, 2nd e^x), and a famous constant (2nd π).

A significant difference between the TI-81 and many scientific calculators is that the TI-81 requires the argument of a function *after* the function, as you would see a formula written in your textbook. For example, on the TI-81 you calculate $\sqrt{16}$ by pressing the keys 2nd $\sqrt{\ }$ 16 in that order.

Here are keystrokes for basic mathematical operations. Try them for practice on your TI-81.

Expression	*Keystrokes*	*Display*
$\sqrt{3^2+4^2}$	2nd $\sqrt{\ }$ (3 x^2 + 4 x^2) ENTER	5
$2\frac{1}{3}$	2 + 3 x^{-1} ENTER	2.333333333
$\lvert -5 \rvert$	2nd ABS (-) 5 ENTER	5
$\log 200$	LOG 200 ENTER	2.301029996
$2.34 \cdot 10^5$	2.34 × 2nd 10^x 5 ENTER	234000

Additional mathematical operations and functions are available from the MATH menu (Figure 1.5). Press MATH to see the various options. You will learn in your mathematics textbook how to apply many of them. As an example, calculate $\sqrt[3]{7}$ by pressing MATH and then *either* 4 *or* ▼ ▼ ▼ ENTER; finally press 7 ENTER to see 1.912931183. To leave the MATH menu and take no other action, press 2nd QUIT or just CLEAR.

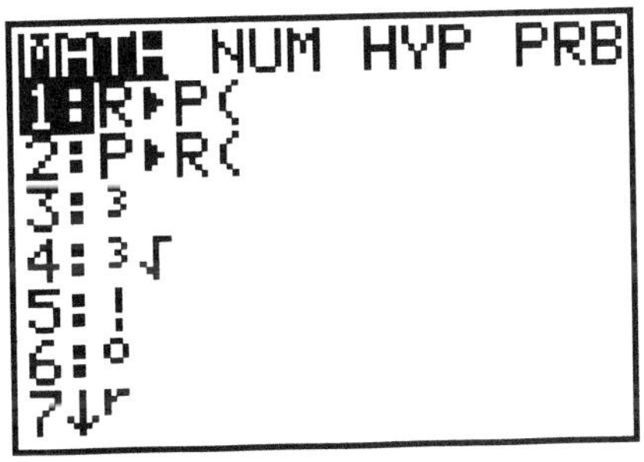

Figure 1.5: MATH menu

The *factorial* of a non-negative integer is the *product* of *all* the integers from 1 up to the given integer. The symbol for factorial is the exclamation point. So 4! (pronounced *four factorial*) is 1·2·3·4 = 24. You will learn more about applications of factorials in your textbook, but for now use the TI-81 to calculate 4! Press these keystrokes: 4 MATH 5 ENTER *or* 4 MATH ▼ ▼ ▼ ▼ ENTER ENTER.

Hyperbolic functions (sinh, cosh, and tanh) and their inverses are available from the HYP sub-menu of the MATH menu. For example, here are the keystrokes to calculate sinh 3: MATH ▶ ▶ 1 3 ENTER.

Note that you can select a sub-menu from the MATH menu by pressing either ◀ or ▶. It is easier to press ◀ once than to press ▶ three times to get to the PRB sub-menu.

1.2 Functions and Graphs

1.2.1 Evaluating Functions: Suppose you receive a monthly salary of \$1975 plus a commission of 10% of sales. Let x = your sales in dollars; then your wages W in dollars are given by the equation $W = 1975 + .10x$. If your January sales were \$2230 and your February sales were \$1865, what was your income during those months?

Here's how to use your TI-81 to perform this task. Press the Y= key at the top of the calculator to display the function editing screen (Figure 1.6). You may enter as many as four different functions for the TI-81 to use at one time. If there is already a function Y_1, press ▲ or ▼ as many times as necessary to move the cursor to Y_1 and then press CLEAR to delete whatever was there. Then enter the expression $1975 + .10x$ by pressing these keys: 1975 + .10 X|T. (The X|T key lets you enter the variable x easily without having to use the ALPHA key.) Now press 2nd QUIT to return to the main calculations screen.

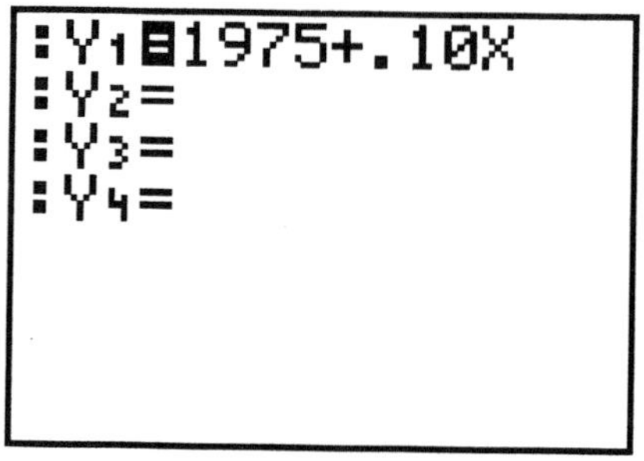

Figure 1.6: Y= screen

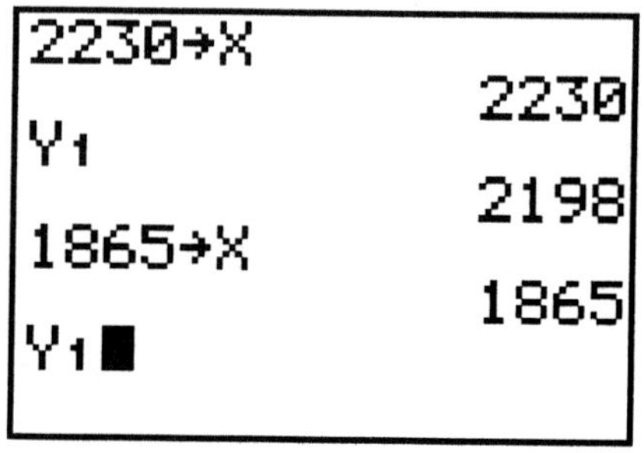

Figure 1.7: Evaluating a function

Assign the value 2230 to the variable x by these keystrokes (see Figure 1.7): 2230 STO▸ X|T ENTER. Next press the following keystrokes to evaluate Y_1 and find January's wages: 2nd Y-VARS 1 ENTER. Repeat these steps to find the February wages. Each time the TI-81 evaluates the function Y_1, it uses the *current* value of x.

Technology Tip: The TI-81 does not require multiplication to be expressed between variables, so xxx means x^3. It is often easier to press two or three x's together than to search for the square key or the cube operation. Of course, expressed multiplication is also not required between a constant and a variable. Hence to enter $2x^3 + 3x^2 - 4x + 5$ in the TI-81, you might save keystrokes and press just these keys: 2 X|T X|T X|T + 3 X|T X|T - 4 X|T + 5.

1.2.2 Functions in a Graph Window: Once you have entered a function in the Y= screen of the TI-81, just press GRAPH to see its graph. The ability to draw a graph contributes substantially to our ability to solve problems.

For example, here is how to graph $y = -x^3 + 4x$. First press Y= and delete anything that may be there by moving with the arrow keys to Y_1 or to any of the other lines and pressing CLEAR wherever necessary.

Then, with the cursor on the top line Y_1, press (-) X|T MATH 3 + 4 X|T to enter the function (as in Figure 1.8). Now press GRAPH and the TI-81 changes to a window with the graph of $y=-x^3+4x$.

Your graph window may look like the one in Figure 1.9 or it may be different. Since the graph of $y=-x^3+4x$ extends infinitely far left and right and also infinitely far up and down, the TI-81 can display only a piece of the actual graph. This displayed rectangular part is called a *viewing rectangle*. You can easily change the viewing rectangle to enhance your investigation of a graph.

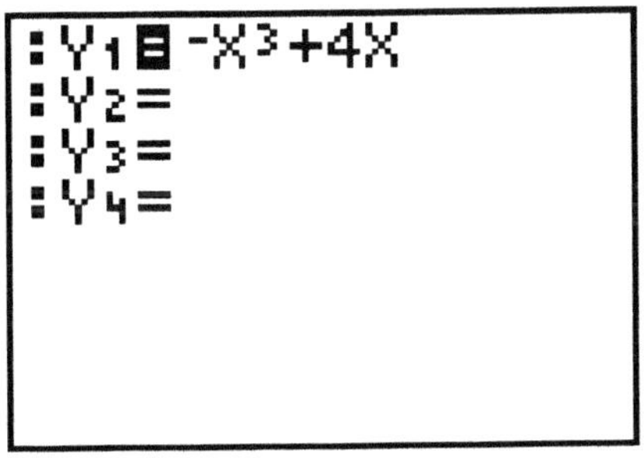

Figure 1.8: Y= screen

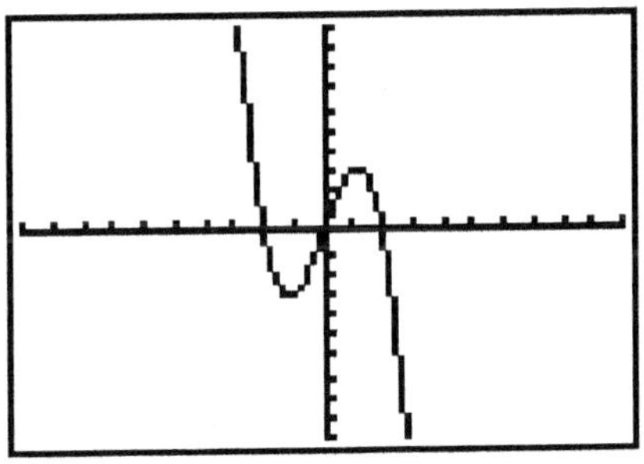

Figure 1.9: Graph of $y=-x^3+4x$

The viewing rectangle in Figure 1.9 shows the part of the graph that extends horizontally from -10 to 10 and vertically from -10 to 10. Press RANGE to see information about your viewing rectangle. Figure 1.10 shows the RANGE screen that corresponds to the viewing rectangle in Figure 1.9. This is the *standard* viewing rectangle for the TI-81.

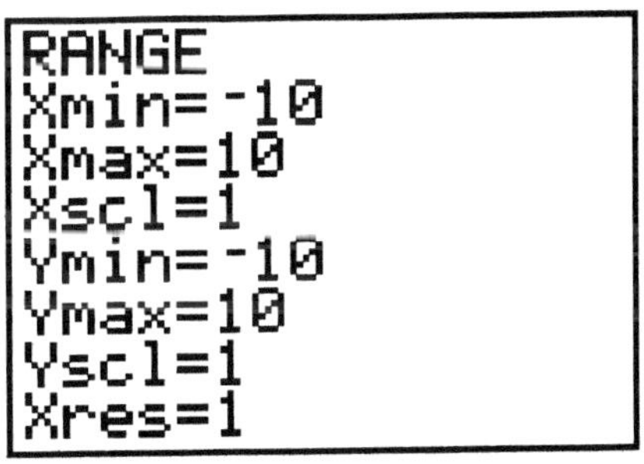

Figure 1.10: Standard RANGE

The variables Xmin and Xmax are the minimum and maximum *x*-values of the viewing rectangle; Ymin and Ymax are its minimum and maximum *y*-values.

Xscl and Yscl set the spacing between tick marks on the axes.

Xres is an integer from 1 to 8 that controls the resolution of the plot and also the speed of plotting. When Xres = 1, the calculator evaluates the function and plots a point 96 times along the *x*-axis. When Xres = 2, the calculator evaluates and plots at every *second* point, 48 times along the x-axis. Keep Xres = 1 to have the best resolution for your graphs.

Use the arrow keys ▲ and ▼ to move up and down from one line to another in this list; pressing the ENTER key will move down the list. Press CLEAR to delete the current value and then enter a new value. You may also edit the entry as you would edit an expression. Remember that a minimum *must* be less than the corresponding maximum or the TI-81 will issue an error message. Also, remember to use the (-) key, not - (which is subtraction), when you want to enter a negative value. The following figures show different RANGE screens and the corresponding viewing rectangle for each one.

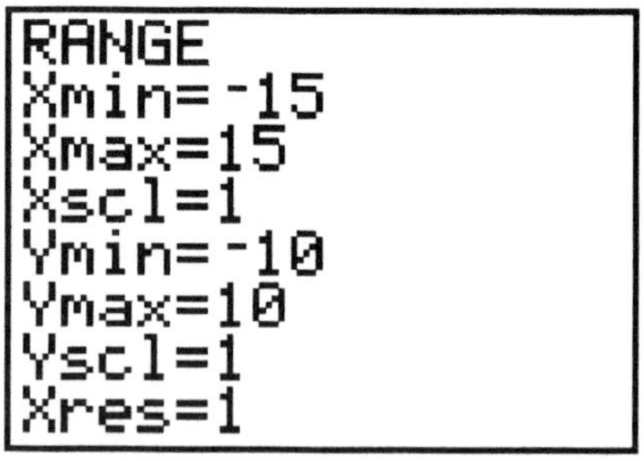

Figure 1.11: Square window

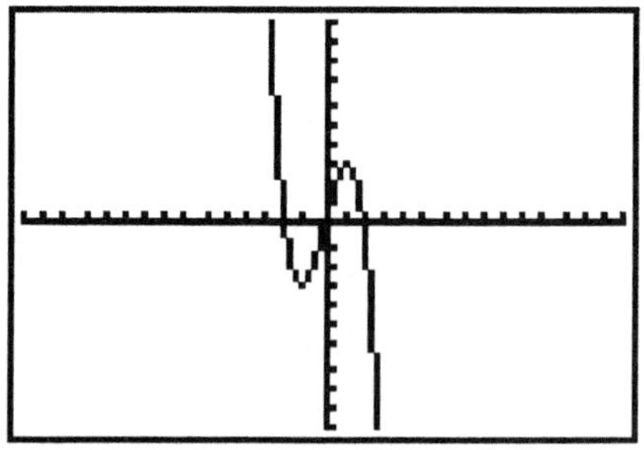

Figure 1.12: Graph of $y = -x^3 + 4x$

To set the range quickly to standard values (see Figure 1.10), press ZOOM 6. To set the viewing rectangle quickly to a square (Figure 1.11), press ZOOM 5. More information about square windows is presented later in Section 1.2.4.

Sometimes you may wish to display grid points corresponding to tick marks on the axes. In the MODE menu (Figure 1.1), use arrow keys to move the blinking cursor to Grid On, then press ENTER and 2nd QUIT GRAPH. Figure 1.15 shows the same graph as in Figure 1.14 but with the grid turned on. In general, you'll want the grid turned *off*, so do that now by pressing MODE, use the arrow keys to move the blinking cursor to Grid Off, and press ENTER.

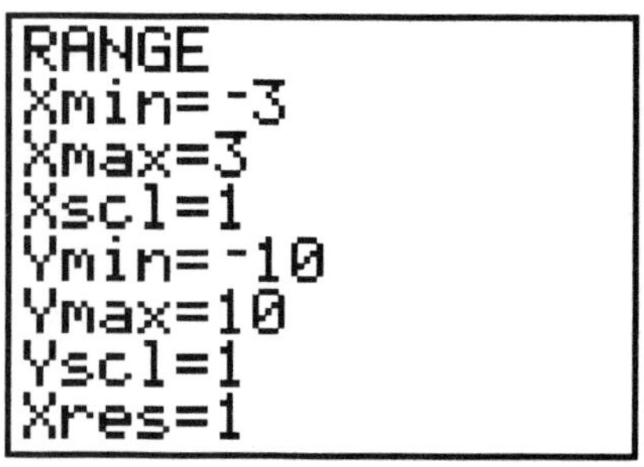

Figure 1.13: Custom window

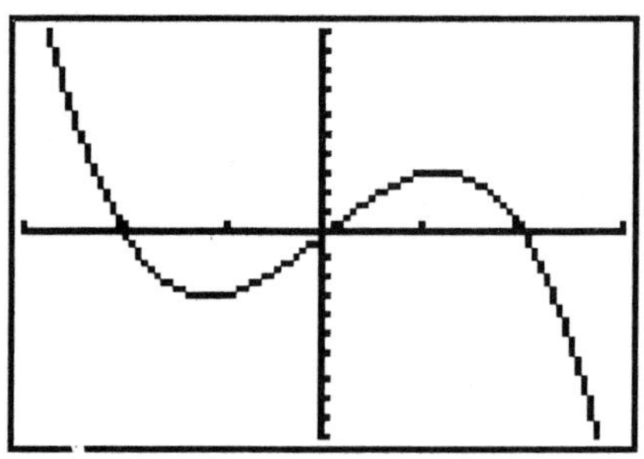

Figure 1.14: Graph of $y = -x^3 + 4x$

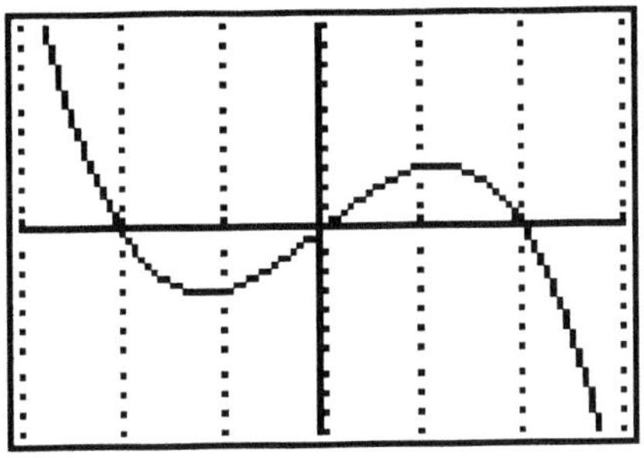

Figure 1.15: Grid turned on for $y = -x^3 + 4x$

1.2.3 The Greatest Integer Function: The greatest integer function, written [[x]], gives the greatest *integer* less than or equal to a number x. On the TI-81, the greatest integer function is called Int and is located under the NUM sub-menu of the MATH menu (see Figure 1.5). So calculate [[6.78]] = 6 by pressing MATH ▶ 4 6.78 ENTER.

To graph y = [[x]], go in the Y= menu, move beside Y_1 and press CLEAR MATH ▶ 4 X|T GRAPH. Figure 1.16 shows this graph in a viewing rectangle from -5 to 5 in both directions.

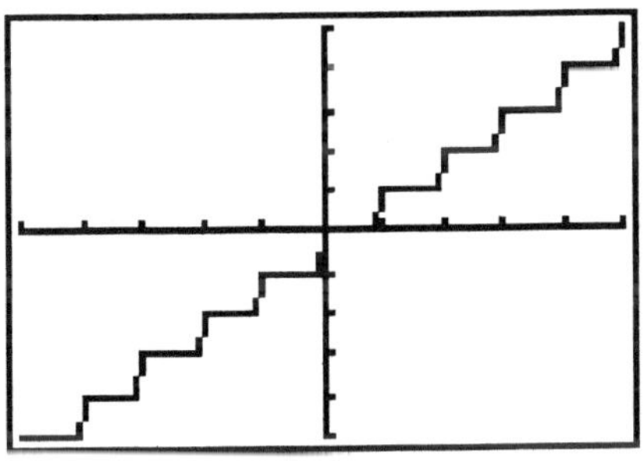

Figure 1.16: Connected graph of y = [[x]]

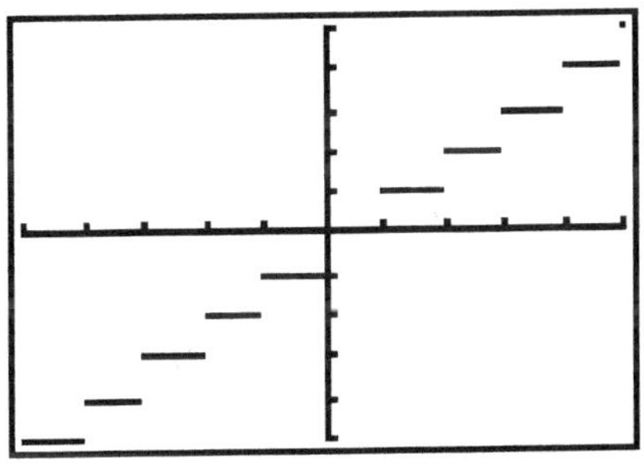

Figure 1.17: Dot graph of y = [[x]]

The true graph of the greatest integer function is a step graph, like the one in Figure 1.17. For the graph of y = [[x]], a segment should *not* be drawn between every pair of successive points. You can change from Connected line to Dot graph on the TI-81 by opening the MODE menu. Move the cursor down to the fifth line; select whichever graph type you require; press ENTER to put it into effect and GRAPH to see the result.

1.2.4 Graphing a Circle: Here is a useful technique for graphs that are not functions, but that can be "split" into a top part and a bottom part, or into multiple parts. Suppose you wish to graph the circle whose equation is $x^2 + y^2 = 36$. First solve for y and get an equation for the top semicircle, $y = \sqrt{36 - x^2}$, and for the

bottom semicircle, $y = -\sqrt{36 - x^2}$. Then graph the two semicircles simultaneously.

The keystrokes to draw this circle's graph follow. Enter $\sqrt{36 - x^2}$ as Y_1 and $-\sqrt{36 - x^2}$ as Y_2 (see Figure 1.18) by pressing Y= CLEAR 2nd √ (36 - X|T x^2) ENTER CLEAR (-) 2nd √ (36 - X|T x^2). Then press GRAPH to draw them both.

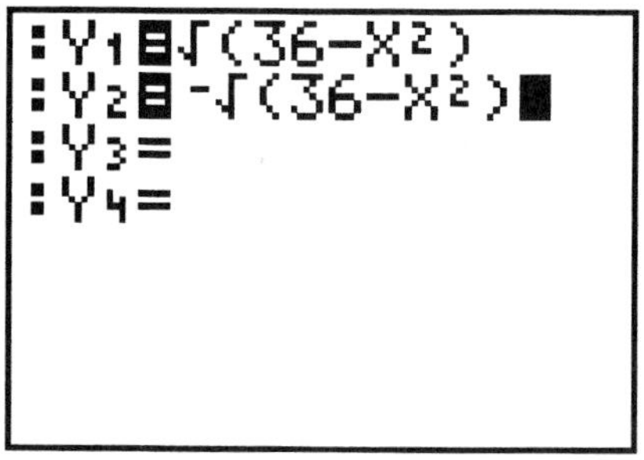

Figure 1.18: Two semicircles

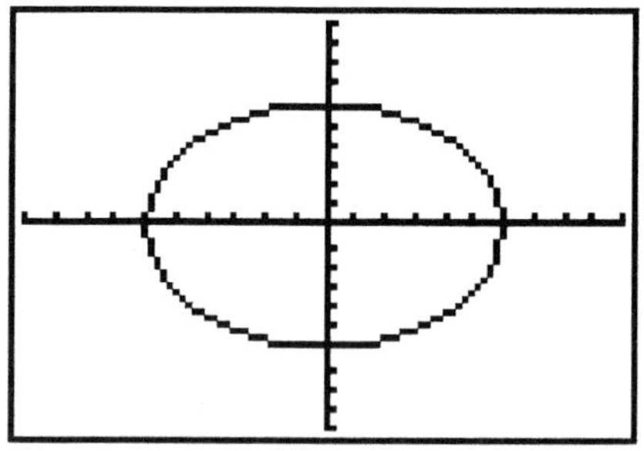

Figure 1.19: Circle's graph - standard view

If your range were set to the standard viewing rectangle, your graph would look like Figure 1.19. Now this does *not* look like a circle, because the units along the axes are not the same. This is where the square viewing rectangle is important. Press ZOOM 5 and see a graph that appears more circular.

Technology Tip: Another way to get a square graph is to change the range variables so that the value of Ymax - Ymin is $\frac{2}{3}$ times Xmax - Xmin. For example, see the RANGE in Figure 1.20 and the corresponding graph in Figure 1.21. The method works because the dimensions of the TI-81's display are such that the ratio of vertical to horizontal is $\frac{2}{3}$.

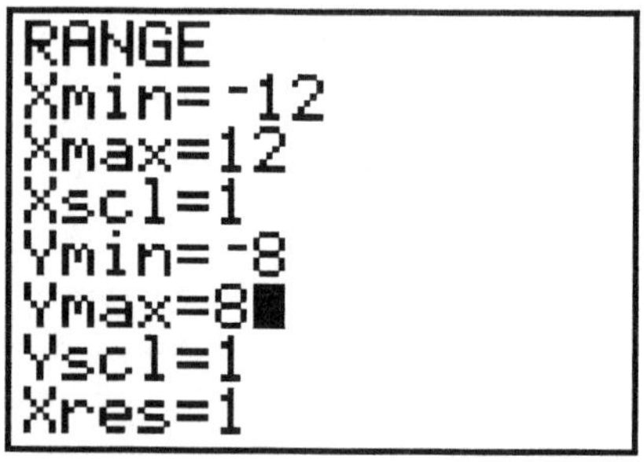

Figure 1.20: $\frac{\text{vertical}}{\text{horizontal}} = \frac{16}{24} = \frac{2}{3}$

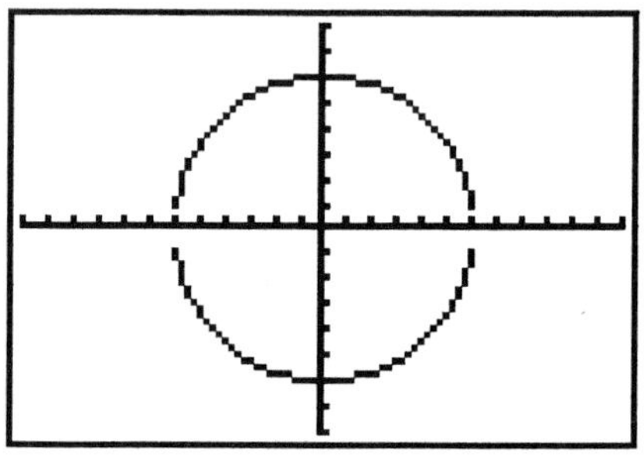

Figure 1.21: A "square" circle

The two semicircles in Figure 1.21 do not meet because of an idiosyncrasy in the way the TI-81 plots a graph.

Back when you entered $\sqrt{36 - x^2}$ as Y_1 and $-\sqrt{36 - x^2}$ as Y_2, you could have entered $-Y_1$ as Y_2 and saved some keystrokes. Try this by going back to the Y= menu and pressing the arrow key to move the cursor down to Y_2. Then press CLEAR (-) 2nd Y-VARS 1. The graph should be just as it was before.

Technology Tip: The square viewing rectangle is also important when you want to judge whether two lines are perpendicular. The intersection of perpendicular lines will always *look* like a right angle in a square viewing rectangle.

1.2.5 ***TRACE:*** Graph $y = -x^3 + 4x$ in the standard viewing rectangle. Press any of the arrow keys ▲ ▼ ◀ ▶ and see the cursor move from the center of the viewing rectangle. The coordinates of the cursor's location are displayed at the bottom of the screen, as in Figure 1.22, in floating decimal format. This cursor is called a *free-moving cursor* because it can move from dot to dot *anywhere* in the graph window.

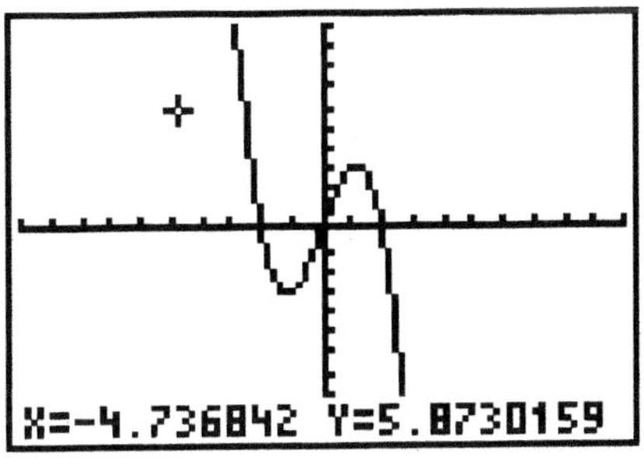

Figure 1.22: Free-moving cursor

Remove the free-moving cursor and its coordinates from the window by pressing GRAPH or ENTER. If you press GRAPH, the next time you press an arrow key the free-moving cursor will appear again from the center of the viewing rectangle. If you press ENTER, the cursor will reappear at the same point you left it.

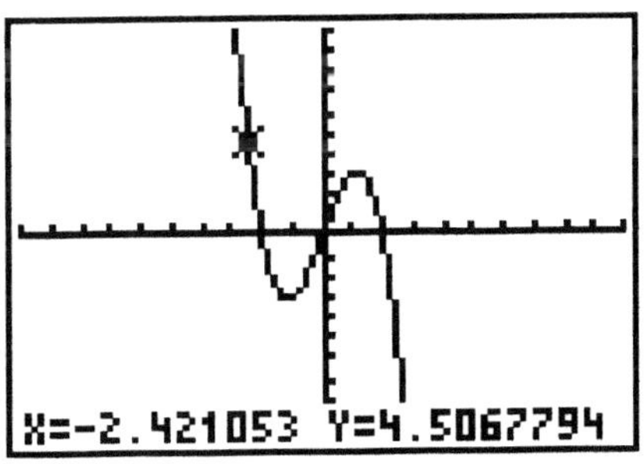

Figure 1.23: Trace on $y = -x^3 + 4x$

Press TRACE to enable the left ◀ and right ▶ arrow keys to move the cursor along the function. The cursor is no longer free-moving, but is now constrained to the function. The coordinates that are displayed belong to points on the function's graph, so the y-coordinate is the calculated value of the function at the corresponding x-coordinate.

Now plot a second function, $y = -.25x$, along with $y = -x^3 + 4x$. Press Y= and enter $-.25x$ for Y_2, then press GRAPH.

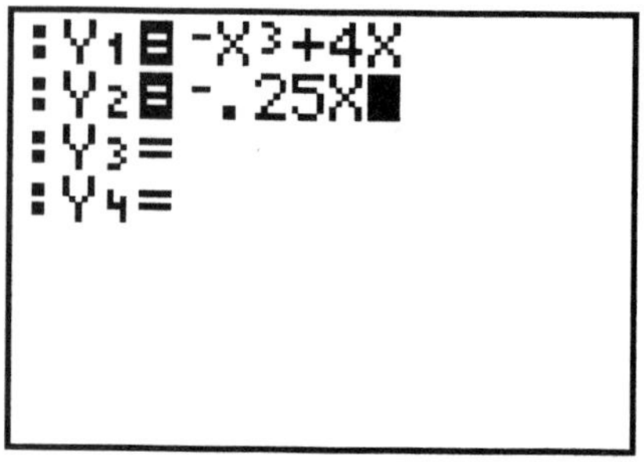

Figure 1.24: Two functions

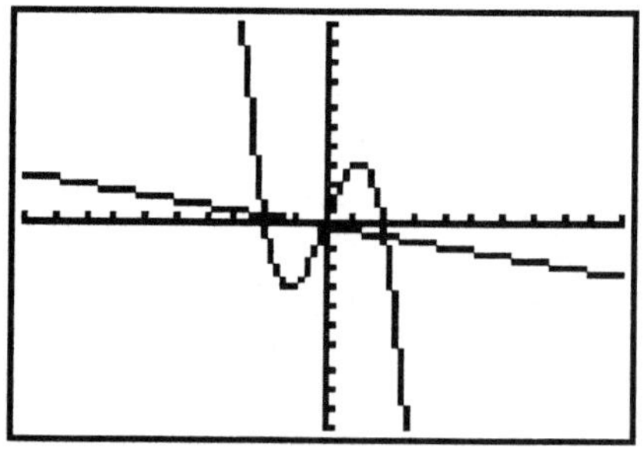

Figure 1.25: $y = -x^3 + 4x$ and $y = -.25x$

Note in Figure 1.24 that the equal signs next to Y_1 and Y_2 are *both* highlighted. This means *both* functions will be graphed. In the Y= screen, move the cursor directly on top of the equal sign next to Y_1 and press ENTER. This equal sign should no longer be highlighted (see Figure 1.26). Now press GRAPH and see that only Y_2 is plotted (Figure 1.27).

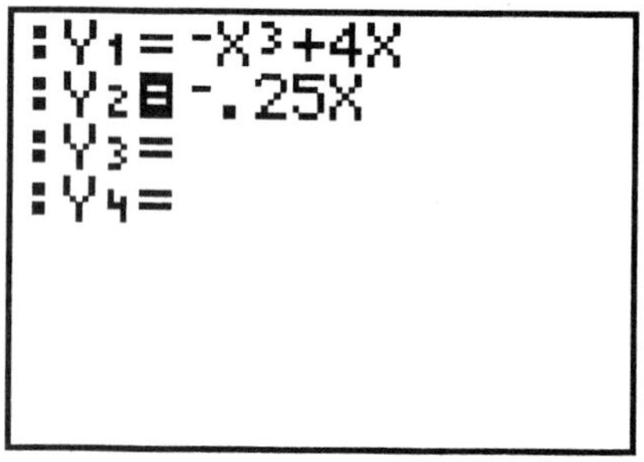

Figure 1.26: Y= screen with only Y_2 active

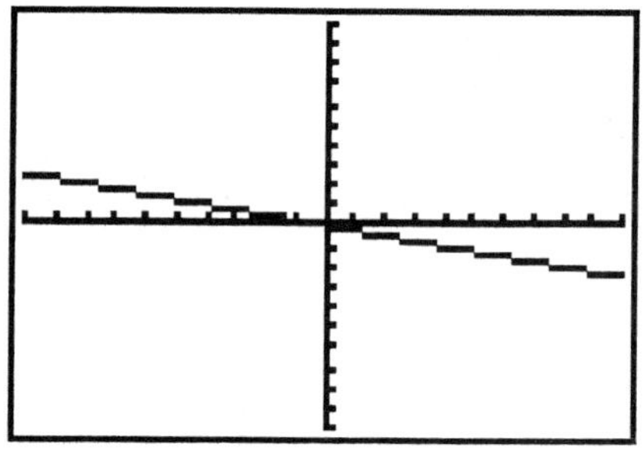

Figure 1.27: Graph of $y = -.25x$

So up to 4 different functions may be stored in the Y= list and any combination of them may be graphed simultaneously. You can make a function active or inactive for graphing by pressing ENTER on its equal sign to highlight (activate) or remove the highlight (deactivate). Go back to the Y= screen and do what is needed in order to graph Y_1 but not Y_2.

Now activate Y_2 again so that both graphs are plotted. Press TRACE and the cursor appears first on the graph of $y = -x^3 + 4x$ because it is higher up in the Y= list. Press the up ▲ or down ▼ arrow key to move the cursor vertically to the graph of $y = -.25x$. Next press the right and left arrow keys to trace along the graph of $y = -.25x$. When more than one function is plotted, you can move the trace cursor vertically from one graph to another in this way.

Technology Tip: By the way, trace along the graph of $y = -.25x$ and press and hold either ◀ or ▶. Eventually you will reach the left or right edge of the window. Keep pressing the arrow key and the TI-81 will allow you to continue the trace by panning the viewing rectangle. Check the RANGE screen to see that Xmin and Xmax are automatically updated.

The TI-81's display has 96 horizontal columns of pixels and 64 vertical rows. So when you trace a curve across a graph window, you are actually moving from Xmin to Xmax in 95 equal jumps, each called Δx. You would calculate the size of each jump to be $\Delta x = \frac{\text{Xmax} - \text{Xmin}}{95}$. Sometimes you may want the jumps to be friendly numbers like .1 or .25 so that, when you trace along the curve, the x-coordinates will be incremented by such a convenient amount. Just set your viewing rectangle for a particular increment Δx by making Xmax = Xmin + 95·Δx. For example, if you want Xmin = -5 and Δx = .3, set Xmax = -5 + 95·.3 = 23.5. Likewise, set Ymax = Ymin + 63·Δy if you want the vertical increment to be some special Δy.

To center your window around a particular point, say (h, k), and also have a certain Δx, set Xmin = h - 47·Δx and Xmax = h + 48·Δx. Likewise, make Ymin = k - 31·Δy and Ymax = k + 32·Δy. For example, to center a window around the origin, (0, 0), with both horizontal and vertical increments of .25, set the range so that Xmin = 0 - 47·.25 = -11.75, Xmax = 0 + 48·.25 = 12, Ymin = 0 - 31·.25 = -7.75, and Ymax = 0 + 32·.25 = 8.

See the benefit by first plotting $y = x^2 + 2x + 1$ in a standard graphing window. Trace near its y-intercept, which is (0, 1), and move towards its x-intercept, which is (-1, 0). Then change to a viewing rectangle from -9 to 10 horizontally and from -6 to 6.6 vertically, and trace again near the intercepts.

1.2.6 ZOOM: Plot again the two graphs, for $y = -x^3 + 4x$ and for $y = -.25x$. There appears to be an intersection near $x = 2$. The TI-81 provides several ways to enlarge the view around this point. You can change the viewing rectangle directly by pressing RANGE and editing the values of Xmin, Xmax, Ymin, and Ymax. Figure 1.29 shows a new viewing rectangle for the range displayed in Figure 1.28. Trace has been turned on and the coordinates of a point on $y = -x^3 + 4x$ that is close to the intersection are displayed.

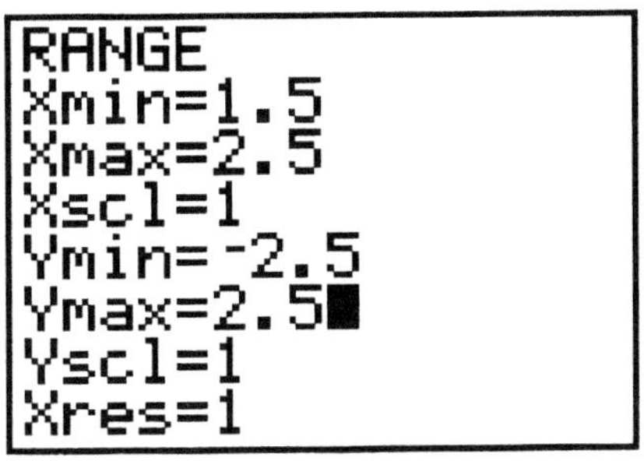

Figure 1.28: New RANGE

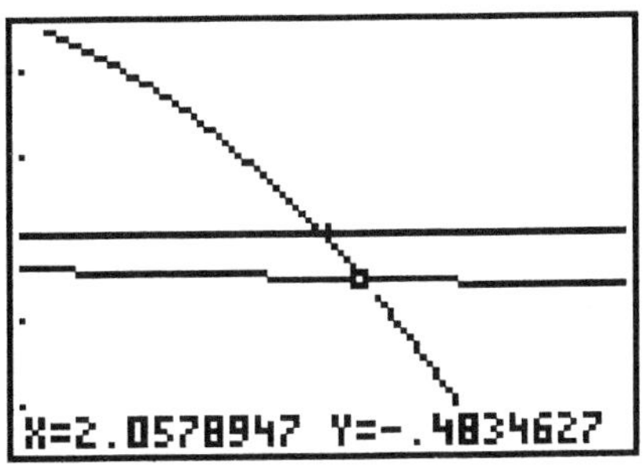

Figure 1.29: Closer view

A more efficient method for enlarging the view is to draw a new viewing rectangle with the cursor. Start again with a graph of the two functions $y = -x^3 + 4x$ and $y = -.25x$ in a standard viewing rectangle (press ZOOM 6 for the standard window, from -10 to 10 along both axes).

Now imagine a small rectangular box around the intersection point, near $x = 2$. Press ZOOM 1 (Figure 1.30) to draw a box to define this new viewing rectangle. Use the arrow keys to move the cursor, whose coordinates are displayed at the bottom of the window, to one corner of the new viewing rectangle you imagine.

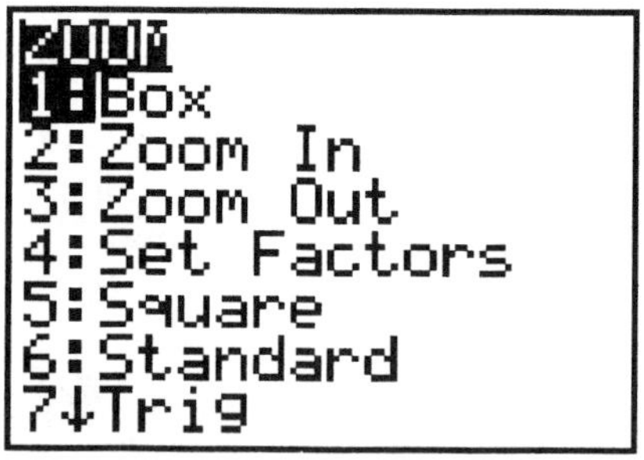

Figure 1.30: ZOOM menu

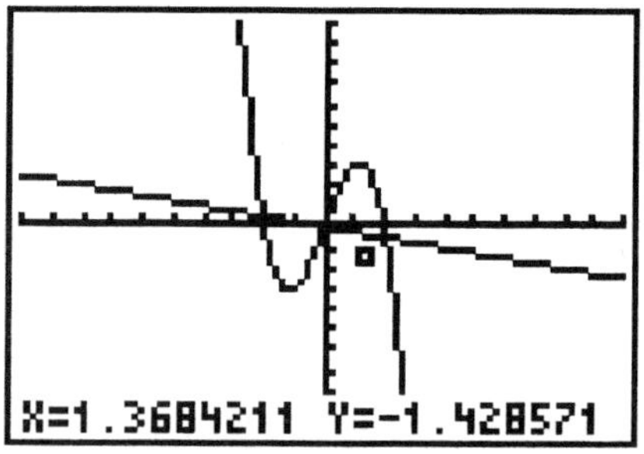

Figure 1.31: One corner selected

Press ENTER to fix the corner where you have moved the cursor; it changes shape and becomes a blinking square (Figure 1.31). Use the arrow keys again to move the cursor to the diagonally opposite corner of the new rectangle (Figure 1.32). If this box looks all right to you, press ENTER. The rectangular area you have enclosed will now enlarge to fill the graph window (Figure 1.33).

You may cancel the zoom any time *before* you press this last ENTER. Press 2nd QUIT to cancel the zoom and return to the home screen, or select another screen by pressing GRAPH or ZOOM and also cancel the zoom.

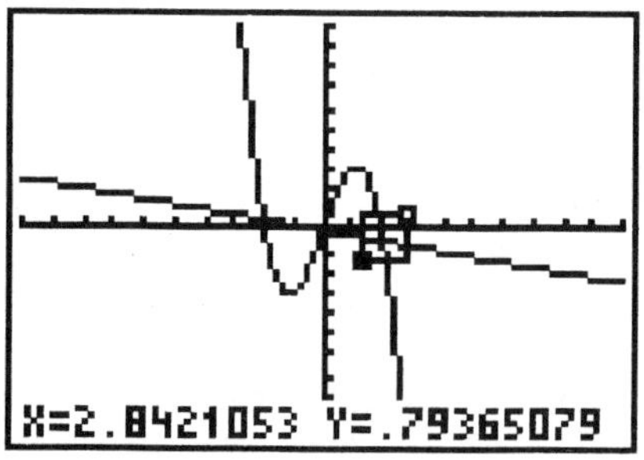

Figure 1.32: Box drawn

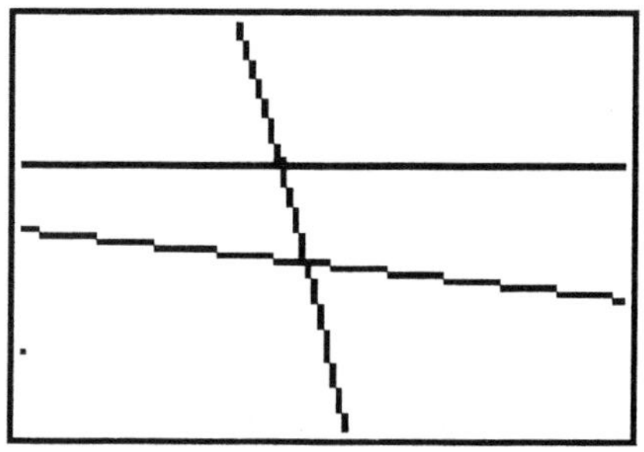

Figure 1.33: New viewing rectangle

You can also gain a quick magnification of the graph around the cursor's location. Return once more to the standard range for the graph of the two functions $y = -x^3 + 4x$ and $y = -.25x$. Press ZOOM 2 and then press arrow keys to move the cursor as close as you can to the point of intersection near $x = 2$ (see Figure 1.34). Then press ENTER and the calculator draws a magnified graph, centered at the cursor's position (Figure 1.35). The range variables are changed to reflect this new viewing rectangle. Look in the RANGE menu to check.

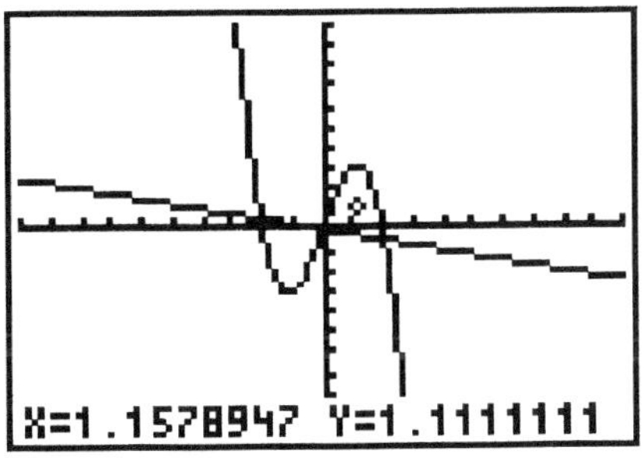

Figure 1.34: Before a zoom in

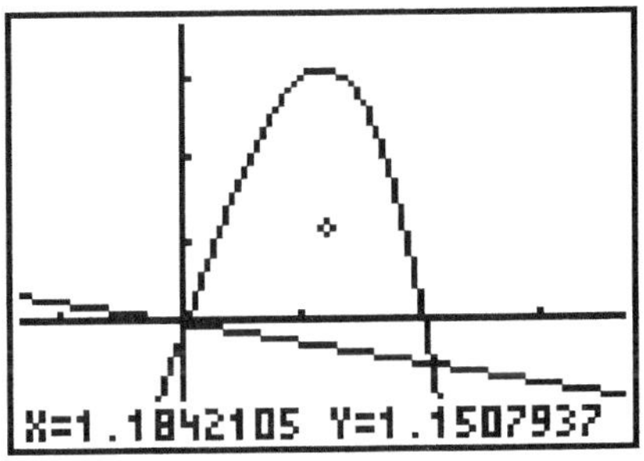

Figure 1.35: After a zoom in

As you see in the ZOOM menu (Figure 1.30), the TI-81 can Zoom In (press ZOOM 2) or Zoom Out (press ZOOM 3). Zoom out to see a larger view of the graph, centered at the cursor position. You can change the horizontal and vertical scale of the magnification by pressing ZOOM 4 (see Figure 1.36) and editing XFact and YFact, the horizontal and vertical magnification factors.

The default zoom factor is 4 in both directions. It is not necessary for XFact and YFact to be equal. Sometimes, you may prefer to zoom in one direction only, so the other factor should be set to 1. As usual, press 2nd QUIT to leave the ZOOM menu.

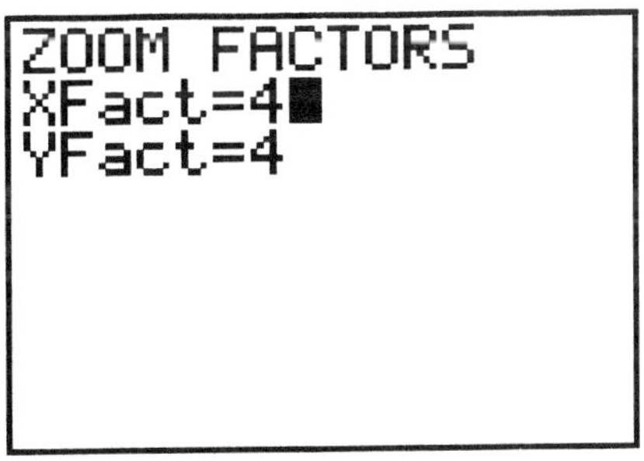

Figure 1.36: Set zoom factors

Technology Tip: If you should zoom in too much and lose the curve, zoom back to the standard viewing rectangle and start over.

1.2.7 Relative Minimums and Maximums: Graph $y = -x^3 + 4x$ once again in the standard viewing rectangle (Figure 1.9). This function appears to have a relative minimum near $x = -1$ and a relative maximum near $x = 1$. You may zoom and trace to approximate these extreme values.

First trace along the curve near the local minimum. Notice by how much the x-values and y-values change as you move from point to point. Trace along the curve until the y-coordinate is as *small* as you can get it, so that you are as close as possible to the local minimum, and zoom in (press ZOOM 2 or use a zoom box). Now trace again along the curve and, as you move from point to point, see that the coordinates change by smaller amounts than before. Keep zooming and tracing until you find the coordinates of the local minimum point as accurately as you need them, approximately (-1.15, -3.08).

Follow a similar procedure to find the local maximum. Trace along the curve until the y-coordinate is as *great* as you can get it, so that you are as close as possible to the local maximum, and zoom in. The local maximum point on the graph of $y=-x^3+4x$ is approximately (1.15, 3.08).

1.3 Solving Equations and Inequalities

1.3.1 Intercepts and Intersections: Tracing and zooming are also used to locate an x-intercept of a graph, where a curve crosses the x-axis. For example, the graph of $y=x^3-8x$ crosses the x-axis three times (see Figure 1.37). After tracing over to the x-intercept point that is furthest to the left, zoom in (Figure 1.38). Continue this process until you have located all three intercepts with as much accuracy as you need. The three x-intercepts of $y=x^3-8x$ are approximately -2.828, 0, and 2.828.

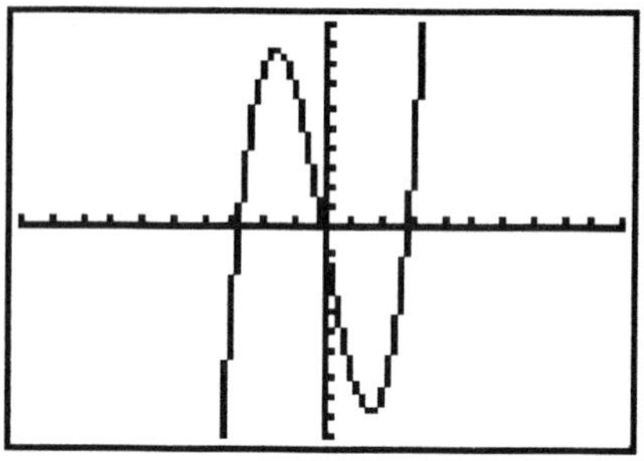

Figure 1.37: Graph of $y=x^3-8x$

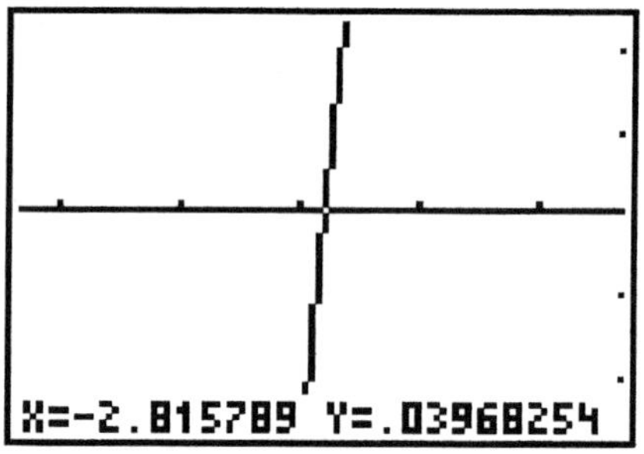

Figure 1.38: An x-intercept of $y=x^3-8x$

Technology Tip: As you zoom in, you may also wish to change the spacing between tick marks on the x-axis so that the viewing rectangle shows scale marks near the intercept point. Then the accuracy of your approximation will be such that the error is less than the distance between two tick marks. Change the x-scale on the TI-81 from the RANGE menu. Move the cursor down to Xscl and enter an appropriate value.

TRACE and ZOOM are especially important for locating the intersection points of two graphs, say the graphs of $y=-x^3+4x$ and $y=-.25x$. Trace along one of the graphs until you arrive close to an intersection point. Then press ▲ or ▼ to jump to the other graph. Notice that the x-coordinate does not change, but the y-coordinate is likely to be different (see Figures 1.39 and 1.40).

When the two y-coordinates are as close as they can get, you have come as close as you now can to the point of intersection. So zoom in around the intersection point, then trace again until the two y-coordinates are as close as possible. Continue this process until you have located the point of intersection with as much accuracy as necessary.

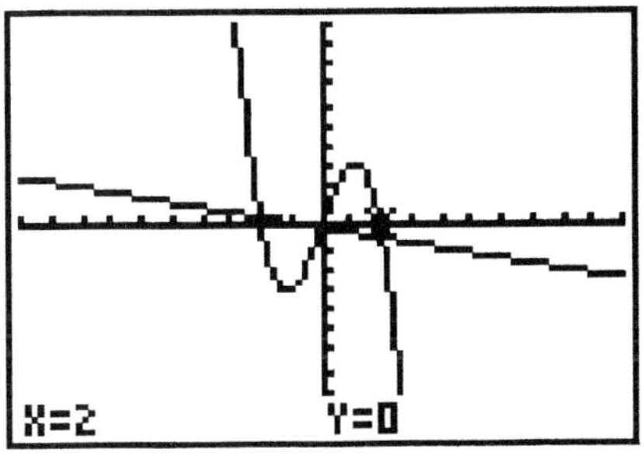

Figure 1.39: Trace on $y=-x^3+4x$

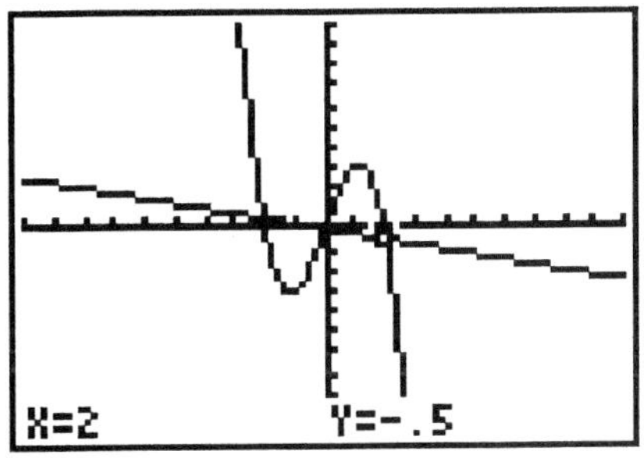

Figure 1.40: Trace on $y=-.25x$

1.3.2 Solving Equations by Graphing: Suppose you need to solve the equation $24x^3-36x+17=0$. First graph $y=24x^3-36x+17$ in a window large enough to exhibit *all* its x-intercepts, corresponding to all its roots. Then use trace and zoom to locate each one. In fact, this equation has just one solution, approximately x = -1.414.

Remember that when an equation has more than one x-intercept, it may be necessary to change the viewing rectangle a few times to locate all of them.

Technology Tip: To solve an equation like $24x^3+17=36x$, you may first transform it into standard form, $24x^3-36x+17=0$, and proceed as above. However, you may also graph the *two* functions $y=24x^3+17$ and $y=36x$, then zoom and trace to locate their point of intersection.

1.3.3 Solving Systems by Graphing: The solutions to a system of equations correspond to the points of intersection of their graphs (Figure 1.41). For example, to solve the system $y=x^2-3x-4$ and $y=x^3+3x^2-2x-1$, first graph them together. Then zoom and trace to locate their point of intersection, approximately (-2.17, 7.25).

You must judge whether the two current y-coordinates are sufficiently close for x = -2.17 or whether you should continue to zoom and trace to improve the approximation.

The solutions of the system of two equations $y=x^3+3x^2-2x-1$ and $y=x^2-3x-4$ correspond to the solutions of the single equation $x^3+3x^2-2x-1=x^2-3x-4$, which simplifies to $x^3+2x^2+x+3=0$. So you may also graph $y=x^3+2x^2+x+3$ and find its x-intercepts to solve the system.

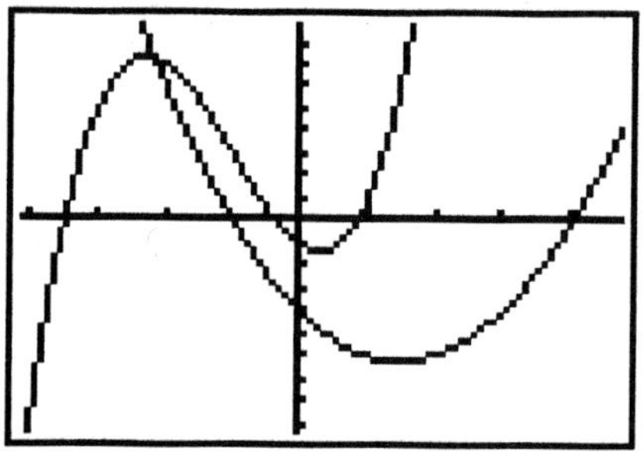

Figure 1.41: Solving a system of equations

1.3.4 Solving Inequalities by Graphing: Consider the inequality $1-\frac{3x}{2}\geq x-4$. To solve it with your TI-81, graph the two functions $y=1-\frac{3x}{2}$ and $y=x-4$ (Figure 1.42). First locate their point of intersection, at $x = 2$. The inequality is true when the graph of $y=1-\frac{3x}{2}$ lies *above* the graph of $y=x-4$, and that occurs for $x < 2$. So the solution is the half-line $x\leq 2$, or $(-\infty, 2]$.

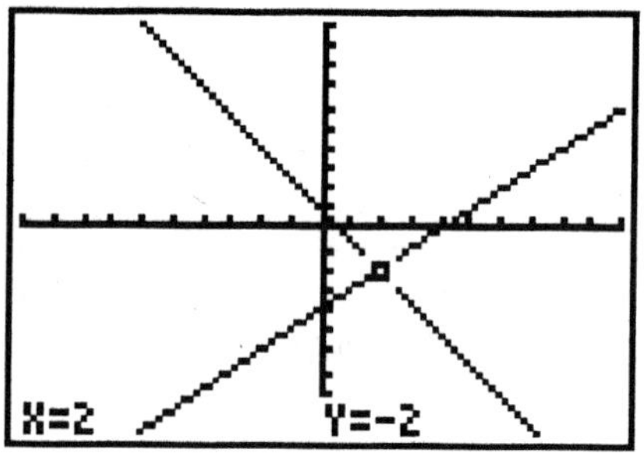

Figure 1.42: Solving $1-\frac{3x}{2}\geq x-4$

The TI-81 is capable of shading the region above or below a graph or between two graphs. For example, to graph $y\geq x^2-1$, first graph the function $y=x^2-1$ as Y_1. Then press 2nd DRAW 7 2nd Y-VARS 1 ALPHA , 10 ALPHA , 2) ENTER (see Figure 1.43). These keystrokes instruct the TI-81 to shade the region *above* $y=x^2-1$ and *below* $y = 10$ (chosen because this is the greatest y-value in the graph window) with shading resolution value of 2. The result is shown in Figure 1.44.

To clear the shading, press 2nd DRAW 1 ENTER.

Now use shading to solve the previous inequality, $1-\frac{3x}{2}\geq x-4$. The function whose graph forms the lower boundary is named *first* in the SHADE command (see Figure 1.45). To enter this in your TI-81, press these keys: 2nd DRAW 7 X|T - 4 ALPHA , 1 - 3 X|T ÷ 2 ALPHA , 2) ENTER (Figure 1.46). The shading extends left from $x = 2$, hence the solution to $1-\frac{3x}{2} \ge x-4$ is the half-line $x \le 2$, or $(-\infty, 2]$.

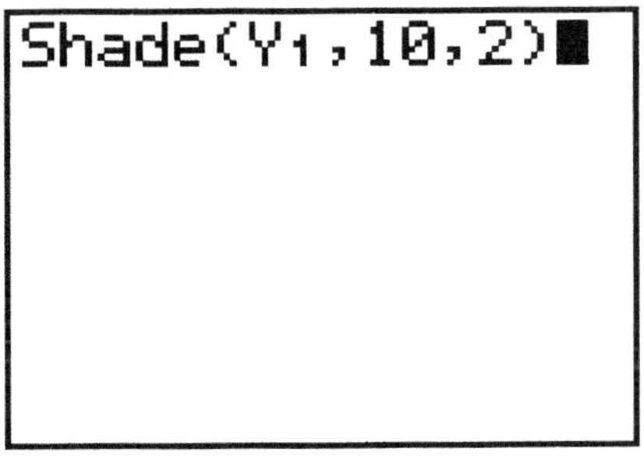

Figure 1.43: DRAW Shade

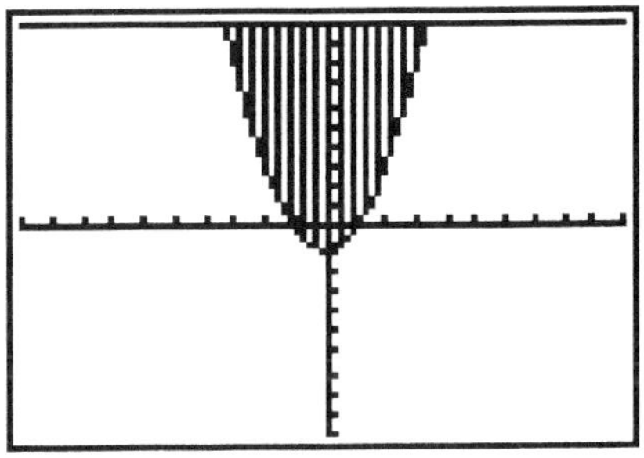

Figure 1.44: Graph of $y \ge x^2 - 1$

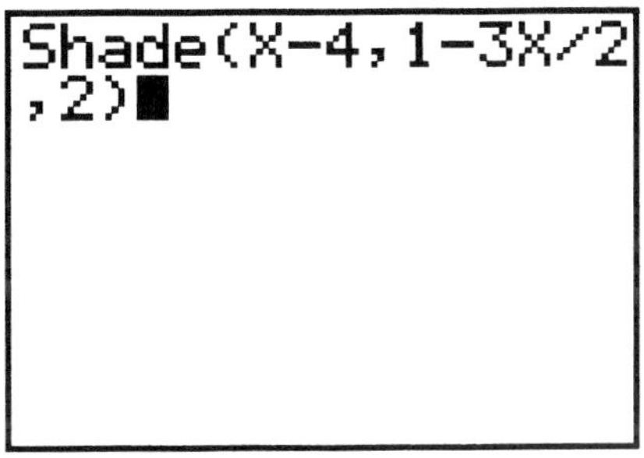

Figure 1.45: DRAW Shade command

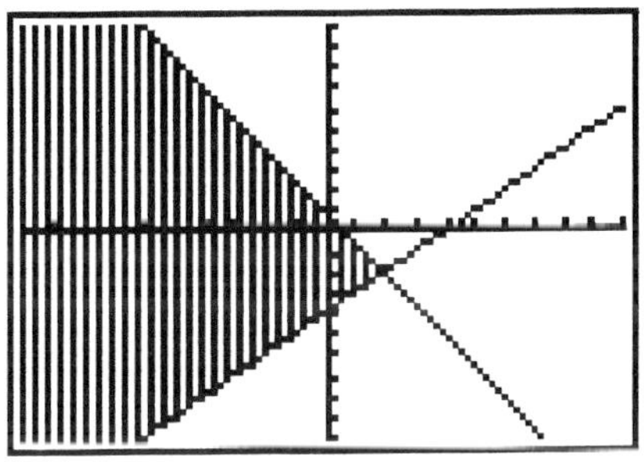

Figure 1.46: Graph of $1-\frac{3x}{2} \ge x-4$

More information about the DRAW menu is in the TI-81 manual.

1.4 Trigonometry

1.4.1 Degrees and Radians: The trigonometric functions can be applied to angles measured either in radians or degrees, but you should take care that the TI-81 is configured for whichever measure you need. Press MODE to see the current settings. Press ▼ twice and move down to the third line of the mode menu where angle measure is selected. Then press ◄ or ► to move between the displayed options. When the blinking cursor is on the measure you want, press ENTER to select it. Then press 2nd QUIT to leave the mode menu.

It's a good idea to check the angle measure setting before executing a calculation that depends on a particular measure. You may change a mode setting at any time and not interfere with pending calculations. Try the following keystrokes to see this in action.

Expression	*Keystrokes*	*Display*
$\sin 45°$	MODE ▼ ▼ ▶ ENTER	
	2nd QUIT SIN 45 ENTER	.7071067812
$\sin \pi°$	SIN 2nd π ENTER	.0548036651
$\sin \pi$	SIN 2nd π MODE ▼ ▼	
	ENTER 2nd QUIT ENTER	0
$\sin 45$	SIN 45 ENTER	.8509035245
$\sin \frac{\pi}{6}$	SIN (2nd $\pi \div 6$) ENTER	.5

The first line of keystrokes sets the TI-81 in degree mode and calculates the sine of 45 *degrees*. While the calculator is still in degree mode, the second line of keystrokes calculates the sine of π *degrees*, 3.1415°. The third line changes to radian mode just before calculating the sine of π *radians*. The fourth line calculates the sine of 45 *radians* (the calculator is already in radian mode).

The TI-81 makes it possible to mix degrees and radians in a calculation. Execute these keystrokes to calculate $\tan 45° + \sin \frac{\pi}{6}$ as shown in Figure 1.47: TAN 45 MATH 6 + SIN (2nd $\pi \div 6$) MATH 7 ENTER. Do you get 1.5 whether your calculator is set *either* in degree mode *or* in radian mode?

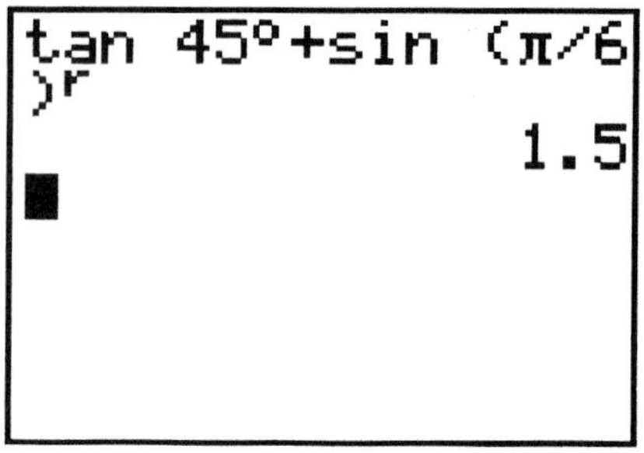

Figure 1.47: Angle measure

1.4.2 Graphs of Trigonometric Functions: When you graph a trigonometric function, you need to pay careful attention to the choice of graph window. For example, graph $y = \dfrac{\sin 30x}{30}$ in the standard viewing rectangle. Trace along the curve to see where it is. Zoom in to a better window, or use the period and amplitude to establish better RANGE values.

Technology Tip: Since $\pi \approx 3.1$, set Xmin = 0 and Xmax = 6.3 to cover the interval from 0 to 2π.

Next graph $y = \tan x$ in the standard window. The TI-81 plots consecutive points and then connects them with a segment, so the graph is not exactly what you should expect. You may wish to change from Connected line to Dot graph (see Section 1.2.3) when you plot the tangent function.

1.5 Differentiation

1.5.1 Limits: Suppose you need to find this limit: $\lim\limits_{x \to 0} \dfrac{\sin 4x}{x}$. Plot the graph of $f(x) = \dfrac{\sin 4x}{x}$ in a convenient viewing rectangle (see Figure 1.48) that contains the point where the function appears to intersect the line $x = 0$ (because you want the limit as $x \to 0$). Your graph should lend support to the conclusion that $\lim\limits_{x \to 0} \dfrac{\sin 4x}{x} = 4$.

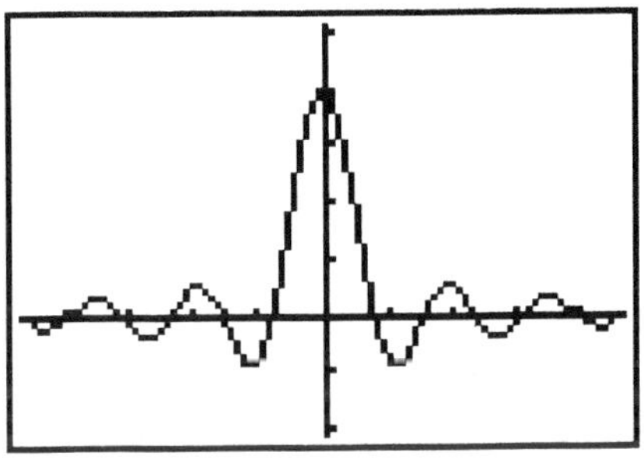

Figure 1.48: Checking $\lim\limits_{x \to 0} \dfrac{\sin 4x}{x} = 4$

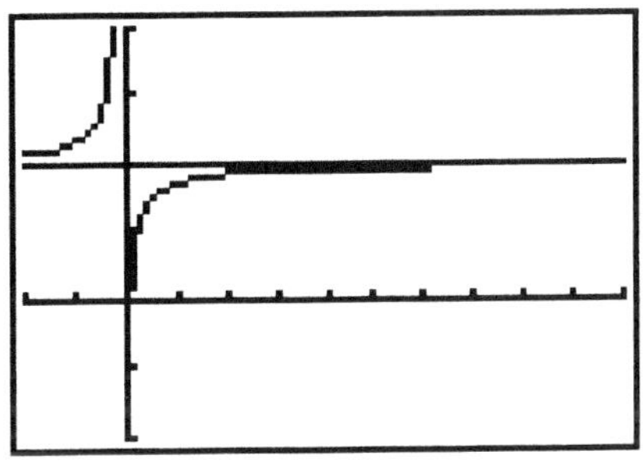

Figure 1.49: Checking $\lim\limits_{x \to \infty} \dfrac{2x-1}{x+1} = 2$

To test the reasonableness of the conclusion that $\lim\limits_{x \to \infty} \dfrac{2x-1}{x+1} = 2$, evaluate the function $f(x) = \dfrac{2x-1}{x+1}$ for several large positive values of x (since you want the limit as $x \to \infty$). For example, evaluate $f(100)$, $f(1000)$, and $f(10{,}000)$. Another way to test the reasonableness of this result is to examine the graph of $f(x) = \dfrac{2x-1}{x+1}$ in a viewing rectangle that extends over large values of x. See, as in Figure 1.49 (where the viewing rectangle extends horizontally from -20 to 100), whether the graph is asymptotic to the horizontal line $y = 2$ (enter $\dfrac{2x-1}{x+1}$ for Y_1 and 2 for Y_2).

1.5.2 Numerical Derivatives: The derivative of a function f at x can be defined as the limit of the slopes of secant lines, so $f'(x) = \lim\limits_{\Delta x \to 0} \dfrac{f(x+\Delta x) - f(x-\Delta x)}{2\Delta x}$. And for small values of Δx, the expression

$\dfrac{f(x+\Delta x)-f(x-\Delta x)}{2\Delta x}$ gives a good approximation to the limit.

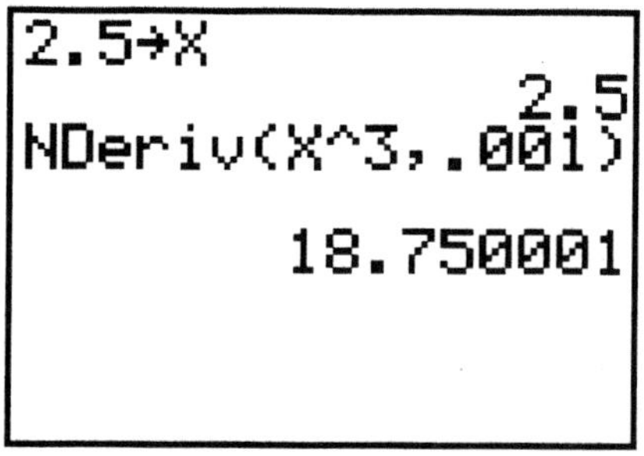

Figure 1.50: Using NDeriv(

The TI-81 has a function NDeriv(in the MATH menu to calculate the *symmetric difference*, $\dfrac{f(x+\Delta x)-f(x-\Delta x)}{2\Delta x}$. So to find a numerical approximation to $f'(2.5)$ when $f(x)=x^3$ and with Δx = 0.001, first save 2.5 for x, then press MATH 8 X|T ^ 3 ALPHA , .001) ENTER as shown in Figure 1.50.

Technology Tip: It is sometimes helpful to plot both a function and its derivative together. In Figure 1.52, the function $f(x)=\dfrac{5x-2}{x^2+1}$ and its numerical derivative (actually, an approximation to the derivative given by the symmetric difference) are graphed. You can duplicate this graph by first entering $\dfrac{5x-2}{x^2+1}$ for Y_1 and then entering its numerical derivative for Y_2 by pressing MATH 8 2nd Y-VARS 1 ALPHA , .001), as you see in Figure 1.51.

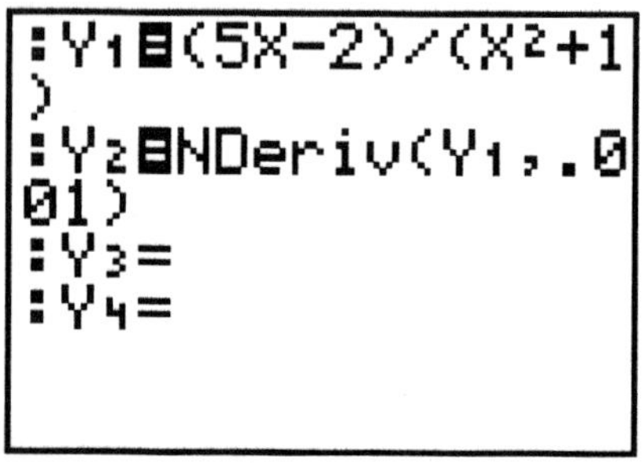

Figure 1.51: Entering $f(x)$ and $f'(x)$

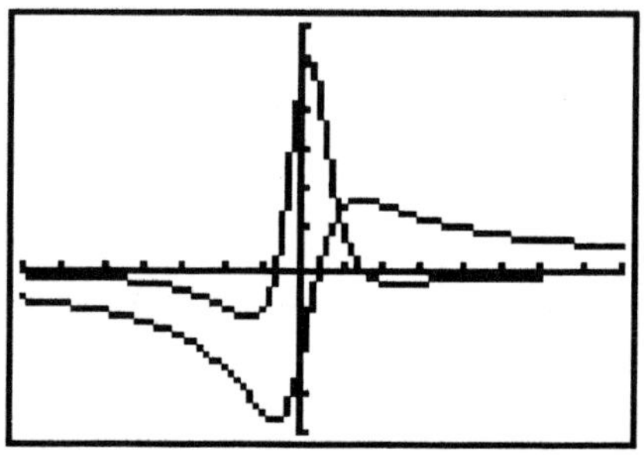

Figure 1.52: Graphs of $f(x)$ and $f'(x)$

Technology Tip: To approximate the *second* derivative $f''(x)$ of a function $y=f(x)$ or to plot the second derivative, first enter the expression for Y_1 and its derivative for Y_2 as above. Then enter the second derivative for Y_3 by pressing MATH 8 2nd Y-VARS 1 2 , X,T,θ , X,T,θ).

1.5.3 Newton's Method: With your TI-81, you may iterate using Newton's Method to find the zeros of a function. Recall that Newton's Method determines each successive approximation by the formula $x_{n+1} = x_n - \dfrac{f(x_n)}{f'(x_n)}$.

As an example of the technique, consider $f(x) = 2x^3 + x^2 - x + 1$. Enter this function as Y_1. A look at its graph suggests that it has a zero near x = -1, so start the iteration by storing -1 as x (see Figure 1.53). Then press these keystrokes: X|T - 2nd Y-VARS 1 ÷ MATH 8 2nd Y-VARS 1 ALPHA , .001) STO► X|T. Press ENTER repeatedly until two successive approximations differ by less than some predetermined value, say 0.0001. Note that each time you press ENTER, the TI-81 will use its *current* value of x, and that value is changing as you continue the iteration.

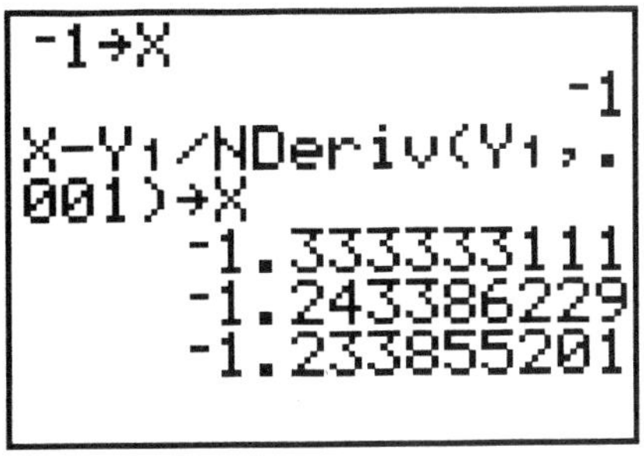

Figure 1.53: Newton's Method

Technology Tip: Newton's Method is sensitive to your seed value for x, so look carefully at the function's graph to make a good first estimate. Also, remember that the method sometimes fails to converge!

You may want to save the Newton's Method formula as a short program. See Section 1.9 or your calculator's manual for further information on programming the TI-81.

1.6 Sequences

1.6.1 Iteration: The ANS feature enables you to perform iterations to evaluate a function repeatedly. As an example, calculate $\dfrac{n-1}{3}$ for $n = 27$. Then calculate $\dfrac{n-1}{3}$ for n = the answer to the previous calculation. Continue to use each answer as n in the *next* calculation. Here are keystrokes to accomplish this iteration on the TI-81 calculator (see the results in Figure 1.54). Notice that when you use ANS in place of n in a formula, it is sufficient to press ENTER to continue an iteration.

Iteration	*Keystrokes*	*Display*
1	27 ENTER	27

2	(ANS - 1) ÷ 3 ENTER	8.666666667
3	ENTER	2.555555556
4	ENTER	.5185185185
5	ENTER	-.1604938272

Press ENTER several more times and see what happens with this iteration. You may wish to try it again with a different starting value.

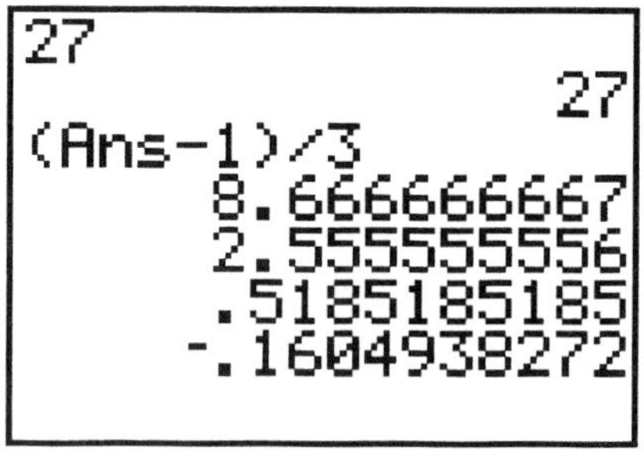

Figure 1.54: Iteration

1.6.2 Arithmetic and Geometric Sequences: Use iteration with the ANS variable to determine the *n*-th term of a sequence. For example, find the 18th term of an *arithmetic* sequence whose first term is 7 and whose common difference is 4. Enter the first term 7, then start the progression with the recursion formula, ANS + 4 ENTER. This yields the 2nd term, so press ENTER sixteen more times to find the 18th term. For a *geometric* sequence whose common ratio is 4, start the progression with ANS × 4 ENTER.

Of course, you could also use the *explicit* formula for the *n*-th term of an arithmetic sequence, $t_n = a + (n-1)d$. First enter values for the variables *a*, *d*, and *n*, then evaluate the formula by pressing ALPHA A + (ALPHA N - 1) ALPHA D ENTER. For a geometric sequence whose *n*-th term is given by $t_n = a \cdot r^{n-1}$, enter values for the variables *a*, *r*, and *n*, then evaluate the formula by pressing ALPHA A ALPHA R ^ (ALPHA N - 1) ENTER.

1.7 Integration

1.7.1 Approximating Definite Integrals: See Section 1.9 for a sample program that uses left and right Riemann Sums as well as the Midpoint Rule, the Trapezoid Rule, and Simpson's Rule to enable the TI-81 to approximate definite integrals.

1.7.2 Areas: To find the area under the graph of a function $y = f(x)$ between $x = A$ and $x = B$, enter the expression $f(x)$ for Y_1 and run the program INTEGRAL listed in Section 1.9. The program itself will prompt you for the endpoints A and B of the interval.

Technology Tip: Suppose that you want to find the area between two functions, $y = f(x)$ and $y = g(x)$, from $x = A$ to $x = B$. If $f(x) \geq g(x)$ for $A \leq x \leq B$, then enter the expression $f(x) - g(x)$ for Y_1 and run the program INTEGRAL.

1.8 Parametric and Polar Graphs

1.8.1 Graphing Parametric Equations: The TI-81 plots parametric equations as easily as it plots functions. Just use the MODE menu (Figure 1.1), go to the fourth line from the top, and change the setting from Function to Param. Be sure, if the independent parameter is an angle measure, that MODE is set to whichever you need, Rad or Deg.

For example, here are the keystrokes needed to graph the parametric equations $x = \cos^3 t$ and $y = \sin^3 t$. First check that angles are currently being measured in radians. Change to parametric mode and press Y= to examine the new parametric equation menu (Figure 1.55). Enter the two parametric equations by pressing (COS X|T) ^ 3 ENTER (SIN X|T) ^ 3 ENTER. Now, when you press the variable key X|T, you get a T because the calculator is in parametric mode.

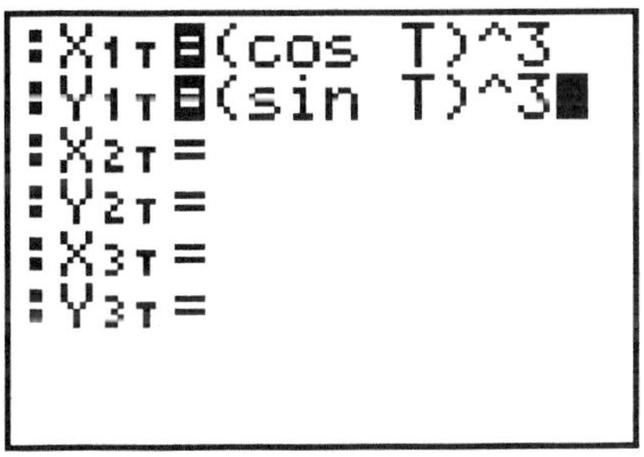

Figure 1.55: Parametric Y= menu

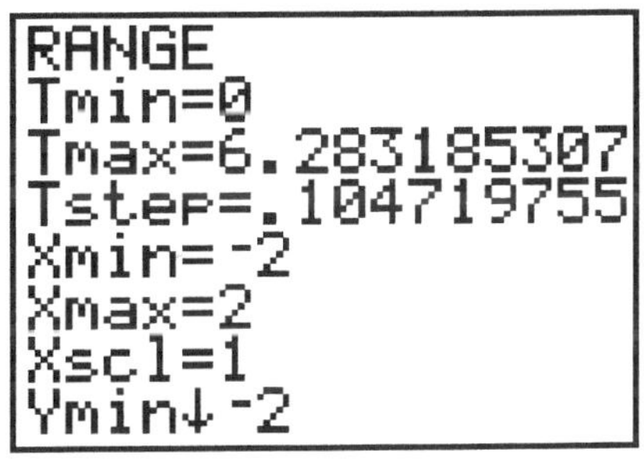

Figure 1.56: Parametric RANGE menu

Also look at the new RANGE menu (Figure 1.56). In the standard window, the values of T go from 0 to 2π in steps of $\frac{\pi}{30} = .1047$, with the view from -10 to 10 in both directions. But here the viewing rectangle has been changed to extend from -2 to 2 in both directions. Press GRAPH to see the parametric graph (Figure 1.57).

You may ZOOM and TRACE along parametric graphs just as you did with function graphs. As you trace along this graph, notice that the cursor moves in the *counterclockwise* direction as T increases.

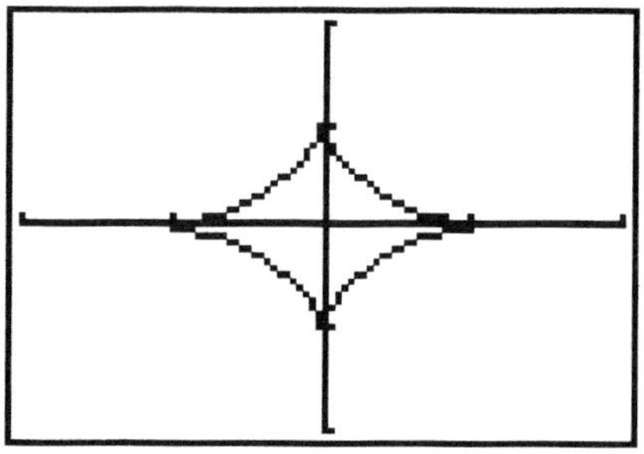

Figure 1.57: Parametric graph of $x = \cos^3 t$ and $y = \sin^3 t$

1.8.2 Rectangular-Polar Coordinate Conversion: The MATH menu (Figure 1.5) provides functions for converting between rectangular and polar coordinate systems. These functions use the current MODE settings, so it is a good idea to check the default angle measure before any conversion. Of course, you may use the MATH menu to override the current angle measure setting, as explained in Section 1.4.1. For the following examples, the TI-81 is set to radian measure.

Given rectangular coordinates $(x, y) = (4, -3)$, convert *from* these rectangular coordinates *to* polar coordinates (r, θ) by pressing MATH 1 4 ALPHA , (-) 3) ENTER. The value of r is displayed; press ALPHA θ ENTER to display the value of θ.

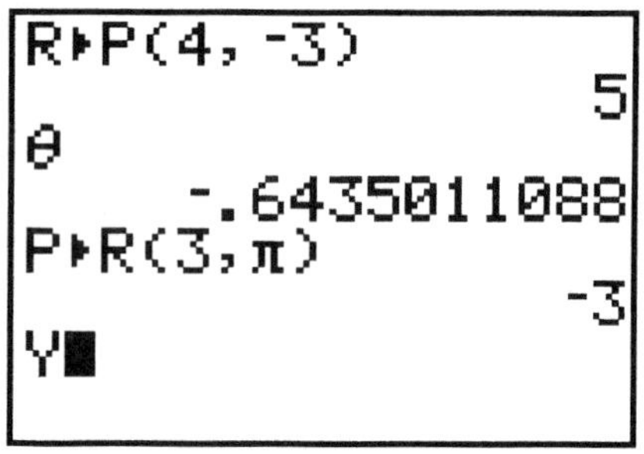

Figure 1.58: Coordinate conversions

Suppose $(r, \theta) = (3, \pi)$. To convert *from* these polar coordinates *to* rectangular coordinates (x, y), press MATH 2 3 ALPHA , 2nd π) ENTER. The x-coordinate is displayed; press ALPHA Y ENTER to display the y-coordinate.

1.8.3 Graphing Polar Equations: The TI-81 graphs a polar function when you write it in parametric form. For example, to graph $r = 4\sin\theta$, enter the parametric equations $x = (4\sin t)\cos t$ and $y = (4\sin t)\sin t$. While you are changing MODE to parametric, also change the last MODE menu item to Polar (see below for the reason). Choose a good viewing rectangle and an appropriate range for the parameter t. In Figure 1.59, the graphing window is square and extends from -6 to 6 horizontally and from -4 to 4 vertically.

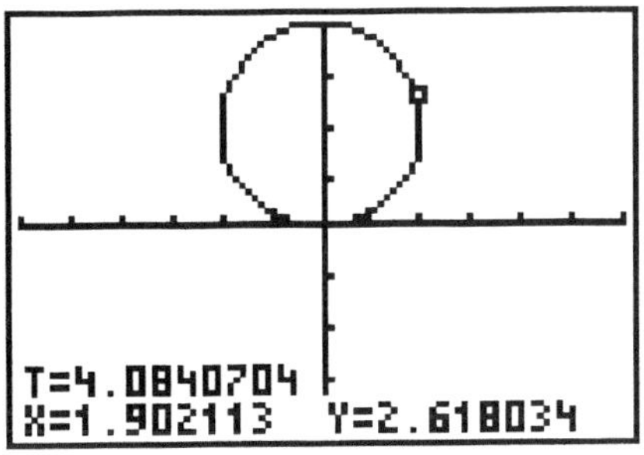

Figure 1.59: Polar graph of $r = 4\sin\theta$

Figure 1.59 shows *rectangular* coordinates of the cursor's location on the graph. When you change MODE to Polar, you are able to trace along a parametric curve and see the *polar* coordinates of the cursor's location.

1.10 Programming

1.10.1 Entering a Program: The TI-81 is a programmable calculator that can store sequences of commands for later replay. Here's an example to show you how to enter a useful program that performs numerical integration by several methods: left and right Riemann Sums as well as the Midpoint Rule, the Trapezoid Rule, and Simpson's Rule.

Press PRGM to access the programming menu. The TI-81 has space for up to 37 programs, each named by a number or letter. If a program area is empty, there will be nothing to the right of its name in the PRGM window. You may ERASE a program area to make one clear by pressing ▶ ▶ and then the number or letter of the program. When you see a clear program area, press ▶ or ◀ as many times as necessary to move the cursor to EDIT; then press the key corresponding to its number or letter. For example, to edit program 5, press 5; to edit program B, press ALPHA B.

For convenience, the cursor is now a blinking **A**, indicating that the calculator is set to receive alphabetic characters. Enter a descriptive title of up to eight characters, letters or numerals, and end by pressing ENTER. Let's call this program INTEGRAL. Since its name is exactly eight letters, no ENTER is needed at the end.

In a program, each line begins with a colon : supplied automatically by the calculator. Any command you could enter directly in the TI-81's home screen can be entered as a line in a program. There are also special programming commands.

Enter the program INTEGRAL by pressing the keystrokes given in the listing below.

Program Line	*Keystrokes*
: Disp "Lower Limit"	PRGM ▶ 1 2nd A-LOCK " L O W E R ␣ L I M I T " ENTER
displays the words *Lower Limit* on the TI-81 screen	
: Input A	PRGM ▶ 2 ALPHA A ENTER
waits for you to input a value that will be assigned to the variable *A*	
: Disp "Upper Limit"	PRGM ▶ 1 2nd A-LOCK " U P P E R ␣ L I M I T " ENTER
: Input B	PRGM ▶ 2 ALPHA B ENTER
: Disp "Subdivisions"	PRGM ▶ 1 2nd A-LOCK " S U B D I V I S I O N S " ENTER
: Input N	PRGM ▶ 2 ALPHA N ENTER
: (B - A)/2N → D	(ALPHA B - ALPHA A) ÷ 2 ALPHA N STO▸ D ENTER
calculates $\frac{1}{2}\Delta x$ and stores its value as *D*	
: 0 → L	0 STO▸ L ENTER
uses the variable *L* with the left Riemann Sum	
: 0 → M	0 STO▸ M ENTER
uses the variable *M* with the Midpoint Rule	
: 0 → C	0 STO▸ C ENTER
uses the variable *C* to keep track of the subdivisions	
: A → X	ALPHA A STO▸ X ENTER
starts off at the lower limit	
: Disp "Riemann Sums"	PRGM ▶ 1 2nd A-LOCK " R I E M A N N ␣ S U M S " ENTER
: Lbl 1	PRGM 1 1 ENTER
jumping point for the Goto command below	
: L + Y_1 → L	ALPHA L + 2nd Y-VARS 1 STO▸ L ENTER
adds the value of the function at the *left* endpoint of the current subdivision	
: X + D → X	ALPHA X + ALPHA D STO▸ X ENTER
increments by $\frac{1}{2}\Delta x$ to the *midpoint* of the subdivision	

: M + Y_1 → M ALPHA M + 2nd Y-VARS 1 STO▸ M ENTER

adds the value of the function at the *midpoint* of the current subdivision

: X + D → X ALPHA X + ALPHA D STO▸ X ENTER

increments by another $\frac{1}{2}\Delta x$ to the left endpoint of the *next* subdivision

: C + 1 → C ALPHA C + 1 STO▸ C ENTER

counts up one subdivision

: If C > N PRGM 3 ALPHA C 2nd TEST 3 ALPHA N ENTER

tests whether the *last* subdivision has been reached:

: Goto 1 PRGM 2 1 ENTER

if not, then go back and calculate another rectangular area;
if yes, then continue on to the next instruction

: Disp " Left" PRGM ▶ 1 2nd A-LOCK " ␣ L E F T " ENTER

: 2DL → L 2 ALPHA D ALPHA L STO▸ L ENTER

calculates left Riemann Sum

: Disp L PRGM ▶ 1 ALPHA L ENTER

: Pause PRGM 6 ENTER

during program execution, waits for you to press ENTER

: Disp " Right" PRGM ▶ 1 2nd A-LOCK " ␣ R I G H T " ENTER

: L + $2DY_1$ → R ALPHA L + 2 ALPHA D 2nd Y-VARS 1 STO▸ R ENTER

: A → X ALPHA A STO▸ X ENTER

: R - $2DY_1$ → R ALPHA R - 2 ALPHA D 2nd Y-VARS 1 STO▸ R ENTER

calculates right Riemann Sum

: Disp R PRGM ▶ 1 ALPHA R ENTER

: Pause PRGM 6 ENTER

: Disp "Midpoint Rule" PRGM ▶ 1 2nd A-LOCK " M I D P O I N T ␣ R U L E " ENTER

: 2DM → M 2 ALPHA D ALPHA M STO▸ M ENTER

calculates numerical integral by Midpoint Rule

: Disp M	PRGM ▶ 1 ALPHA M ENTER
: Pause	PRGM 6 ENTER
: Disp "Trapezoid Rule"	PRGM ▶ 1 2nd A-LOCK " T R A P E Z O I D ␣ R U L E " ENTER
: (L + R)/2 → T	(ALPHA L + ALPHA R) ÷ 2 STO▶ T ENTER

calculates numerical integral by Trapezoid Rule (average left and right Riemann Sums)

: Disp T	PRGM ▶ 1 ALPHA T ENTER
: Pause	PRGM 6 ENTER
: Disp "Simpsons Rule"	PRGM ▶ 1 2nd A-LOCK " S I M P S O N S ␣ R U L E " ENTER
: (2M + T)/3 → S	(2 ALPHA M + ALPHA T) ÷ 3 STO▶ S ENTER

calculates numerical integral by Simpson's Rule ($\frac{2}{3}$ Midpoint and $\frac{1}{3}$ Trapezoid)

: Disp S	PRGM ▶ 1 ALPHA S ENTER

When you have finished, press 2nd QUIT to leave the program editor.

1.10.2 Executing a Program: To execute the program just entered, press PRGM and then the number or letter that it was named. If you have forgotten its name, use the arrow keys to move through the program listing to find its description INTEGRAL. Then press ENTER to select this program and ENTER again to execute it.

The program INTEGRAL has been written to calculate $\int_A^B f(x)\,dx$ for N subdivisions of the interval $[A, B]$. You must enter the expression $f(x)$ as Y_1 before running this program. The program itself will prompt you for A, B, and N.

If you need to interrupt a program during execution, press ON.

The instruction manual for your TI-81 gives detailed information about programming. Refer to it to learn more about programming and how to use other features of your calculator.

CHAPTER 2

Texas Instruments TI-82 Graphics Calculator

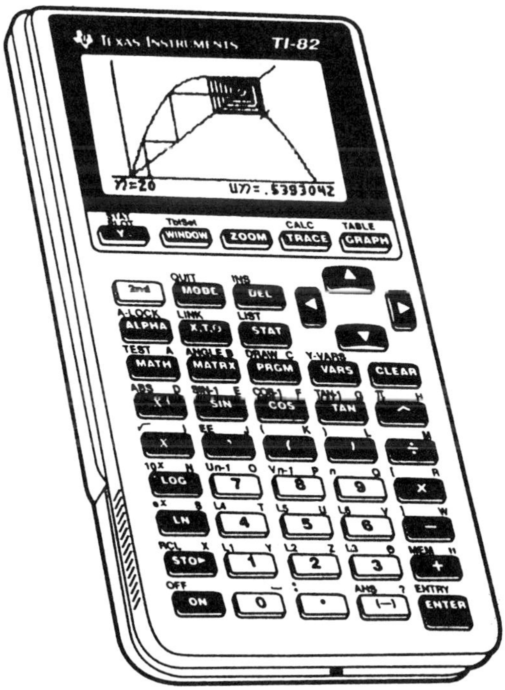

2.1 Getting started with the TI-82

2.1.1 Basics: Press the ON key to begin using your TI-82 calculator. If you need to adjust the display contrast, first press 2nd, then press and hold ▲ (the *up* arrow key) to increase the contrast or ▼ (the *down* arrow key) to decrease the contrast. As you press and hold ▲ or ▼, an integer between 0 (lightest) and 9 (darkest) appears in the upper right corner of the display. When you have finished with the calculator, turn it off to conserve battery power by pressing 2nd and then OFF.

Check the TI-82's settings by pressing MODE. If necessary, use the arrow keys to move the blinking cursor to a setting you want to change. Press ENTER to select a new setting. To start with, select the options along the left side of the MODE menu as illustrated in Figure 2.1: normal display, floating decimals, radian measure, function graphs, connected lines, sequential plotting, and full screen display. Details on alternative options will be given later in this guide. For now, leave the MODE menu by pressing CLEAR.

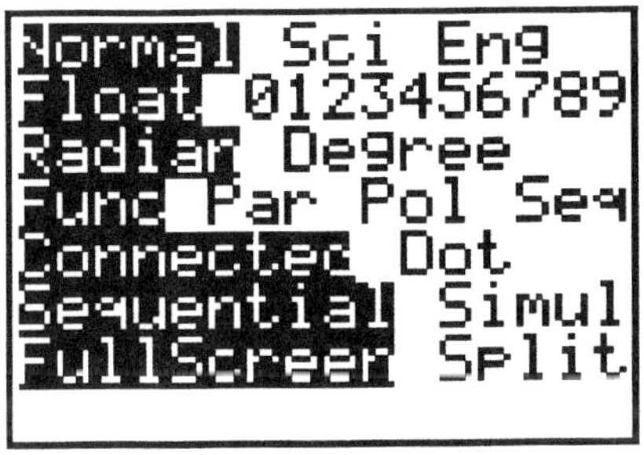

Figure 2.1: MODE menu

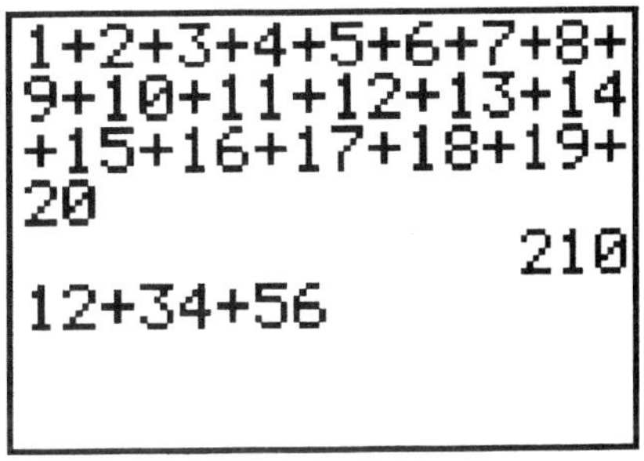

Figure 2.2: Home screen

2.1.2 Editing: One advantage of the TI-82 is that up to 8 lines are visible at one time, so you can *see* a long calculation. For example, type this sum (see Figure 2.2):

$$1 + 2 + 3 + 4 + 5 + 6 + 7 + 8 + 9 + 10 + 11 + 12 + 13 + 14 + 15 + 16 + 17 + 18 + 19 + 20$$

Then press ENTER to see the answer, too.

Often we do not notice a mistake until we see how unreasonable an answer is. The TI-82 permits you to re-display an entire calculation, edit it easily, then execute the *corrected* calculation.

Suppose you had typed 12 + 34 + 56 as in Figure 2.2 but had *not* yet pressed ENTER, when you realize that 34 should have been 74. Simply press ◀ (the *left* arrow key) as many times as necessary to move the blinking cursor left to 3, then type 7 to write over it. On the other hand, if 34 should have been 384, move the cursor back to 4, press 2nd INS (the cursor changes to a blinking underline) and then type 8 (inserts at the cursor position and other characters are pushed to the right). If the 34 should have been 3 only, move the cursor to 4 and press DEL to delete it.

Even if you had pressed ENTER, you may still edit the previous expression. Press 2nd and then ENTRY to *recall* the last expression that was entered. Now you can change it. In fact, the TI-82 retains many prior entries in a "last entry" storage area. Press 2nd ENTRY repeatedly until the previous line you want replaces the current line.

Technology Tip: When you need to evaluate a formula for different values of a variable, use the editing feature to simplify the process. For example, suppose you want to find the balance in an investment account if there is now \$5000 in the account and interest is compounded annually at the rate of 8.5%. The formula for the balance is $P(1+\frac{r}{n})^{nt}$, where P = principal, r = rate of interest (expressed as a decimal), n = number of times interest is compounded each year, and t = number of years. In our example, this becomes $5000(1+.085)^t$. Here are the keystrokes for finding the balance after t = 3, 5, and 10 years.

Years	*Keystrokes*	*Balance*
3	5000 (1 + .085) ^ 3 ENTER	\$6386.45
5	2nd ENTRY ◄ 5 ENTER	\$7518.28
10	2nd ENTRY ◄ 10 ENTER	\$11,304.92

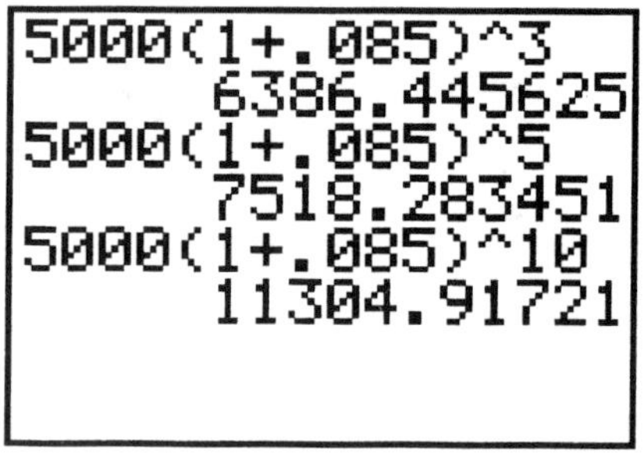

Figure 2.3: Editing expressions

Then to find the balance from the same initial investment but after 5 years when the annual interest rate is 7.5%, press these keys to change the last calculation above: 2nd ENTRY ◄ DEL ◄ 5 ◄ ◄ ◄ ◄ ◄ 7 ENTER.

2.1.3 Key Functions: Most keys on the TI-82 offer access to more than one function, just as the keys on a computer keyboard can produce more than one letter ("g" and "G") or even quite different characters ("5" and "%"). The primary function of a key is indicated on the key itself, and you access that function by a simple press on the key.

To access the *second* function indicated to the *left* above a key, first press 2nd (the cursor changes to a blinking ↑) and *then* press the key. For example, to calculate $\sqrt{25}$, press 2nd $\sqrt{\ }$ 25 ENTER.

When you want to use a letter or other character printed to the *right* above a key, first press ALPHA (the cursor changes to a blinking **A**) and then the key. For example, to use the letter K in a formula, press ALPHA K. If you need several letters in a row, press 2nd A-LOCK, which is like **CAPS LOCK** on a computer keyboard, and then press all the letters you want. Remember to press ALPHA when you are finished and want to restore the keys to their primary functions.

2.1.4 Order of Operations: The TI-82 performs calculations according to the standard algebraic rules. Working outwards from inner parentheses, calculations are performed from left to right. Powers and roots are evaluated first, followed by multiplications and divisions, and then additions and subtractions.

Note that the TI-82 distinguishes between *subtraction* and the *negative sign*. If you wish to enter a negative number, it is necessary to use the (-) key. For example, you would evaluate $-5-(4\cdot-3)$ by pressing (-) 5 - (4 × (-) 3) ENTER to get 7.

Enter these expressions to practice using your TI-82.

Expression	*Keystrokes*	*Display*
$7-5\cdot3$	7 - 5 × 3 ENTER	-8
$(7-5)\cdot3$	(7 - 5) × 3 ENTER	6
$120-10^2$	120 - 10 x² ENTER	20
$(120-10)^2$	(120 - 10) x² ENTER	12100
$\frac{24}{2^3}$	24 ÷ 2 ^ 3 ENTER	3
$\left(\frac{24}{2}\right)^3$	(24 ÷ 2) ^ 3 ENTER	1728
$(7--5)\cdot-3$	(7 - (-) 5) × (-) 3 ENTER	-36

2.1.5 Algebraic Expressions and Memory: Your calculator can evaluate expressions such as $\frac{N(N+1)}{2}$ *after* you have entered a value for N. Suppose you want $N = 200$. Press 200 STO▸ ALPHA N ENTER to store the value 200 in memory location N. Whenever you use N in an expression, the calculator will substitute the value 200 until you make a change by storing *another* number in N. Next enter the expression $\frac{N(N+1)}{2}$ by typing ALPHA N (ALPHA N + 1) ÷ 2 ENTER. For $N = 200$, you will find that $\frac{N(N+1)}{2} = 20100$.

The contents of any memory location may be revealed by typing just its letter name and then ENTER. And the TI-82 retains memorized values even when it is turned off, so long as its batteries are good.

2.1.6 Repeated Operations with **ANS:** The result of your *last* calculation is always stored in memory location ANS and replaces any previous result. This makes it easy to use the answer from one computation in another computation. For example, press 30 + 15 ENTER so that 45 is the last result displayed. Then press 2nd ANS ÷ 9 ENTER and get 5 because $\frac{45}{9} = 5$.

With a function like division, you press the ÷ key *after* you enter an argument. For such functions, whenever you would start a new calculation with the previous answer followed by pressing the function key, you may press just the function key. So instead of 2nd ANS ÷ 9 in the previous example, you could have pressed simply ÷ 9 to achieve the same result. This technique also works for these functions: + - × x^2 ^ x^{-1}.

Here is a situation where this is especially useful. Suppose a person makes \$5.85 per hour and you are asked to calculate earnings for a day, a week, and a year. Execute the given keystrokes to find the person's incomes during these periods (results are shown in Figure 2.4):

Pay period	*Keystrokes*	*Earnings*
8-hour day	5.85 × 8 ENTER	\$46.80
5-day week	× 5 ENTER	\$234
52-week year	× 52 ENTER	\$12,168

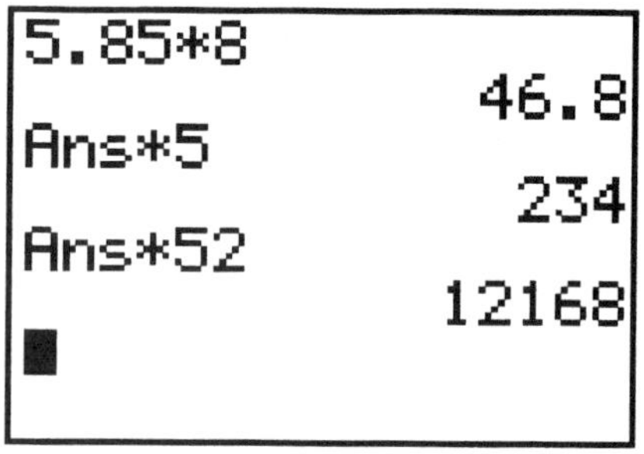

Figure 2.4: ANS variable

2.2.7 The ***MATH*** *Menu:* Operators and functions associated with a scientific calculator are available either immediately from the keys of the TI-82 or by 2nd keys. You have direct key access to common arithmetic operations (x^2, 2nd $\sqrt{\ }$, x^{-1}, ^, 2nd ABS), trigonometric functions (SIN, COS, TAN) and their inverses (2nd SIN^{-1}, 2nd COS^{-1}, 2nd TAN^{-1}), exponential and logarithmic functions (LOG, 2nd 10^x, LN, 2nd e^x), and a famous constant (2nd π).

A significant difference between the TI-82 and many scientific calculators is that the TI-82 requires the argument of a function *after* the function, as you would see a formula written in your textbook. For example, on the TI-82 you calculate $\sqrt{16}$ by pressing the keys 2nd $\sqrt{\ }$ 16 in that order.

Here are keystrokes for basic mathematical operations. Try them for practice on your TI-82.

Expression	*Keystrokes*	*Display*
$\sqrt{3^2+4^2}$	2nd $\sqrt{\ }$ (3 x^2 + 4 x^2) ENTER	5
$2\frac{1}{3}$	2 + 3 x^{-1} ENTER	2.333333333
$\|-5\|$	2nd ABS (-) 5 ENTER	5
$\log 200$	LOG 200 ENTER	2.301029996
$2.34 \cdot 10^5$	2.34 × 2nd 10^x 5 ENTER	234000

Additional mathematical operations and functions are available from the MATH menu (Figure 2.5). Press MATH to see the various options. You will learn in your mathematics textbook how to apply many of them. As an example, calculate $\sqrt[3]{7}$ by pressing MATH and then *either* 4 *or* ▼ ▼ ▼ ENTER; finally press 7 ENTER to see 1.912931183. To leave the MATH menu and take no other action, press 2nd QUIT or just CLEAR.

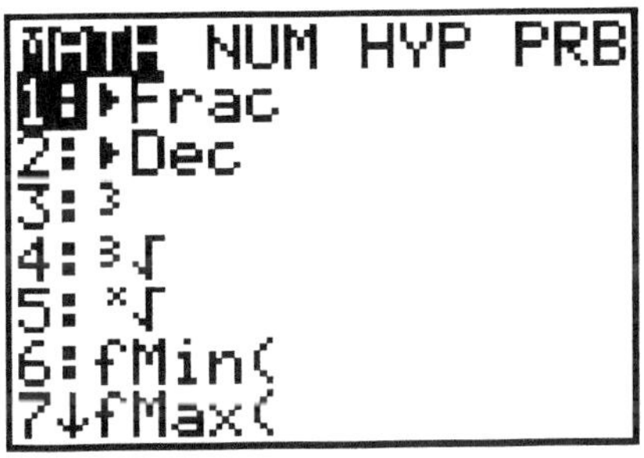

Figure 2.5: MATH menu

The *factorial* of a non-negative integer is the *product* of *all* the integers from 1 up to the given integer. The symbol for factorial is the exclamation point. So 4! (pronounced *four factorial*) is 1·2·3·4 = 24. You will learn more about applications of factorials in your textbook, but for now use the TI-82 to calculate 4! The factorial command is located in the MATH menu's PRB sub-menu. To compute 4!, press these keystrokes: 4 MATH ◀ 4 ENTER *or* 4 MATH ◀ ▼ ▼ ▼ ENTER ENTER.

Hyperbolic functions (sinh, cosh, and tanh) and their inverses are available from the HYP sub-menu of the MATH menu. For example, here are the keystrokes to calculate sinh 3: MATH ▶ ▶ 1 3 ENTER.

Note that you can select a sub-menu from the MATH menu by pressing either ◀ or ▶. It is easier to press ◀ once than to press ▶ three times to get to the PRB sub-menu.

2.2 Functions and Graphs

2.2.1 Evaluating Functions: Suppose you receive a monthly salary of \$1975 plus a commission of 10% of sales. Let x = your sales in dollars; then your wages W in dollars are given by the equation $W = 1975 + .10x$. If your January sales were \$2230 and your February sales were \$1865, what was your income during those months?

Here's how to use your TI-82 to perform this task. Press the Y= key at the top of the calculator to display the function editing screen (Figure 2.6). You may enter as many as ten different functions for the TI-82 to use at one time. If there is already a function Y_1, press ▲ or ▼ as many times as necessary to move the cursor to Y_1 and then press CLEAR to delete whatever was there. Then enter the expression $1975 + .10x$ by pressing these keys: 1975 + .10 X,T,θ. (The X,T,θ key lets you enter the variable X easily without having to use the ALPHA key.) Now press 2nd QUIT to return to the main calculations screen.

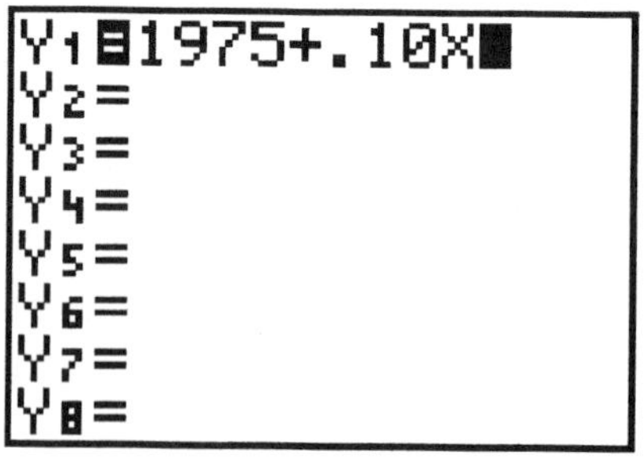

Figure 2.6: Y= screen

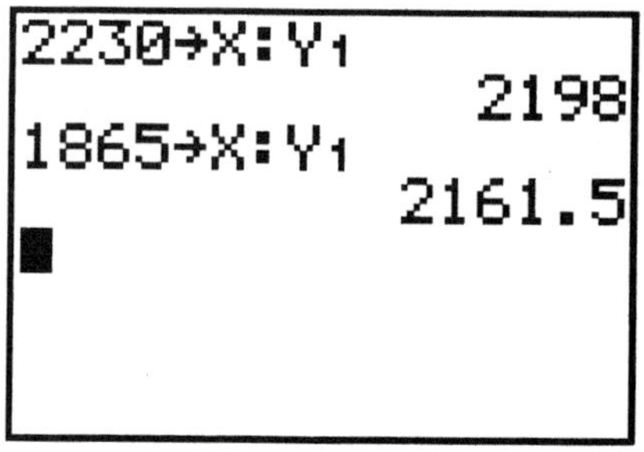

Figure 2.7: Evaluating a function

Assign the value 2230 to the variable x by these keystrokes (see Figure 2.7): 2230 STO▸ X,T,θ. Then press 2nd : to allow another expression to be entered on the same command line. Next press the following keystrokes to evaluate Y_1 and find January's wages: 2nd Y-VARS 1 1 ENTER.

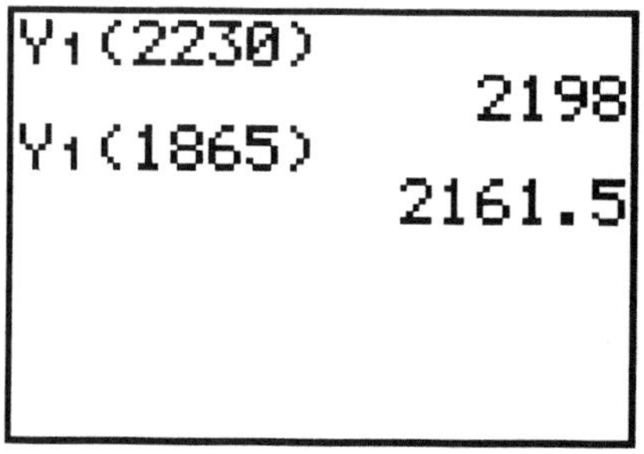

Figure 2.8: Function notation

It is not necessary to repeat all these steps to find the February wages. Simply press 2nd ENTRY to recall the entire previous line and change 2230 to 1865. Each time the TI-82 evaluates the function Y_1, it uses the *current* value of x.

Like your textbook, the TI-82 uses standard function notation. So to evaluate $Y_1(2230)$ when $Y_1(x) = 1975 + .10x$, press 2nd Y-VARS 1 1 (2230) ENTER (see Figure 2.8). Then to evaluate $Y_1(1865)$, press 2nd ENTRY to recall the last line and change 2230 to 1865.

You may also have the TI-82 make a table of values for the function. Press 2nd TblSet to set up the table (Figure 2.9). Move the blinking cursor onto Ask beside Indpnt:, then press ENTER. This configuration permits you to input values for x one at a time. Now press 2nd TABLE, enter 2230 in the x column, and press ENTER (see Figure 2.10). Continue to enter additional values for x and the calculator automatically completes the table with corresponding values of Y_1. Press 2nd QUIT to leave the TABLE screen.

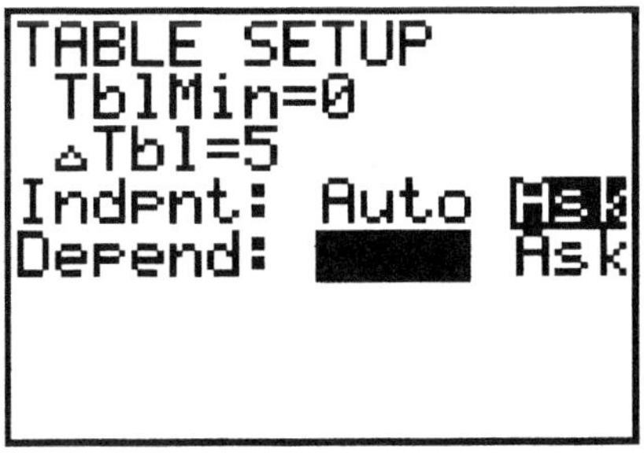

Figure 2.9: TblSet screen

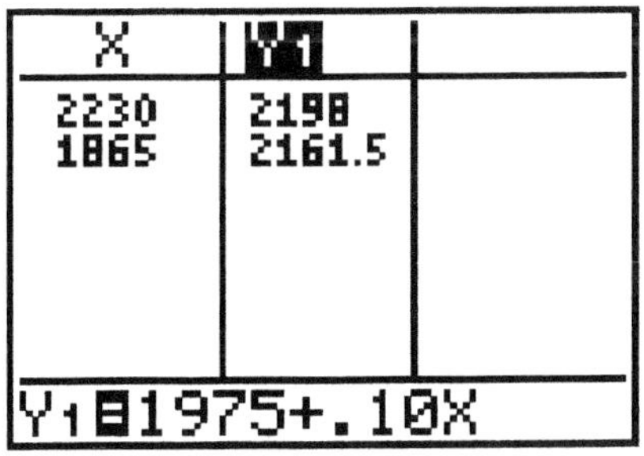

Figure 2.10: Table of values

Technology Tip: The TI-82 does not require multiplication to be expressed between variables, so xxx means x^3. It is often easier to press two or three x's together than to search for the square key or the cube operation. Of course, expressed multiplication is also not required between a constant and a variable. Hence to enter $2x^3 + 3x^2 - 4x + 5$ in the TI-82, you might save keystrokes and press just these keys: 2 X,T,θ X,T,θ X,T,θ + 3 X,T,θ X,T,θ - 4 X,T,θ + 5.

2.2.2 Functions in a Graph Window: Once you have entered a function in the Y= screen of the TI-82, just press GRAPH to see its graph. The ability to draw a graph contributes substantially to our ability to solve problems.

For example, here is how to graph $y = -x^3 + 4x$. First press Y= and delete anything that may be there by moving with the arrow keys to Y_1 or to any of the other lines and pressing CLEAR wherever necessary. Then, with the cursor on the top line Y_1, press (-) X,T,θ MATH 3 + 4 X,T,θ to enter the function (as in Figure 2.11). Now press GRAPH and the TI-82 changes to a window with the graph of $y = -x^3 + 4x$.

While the TI-82 is calculating coordinates for a plot, it displays a busy indicator at the top right of the graph window.

Technology Tip: If you would like to see a function in the Y= menu and its graph in a graph window, both at the same time, open the MODE menu, move the cursor down to the last line, and select Split screen. Your TI-82's screen is now divided horizontally (see Figure 2.11), with an upper graph window and a lower window that can display the home screen or an editing screen. The split screen is also useful when you need to do some calculations as you trace along a graph. For now, restore the TI-82 to FullScreen.

Your graph window may look like the one in Figure 2.12 or it may be different. Since the graph of $y = -x^3 + 4x$ extends infinitely far left and right and also infinitely far up and down, the TI-82 can display only a piece of the actual graph. This displayed rectangular part is called a *viewing rectangle*. You can easily change the viewing rectangle to enhance your investigation of a graph.

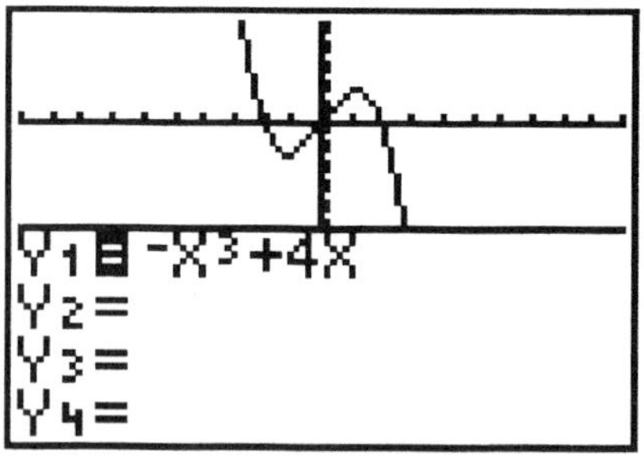

Figure 2.11: Split screen: Y= below

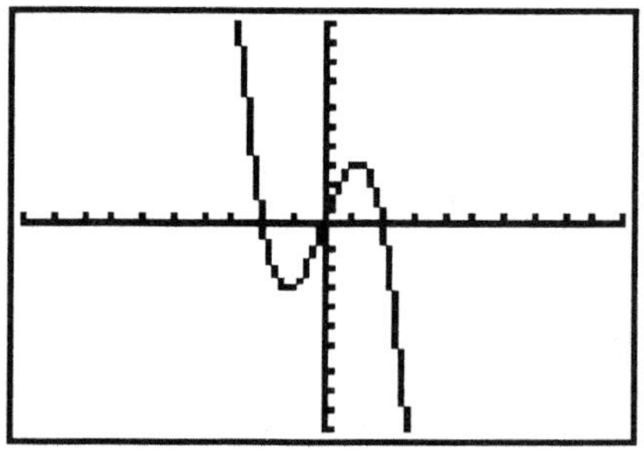

Figure 2.12: Graph of $y = -x^3 + 4x$

The viewing rectangle in Figure 2.12 shows the part of the graph that extends horizontally from -10 to 10 and vertically from -10 to 10. Press WINDOW to see information about your viewing rectangle. Figure 2.13 shows the WINDOW screen that corresponds to the viewing rectangle in Figure 2.12. This is the *standard* viewing rectangle for the TI-82.

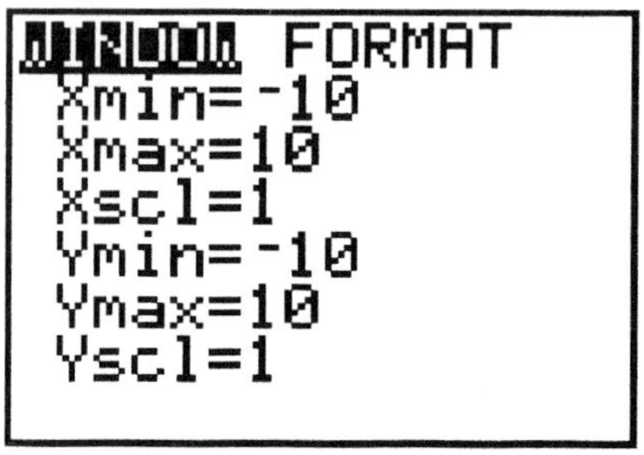

Figure 2.13: Standard WINDOW

The variables Xmin and Xmax are the minimum and maximum x-values of the viewing rectangle; Ymin and Ymax are its minimum and maximum y-values.

Xscl and Yscl set the spacing between tick marks on the axes.

Use the arrow keys ▲ and ▼ to move up and down from one line to another in this list; pressing the ENTER key will move down the list. Press CLEAR to delete the current value and then enter a new value. You may also edit the entry as you would edit an expression. Remember that a minimum *must* be less than the corresponding maximum or the TI-82 will issue an error message. Also, remember to use the (-) key, not - (which is subtraction), when you want to enter a negative value. Figures 2.12-13, 2.14-15, and 2.16-17 show different WINDOW screens and the corresponding viewing rectangle for each one.

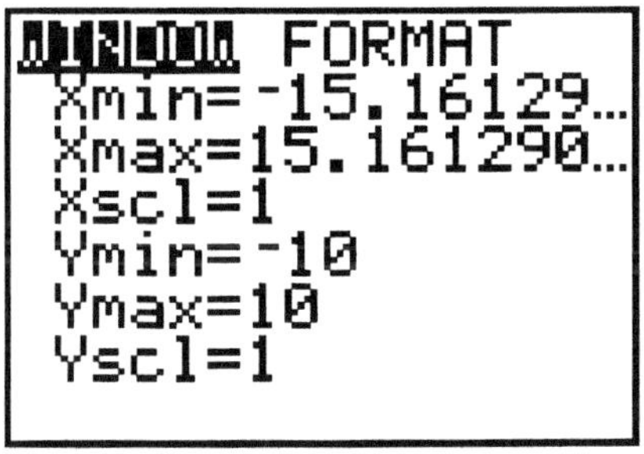

Figure 2.14: Square window

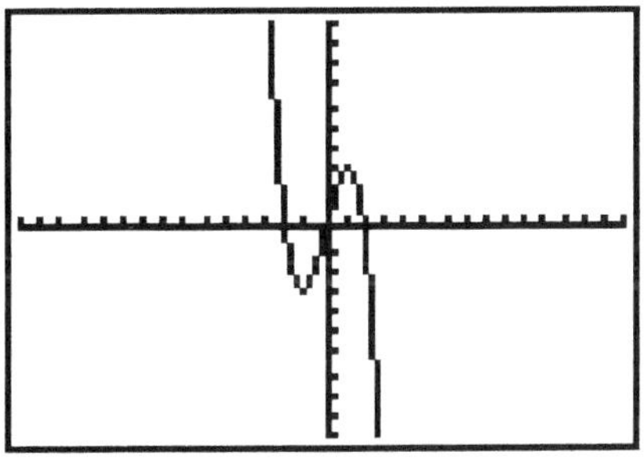

Figure 2.15: Graph of $y=-x^3+4x$

To set the range quickly to standard values (see Figure 2.13), press ZOOM 6. To set the viewing rectangle quickly to a square (Figure 2.14), press ZOOM 5. More information about square windows is presented later in Section 2.2.4.

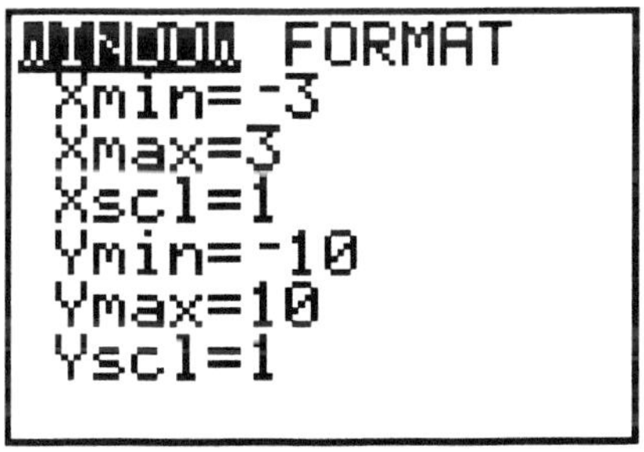

Figure 2.16: Custom window

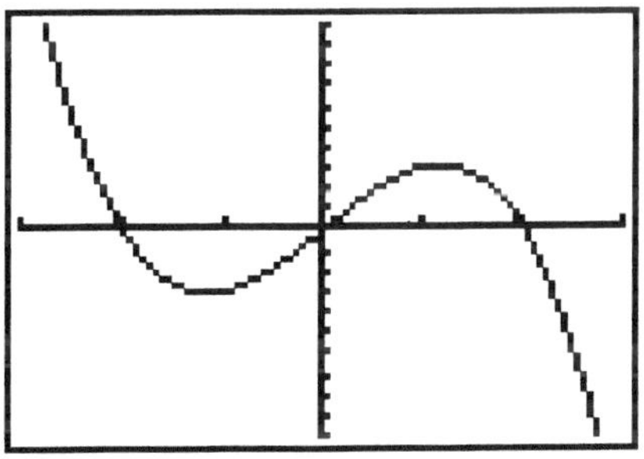

Figure 2.17: Graph of $y=-x^3+4x$

Sometimes you may wish to display grid points corresponding to tick marks on the axes. This and other graph format options may be changed by pressing WINDOW ▶ to display the FORMAT menu (Figure 2.18). Use arrow keys to move the blinking cursor to GridOn; press ENTER and then GRAPH to redraw the graph. Figure 2.19 shows the same graph as in Figure 2.17 but with the grid turned on. In general, you'll want the grid turned *off*, so do that now by pressing WINDOW ▶, use the arrow keys to move the blinking cursor to GridOff, and press ENTER and CLEAR.

Figure 2.18: WINDOW FORMAT menu

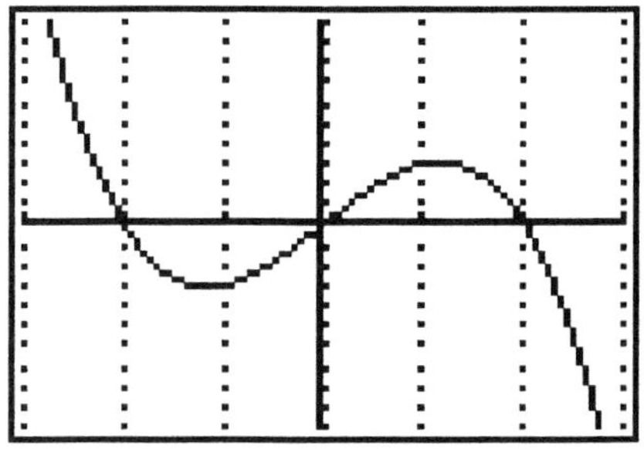

Figure 2.19: Grid turned on for $y = -x^3 + 4x$

2.2.3 The Greatest Integer Function: The greatest integer function, written [[x]], gives the greatest *integer* less than or equal to a number x. On the TI-82, the greatest integer function is called Int and is located under the NUM sub-menu of the MATH menu (see Figure 2.5). So calculate [[6.78]] = 6 by pressing MATH ▶ 4 6.78 ENTER.

To graph y = [[x]], go in the Y= menu, move beside Y_1 and press CLEAR MATH ▶ 4 X,T,θ GRAPH. Figure 2.20 shows this graph in a viewing rectangle from -5 to 5 in both directions.

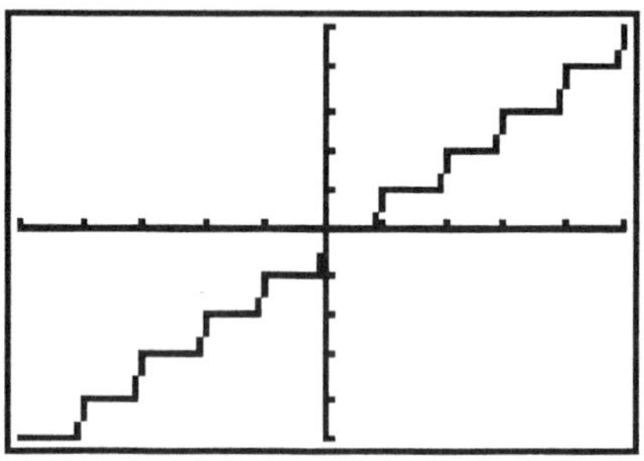

Figure 2.20: Connected graph of y = [[x]]

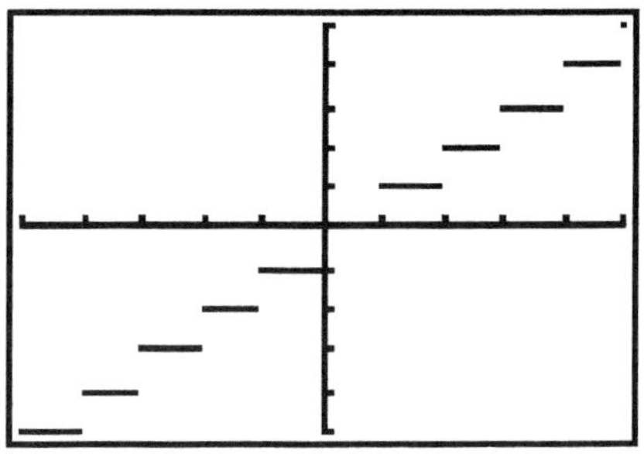

Figure 2.21: Dot graph of y = [[x]]

The true graph of the greatest integer function is a step graph, like the one in Figure 2.21. For the graph of y = [[x]], a segment should *not* be drawn between every pair of successive points. You can change from Connected line to Dot graph on the TI-82 by opening the MODE menu. Move the cursor down to the fifth line; select whichever graph type you require; press ENTER to put it into effect and GRAPH to see the result.

2.2.4 Graphing a Circle: Here is a useful technique for graphs that are not functions, but that can be "split" into a top part and a bottom part, or into multiple parts. Suppose you wish to graph the circle whose equation is $x^2 + y^2 = 36$. First solve for y and get an equation for the top semicircle, $y = \sqrt{36 - x^2}$, and for the

bottom semicircle, $y = -\sqrt{36 - x^2}$. Then graph the two semicircles simultaneously.

The keystrokes to draw this circle's graph follow. Enter $\sqrt{36 - x^2}$ as Y_1 and $-\sqrt{36 - x^2}$ as Y_2 (see Figure 2.22) by pressing Y= CLEAR 2nd $\sqrt{\ }$ (36 - X,T,θ x^2) ENTER CLEAR (-) 2nd $\sqrt{\ }$ (36 - X,T,θ x^2). Then press GRAPH to draw them both.

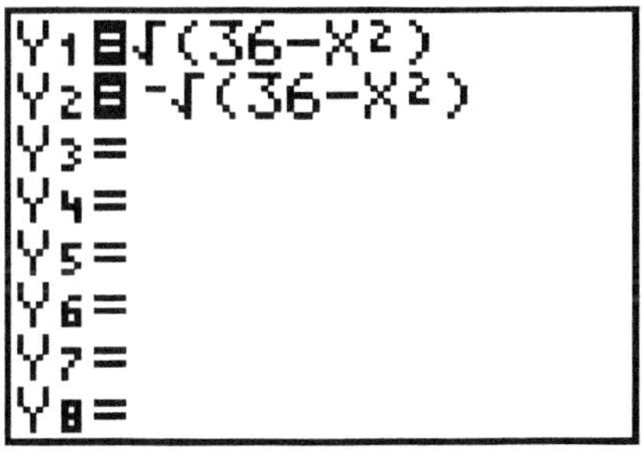

Figure 2.22: Two semicircles

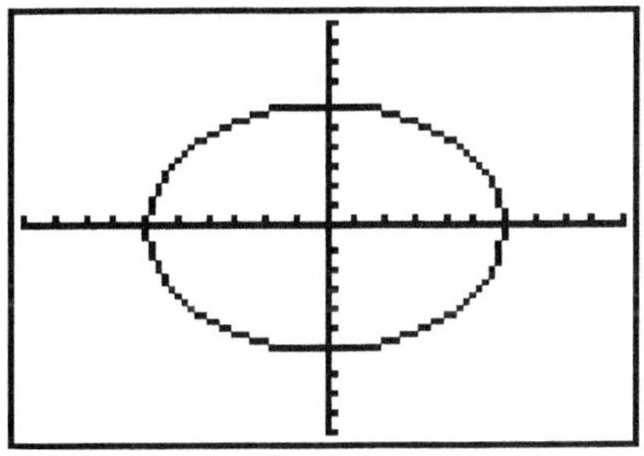
Figure 2.23: Circle's graph - standard view

If your range were set to the standard viewing rectangle, your graph would look like Figure 2.23. Now this does *not* look like a circle, because the units along the axes are not the same. This is where the square viewing rectangle is important. Press ZOOM 5 and see a graph that appears more circular.

Technology Tip: Another way to get a square graph is to change the range variables so that the value of Ymax - Ymin is approximately $\frac{2}{3}$ times Xmax - Xmin. For example, see the WINDOW in Figure 2.24 and the corresponding graph in Figure 2.25. The method works because the dimensions of the TI-82's display are such that the ratio of vertical to horizontal is approximately $\frac{2}{3}$.

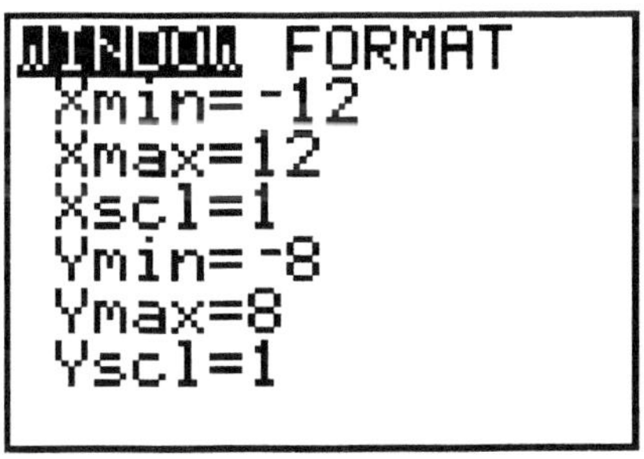

Figure 2.24: $\frac{\text{vertical}}{\text{horizontal}} = \frac{16}{24} = \frac{2}{3}$

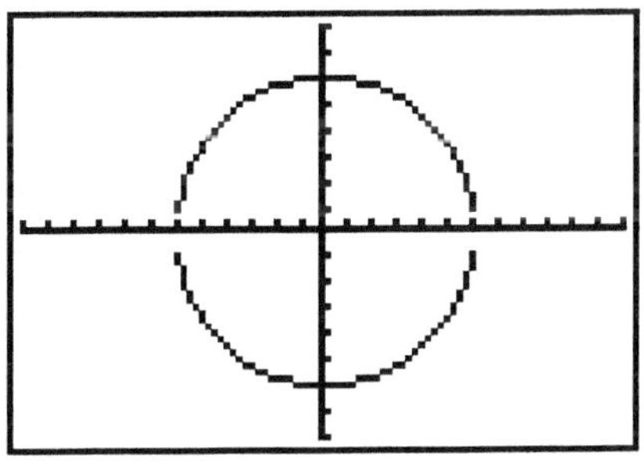
Figure 2.25: A "square" circle

The two semicircles in Figure 2.25 do not meet because of an idiosyncrasy in the way the TI-82 plots a graph.

Back when you entered $\sqrt{36 - x^2}$ as Y_1 and $-\sqrt{36 - x^2}$ as Y_2, you could have entered $-Y_1$ as Y_2 and saved some keystrokes. Try this by going back to the Y= menu and pressing the arrow key to move the cursor down to Y_2. Then press CLEAR (-) 2nd Y-VARS 1 1. The graph should be just as it was before.

Technology Tip: The square viewing rectangle is also important when you want to judge whether two lines are perpendicular. The intersection of perpendicular lines will always *look* like a right angle in a square viewing rectangle.

2.2.5 ***TRACE:*** Graph $y = -x^3 + 4x$ in the standard viewing rectangle. Press any of the arrow keys ▲ ▼ ◀ ▶ and see the cursor move from the center of the viewing rectangle. The coordinates of the cursor's location are displayed at the bottom of the screen, as in Figure 2.26, in floating decimal format. This cursor is called a *free-moving cursor* because it can move from dot to dot *anywhere* in the graph window.

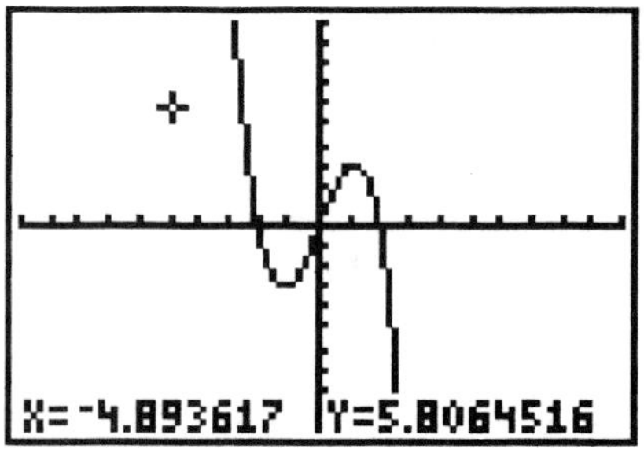

Figure 2.26: Free-moving cursor

Remove the free-moving cursor and its coordinates from the window by pressing GRAPH, CLEAR, or ENTER. Press an arrow key again and the free-moving cursor will reappear at the same point you left it.

Press TRACE to enable the left ◀ and right ▶ arrow keys to move the cursor along the function. The cursor is no longer free-moving, but is now constrained to the function. The coordinates that are displayed belong to points on the function's graph, so the y-coordinate is the calculated value of the function at the corresponding x-coordinate.

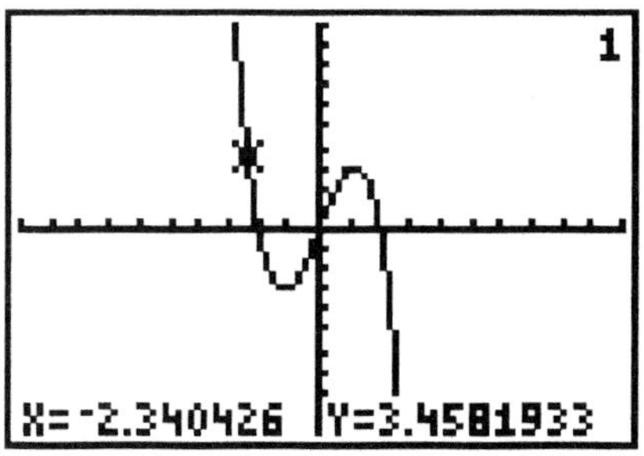

Figure 2.27: Trace on $y = -x^3 + 4x$

Now plot a second function, $y = -.25x$, along with $y = -x^3 + 4x$. Press Y= and enter $-.25x$ for Y_2, then press GRAPH.

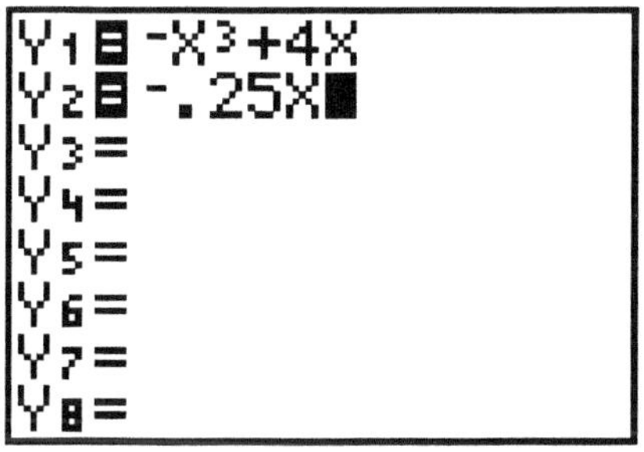

Figure 2.28: Two functions

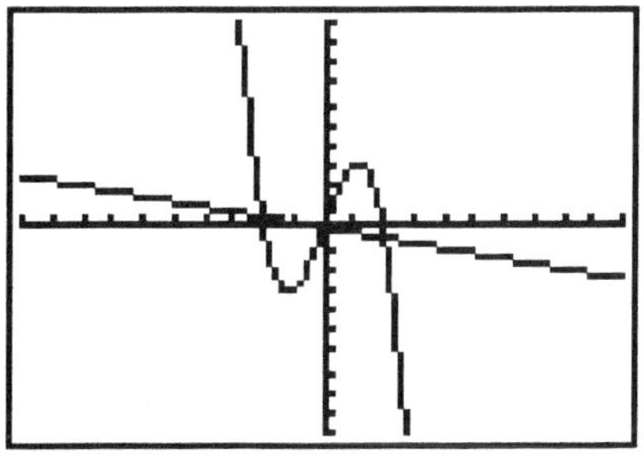

Figure 2.29: $y = -x^3 + 4x$ and $y = -.25x$

Note in Figure 2.28 that the equal signs next to Y_1 and Y_2 are *both* highlighted. This means *both* functions will be graphed. In the Y= screen, move the cursor directly on top of the equal sign next to Y_1 and press ENTER. This equal sign should no longer be highlighted (see Figure 2.30). Now press GRAPH and see that only Y_2 is plotted (Figure 2.31).

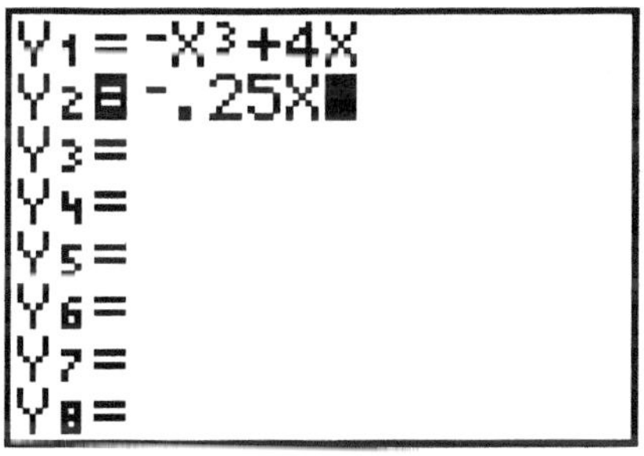

Figure 2.30: Y= screen with only Y_2 active

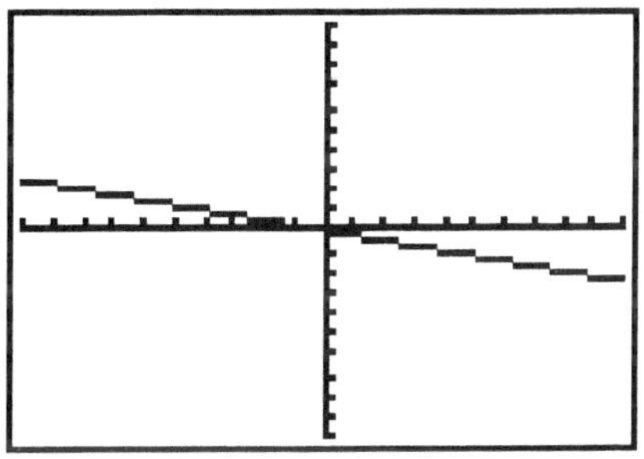

Figure 2.31: Graph of $y = -.25x$

Many different functions may be stored in the Y= list and any combination of them may be graphed simultaneously. You can make a function active or inactive for graphing by pressing ENTER on its equal sign to highlight (activate) or remove the highlight (deactivate). Go back to the Y= screen and do what is needed in order to graph Y_1 but not Y_2.

Now activate Y_2 again so that both graphs are plotted. Press TRACE and the cursor appears first on the graph of $y = -x^3 + 4x$ because it is higher up in the Y= list. You know that the cursor is on this function, Y_1, because of the numeral 1 that is displayed in the upper right corner of the window (see Figure 2.27). Press the up ▲ or down ▼ arrow key to move the cursor vertically to the graph of $y = -.25x$. Now the numeral 2 is displayed in the top right corner of the window. Next press the right and left arrow keys to trace along the graph of $y = -.25x$. When more than one function is plotted, you can move the trace cursor vertically from one graph to another in this way.

Technology Tip: By the way, trace along the graph of $y = -.25x$ and press and hold either ◀ or ▶. Eventually you will reach the left or right edge of the window. Keep pressing the arrow key and the TI-82 will allow you to continue the trace by panning the viewing rectangle. Check the WINDOW screen to see that Xmin and Xmax are automatically updated.

The TI-82's display has 95 horizontal columns of pixels and 63 vertical rows. So when you trace a curve across a graph window, you are actually moving from Xmin to Xmax in 94 equal jumps, each called Δx. You would calculate the size of each jump to be $\Delta x = \frac{\text{Xmax} - \text{Xmin}}{94}$. Sometimes you may want the jumps to be friendly numbers like .1 or .25 so that, when you trace along the curve, the x-coordinates will be incremented by such a convenient amount. Just set your viewing rectangle for a particular increment Δx by making Xmax = Xmin + 94·Δx. For example, if you want Xmin = -5 and Δx = .3, set Xmax = -5 + 94·.3 = 23.2. Likewise, set Ymax = Ymin + 62·Δy if you want the vertical increment to be some special Δy.

To center your window around a particular point, say (h, k), and also have a certain Δx, set Xmin = h - 47·Δx and Xmax = h + 47·Δx. Likewise, make Ymin = k - 31·Δy and Ymax = k + 31·Δy. For example, to center a window around the origin, (0, 0), with both horizontal and vertical increments of .25, set the range so that Xmin = 0 - 47·.25 = -11.75, Xmax = 0 + 47·.25 = 11.75, Ymin = 0 - 31·.25 = -7.75, and Ymax = 0 + 31·.25 = 7.75.

See the benefit by first plotting $y = x^2 + 2x + 1$ in a standard graphing window. Trace near its y-intercept, which is (0, 1), and move towards its x-intercept, which is (-1, 0). Then press ZOOM 4 and trace again near the intercepts.

2.2.6 ZOOM: Plot again the two graphs, for $y = -x^3 + 4x$ and for $y = -.25x$. There appears to be an intersection near $x = 2$. The TI-82 provides several ways to enlarge the view around this point.

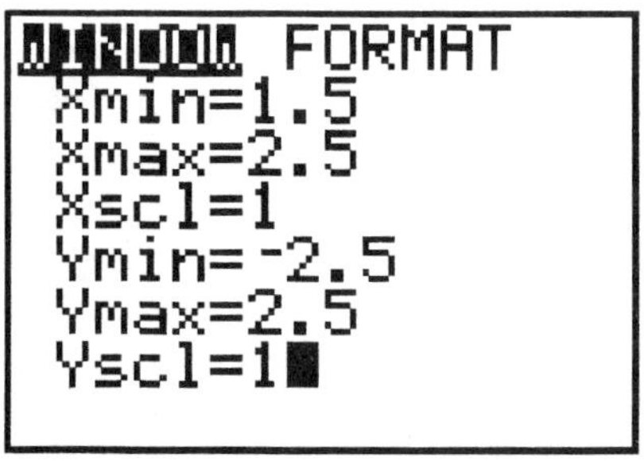

Figure 2.32: New WINDOW

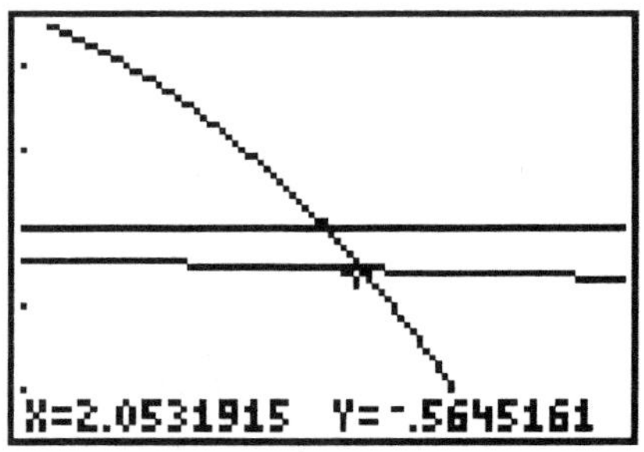

Figure 2.33: Closer view

You can change the viewing rectangle directly by pressing WINDOW and editing the values of Xmin,

Xmax, Ymin, and Ymax. Figure 2.33 shows a new viewing rectangle for the range displayed in Figure 2.32. The cursor has been moved near the point of intersection; move your cursor closer to get the best approximation possible for the coordinates of the intersection.

A more efficient method for enlarging the view is to draw a new viewing rectangle with the cursor. Start again with a graph of the two functions $y=-x^3+4x$ and $y=-.25x$ in a standard viewing rectangle (press ZOOM 6 for the standard window, from -10 to 10 along both axes).

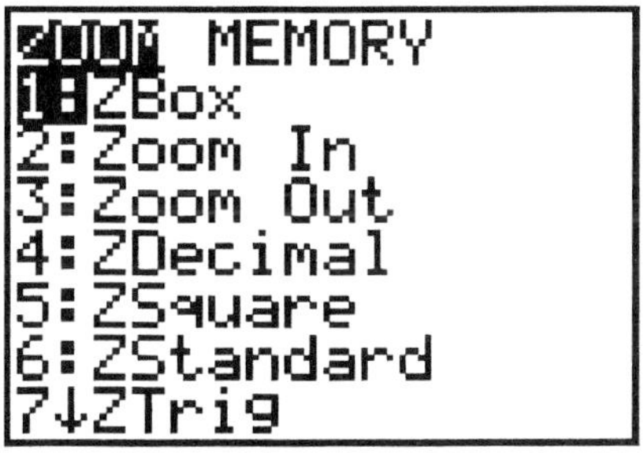

Figure 2.34: ZOOM menu

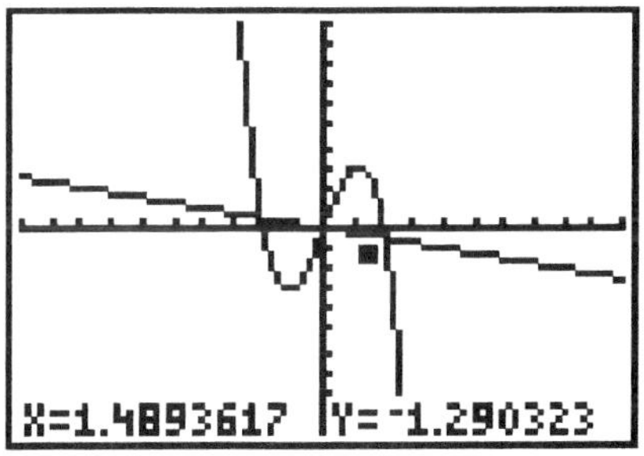

Figure 2.35: One corner selected

Now imagine a small rectangular box around the intersection point, near $x = 2$. Press ZOOM 1 (Figure 2.34) to draw a box to define this new viewing rectangle. Use the arrow keys to move the cursor, whose coordinates are displayed at the bottom of the window, to one corner of the new viewing rectangle you imagine.

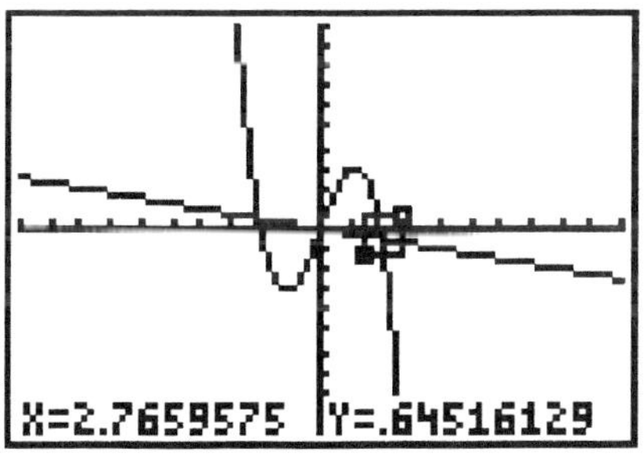

Figure 2.36: Box drawn

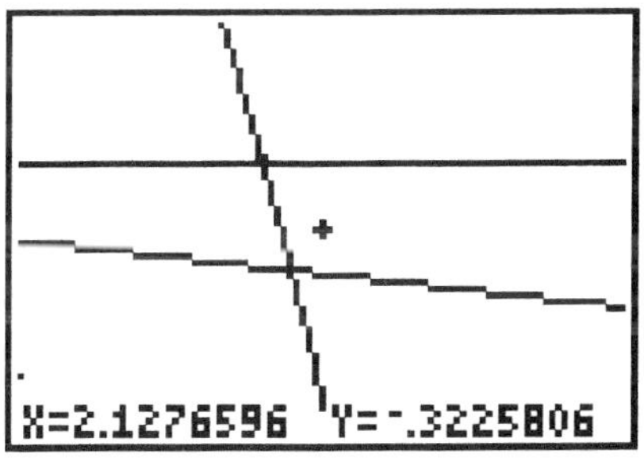

Figure 2.37: New viewing rectangle

Press ENTER to fix the corner where you have moved the cursor; it changes shape and becomes a blinking square (Figure 2.35). Use the arrow keys again to move the cursor to the diagonally opposite corner of the new rectangle (Figure 2.36). If this box looks all right to you, press ENTER. The rectangular area you have enclosed will now enlarge to fill the graph window (Figure 2.37).

You may interrupt the zoom any time *before* you press this last ENTER. Press ZOOM once more and start over. Press CLEAR or GRAPH to cancel the zoom, or press 2nd QUIT to cancel the zoom and return to the home screen.

You can also gain a quick magnification of the graph around the cursor's location. Return once more to the standard window for the graph of the two functions $y = -x^3 + 4x$ and $y = -.25x$. Press ZOOM 2 and then press arrow keys to move the cursor as close as you can to the point of intersection near $x = 2$ (see Figure 2.38). Then press ENTER and the calculator draws a magnified graph, centered at the cursor's position (Figure 2.39). The range variables are changed to reflect this new viewing rectangle. Look in the WINDOW menu to verify this.

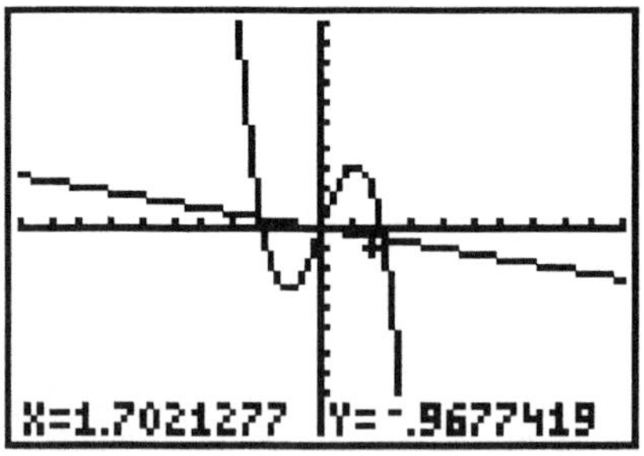

Figure 2.38: Before a zoom in

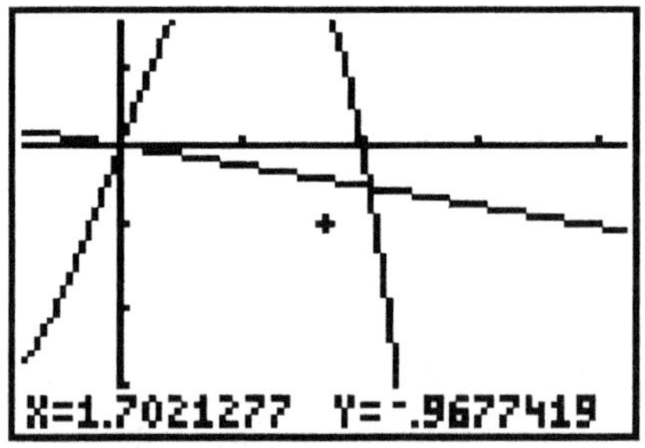

Figure 2.39: After a zoom in

As you see in the ZOOM menu (Figure 2.34), the TI-82 can Zoom In (press ZOOM 2) or Zoom Out (press ZOOM 3). Zoom out to see a larger view of the graph, centered at the cursor position. You can change the horizontal and vertical scale of the magnification by pressing ZOOM ▶ 4 (see Figure 2.41) and editing XFact and YFact, the horizontal and vertical magnification factors.

The default zoom factor is 4 in both directions. It is not necessary for XFact and YFact to be equal. Sometimes, you may prefer to zoom in one direction only, so the other factor should be set to 1. As usual, press 2nd QUIT to leave the ZOOM menu.

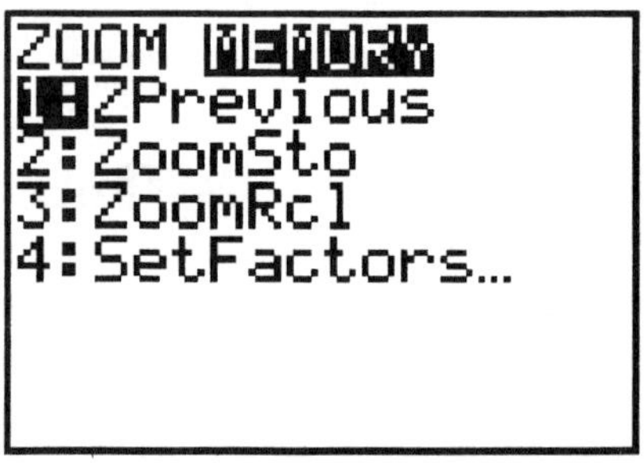

Figure 2.40: ZOOM MEMORY menu

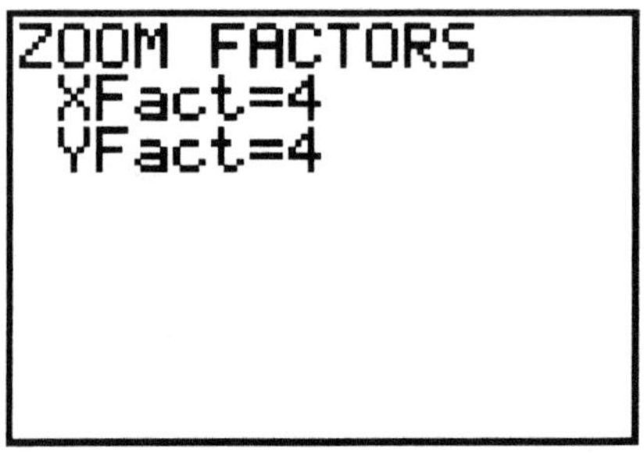

Figure 2.41: ZOOM MEMORY SetFactors...

Technology Tip: The TI-82 remembers the window it displayed before a zoom. So if you should zoom in too much and lose the curve, press ZOOM ▶ 1 to go back to the window before. If you want to execute a series of zooms but then return to a particular window, press ZOOM ▶ 2 to store the current window's dimensions. Later, press ZOOM ▶ 3 to recall the stored window.

2.2.7 Relative Minimums and Maximums: Graph $y = -x^3 + 4x$ once again in the standard viewing rectangle (Figure 2.12). This function appears to have a relative minimum near x = -1 and a relative maximum near x = 1. You may zoom and trace to approximate these extreme values.

First trace along the curve near the local minimum. Notice by how much the x-values and y-values change as you move from point to point. Trace along the curve until the y-coordinate is as *small* as you can get it, so that you are as close as possible to the local minimum, and zoom in (press ZOOM 2 or use a zoom box). Now trace again along the curve and, as you move from point to point, see that the coordinates change by smaller amounts than before. Keep zooming and tracing until you find the coordinates of the local minimum point as accurately as you need them, approximately (-1.15, -3.08).

Follow a similar procedure to find the relative maximum. Trace along the curve until the y-coordinate is as *great* as you can get it, so that you are as close as possible to the relative maximum, and zoom in. The local maximum point on the graph of $y = -x^3 + 4x$ is approximately (1.15, 3.08).

The TI-82 automates the search for relative minimum and relative maximum points. Press 2nd CALC to display the CALCULATE menu (Figure 2.42). Choose 3 to calculate the minimum value of the function and 4 for the maximum. You will be prompted to trace the cursor along the graph first to a point *left* of the minimum/maximum (press ENTER to set this *lower bound*). Then move to a point *right* of the minimum/maximum and set an *upper bound* (as in Figure 2.43) and press ENTER. Note the two arrows marking the lower and upper bounds at the top of the display.

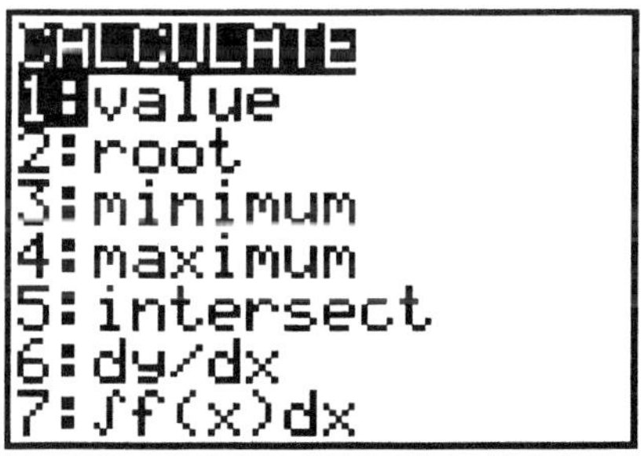

Figure 2.42: CALCULATE menu

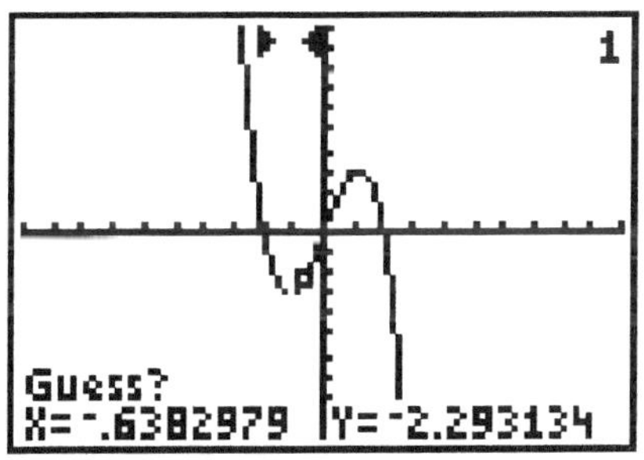

Figure 2.43: Finding a minimum

Next move the cursor along the graph between the two bounds and as close to the minimum/maximum as you can; this serves as a *guess* for the TI-82 to start its search. Good choices for the lower bound, upper bound, and guess can help the calculator work more efficiently and quickly. Press ENTER and the coordinates of the relative minimum/maximum point will be displayed (see Figure 2.44).

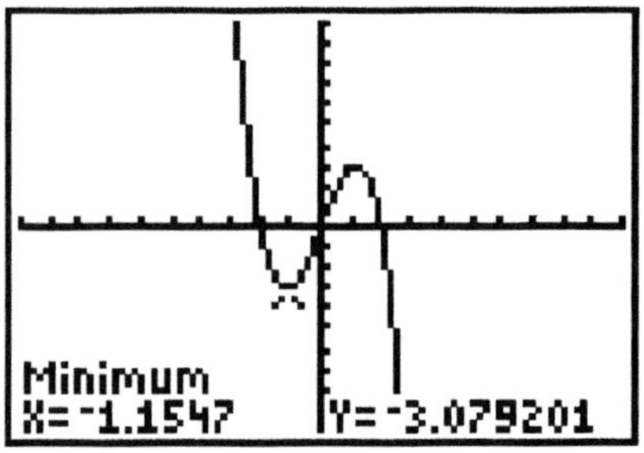

Figure 2.44: Relative minimum on $y = -x^3 + 4x$

2.3 Solving Equations and Inequalities

2.3.1 Intercepts and Intersections: Tracing and zooming are also used to locate an x-intercept of a graph, where a curve crosses the x-axis. For example, the graph of $y = x^3 - 8x$ crosses the x-axis three times (see Figure 2.45). After tracing over to the x-intercept point that is furthest to the left, zoom in (Figure 2.46). Continue this process until you have located all three intercepts with as much accuracy as you need. The three x-intercepts of $y = x^3 - 8x$ are approximately -2.828, 0, and 2.828.

Technology Tip: As you zoom in, you may also wish to change the spacing between tick marks on the x-axis so that the viewing rectangle shows scale marks near the intercept point. Then the accuracy of your approximation will be such that the error is less than the distance between two tick marks. Change the x-scale on the TI-82 from the WINDOW menu. Move the cursor down to Xscl and enter an appropriate value.

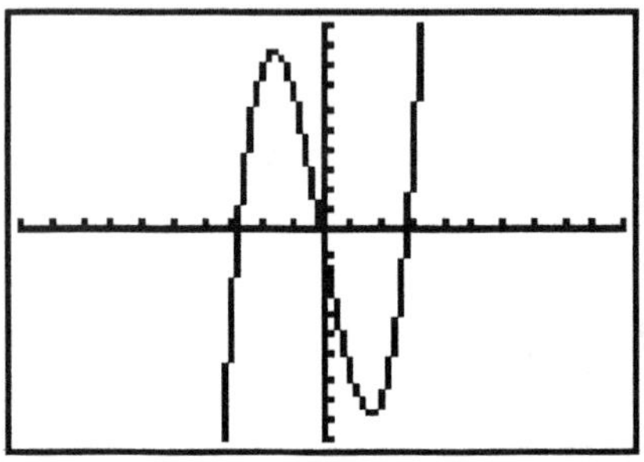

Figure 2.45: Graph of $y = x^3 - 8x$

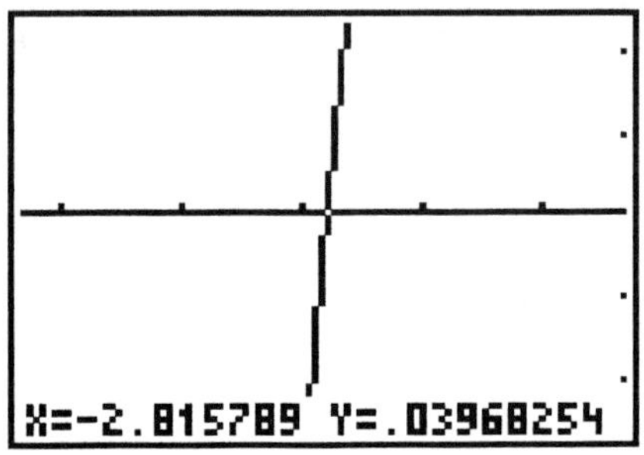

Figure 2.46: An x-intercept of $y = x^3 - 8x$

The x-intercept of a function's graph is a *root* of the equation $f(x) = 0$. So press 2nd CALC to display the CALCULATE menu (Figure 2.42) and choose 2 to find a root of this function. Set a lower bound, upper bound, and guess as described above in Section 2.2.7.

TRACE and ZOOM are especially important for locating the intersection points of two graphs, say the graphs of $y=-x^3+4x$ and $y=-.25x$. Trace along one of the graphs until you arrive close to an intersection point. Then press ▲ or ▼ to jump to the other graph. Notice that the x-coordinate does not change, but the y-coordinate is likely to be different (see Figures 2.47 and 2.48).

When the two y-coordinates are as close as they can get, you have come as close as you now can to the point of intersection. So zoom in around the intersection point, then trace again until the two y-coordinates are as close as possible. Continue this process until you have located the point of intersection with as much accuracy as necessary.

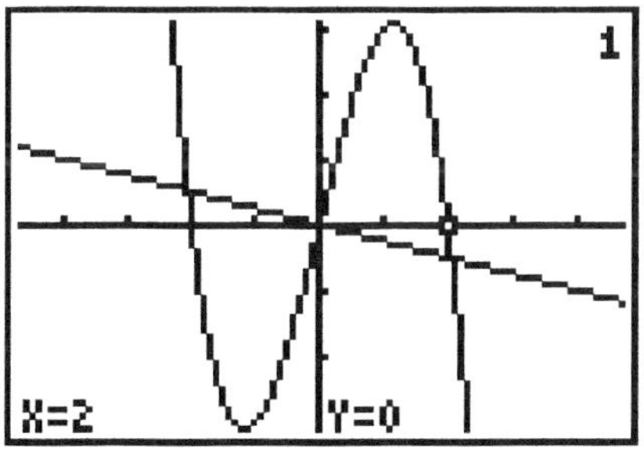

Figure 2.47: Trace on $y=-x^3+4x$

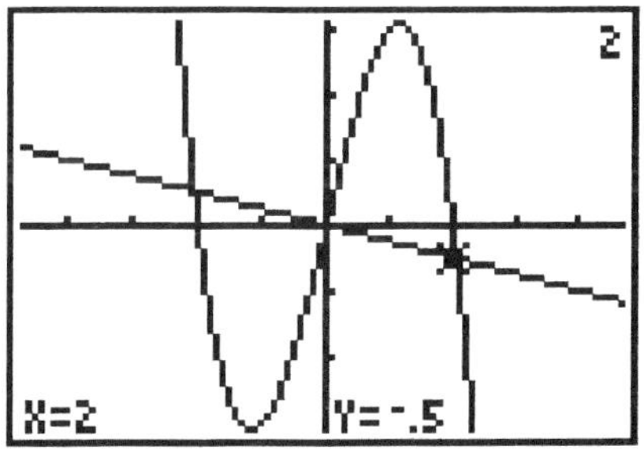

Figure 2.48: Trace on $y=-.25x$

You can also find the point of intersection of two graphs by pressing 2nd CALC 5. Trace with the cursor first along one graph near the intersection and press ENTER; then trace with the cursor along the other graph and press ENTER. Marks + are placed on the graphs at these points. Finally, move the cursor near the point of intersection and press ENTER again. Coordinates of the intersection will be displayed at the bottom of the window.

2.3.2 Solving Equations by Graphing: Suppose you need to solve the equation $24x^3-36x+17=0$. First graph $y=24x^3-36x+17$ in a window large enough to exhibit *all* its x-intercepts, corresponding to all its roots. Then use trace and zoom, or the TI-82's root finder, to locate each one. In fact, this equation has just one solution, approximately x = -1.414.

Remember that when an equation has more than one x-intercept, it may be necessary to change the viewing rectangle a few times to locate all of them.

Technology Tip: To solve an equation like $24x^3+17=36x$, you may first transform it into standard form, $24x^3-36x+17=0$, and proceed as above. However, you may also graph the *two* functions $y=24x^3+17$ and $y=36x$, then zoom and trace to locate their point of intersection.

2.3.3 Solving Systems by Graphing: The solutions to a system of equations correspond to the points of intersection of their graphs (Figure 2.49). For example, to solve the system $y=x^2-3x-4$ and $y=x^3+3x^2-2x-1$, first graph them together. Then zoom and trace, or use the intersect option in the

CALC menu, to locate their point of intersection, approximately (-2.17, 7.25).

You must judge whether the two current y-coordinates are sufficiently close for x = -2.17 or whether you should continue to zoom and trace to improve the approximation.

The solutions of the system of two equations $y=x^3+3x^2-2x-1$ and $y=x^2-3x-4$ correspond to the solutions of the single equation $x^3+3x^2-2x-1=x^2-3x-4$, which simplifies to $x^3+2x^2+x+3=0$. So you may also graph $y=x^3+2x^2+x+3$ and find its x-intercepts to solve the system.

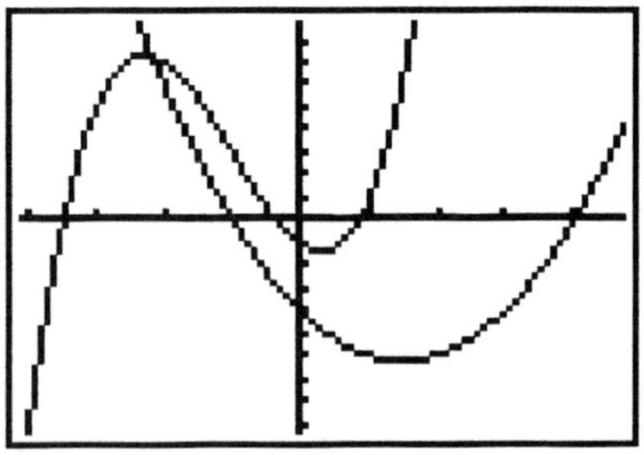

Figure 2.49: Solving a system of equations

2.3.4 Solving Inequalities by Graphing: Consider the inequality $1-\frac{3x}{2}\geq x-4$. To solve it with your TI-82, graph the two functions $y=1-\frac{3x}{2}$ and $y=x-4$ (Figure 2.50). First locate their point of intersection, at x = 2. The inequality is true when the graph of $y=1-\frac{3x}{2}$ lies *above* the graph of $y=x-4$, and that occurs for x < 2. So the solution is the half-line $x\leq 2$, or $(-\infty, 2]$.

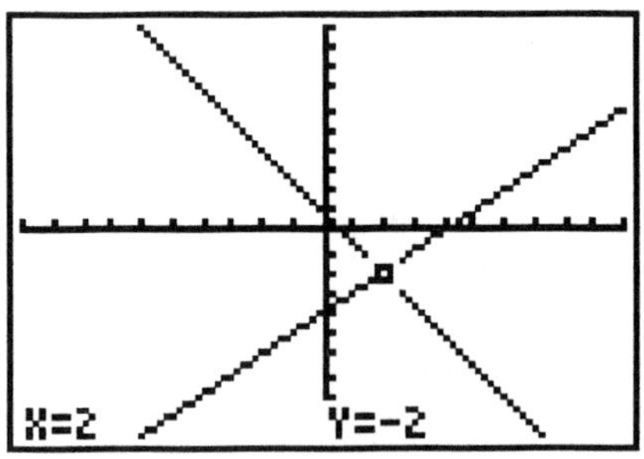

Figure 2.50: Solving $1-\frac{3x}{2}\geq x-4$

The TI-82 is capable of shading the region above or below a graph or between two graphs. For example, to graph $y \ge x^2 - 1$, first graph the function $y = x^2 - 1$ as Y_1. Then press 2nd DRAW 7 2nd Y-VARS 1 1 , 10 , 2) ENTER (see Figure 2.51). These keystrokes instruct the TI-82 to shade the region *above* $y = x^2 - 1$ and *below* y = 10 (chosen because this is the greatest *y*-value in the graph window) with shading resolution value of 2. The result is shown in Figure 2.52.

To clear the shading, press 2nd DRAW 1.

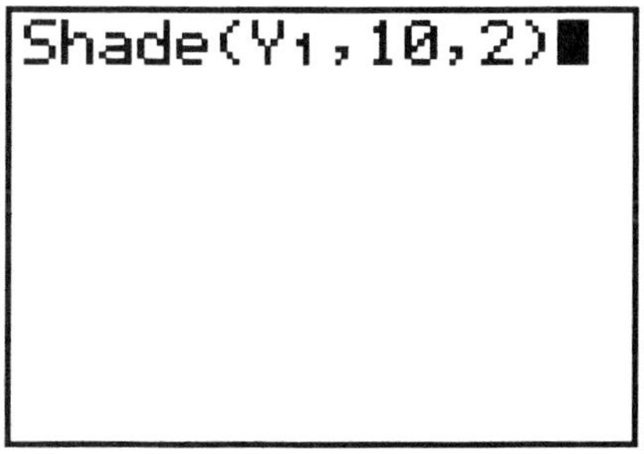

Figure 2.51: DRAW Shade

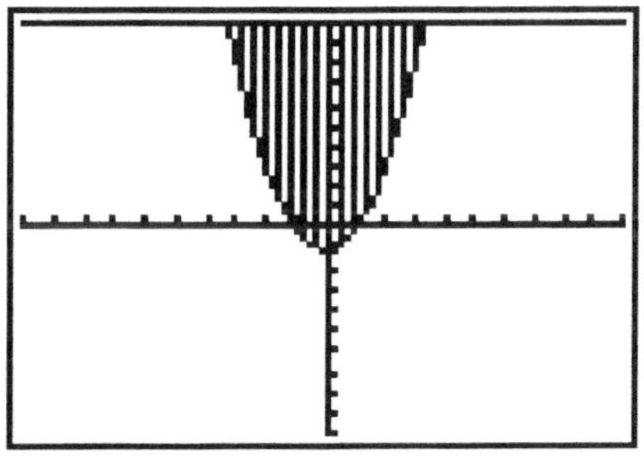

Figure 2.52: Graph of $y \ge x^2 - 1$

Now use shading to solve the previous inequality, $1 - \frac{3x}{2} \ge x - 4$. The function whose graph forms the lower boundary is named *first* in the SHADE command (see Figure 2.53). To enter this in your TI-82, press these keys: 2nd DRAW 7 X,T,θ - 4 , 1 - 3 X,T,θ ÷ 2 , 2) ENTER (Figure 2.54). The shading extends left from x = 2, hence the solution to $1 - \frac{3x}{2} \ge x - 4$ is the half-line $x \le 2$, or $(-\infty, 2]$.

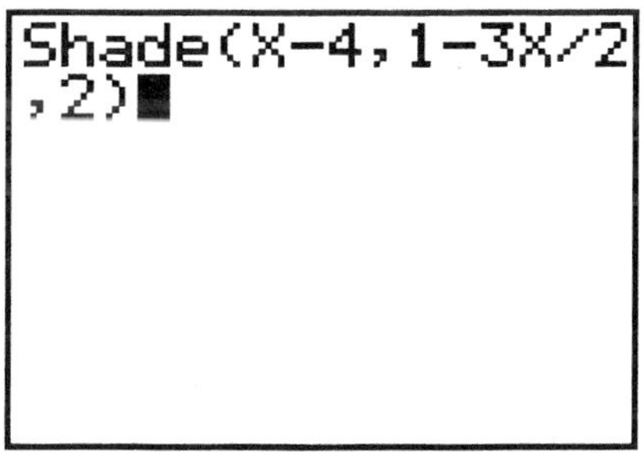

Figure 2.53: DRAW Shade command

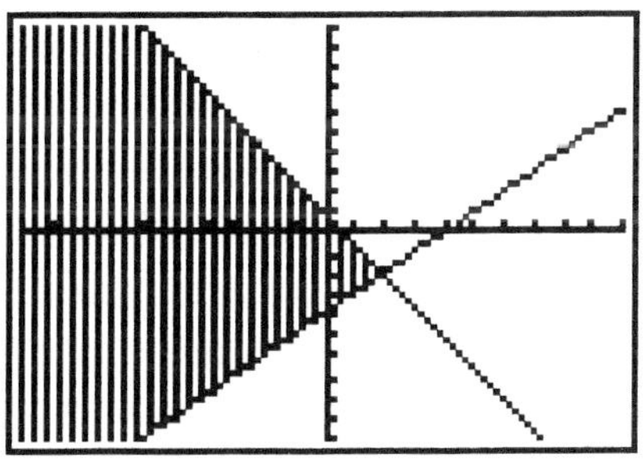

Figure 2.54: Graph of $1 - \frac{3x}{2} \ge x - 4$

More information about the DRAW menu is in the TI-82 manual.

2.4 Trigonometry

2.4.1 Degrees and Radians: The trigonometric functions can be applied to angles measured either in radians or degrees, but you should take care that the TI-82 is configured for whichever measure you need. Press MODE to see the current settings. Press ▼ twice and move down to the third line of the mode menu where angle measure is selected. Then press ◀ or ▶ to move between the displayed options. When the blinking cursor is on the measure you want, press ENTER to select it. Then press CLEAR or 2nd QUIT to leave the mode menu.

It's a good idea to check the angle measure setting before executing a calculation that depends on a particular measure. You may change a mode setting at any time and not interfere with pending calculations. Try the following keystrokes to see this in action.

Expression	*Keystrokes*	*Display*
$\sin 45°$	MODE ▼ ▼ ▶ ENTER 2nd QUIT SIN 45 ENTER	.7071067812
$\sin \pi°$	SIN 2nd π ENTER	.0548036651
$\sin \pi$	SIN 2nd π MODE ▼ ▼ ENTER 2nd QUIT ENTER	0
$\sin 45$	SIN 45 ENTER	.8509035245
$\sin \frac{\pi}{6}$	SIN (2nd π ÷ 6) ENTER	.5

The first line of keystrokes sets the TI-82 in degree mode and calculates the sine of 45 *degrees*. While the calculator is still in degree mode, the second line of keystrokes calculates the sine of π *degrees*, 3.1415°. The third line changes to radian mode just before calculating the sine of π *radians*. The fourth line calculates the sine of 45 *radians* (the calculator is already in radian mode).

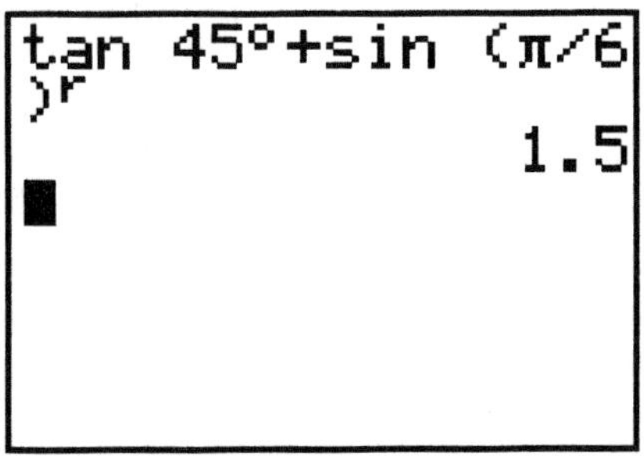

Figure 2.55: Angle measure

The TI-82 makes it possible to mix degrees and radians in a calculation. Execute these keystrokes to calculate $\tan 45° + \sin\frac{\pi}{6}$ as shown in Figure 2.55: TAN 45 2nd ANGLE 1 + SIN (2nd π ÷ 6) 2nd ANGLE 3 ENTER. Do you get 1.5 whether your calculator is set *either* in degree mode *or* in radian mode?

2.4.2 Graphs of Trigonometric Functions: When you graph a trigonometric function, you need to pay careful attention to the choice of graph window. For example, graph $y = \dfrac{\sin 30x}{30}$ in the standard viewing rectangle. Trace along the curve to see where it is. Zoom in to a better window, or use the period and amplitude to establish better WINDOW values.

Technology Tip: Since $\pi \approx 3.1$, set Xmin = 0 and Xmax = 6.3 to cover the interval from 0 to 2π.

Next graph $y = \tan x$ in the standard window first, then press ZOOM 7 to change to a special window for trigonometric functions in which the horizontal increment is $\frac{\pi}{24}$. The TI-82 plots consecutive points and then connects them with a segment, so the graph is not exactly what you should expect. You may wish to change from Connected line to Dot graph (see Section 2.2.3) when you plot the tangent function.

2.5 Differentiation

2.5.1 Limits: Suppose you need to find this limit: $\lim_{x\to 0} \dfrac{\sin 4x}{x}$. Plot the graph of $f(x) = \dfrac{\sin 4x}{x}$ in a convenient viewing rectangle that contains the point where the function appears to intersect the line $x = 0$ (because you want the limit as $x \to 0$). Your graph should lend support to the conclusion that $\lim_{x\to 0} \dfrac{\sin 4x}{x} = 4$.

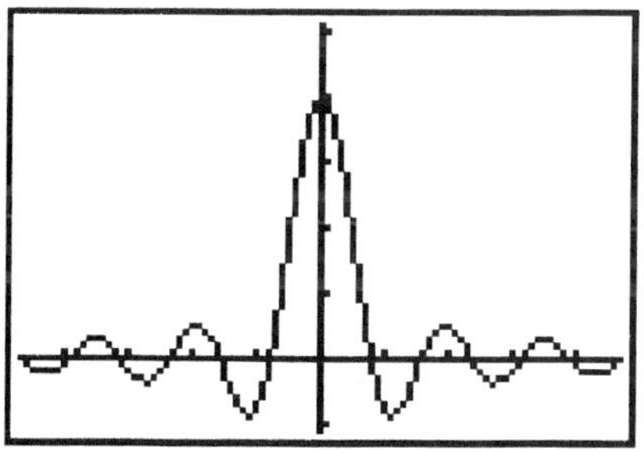

Figure 2.56: Checking $\lim_{x\to 0} \dfrac{\sin 4x}{x} = 4$

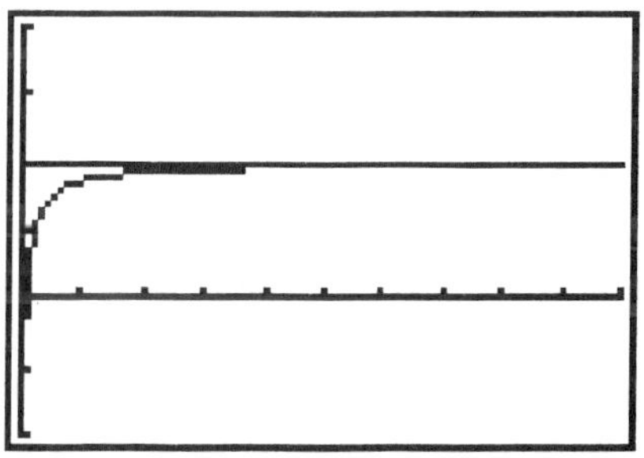

Figure 2.57: Checking $\lim_{x\to\infty} \dfrac{2x-1}{x+1} = 2$

To test the reasonableness of the conclusion that $\lim_{x\to\infty} \dfrac{2x-1}{x+1} = 2$, evaluate the function $f(x) = \dfrac{2x-1}{x+1}$ for several large positive values of x (since you want the limit as $x \to \infty$). For example, evaluate *f*(100), *f*(1000), and *f*(10,000). Another way to test the reasonableness of this result is to examine the graph of

$f(x) = \frac{2x-1}{x+1}$ in a viewing rectangle that extends over large values of x. See, as in Figure 2.57 (where the viewing rectangle extends horizontally from 0 to 100), whether the graph is asymptotic to the horizontal line $y = 2$ (enter $\frac{2x-1}{x+1}$ for Y_1 and 2 for Y_2).

2.5.2 Numerical Derivatives: The derivative of a function f at x can be defined as the limit of the slopes of secant lines, so $f'(x) = \lim_{\Delta x \to 0} \frac{f(x+\Delta x) - f(x-\Delta x)}{2\Delta x}$. And for small values of Δx, the expression $\frac{f(x+\Delta x) - f(x-\Delta x)}{2\Delta x}$ gives a good approximation to the limit.

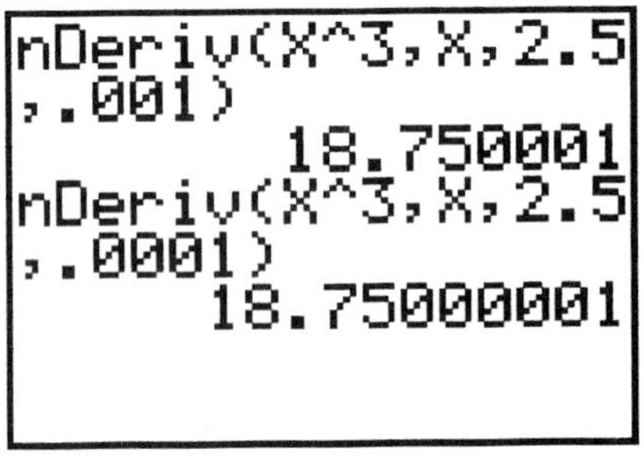

Figure 2.58: Using nDeriv(

The TI-82 has a function nDeriv(in the MATH menu to calculate the *symmetric difference*, $\frac{f(x+\Delta x) - f(x-\Delta x)}{2\Delta x}$. So to find a numerical approximation to $f'(2.5)$ when $f(x) = x^3$ and with Δx = 0.001, press MATH 8 X,T,θ ^ 3 , ALPHA X , 2.5 , .001) ENTER as shown in Figure 2.58. The format of this command is nDeriv(*expression, variable, value,* Δx). The same derivative is also approximated in Figure 2.58 using $\Delta x = 0.0001$. For most purposes, $\Delta x = 0.001$ gives a very good approximation to the derivative and is the TI-82's default. So if you do use $\Delta x = 0.001$, just enter nDeriv(*expression, variable, value*).

Technology Tip: It is sometimes helpful to plot both a function and its derivative together. In Figure 2.60, the function $f(x) = \frac{5x-2}{x^2+1}$ and its numerical derivative (actually, an approximation to the derivative given by the symmetric difference) are graphed. You can duplicate this graph by first entering $\frac{5x-2}{x^2+1}$ for Y_1 and then entering its numerical derivative for Y_2 by pressing MATH 8 2nd Y-VARS 1 1 , X,T,θ , X,T,θ), as you see in Figure 2.59.

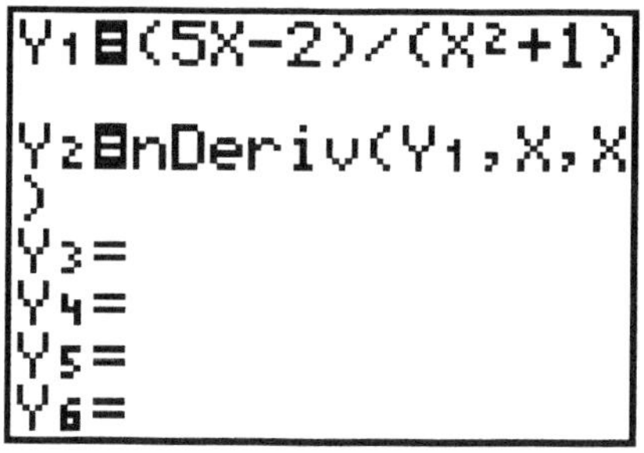

Figure 2.59: Entering $f(x)$ and $f'(x)$

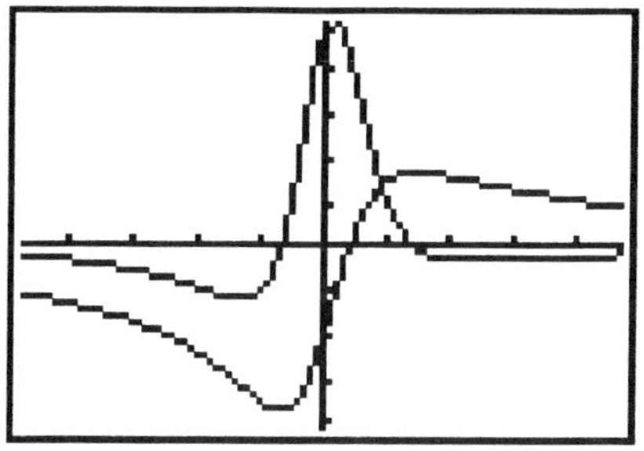

Figure 2.60: Graphs of $f(x)$ and $f'(x)$

Technology Tip: To approximate the *second* derivative $f''(x)$ of a function $y = f(x)$ or to plot the second derivative, first enter the expression for Y_1 and its derivative for Y_2 as above. Then enter the second derivative for Y_3 by pressing MATH 8 2nd Y-VARS 1 2 , X,T,θ , X,T,θ).

You may also approximate a derivative while you are examining the graph of a function. When you are in a graph window, press 2nd CALC 6, then use the arrow keys to trace along the curve to a point where you want the derivative (see Figure 2.61 for the graph of $f(x) = \frac{5x-2}{x^2+1}$ at x = -2.3) and press ENTER. The TI-82 uses $\Delta x = 0.001$ for this approximation.

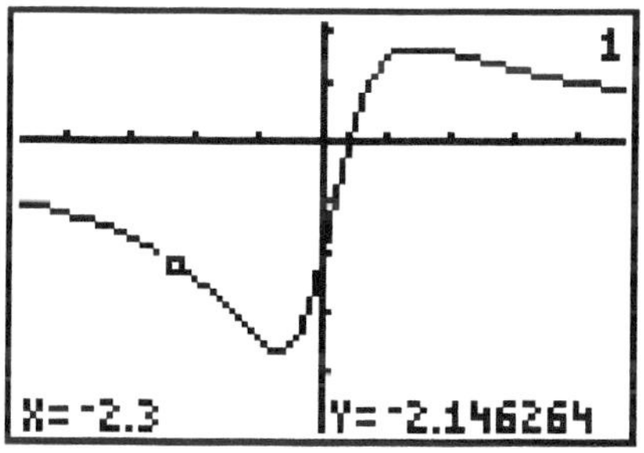

Figure 2.61: $f(x) = \frac{5x-2}{x^2+1}$ at x = -2.3

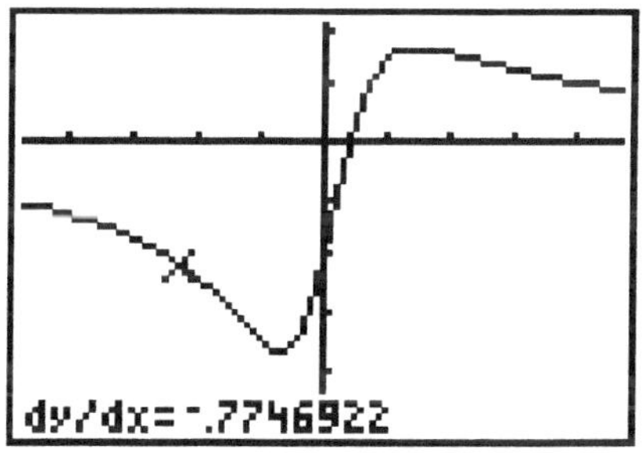

Figure 2.62: dy/dx

2.5.3 Newton's Method: With your TI-82, you may iterate using Newton's Method to find the zeros of a function. Recall that Newton's Method determines each successive approximation by the formula $x_{n+1} = x_n - \frac{f(x_n)}{f'(x_n)}$.

As an example of the technique, consider $f(x) = 2x^3 + x^2 - x + 1$. Enter this function as Y_1. A look at its graph suggests that it has a zero near x = -1, so start the iteration by storing -1 as x (see Figure 2.63). Then press these keystrokes: X,T,θ - 2nd Y-VARS 1 1 ÷ MATH 8 2nd Y-VARS 1 1 , X,T,θ , X,T,θ) STO▸ X,T,θ.

Press ENTER repeatedly until two successive approximations differ by less than some predetermined value, say 0.0001. Note that each time you press ENTER, the TI-82 will use its *current* value of x, and that value is changing as you continue the iteration.

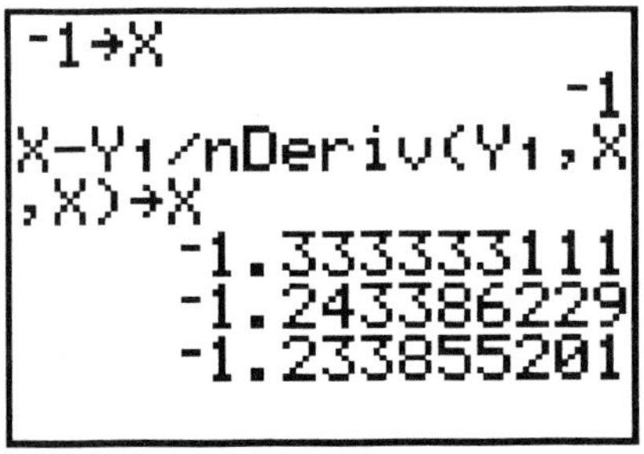

Figure 2.63: Newton's Method

Technology Tip: Newton's Method is sensitive to your seed value for x, so look carefully at the function's graph to make a good first estimate. Also, remember that the method sometimes fails to converge!

You may want to save the Newton's Method formula as a short program. See Section 2.9 or your calculator's manual for further information on programming the TI-82.

2.6 Sequences

2.6.1 Iteration: The ANS feature enables you to perform iterations to evaluate a function repeatedly. As an example, calculate $\frac{n-1}{3}$ for $n = 27$. Then calculate $\frac{n-1}{3}$ for n = the answer to the previous calculation. Continue to use each answer as n in the *next* calculation. Here are keystrokes to accomplish this iteration on the TI-82 calculator (see the results in Figure 2.64). Notice that when you use ANS in place of n in a formula, it is sufficient to press ENTER to continue an iteration.

Iteration	*Keystrokes*	*Display*
1	27 ENTER	27
2	(2nd ANS - 1) ÷ 3 ENTER	8.666666667
3	ENTER	2.555555556
4	ENTER	.5185185185
5	ENTER	-.1604938272

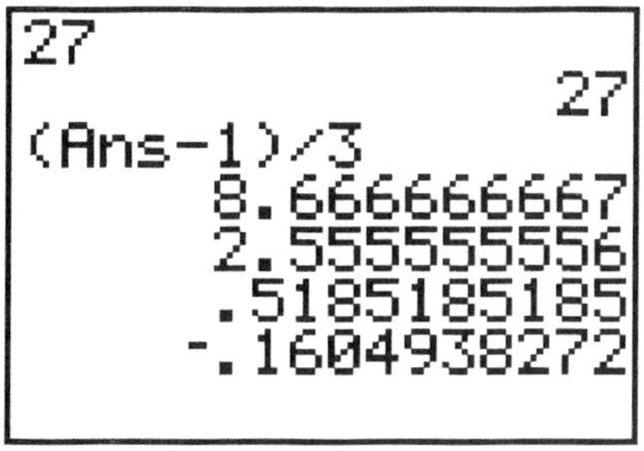

Figure 2.64: Iteration

Press ENTER several more times and see what happens with this iteration. You may wish to try it again with a different starting value.

2.6.2 Arithmetic and Geometric Sequences: Use iteration with the ANS variable to determine the n-th term of a sequence. Enter the first term 7, then start the progression with the recursion formula, 2nd ANS + 4 ENTER. This yields the 2nd term, so press ENTER sixteen more times to find the 18th term. For a *geometric* sequence whose common ratio is 4, start the progression with 2nd ANS × 4 ENTER.

You can also define the sequence recursively with the TI-82 by selecting Seq in the MODE menu (see Figure 2.1). Once again, let's find the 18th term of an *arithmetic* sequence whose first term is 7 and whose common difference is 4. Press MODE ▼ ▼ ▼ ▶ ▶ ▶ ENTER 2nd QUIT. Then press Y= to edit either of the TI-82's two sequences, u_n and v_n. Make $u_n = u_{n-1} + 4$ by pressing 2nd u_{n-1} + 4. Now make u_1 = 7 by pressing WINDOW and setting U*n*Start = 7 and *n*Start = 1 (because the first term is u_1 where n = 1). Press 2nd QUIT to leave this menu and return to the home screen. To find the 18th term of this sequence, calculate u_{18} by pressing 2nd Y-VARS 4 1 (18) ENTER (see Figure 2.65).

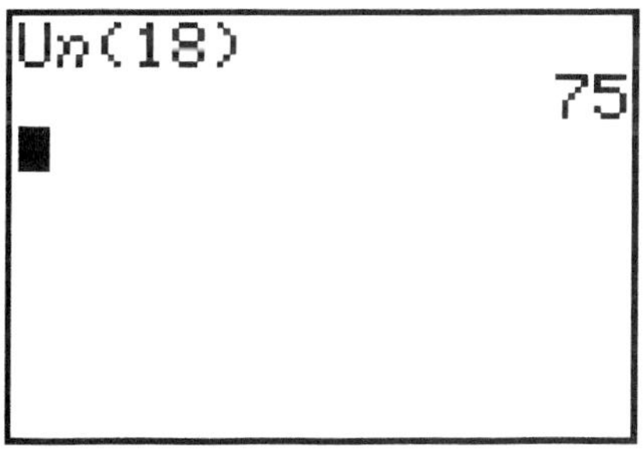

Figure 2.65: Sequence mode

Of course, you could use the *explicit* formula for the n-th term of an arithmetic sequence, $t_n = a + (n-1)d$. First enter values for the variables a, d, and n, then evaluate the formula by pressing ALPHA A + (ALPHA

N - 1) ALPHA D ENTER. For a geometric sequence whose n-th term is given by $t_n = a \cdot r^{n-1}$, enter values for the variables a, r, and n, then evaluate the formula by pressing ALPHA A ALPHA R ^ (ALPHA N - 1) ENTER.

To use the explicit formula in Seq MODE, make $u_n = 7 + (n-1) \cdot 4$ by pressing Y= and then 7 + (2nd n - 1) × 4. Once more, calculate u_{18} by pressing 2nd Y-VARS 4 1 (18) ENTER.

There are more instructions for using sequence mode in the TI-82 manual.

2.7 Integration

2.7.1 Approximating Definite Integrals: The TI-82 has the function fnInt(in the MATH menu to approximate an integral. So to find a numerical approximation to $\int_0^1 \cos x^2 dx$ with a tolerance of 0.001 (which controls the accuracy of the approximation), press MATH 9 COS X,T,θ x² , X,T,θ , 0 , 1 , .001) ENTER as shown in Figure 2.66. The format of this command is fnInt(*expression, variable, lower limit, upper limit, tolerance*). The same integral is also approximated in Figure 2.66 using a tolerance of 0.00001, the TI-82's default that is used when no other tolerance is specified.

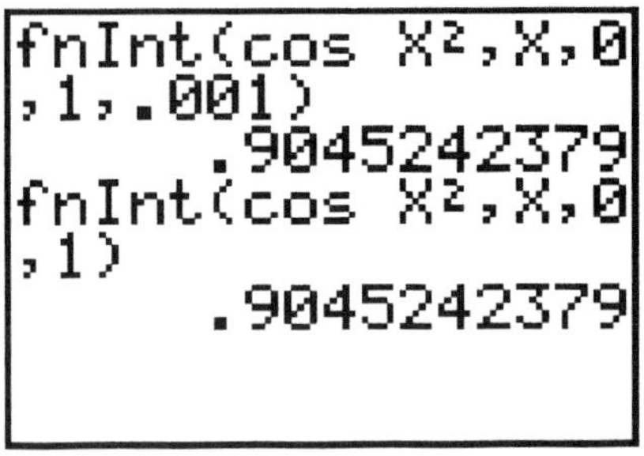

Figure 2.66: fnInt(

2.7.2 Areas: You may approximate the area under the graph of a function $y = f(x)$ between $x = A$ and $x = B$ with your TI-82. For example, here are keystrokes for finding the area under the graph of the function $y = \cos x^2$ between $x = 0$ and $x = 1$. This area is represented by the definite integral $\int_0^1 \cos x^2 dx$. So graph $f(x) = \cos x^2$ and press 2nd CALC 7. Use the arrow keys to trace along the curve to the lower limit and press ENTER; then trace again to the upper limit (see Figure 2.67) and press ENTER. The region under the graph between the lower limit and the upper limit is shaded and the area is displayed as in Figure 2.68. The TI-82 uses fnInt(with the default tolerance of 10^{-5} in this calculation.

Technology Tip: When approximating the area under $f(x) = \cos x^2$ between $x = 0$ and $x = 1$, you must trace along the curve to *exactly* where $x = 0$ and $x = 1$. Now to trace along the curve to $x = a$, the viewing rectangle must be chosen so that the function is evaluated at $x = a$. The window shown in Figure 2.67 was made first by pressing ZOOM 4 *[ZDecimal]*, then by changing its vertical dimensions to appropriate values. By contrast, find the area under $f(x) = \cos x^2$ between $x = 0$ and $x = 1$ in the ZOOM 7 *[ZTrig]* window.

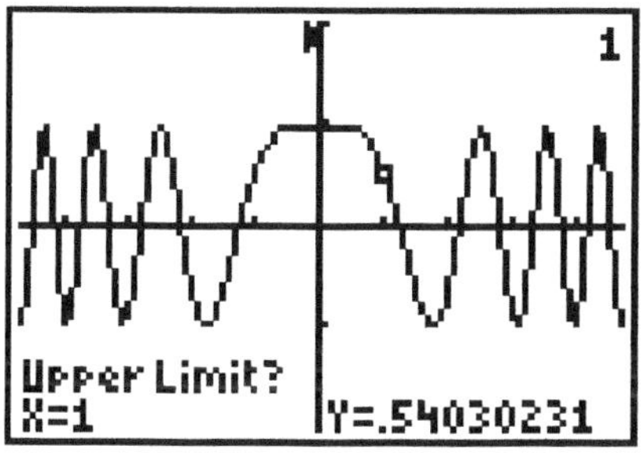

Figure 2.67: Setting the upper limit

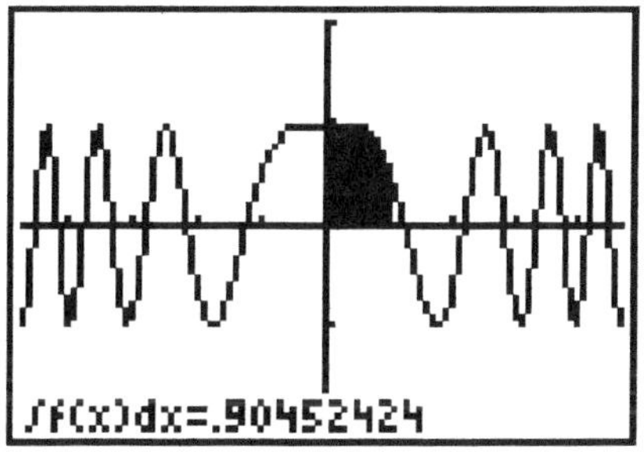

Figure 2.68: ∫f(x)dx

Technology Tip: Suppose that you want to find the area between two functions, $y = f(x)$ and $y = g(x)$, from $x = A$ to $x = B$. If $f(x) \geq g(x)$ for $A \leq x \leq B$, then enter the expression $f(x) - g(x)$ for Y_1 and proceed as before to find the required area.

See Section 2.9 for a sample TI-82 program that uses left and right Riemann Sums as well as the Midpoint Rule, the Trapezoid Rule, and Simpson's Rule to approximate definite integrals.

2.8 Parametric and Polar Graphs

2.8.1 Graphing Parametric Equations: The TI-82 plots up to six pairs of parametric equations as easily as it plots functions. Just use the MODE menu (Figure 2.1), go to the fourth line from the top, and change the setting to Par. Be sure, if the independent parameter is an angle measure, that MODE is set to whichever you need, Rad or Deg.

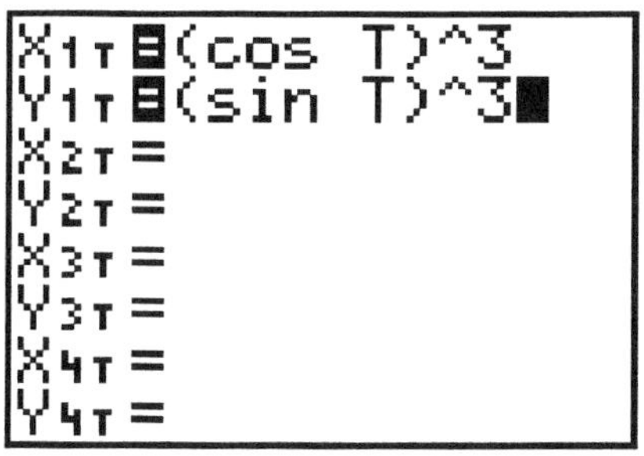

Figure 2.69: Parametric Y= menu

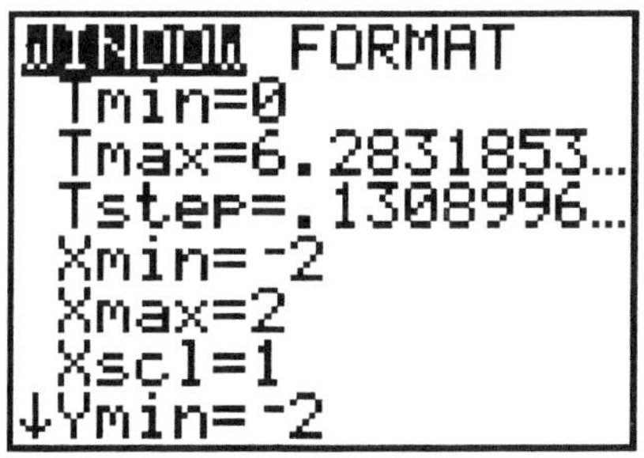

Figure 2.70: Parametric WINDOW menu

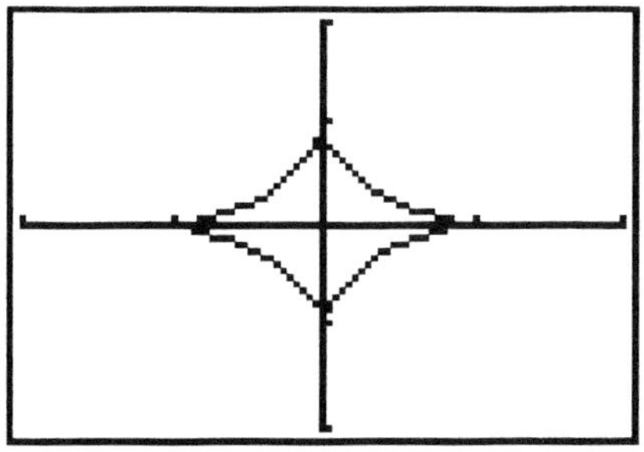

Figure 2.71: Parametric graph of $x=\cos^3 t$ and $y=\sin^3 t$

For example, here are the keystrokes needed to graph the parametric equations $x=\cos^3 t$ and $y=\sin^3 t$. First check that angles are currently being measured in radians. Change to parametric mode and press Y= to examine the new parametric equation menu (Figure 2.69). Enter the two parametric equations for X1T and Y1T by pressing (COS X,T,θ) ^ 3 ENTER (SIN X,T,θ) ^ 3 ENTER. Now, when you press the variable key X,T,θ, you get a T because the calculator is in parametric mode.

Also look at the new WINDOW menu (Figure 2.70). In the standard window, the values of T go from 0 to 2π in steps of $\frac{\pi}{24}=.1309$, with the view from -10 to 10 in both directions. But here the viewing rectangle has been changed to extend from -2 to 2 in both directions. Press GRAPH to see the parametric graph (Figure 2.71).

You may ZOOM and TRACE along parametric graphs just as you did with function graphs. As you trace along this graph, notice that the cursor moves in the *counterclockwise* direction as T increases.

2.8.2 Rectangular-Polar Coordinate Conversion: The 2nd ANGLE menu provides functions for converting between rectangular and polar coordinate systems. These functions use the current MODE settings, so it is a good idea to check the default angle measure before any conversion. Of course, you may use the MATH menu to override the current angle measure setting, as explained in Section 2.4.1. For the following examples, the TI-82 is set to radian measure.

Given rectangular coordinates $(x,y)=(4,-3)$, convert *from* these rectangular coordinates *to* polar coordinates (r,θ) by pressing 2nd ANGLE 5 4 , (-) 3) ENTER to display the value of r. The value of θ is displayed after you press 2nd ANGLE 6 4 , (-) 3) ENTER.

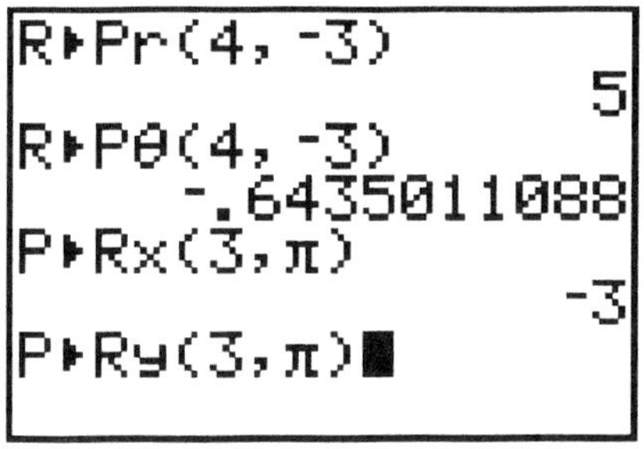

Figure 2.72: Coordinate conversions

Suppose $(r, \theta) = (3, \pi)$. To convert *from* these polar coordinates *to* rectangular coordinates (x, y), press 2nd ANGLE 7 3 , 2nd π) for the x-coordinate; next press 2nd ANGLE 8 3 , 2nd π) ENTER to display the y-coordinate.

2.8.3 Graphing Polar Equations: The TI-82 graphs a polar function in the form $r = f(\theta)$. In the fourth line of the MODE menu, select Pol for polar graphs. You may now graph up to six different polar functions at a time.

For example, to graph $r = 4\sin\theta$, press Y= for the polar graph editing screen. Then enter the expression $4\sin\theta$ for r1 by pressing 4 sin X,T,θ; note that the X,T,θ key produces θ in polar mode. Choose a good viewing rectangle and an appropriate interval and increment for θ. In Figure 2.73, the viewing rectangle is roughly "square" and extends from -6 to 6 horizontally and from -4 to 4 vertically.

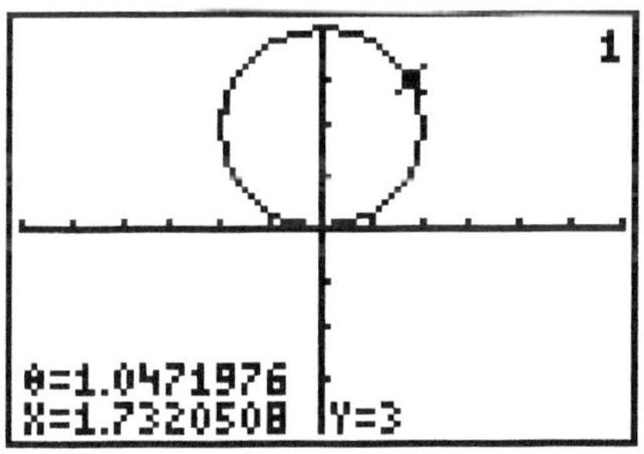

Figure 2.73: Polar graph of $r = 4\sin\theta$

Figure 2.73 shows *rectangular* coordinates of the cursor's location on the graph. You may sometimes wish to trace along the curve and see *polar* coordinates of the cursor's location. The first line of the WINDOW FORMAT menu (Figure 2.18) has options for displaying the cursor's position in rectangular RectGC or polar PolarGC form.

2.10 Programming

2.10.1 Entering a Program: The TI-82 is a programmable calculator that can store sequences of commands for later replay. Here's an example to show you how to enter a useful program that performs numerical integration by several methods: left and right Riemann Sums as well as the Midpoint Rule, the Trapezoid Rule, and Simpson's Rule.

Press PRGM to access the programming menu. The TI-82 has space for many programs, each called by a name you give it. Create a new program now, so press PRGM ◀ 1.

For convenience, the cursor is a blinking **A**, indicating that the calculator is set to receive alphabetic characters. Enter a descriptive title of up to eight characters, letters or numerals (but the first character must be a letter). Name this program INTEGRAL and press ENTER to go to the program editor.

In the program, each line begins with a colon : supplied automatically by the calculator. Any command you could enter directly in the TI-82's home screen can be entered as a line in a program. There are also special programming commands.

Figure 2.74: Part of program INTEGRAL

Input the program INTEGRAL by pressing the keystrokes given in the listing below. You may interrupt program input at any stage by pressing 2nd QUIT. To return later for more editing, press PRGM ▶, move the cursor down to this program's name, and press ENTER.

Program Line | *Keystrokes*

: Disp "Lower Limit" PRGM ▶ 3 2nd A-LOCK " L O W E R ␣ L I M I T " ENTER

displays the words *Lower Limit* on the TI-81 screen

: Input A PRGM ▶ 1 ALPHA A ENTER

waits for you to input a value that will be assigned to the variable *A*

: Disp "Upper Limit" PRGM ▶ 3 2nd A-LOCK " U P P E R ␣ L I M I T " ENTER

: Input B PRGM ▶ 1 ALPHA B ENTER

: Disp "Subdivisions" PRGM ▶ 3 2nd A-LOCK " S U B D I V I S I O N S " ENTER

: Input N PRGM ▶ 1 ALPHA N ENTER

: (B - A)/N → D (ALPHA B - ALPHA A) ÷ ALPHA N STO▸ ALPHA D ENTER

calculates Δx and stores its value as *D*

: 0 → L 0 STO▸ ALPHA L ENTER

uses the variable *L* with the left Riemann Sum

: 0 → M 0 STO▸ ALPHA M ENTER

uses the variable *M* with the Midpoint Rule

: 0 → C 0 STO▸ ALPHA C ENTER

uses the variable *C* to keep track of the subdivisions

: Disp "Riemann Sums" PRGM ▶ 3 2nd A-LOCK " R I E M A N N ␣ S U M S " ENTER

: While C<N PRGM 5 ALPHA C 2nd TEST 5 ALPHA N ENTER

initiates a conditional loop

: L + Y_1(A + CD) → L ALPHA L + 2nd Y-VARS 1 1 (ALPHA A + ALPHA C ALPHA D) STO▸ ALPHA L ENTER

adds the value of the function at the *left* endpoint of the current subdivision

: M + Y_1(A + (C + .5)·D) → M
ALPHA M + 2nd Y-VARS 1 1 (ALPHA A + (ALPHA C + .5) × ALPHA D) STO▸ ALPHA M ENTER

adds the value of the function at the *midpoint* of the current subdivision

: C + 1 → C ALPHA C + 1 STO▸ C ENTER

counts up one subdivision

: End PRGM 7 ENTER

terminates the While loop

: Disp " Left" PRGM ▶ 3 2nd A-LOCK " ␣ L E F T " ENTER

: DL → L ALPHA D ALPHA L STO▸ ALPHA L ENTER

calculates left Riemann Sum

: Disp L PRGM ▶ 3 ALPHA L ENTER

: Pause	PRGM 8 ENTER

during program execution, waits for you to press ENTER

: Disp " Right"	PRGM ▶ 3 2nd A-LOCK " ␣ R I G H T " ENTER
: L + DY$_1$(B) - DY$_1$(A) → R	ALPHA L + ALPHA D 2nd Y-VARS 1 1 (ALPHA B) - ALPHA D 2nd Y-VARS 1 1 (ALPHA A) STO▸ ALPHA R ENTER

calculates right Riemann Sum

: Disp R	PRGM ▶ 3 ALPHA R ENTER
: Pause	PRGM 8 ENTER
: Disp "Midpoint Rule"	PRGM ▶ 3 2nd A-LOCK " M I D P O I N T ␣ R U L E " ENTER
: DM → M	ALPHA D ALPHA M STO▸ ALPHA M ENTER

calculates numerical integral by Midpoint Rule

: Disp M	PRGM ▶ 3 ALPHA M ENTER
: Pause	PRGM 8 ENTER
: Disp "Trapezoid Rule"	PRGM ▶ 3 2nd A-LOCK " T R A P E Z O I D ␣ R U L E " ENTER
: (L + R)/2 → T	(ALPHA L + ALPHA R) ÷ 2 STO▸ ALPHA T ENTER

calculates numerical integral by Trapezoid Rule (average left and right Riemann Sums)

: Disp T	PRGM ▶ 3 ALPHA T ENTER
: Pause	PRGM 8 ENTER
: Disp "Simpsons Rule"	PRGM ▶ 3 2nd A-LOCK " S I M P S O N S ␣ R U L E " ENTER
: (2M + T)/3 → S	(2 ALPHA M + ALPHA T) ÷ 3 STO▸ ALPHA S ENTER

calculates numerical integral by Simpson's Rule ($\frac{2}{3}$ Midpoint and $\frac{1}{3}$ Trapezoid)

: Disp S	PRGM ▶ 3 ALPHA S ENTER

When you have finished, press 2nd QUIT to leave the program editor.

You may remove a program from memory by pressing 2nd MEM 2 *[Delete...]* 6 *[Prgm...]*. Then move the cursor to the program's name and press ENTER to delete the entire program.

2.10.2 Executing a Program: To execute the program just entered, press PRGM and then the number or letter that it was named. If you have forgotten its name, use the arrow keys to move through the program listing to find its description INTEGRAL. Then press ENTER to select this program and ENTER again to execute it.

The program INTEGRAL has been written to calculate $\int_A^B f(x)\,dx$ for N subdivisions of the interval $[A, B]$. You must enter the expression $f(x)$ as Y_1 before running this program. The program itself will prompt you for A, B, and N.

If you need to interrupt a program during execution, press ON.

The instruction manual for your TI-82 gives detailed information about programming. Refer to it to learn more about programming and how to use other features of your calculator.

CHAPTER 3

Texas Instruments TI-85 Advanced Scientific Calculator

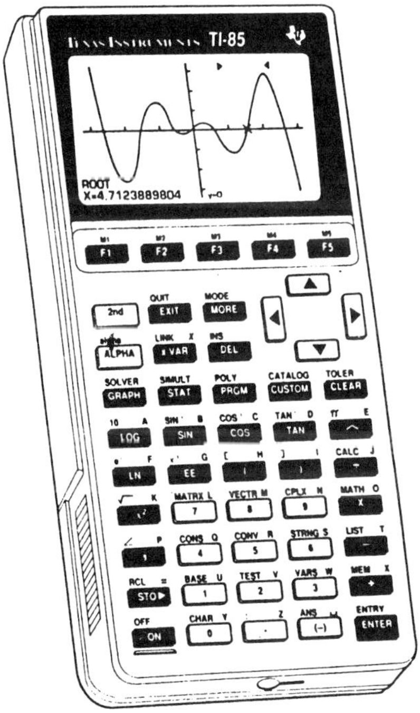

3.1 Getting started with the TI-85

3.1.1 Basics: Press the ON key to begin using your TI-85 calculator. If you need to adjust the display contrast, first press 2nd, then press and hold ▲ (the *up* arrow key) to increase the contrast or ▼ (the *down* arrow key) to decrease the contrast. As you press and hold ▲ or ▼, an integer between 0 (lightest) and 9 (darkest) appears in the upper right corner of the display. When you have finished with the calculator, turn it off to conserve battery power by pressing 2nd and then OFF.

Check the TI-85's settings by pressing 2nd MODE. If necessary, use the arrow keys to move the blinking cursor to a setting you want to change. Press ENTER to select a new setting. To start with, select the options along the left side of the MODE menu as illustrated in Figure 3.1: normal display, floating decimals, radian measure, rectangular coordinates, function graphs, decimal number system, rectangular vectors, and differentiation type. Details on alternative options will be given later in this guide. For now, leave the MODE menu by pressing EXIT or 2nd QUIT or CLEAR.

Figure 3.1: MODE menu

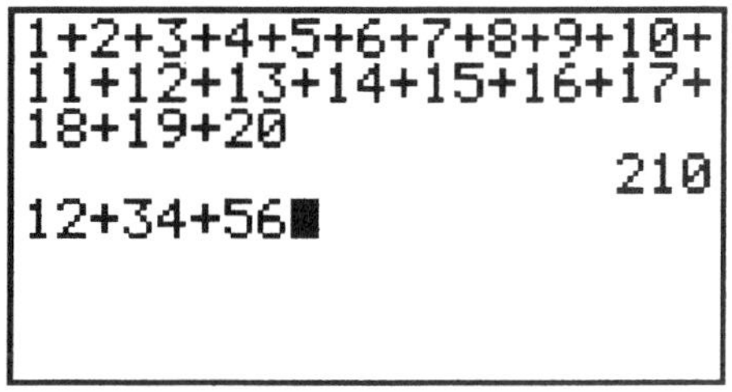

Figure 3.2: Home screen

3.1.2 Editing: One advantage of the TI-85 is that up to 8 lines are visible at one time, so you can *see* a long calculation. For example, type this sum (see Figure 3.2):

$$1 + 2 + 3 + 4 + 5 + 6 + 7 + 8 + 9 + 10 + 11 + 12 + 13 + 14 + 15 + 16 + 17 + 18 + 19 + 20$$

Then press ENTER to see the answer, too.

Often we do not notice a mistake until we see how unreasonable an answer is. The TI-85 permits you to redisplay an entire calculation, edit it easily, then execute the *corrected* calculation.

Suppose you had typed 12 + 34 + 56 as in Figure 3.2 but had *not* yet pressed ENTER, when you realize that 34 should have been 74. Simply press ◀ (the *left* arrow key) as many times as necessary to move the blinking cursor left to 3, then type 7 to write over it. On the other hand, if 34 should have been 384, move the cursor back to 4, press 2nd INS (the cursor changes to a blinking underline) and then type 8 (inserts at the cursor position and other characters are pushed to the right). If the 34 should have been 3 only, move the cursor to 4 and press DEL to delete it.

While you are editing an expression, pressing the *up* (or *down*) arrow key causes the cursor to jump quickly to the *left* (or *right*) end of the expression.

Even if you had pressed ENTER, you may still edit the previous expression. Press 2nd and then ENTRY to *recall* the last expression that was entered. Now you can change it.

Technology Tip: When you need to evaluate a formula for different values of a variable, use the editing feature to simplify the process. For example, suppose you want to find the balance in an investment account if there is now \$5000 in the account and interest is compounded annually at the rate of 8.5%. The formula for the balance is $P(1+\frac{r}{n})^{nt}$, where P = principal, r = rate of interest (expressed as a decimal), n = number of times interest is compounded each year, and t = number of years. In our example, this becomes $5000(1+.085)^t$. Here are the keystrokes for finding the balance after t = 3, 5, and 10 years.

Years	*Keystrokes*	*Balance*
3	5000 (1 + .085) ^ 3 ENTER	\$6386.45
5	2nd ENTRY ◀ 5 ENTER	\$7518.28
10	2nd ENTRY ◀ 10 ENTER	\$11,304.92

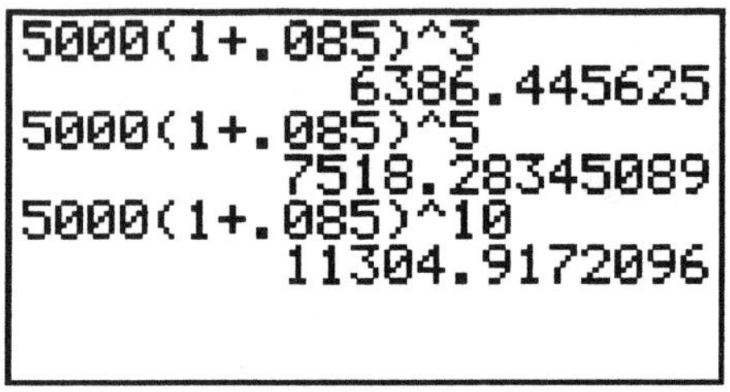

Figure 3.3: Editing expressions

Then to find the balance from the same initial investment but after 5 years when the annual interest rate is 7.5%, press these keys to change the last calculation above: 2nd ENTRY ◀ DEL ◀ 5 ◀ ◀ ◀ ◀ ◀ 7 ENTER.

3.1.3 Key Functions: Most keys on the TI-85 offer access to more than one function, just as the keys on a computer keyboard can produce more than one letter ("g" and "G") or even quite different characters ("5" and "%"). The primary function of a key is indicated on the key itself, and you access that function by a simple press on the key.

To access the *second* function indicated to the *left* above a key, first press 2nd (the cursor changes to a blinking ↑) and *then* press the key. For example, to calculate $\sqrt{25}$, press 2nd $\sqrt{\ }$ 25 ENTER.

When you want to use a capital letter or other character printed to the *right* above a key, first press ALPHA (the cursor changes to a blinking **A**) and then the key. For example, to use the letter K in a formula, press ALPHA K. If you need several letters in a row, press ALPHA twice in succession, which is like pressing

CAPS LOCK on a computer keyboard, and then press all the letters you want. Remember to press ALPHA when you are finished and want to restore keys to their primary functions. To type lowercase letters, press 2nd alpha (the cursor changes to a blinking **a**). To lock in lowercase letters, press 2nd alpha 2nd alpha or 2nd alpha ALPHA. To unlock from lowercase, press ALPHA ALPHA (you'll see the cursor change from blinking **a** to blinking **A** and then to the standard blinking rectangle).

3.1.4 Order of Operations: The TI-85 performs calculations according to the standard algebraic rules. Working outwards from inner parentheses, calculations are performed from left to right. Powers and roots are evaluated first, followed by multiplications and divisions, and then additions and subtractions.

Note that the TI-85 distinguishes between *subtraction* and the *negative sign*. If you wish to enter a negative number, it is necessary to use the (-) key. For example, you would evaluate $-5-(4\cdot-3)$ by pressing (-) 5 - (4 × (-) 3) ENTER to get 7.

Enter these expressions to practice using your TI-85.

Expression	*Keystrokes*	*Display*
$7-5\cdot3$	7 - 5 × 3 ENTER	-8
$(7-5)\cdot3$	(7 - 5) × 3 ENTER	6
$120-10^2$	120 - 10 x² ENTER	20
$(120-10)^2$	(120 - 10) x² ENTER	12100
$\frac{24}{2^3}$	24 ÷ 2 ^ 3 ENTER	3
$\left(\frac{24}{2}\right)^3$	(24 ÷ 2) ^ 3 ENTER	1728
$(7--5)\cdot-3$	(7 - (-) 5) × (-) 3 ENTER	-36

3.1.5 Algebraic Expressions and Memory: Your calculator can evaluate expressions such as $\frac{N(N+1)}{2}$ *after* you have entered a value for N. Suppose you want $N = 200$. Press 200 STO▸ N ENTER to store the value 200 in memory location N. (The STO▸ key prepares the TI-85 for an alphabetical entry, so it is *not* necessary to press ALPHA also.) Whenever you use N in an expression, the calculator will substitute the value 200 until you make a change by storing *another* number in N. Next enter the expression $\frac{N(N+1)}{2}$ by typing ALPHA N (ALPHA N + 1) ÷ 2 ENTER. For $N = 200$, you will find that $\frac{N(N+1)}{2} = 20100$.

The contents of any memory location may be revealed by typing just its letter name and then ENTER. And the TI-85 retains memorized values even when it is turned off, so long as its batteries are good.

A variable name in the TI-85 can be a single letter, or a string of up to eight characters that begins with a letter followed by other letters, numerals, and various symbols. Variable names are case sensitive, which means that length and Length and LENGTH may represent *different* quantities.

3.1.6 Repeated Operations with ANS: The result of your *last* calculation is always stored in memory location ANS and replaces any previous result. This makes it easy to use the answer from one computation in another computation. For example, press 30 + 15 ENTER so that 45 is the last result displayed. Then press 2nd ANS ÷ 9 ENTER and get 5 because $\frac{45}{9} = 5$.

With a function like division, you press the ÷ key *after* you enter an argument. For such functions, whenever you would start a new calculation with the previous answer followed by pressing the function key, you may press just the function key. So instead of 2nd ANS ÷ 9 in the previous example, you could have pressed simply ÷ 9 to achieve the same result. This technique also works for these functions: + - × x^2 ^ x^{-1}.

Here is a situation where this is especially useful. Suppose a person makes $5.85 per hour and you are asked to calculate earnings for a day, a week, and a year. Execute the given keystrokes to find the person's incomes during these periods (results are shown in Figure 3.4):

Pay period	*Keystrokes*	*Earnings*
8-hour day	5.85 × 8 ENTER	$46.80
5-day week	× 5 ENTER	$234
52-week year	× 52 ENTER	$12,168

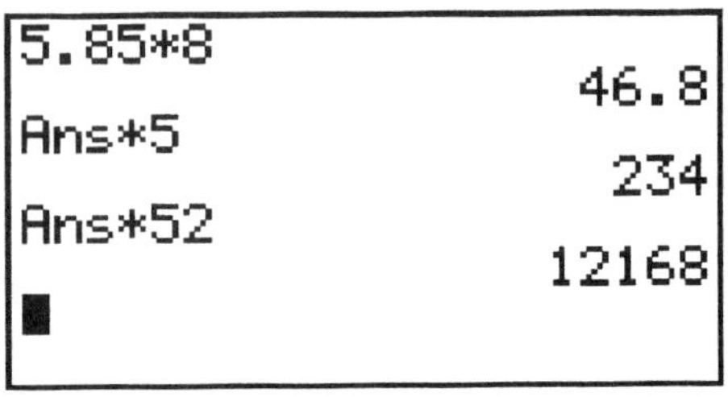

Figure 3.4: ANS variable

3.1.7 The MATH Menu: Operators and functions associated with a scientific calculator are available either immediately from the keys of the TI-85 or by 2nd keys. You have direct key access to common arithmetic operations (x^2, 2nd $\sqrt{\ }$, 2nd x^{-1}, and ^), trigonometric functions (SIN, COS, TAN) and their inverses (2nd SIN^{-1}, 2nd COS^{-1}, 2nd TAN^{-1}), exponential and logarithmic functions (LOG, 2nd 10^x, LN, 2nd e^x), and a famous constant (2nd π).

A significant difference between the TI-85 and many scientific calculators is that the TI-85 requires the argument of a function *after* the function, as you would see a formula written in your textbook. For example, on the TI-85 you calculate $\sqrt{16}$ by pressing the keys 2nd $\sqrt{\ }$ 16 in that order.

Here are keystrokes for basic mathematical operations. Try them for practice on your TI-85.

Expression	*Keystrokes*	*Display*
$\sqrt{3^2+4^2}$	2nd $\sqrt{\ }$ (3 x^2 + 4 x^2) ENTER	5
$2\frac{1}{3}$	2 + 3 2nd x^{-1} ENTER	2.33333333333
$\log 200$	LOG 200 ENTER	2.30102999566
$2.34 \cdot 10^5$	2.34 × 2nd 10^x 5 ENTER	234000
	or 2.34 × 10 ^ 5 ENTER	

Additional mathematical operations and functions are available from the MATH menu (Figure 3.5). Press 2nd MATH to see the various options that are listed across the bottom of the screen. These options are activated by pressing corresponding menu keys, F1 through F5.

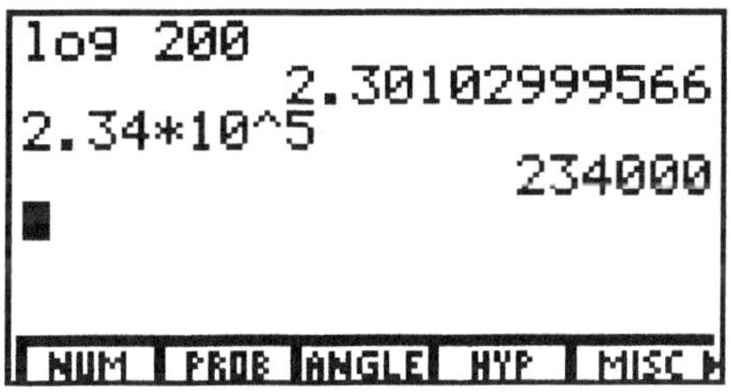

Figure 3.5: Basic MATH menu

For example, F1 brings up the NUM menu of numerical functions. You will learn in your mathematics textbook how to apply many of them. Note that the basic MATH menu items have moved up a line; these options are now available by pressing 2nd M1 through 2nd M5. As an example, determine $|-5|$ by pressing 2nd MATH F1 and then F5 (-) 5 ENTER (see Figure 3.6).

Next calculate $\sqrt[3]{7}$ by pressing 2nd MATH F5 (when the MATH NUM menu is displayed, as in Figure 3.6; press just 2nd M5) to access the MISC menu of miscellaneous mathematical functions. The arrow at the right end of this menu indicates there are more items that you can access. You may press the MORE key repeatedly to move down the row of options and back again. To calculate $\sqrt[3]{7}$, press 2nd MATH F5 MORE 3 F4 [$^x\sqrt{\ }$] 7 ENTER to see 1.9129 (Figure 3.7). To leave the MATH menu or any other menu and take no further action, press EXIT a couple of times.

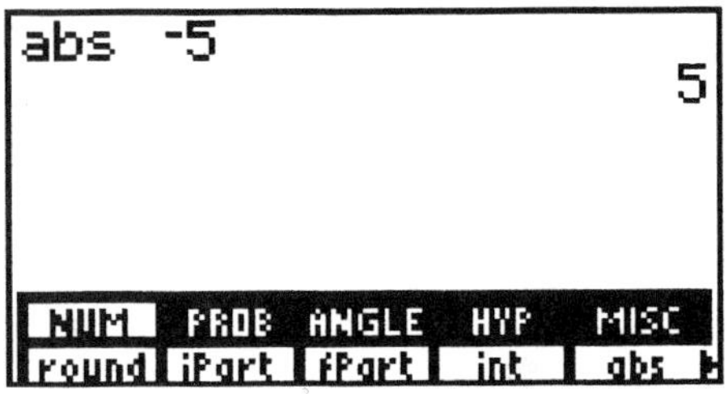

Figure 3.6: MATH NUM menu

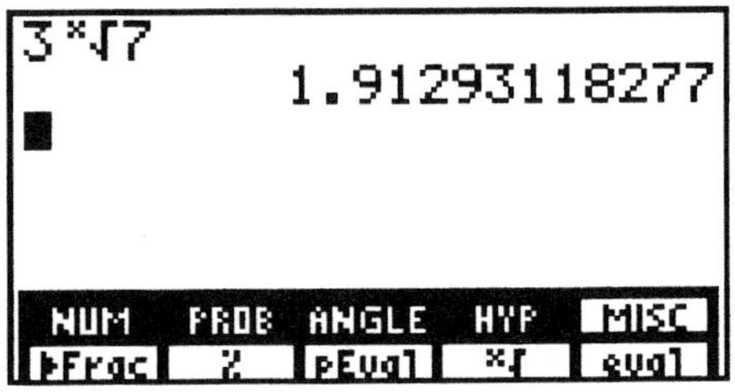

Figure 3.7: MATH MISC menu

The *factorial* of a non-negative integer is the *product* of *all* the integers from 1 up to the given integer. The symbol for factorial is the exclamation point. So 4! (pronounced *four factorial*) is 1·2·3·4 = 24. You will learn more about applications of factorials in your textbook, but for now use the TI-85 to calculate 4! Press these keystrokes: 2nd MATH F2 *[PROB]* 4 F1 *[!]* ENTER.

Hyperbolic functions (sinh, cosh, and tanh) and their inverses are available from the HYP sub-menu of the MATH menu. For example, here are the keystrokes to calculate sinh 3: 2nd MATH F4 F1 3 ENTER.

3.2 Functions and Graphs

3.2.1 Evaluating Functions: Suppose you receive a monthly salary of \$1975 plus a commission of 10% of sales. Let x = your sales in dollars; then your wages W in dollars are given by the equation $W = 1975 + .10x$. If your January sales were \$2230 and your February sales were \$1865, what was your income during those months?

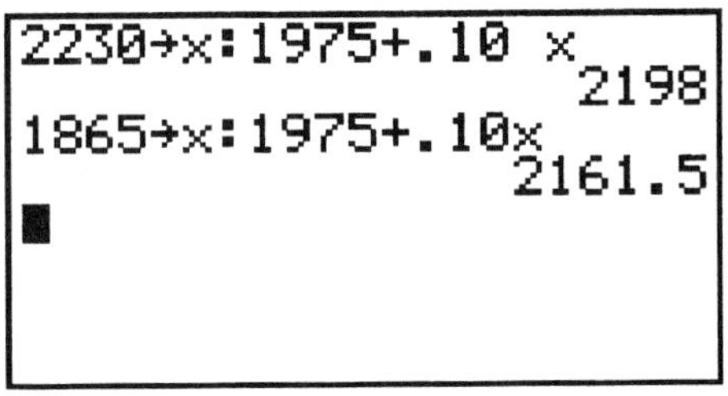

Figure 3.8: Evaluating a function

Here's how to use your TI-85 to perform this task. First press EXIT and CLEAR as necessary to get a blank home screen. Then set $x = 2230$ by pressing 2230 STO▸ x-VAR. (The x-VAR key makes it easy to produce a lower case x for a variable name without having to use the 2nd alpha key.) Then press ALPHA to leave alphabetic entry and 2nd : to allow another expression to be entered on the same command line. Finally, enter the expression $1975 + .10x$ by pressing these keys: 1975 + .10 x-VAR. Now press ENTER to calculate the answer (Figure 3.8).

It is not necessary to repeat all these steps to find the February wages. Simply press 2nd ENTRY to recall the entire previous line and change 2230 to 1865.

Technology Tip: The TI-85 does not require multiplication to be expressed between variables, so xxx means x^3. It is often easier to press two or three x's together than to search for the square key or the power key. Of course, expressed multiplication is also not required between a constant and a variable. Hence to enter $2x^3+3x^2-4x+5$ in the TI-85, you might save some keystrokes and press just these keys: 2 x-VAR x-VAR x-VAR + 3 x-VAR x-VAR - 4 x-VAR + 5.

3.2.2 Functions in a Graph Window: On the TI-85, once you have entered a function, you can easily generate its graph. The ability to draw a graph contributes substantially to our ability to solve problems.

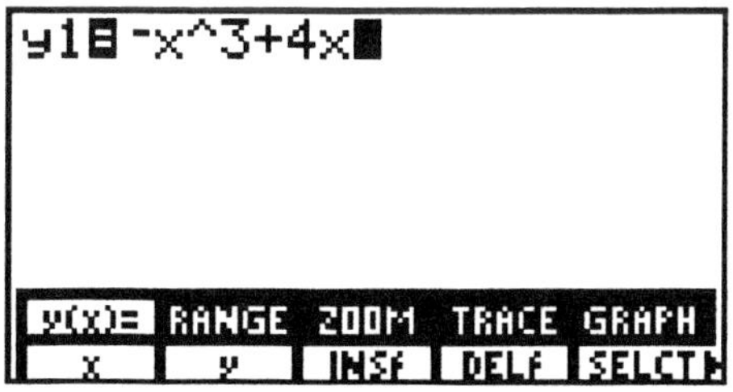

Figure 3.9: y(x)= screen

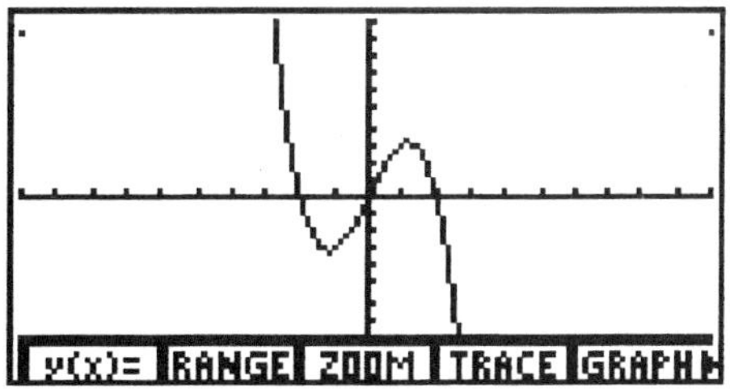

Figure 3.10: Graph of $y=-x^3+4x$

Here is how to graph $y=-x^3+4x$. First press the GRAPH key and then F1 to select y(x)=. This give you access to the function editing screen (Figure 3.9). Press F4 *[DELf]* as many times as necessary to delete any functions that may be there already. Then, with the cursor on the top line to the right of y1=, press (-) F1 ^ 3 + 4 F1 to enter the function. As you see, the TI-85 uses lower-case letters for its graphing variables, just like your mathematics textbook. Note that pressing F1 in this menu is the same as pressing either x-VAR or 2nd alpha X. Now press 2nd M5 *[GRAPH]* and the TI-85 changes to a window with the graph of $y=-x^3+4x$ (Figure 3.10).

While the TI-85 is calculating coordinates for a plot, it displays a busy indicator at the top right of the graph window.

Your graph window may look like the one in Figure 3.10 or it may be different. Since the graph of $y=-x^3+4x$ extends infinitely far left and right and also infinitely far up and down, the TI-85 can display only a piece of the actual graph. This displayed rectangular part is called a *viewing rectangle*. You can easily change the viewing rectangle to enhance your investigation of a graph.

The viewing rectangle in Figure 3.10 shows the part of the graph that extends horizontally from -10 to 10 and vertically from -10 to 10. Press F2 *[RANGE]* to see information about your viewing rectangle. Figure 3.11 shows the RANGE screen that corresponds to the viewing rectangle in Figure 3.10. This is the *standard* viewing rectangle for the TI-85.

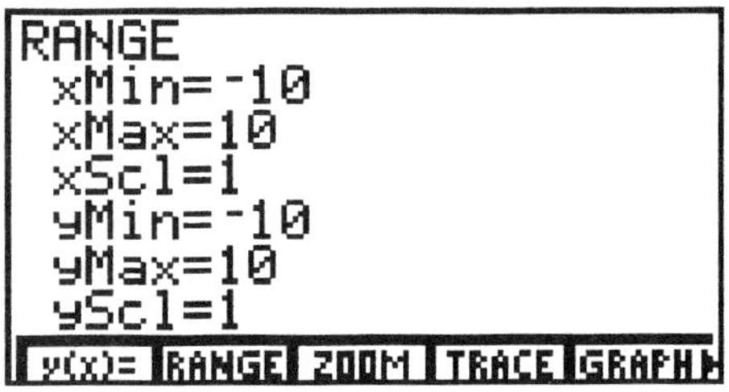

Figure 3.11: Standard RANGE

The variables xMin and xMax are the minimum and maximum x-values of the viewing rectangle; yMin and yMax are its minimum and maximum y-values.

xScl and yScl set the spacing between tick marks on the axes.

Use the arrow keys ▲ and ▼ to move up and down from one line to another in this list; pressing the ENTER key will move down the list. Press CLEAR to delete the current value and then enter a new value. You may also edit the entry as you would edit an expression. Remember that a minimum *must* be less than the corresponding maximum or the TI-85 will issue an error message. Also, remember to use the (-) key, not - (which is subtraction), when you want to enter a negative value. Figures 3.10-11, 3.12-13, and 3.14-15 show different RANGE screens and the corresponding viewing rectangle for each one.

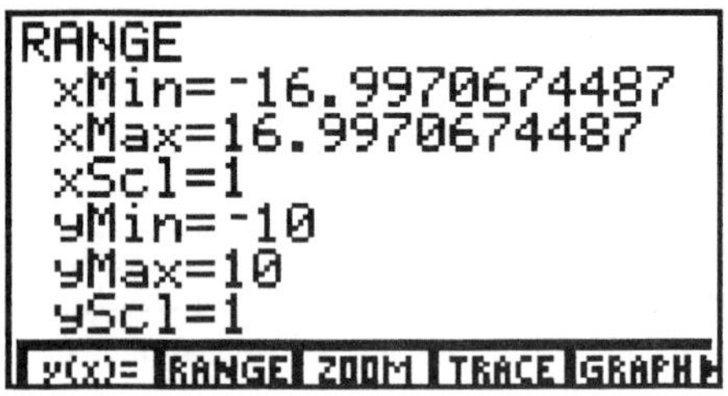

Figure 3.12: Square window

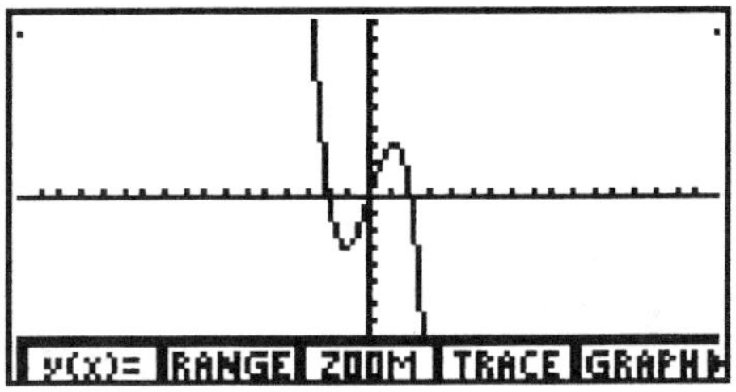

Figure 3.13: Graph of $y = -x^3 + 4x$

To set the range quickly to standard values (see Figure 3.11), press F3 F4 *[ZOOM ZSTD]*

To set the viewing rectangle quickly to a "square" window (Figure 3.12), in which the horizontal and vertical axes have the same scale, press F3 MORE F2 *[ZOOM ZSQR]* in the GRAPH menu. More information about square windows is presented later in Section 3.2.4.

Sometimes you may wish to display grid points corresponding to tick marks on the axes. This and other graph format options may be changed by pressing GRAPH MORE F3 (Figure 3.16). Use arrow keys to move the blinking cursor to GridOn, then press ENTER and EXIT. Figure 3.17 shows the same graph as in Figure 3.15 but with the grid turned on. In general, you'll want the grid turned *off*, so do that now by pressing GRAPH MORE F3 again, use the arrow keys to move the blinking cursor to GridOff, and press ENTER EXIT.

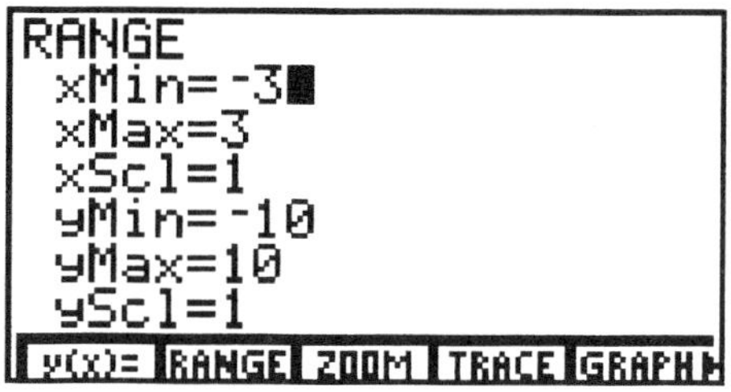

Figure 3.14: Custom window

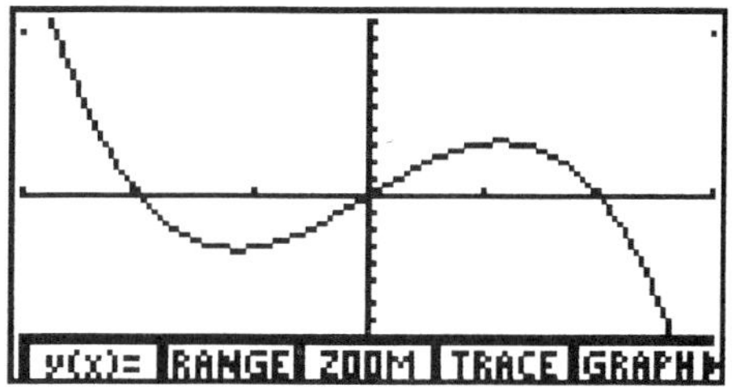

Figure 3.15: Graph of $y=-x^3+4x$

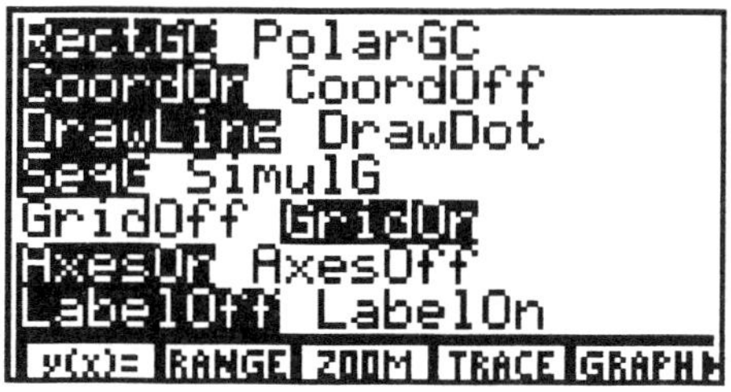

Figure 3.16: GRAPH FORMT menu

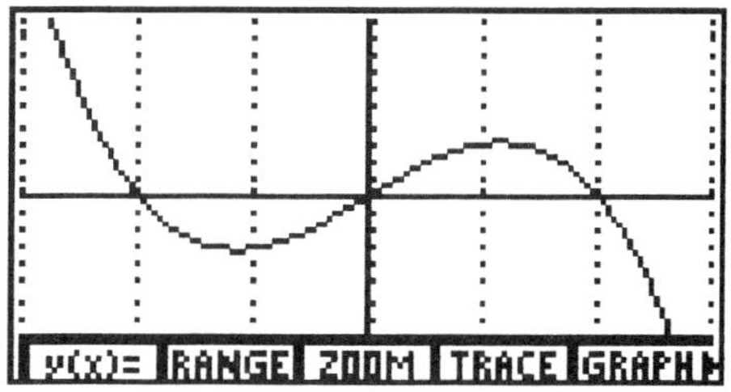

Figure 3.17: Grid on

3.2.3 The Greatest Integer Function: The greatest integer function, written [[x]], gives the greatest *integer* less than or equal to a number x. On the TI-85, the greatest integer function is called int and is located under the NUM sub-menu of the MATH menu (see Figure 3.5). So calculate [[6.78]] = 6 by pressing 2nd MATH F1 F4 6.78 ENTER.

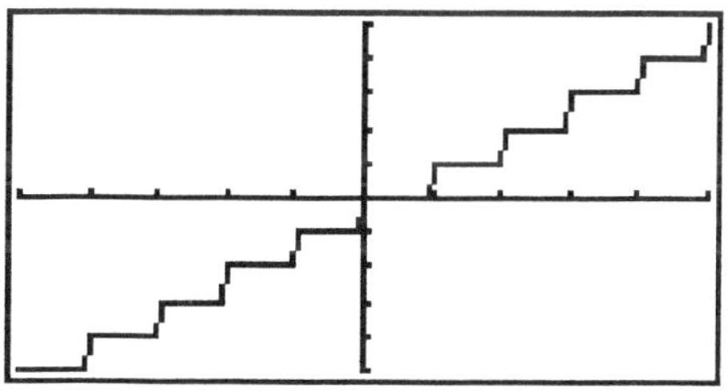

Figure 3.18: DrawLine graph of y = [[x]]

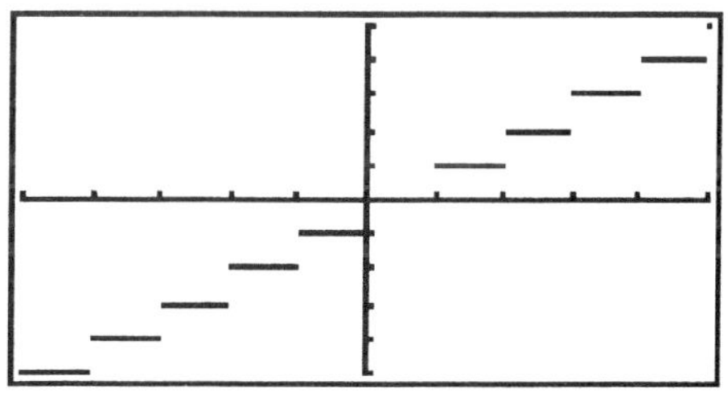

Figure 3.19: DrawDot graph of y = [[x]]

To graph y = [[x]], go in the y(x)= menu, move beside y1 and press CLEAR 2nd MATH F1 F4 EXIT F1 2nd M5. Figure 3.18 shows this graph in a viewing rectangle from -5 to 5 in both directions. The bottom menu line has been cleared by pressing CLEAR once; you may restore it by pressing GRAPH again.

The true graph of the greatest integer function is a step graph, like the one in Figure 3.19. Calculators like the TI-85 graph a function by plotting points, then connecting successive points with segments. For the graph of $y = [[x]]$, a segment should *not* be drawn between every pair of successive points. You can change from DrawLine to DrawDot format on the TI-85 by opening the GRAPH FORMT menu (Figure 3.16).

3.2.4 Graphing a Circle: Here is a useful technique for graphs that are not functions, but that can be "split" into a top part and a bottom part, or into multiple parts. Suppose you wish to graph the circle whose equation is $x^2 + y^2 = 36$. First solve for y and get an equation for the top semicircle, $y = \sqrt{36 - x^2}$, and for the bottom semicircle, $y = -\sqrt{36 - x^2}$. Then graph the two semicircles simultaneously.

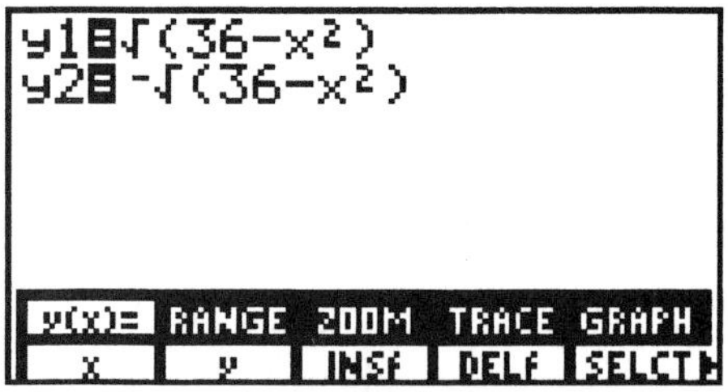

Figure 3.20: Two semicircles

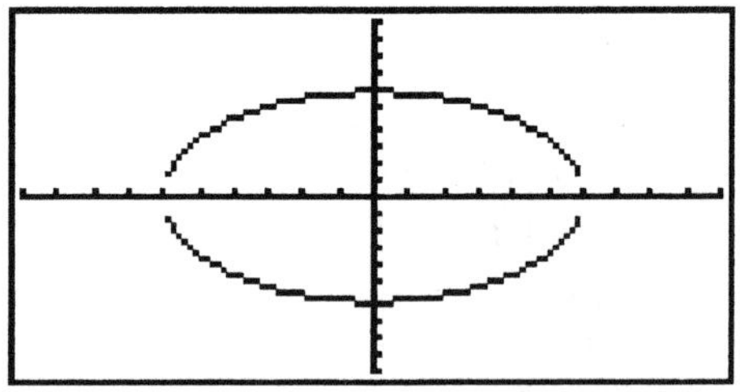
Figure 3.21: Circle's graph - standard view

The keystrokes to draw this circle's graph follow. Enter $\sqrt{36 - x^2}$ as y1 and $-\sqrt{36 - x^2}$ as y2 (see Figure 3.20) by pressing GRAPH F1 CLEAR 2nd √ (36 - F1 x²) ENTER (-) 2nd √ (36 - F1 x²). Then press 2nd M5 to draw them both.

If your range were set to the standard viewing rectangle, your graph would look like Figure 3.21. Now this does *not* look like a circle, because the units along the axes are not the same. This is where the square viewing rectangle is important. Press F3 MORE F2 and see a graph that appears more circular.

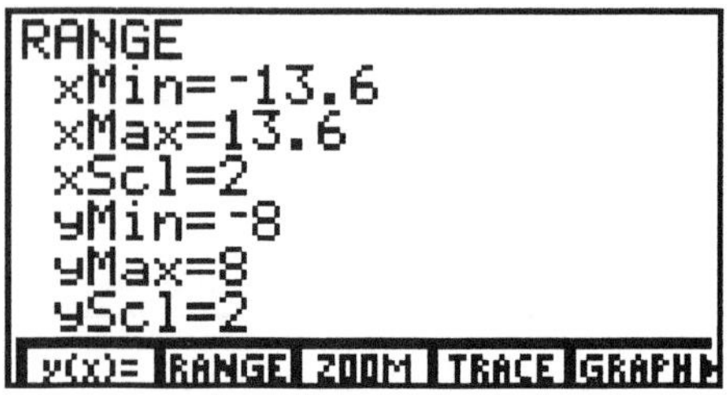

Figure 3.22: $\frac{\text{vertical}}{\text{horizontal}} = \frac{16}{27.2} = \frac{10}{17}$

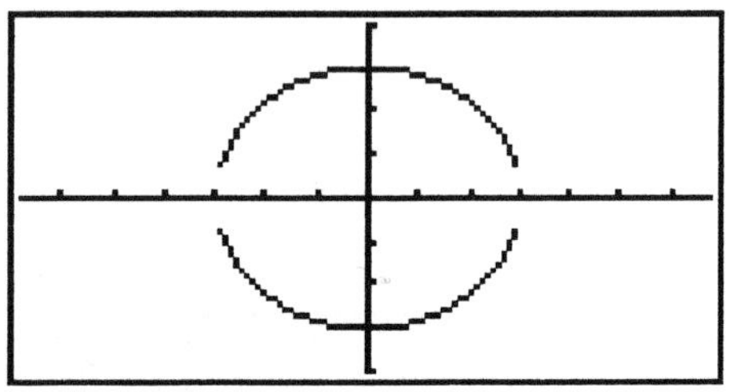
Figure 3.23: A "square" circle

Technology Tip: Another way to get a square graph is to change the range variables so that the value of yMax - yMin is approximately $\frac{10}{17}$ times xMax - xMin. For example, see the RANGE in Figure 3.22 and the corresponding graph in Figure 3.23. The method works because the dimensions of the TI-85's display are such that the ratio of vertical to horizontal is approximately $\frac{10}{17}$.

The two semicircles in Figure 3.23 do not meet because of an idiosyncrasy in the way the TI-85 plots a graph.

Back when you entered $\sqrt{36-x^2}$ as y1 and $-\sqrt{36-x^2}$ as y2, you could have entered -y1 for y2 and saved some keystrokes. Try this by going back to the y(x)= menu and pressing the arrow key to move the cursor down to y2. Then press CLEAR (-) 2nd VARS MORE F3 ENTER. The graph should be just as it was before.

Technology Tip: The square viewing rectangle is also important when you want to judge whether two lines are perpendicular. The intersection of perpendicular lines will always *look* like a right angle in a square viewing rectangle.

3.2.5 TRACE: Graph $y=-x^3+4x$ in the standard viewing rectangle. Press any of the arrow keys ▲ ▼ ◀ ▶ and see the cursor move from the center of the viewing rectangle. The coordinates of the cursor's location are displayed at the bottom of the screen, as in Figure 3.24, in floating decimal format. This cursor is called a *free-moving cursor* because it can move from dot to dot *anywhere* in the graph window.

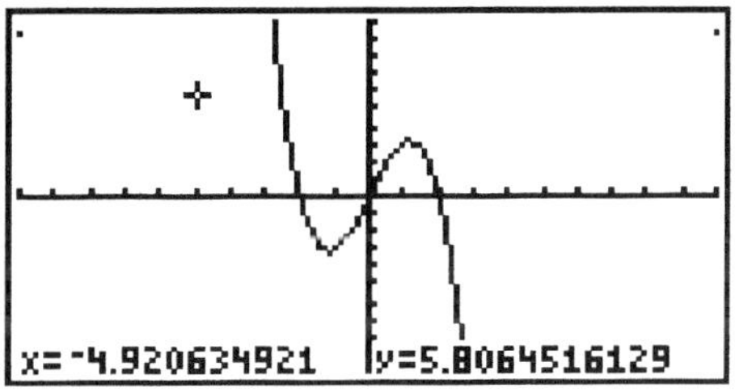

Figure 3.24: Free-moving cursor

Remove the free-moving cursor and its coordinates from the window by pressing ENTER, CLEAR, or GRAPH (this also restores the GRAPH menu line). An advantage of pressing ENTER or CLEAR to remove the free-moving cursor is that, if you press an arrow key once again, the cursor will reappear at the same point you left it.

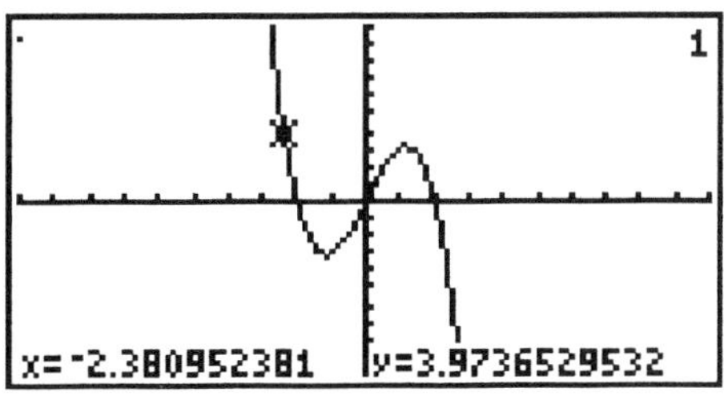

Figure 3.25: Trace on $y=-x^3+4x$

Press F4 *[TRACE]* to enable the left ◀ and right ▶ arrow keys to move the cursor along the function. The cursor is no longer free-moving, but is now constrained to the function. The coordinates that are displayed belong to points on the function's graph, so the *y*-coordinate is the calculated value of the function at the corresponding *x*-coordinate.

Now plot a second function, $y = -.25x$, along with $y = -x^3 + 4x$. Press GRAPH F1 for the y(x)= menu and enter $-.25x$ for y2, then press 2nd M5 to see their graphs (Figure 3.27).

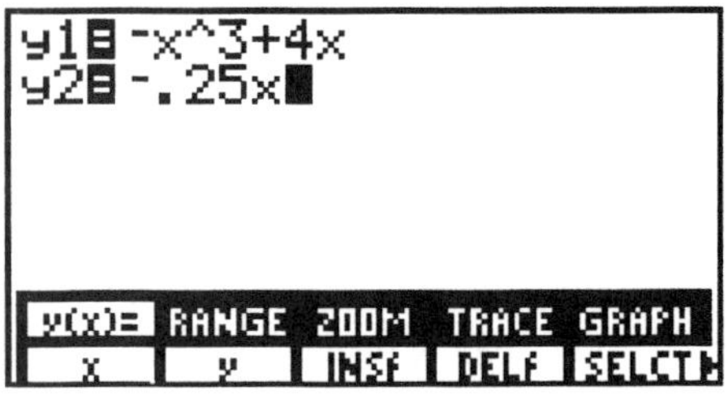

Figure 3.26: Two functions

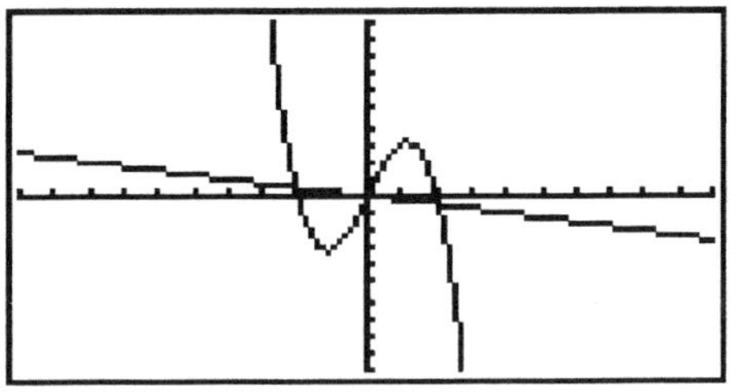

Figure 3.27: $y = -x^3 + 4x$ and $y = -.25x$

Note in Figure 3.26 that the equal signs next to y1 and y2 are *both* highlighted. This means *both* functions will be graphed. In the y(x)= screen, move the cursor to y1 and press F5 *[SELCT]* to turn function selection *off*. The equal sign beside y1 should no longer be highlighted (see Figure 3.28). The SELCT command operates as a toggle switch; executing it once more sets function selection *on*. Now press 2nd M5 *[GRAPH]* and see that only y2 is plotted.

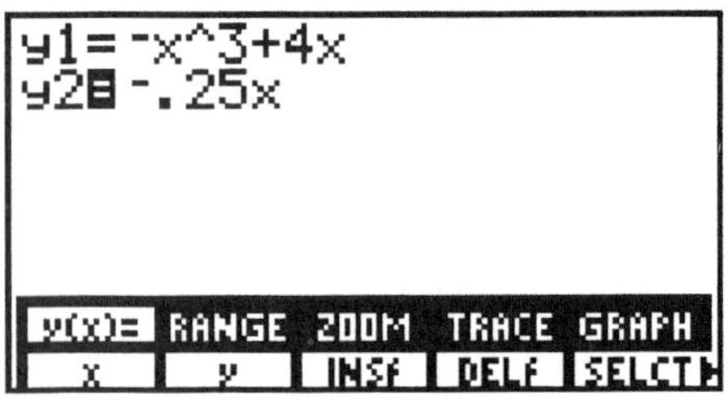

Figure 3.28: y(x)= screen with only y2 active

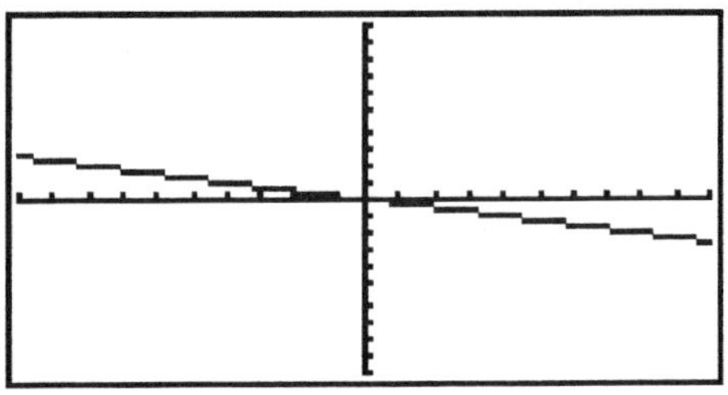

Figure 3.29: Graph of $y = -.25x$

Many different functions may be stored in the y(x)= list and any combination of them may be graphed simultaneously. You can make a function active or inactive for graphing by pressing SELCT to highlight (activate) or remove the highlight (deactivate). Go back to the y(x)= screen and do what is needed in order to graph y1 but not y2.

Now activate y2 again so that both graphs are plotted. Press GRAPH F4 *[TRACE]* and the cursor appears first on the graph of $y = -x^3 + 4x$ because it is higher up in the y(x)= list. You know that the cursor is on this function, y1, because of the numeral 1 displayed in the upper right corner of the window (see Figure

3.25). Press the up ▲ or down ▼ arrow key to move the cursor vertically to the graph of $y = -.25x$. Now the numeral 2 is displayed in the top right corner of the window. When more than one function is plotted, you can move the trace cursor vertically from one graph to another in this way. Next press the right and left arrow keys to trace along the graph of $y = -.25x$.

Technology Tip: By the way, trace along the graph of $y = -.25x$ and press and hold either ◀ or ▶. Eventually you will reach the *left* or *right* edge of the window. Keep pressing the arrow key and the TI-85 will allow you to continue the trace by panning the viewing rectangle. Check the RANGE screen to see that xMin and xMax are automatically updated.

If you trace along the graph of $y = -x^3 + 4x$, the cursor will eventually move *above* or *below* the viewing rectangle. The cursor's coordinates on the graph will still be displayed, though the cursor itself can no longer be seen.

When you are tracing along a graph, press ENTER and the window will quickly pan over so that the cursor's position on the function is centered in a new viewing rectangle. This feature is especially helpful when you trace near or beyond the edge of the current viewing rectangle.

The TI-85's display has 127 horizontal columns of pixels and 63 vertical rows. So when you trace a curve across a graph window, you are actually moving from xMin to xMax in 126 equal jumps, each called Δx. You would calculate the size of each jump to be $\Delta x = \frac{\text{xMax} - \text{xMin}}{126}$. Sometimes you may want the jumps to be friendly numbers like .1 or .25 so that, when you trace along the curve, the x-coordinates will be incremented by such a convenient amount. Just set your viewing rectangle for a particular increment Δx by making xMax = xMin + 126·Δx. For example, if you want xMin = -15 and Δx = .25, set xMax = -15 + 126·.25 = 16.5. Likewise, set yMax = yMin + 62·Δy if you want the vertical increment to be some special Δy.

To center your window around a particular point, say (h, k), and also have a certain Δx, set xMin = h - 63·Δx and xMax = h + 63·Δx. Likewise, make yMin = k - 31·Δy and yMax = k + 31·Δy. For example, to center a window around the origin, (0, 0), with both horizontal and vertical increments of .25, set the range so that xMin = 0 - 63·.25 = -15.75, xMax = 0 + 63·.25 = 15.75, yMin = 0 - 31·.25 = -7.75, and yMax = 0 + 31·.25 = 7.75.

See the benefit by first plotting $y = x^2 + 2x + 1$ in a standard graphing window. Trace near its y-intercept, which is (0, 1), and move towards its x-intercept, which is (-1, 0). Then change to a viewing rectangle that extends from -6.3 to 6.3 horizontally and from -3.1 to 3.1 vertically (center at the origin, Δx and Δy both .1), and trace again from the y-intercept. The TI-85 makes it easy to get this particular viewing rectangle: press GRAPH F3 MORE F4 *[ZOOM ZDECM]*.

3.2.6 ZOOM: Plot again the two graphs, for $y = -x^3 + 4x$ and for $y = -.25x$. There appears to be an intersection near $x = 2$. The TI-85 provides several ways to enlarge the view around this point. You can change the viewing rectangle directly by pressing RANGE and editing the values of xMin, xMax, yMin, and yMax. Figure 3.31 shows a new viewing rectangle for the range displayed in Figure 3.30. Trace has been turned on and the coordinates are displayed for a point on $y=-x^3+4x$ that is close to the intersection.

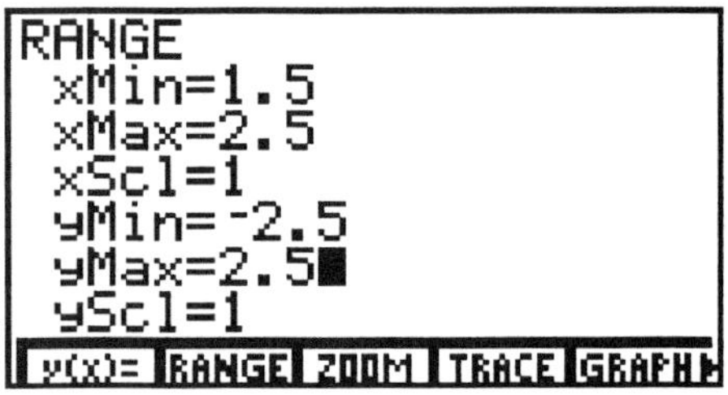

Figure 3.30: New RANGE

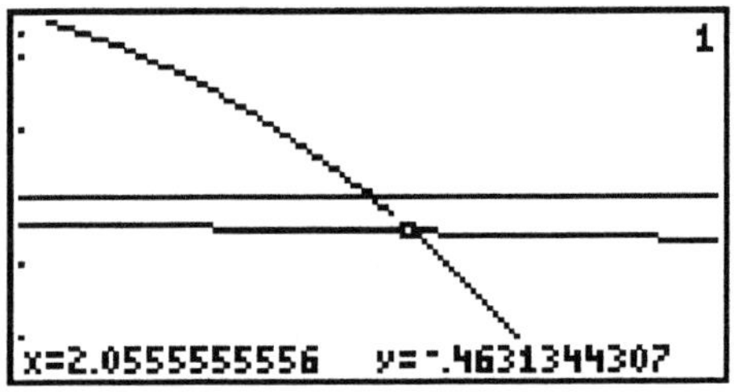

Figure 3.31: Closer view

A more efficient method for enlarging the view is to draw a new viewing rectangle with the cursor. Start again with a graph of the two functions $y=-x^3+4x$ and $y=-.25x$ in a standard viewing rectangle (press GRAPH F3 F4 for the standard window, from -10 to 10 along both axes).

First of all, imagine a small rectangular box around the intersection point, near $x = 2$. Press GRAPH F3 F1 *[ZOOM BOX]* to enable drawing a box (Figure 3.32) to define a new viewing rectangle. Use the arrow keys to move the cursor, whose coordinates are displayed at the bottom of the window, to one corner of the new viewing rectangle you are imagining (Figure 3.33).

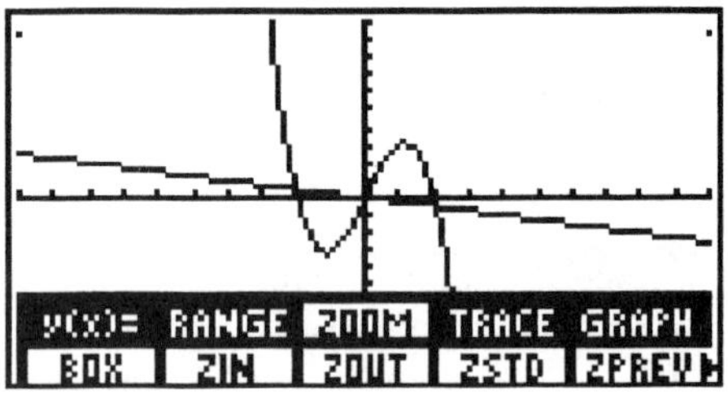

Figure 3.32: ZOOM menu

Figure 3.33: One corner selected

Press ENTER to fix the corner where you have moved the cursor; it changes shape and becomes a blinking square. Use the arrow keys again to move the cursor to the diagonally opposite corner of the new rectangle (Figure 3.34). If this box looks all right to you, press ENTER. The rectangular area you have enclosed will now enlarge to fill the graph window (Figure 3.35).

You may cancel the zoom any time *before* you press this last ENTER. Just press EXIT or GRAPH to interrupt the zoom and return to the current graph window. Even if you did execute the zoom, you may still return to the previous viewing rectangle by pressing F5 *[ZPREV]* in the ZOOM menu.

You can also gain a quick magnification of the graph around the cursor's location. Return once more to the standard range for the graph of the two functions $y=-x^3+4x$ and $y=-.25x$. Start the zoom by pressing GRAPH F3 F2 *[ZOOM ZIN]*; next use the arrow keys to move the cursor as close as you can to the point of intersection near $x = 2$ (see Figure 3.36). Then press ENTER and the calculator draws a magnified graph, centered at the cursor's position (Figure 3.37). The range variables are changed to reflect this new viewing rectangle. Look in the RANGE menu to check.

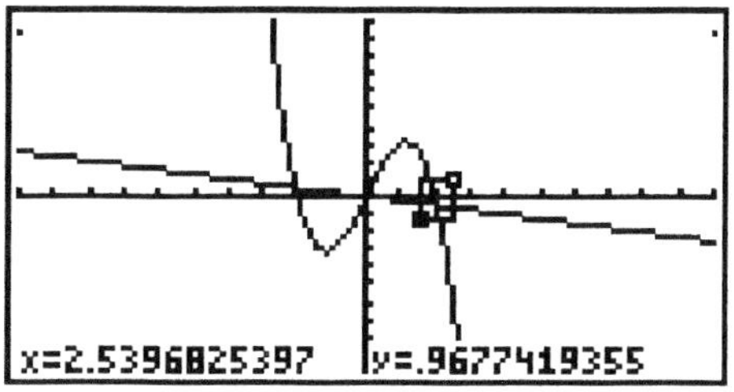

Figure 3.34: Box drawn

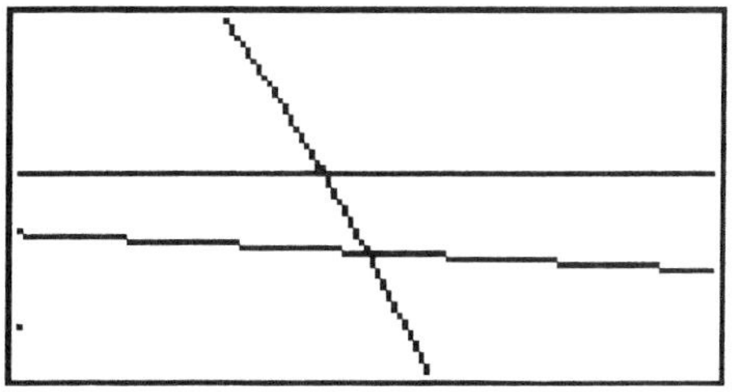
Figure 3.35: New viewing rectangle

As you see in the ZOOM menu (Figure 3.32), the TI-85 can zoom in *[ZIN]* and zoom out *[ZOUT]*. You would zoom out to see a larger view of the graph, centered at the cursor position. You can change the horizontal and vertical scale of the magnification by pressing GRAPH F3 MORE MORE F1 *[ZOOM ZFACT]* (see Figure 3.38) and editing xFact and yFact, the horizontal and vertical magnification factors.

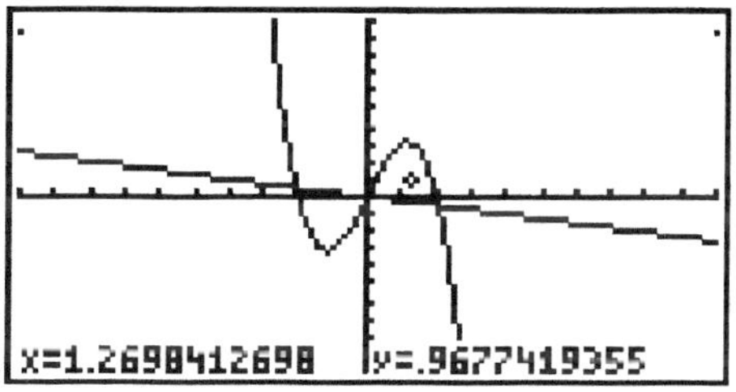

Figure 3.36: Before a zoom in

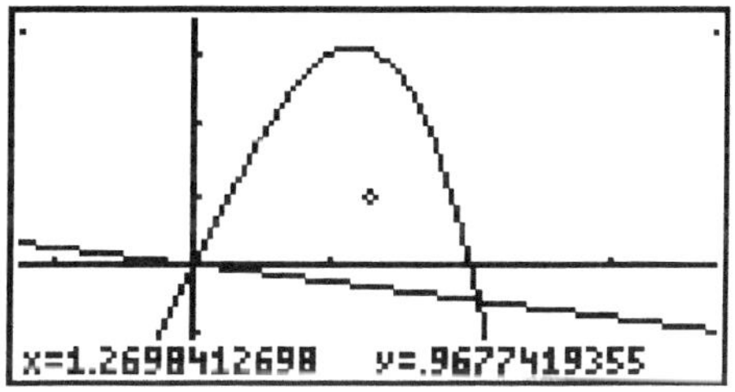

Figure 3.37: After a zoom in

The default zoom factor is 4 in both directions. It is not necessary for xFact and yFact to be equal. Sometimes, you may prefer to zoom in one direction only, so the other factor should be set to 1. Press GRAPH or EXIT to leave the ZOOM FACTORS menu.

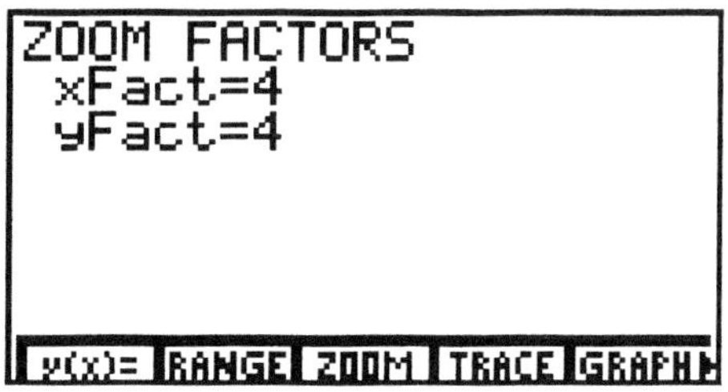

Figure 3.38: Set zoom factors

Technology Tip: If you should zoom in too much and lose the curve, zoom back to the standard viewing rectangle and start over.

3.2.7 Relative Minimums and Maximums: Graph $y=-x^3+4x$ once again by itself in the standard viewing rectangle (Figure 3.10). This function appears to have a relative minimum near x = -1 and a relative maximum near x = 1. You may zoom and trace to approximate these extreme values.

First trace along the curve near the local minimum. Notice by how much the x-values and y-values change as you move from point to point. Trace along the curve until the y-coordinate is as *small* as you can get it, so that you are as close as possible to the local minimum, and zoom in (use either ZIN or a zoom box). Now trace again along the curve and, as you move from point to point, see that the coordinates change by smaller amounts than before. Keep zooming and tracing until you find the coordinates of the local minimum point as accurately as you need them, approximately (-1.15, -3.08).

Follow a similar procedure to find the local maximum. Trace along the curve until the y-coordinate is as *great* as you can get it, so that you are as close as possible to the local maximum, and zoom in. The local maximum point on the graph of $y=-x^3+4x$ is approximately (1.15, 3.08).

Technology Tip: Trace along the function as near as possible to the minimum or maximum point and press ENTER to center the window at the cursor's location. Then you will not need to move the cursor again after you press ZIN.

The TI-85 automates the search for relative minimum and relative maximum points. Press GRAPH MORE F1 to display the menu (Figure 3.39). Since you wish to find a *local* extremum, it is necessary to restrict the interval. Otherwise, the TI-85 will locate extreme points within the entire current viewing rectangle. So press F1 and move the cursor to a point *left* of the minimum/maximum; press ENTER to set this as a *lower bound*. Next press F2 and move to a point *right* of the minimum/maximum; press ENTER to set an *upper bound* (as in Figure 3.40). Note the two arrows marking the lower and upper bounds at the top of the display.

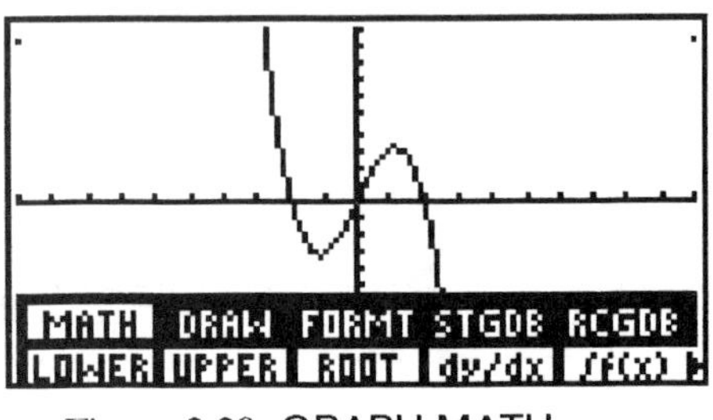

Figure 3.39: GRAPH MATH menu

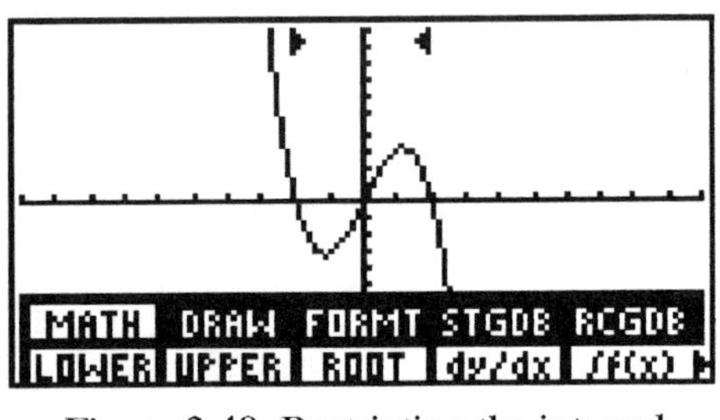

Figure 3.40: Restricting the interval

Technology Tip: The object is to restrict the interval to one in which the *relative* minimum/maximum is also the minimum/maximum overall. For the function $y=-x^3+4x$, you can set bounds that serve for locating both the local minimum and the local maximum. But for many functions, it will be necessary to set different bounds for each local extremum.

Next press MORE and either F1 to locate a minimum or F2 to locate a maximum point within the interval. If necessary, move the cursor to the desired graph. Then press ENTER; the coordinates of the relative minimum/maximum point will be displayed (see Figure 3.41) and the point itself will be marked.

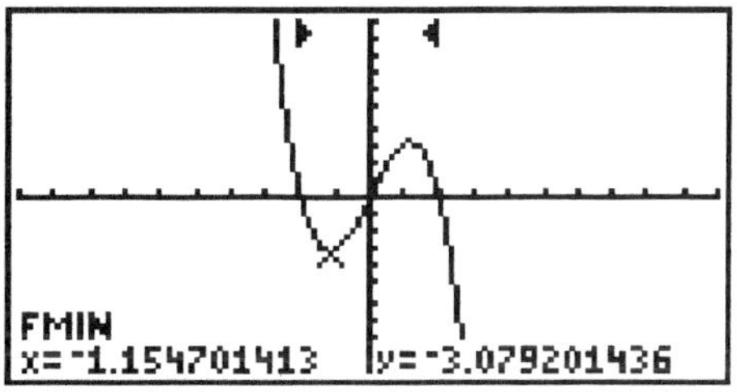

Figure 3.41: Relative minimum on $y = -x^3 + 4x$

3.3 Solving Equations and Inequalities

3.3.1 Intercepts and Intersections: Tracing and zooming are also used to locate an x-intercept of a graph, where a curve crosses the x-axis. For example, the graph of $y = x^3 - 8x$ crosses the x-axis three times (see Figure 3.42). After tracing over to the x-intercept point that is furthest to the left, zoom in (Figure 3.43). Continue this process until you have located all three intercepts with as much accuracy as you need. The three x-intercepts of $y = x^3 - 8x$ are approximately -2.828, 0, and 2.828.

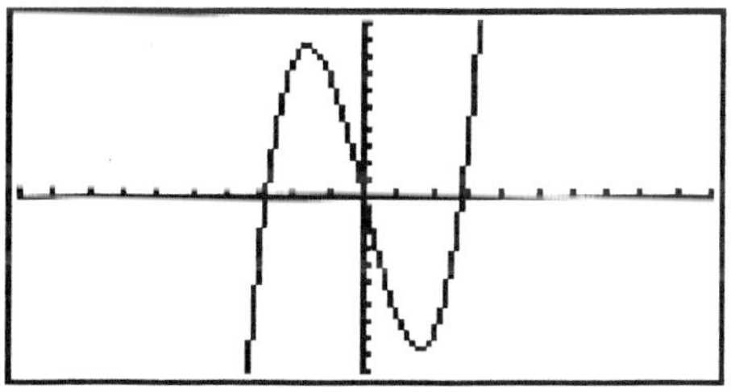

Figure 3.42: Graph of $y = x^3 - 8x$

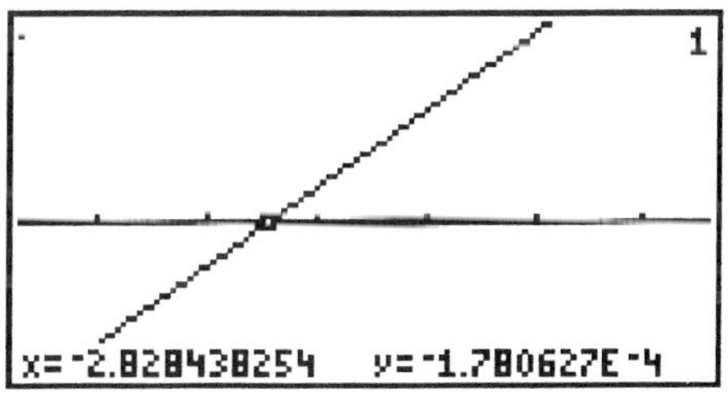

Figure 3.43: An x-intercept of $y = x^3 - 8x$

Technology Tip: As you zoom in, you may also wish to change the spacing between tick marks on the x-axis so that the viewing rectangle shows scale marks near the intercept point. Then the accuracy of your approximation will be such that the error is less than the distance between two tick marks. Change the x-scale on the TI-85 from the GRAPH F2 *[RANGE]* menu. Move the cursor down to xScl and enter an appropriate value.

TRACE and ZOOM are especially important for locating the intersection points of two graphs, say the graphs of $y = -x^3 + 4x$ and $y = -.25x$. Trace along one of the graphs until you arrive close to an intersection point. Then press ▲ or ▼ to jump to the other graph. Notice that the x-coordinate does not change, but the y-coordinate is likely to be different (see Figures 3.44 and 3.45).

When the two y-coordinates are as close as they can get, you have come as close as you now can to the point of intersection. So zoom in around the intersection point, then trace again until the two y-coordinates are as close as possible. Continue this process until you have located the point of intersection with as much accuracy as necessary.

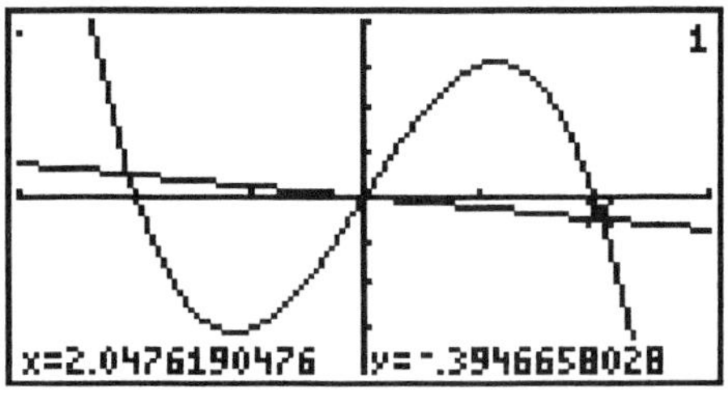

Figure 3.44: Trace on $y = -x^3 + 4x$

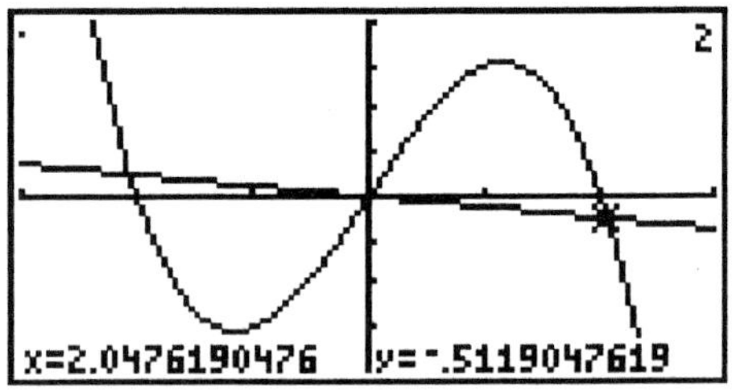

Figure 3.45: Trace on $y = -.25x$

You can also find the point of intersection of two graphs by pressing GRAPH MORE F1 MORE F5 *[ISECT]*. First move the cursor vertically to one graph and press ENTER. Next move the cursor vertically to select the other graph, trace near the intersection point, and press ENTER. Coordinates of the intersection will be displayed at the bottom of the window. Before locating the intersection, you may wish to restrict the interval by setting lower and upper bounds, as in Section 3.2.7 above.

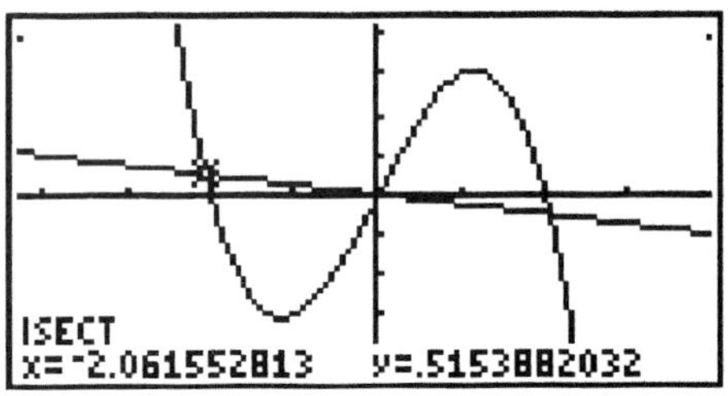

Figure 3.46: An intersection of $y = -x^3 + 4x$ and $y = -.25x$

3.3.2 Solving Equations by Graphing: Suppose you need to solve the equation $24x^3 - 36x + 17 = 0$. First graph $y = 24x^3 - 36x + 17$ in a window large enough to exhibit *all* its x-intercepts, corresponding to all its roots. Then use trace and zoom to locate each one. In fact, this equation has just one solution, approximately x = -1.414.

Remember that when an equation has more than one x-intercept, it may be necessary to change the viewing rectangle a few times to locate all of them.

The TI-85 also has a ROOT function in the GRAPH MATH menu. First, if desired, restrict the interval by setting lower and upper bounds. Then press GRAPH MORE F1 F3, trace with the cursor near a root, and press ENTER.

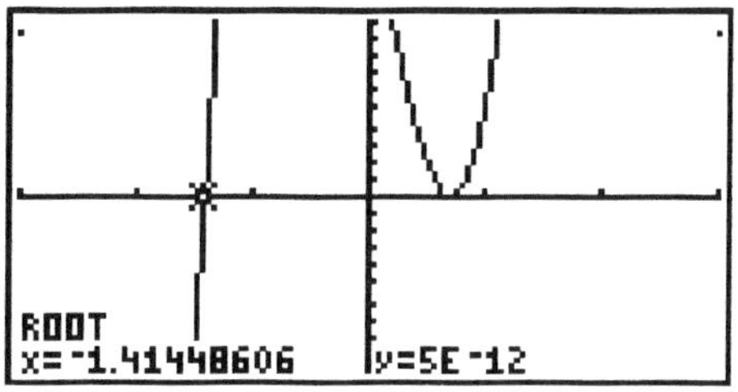

Figure 3.47: Root of $y = 24x^3 - 36x + 17$

Technology Tip: To solve an equation like $24x^3 + 17 = 36x$, you may first transform it into standard form, $24x^3 - 36x + 17 = 0$, and proceed as above to search for its x-intercepts. However, you may also graph the *two* functions $y = 24x^3 + 17$ and $y = 36x$, then zoom and trace to locate their point of intersection.

3.3.3 Solving Systems by Graphing: The solutions to a system of equations correspond to the points of intersection of their graphs (Figure 3.48). For example, to solve the system $y = x^2 - 3x - 4$ and $y = x^3 + 3x^2 - 2x - 1$, first graph them together. Then zoom and trace, or use the ISECT command from the GRAPH MATH menu, to locate their point of intersection, approximately (-2.17, 7.25).

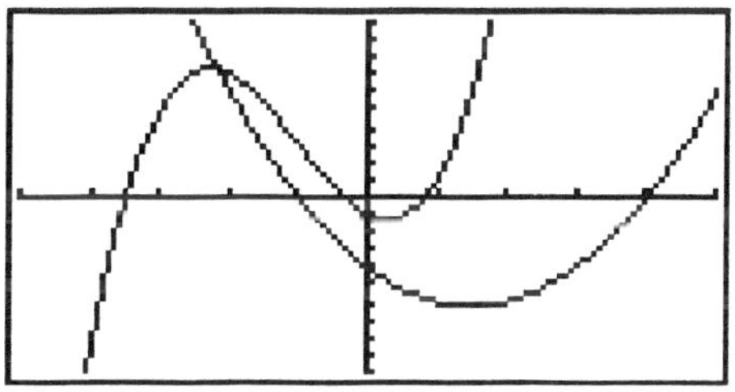

Figure 3.48: Solving a system of equations

You must judge whether the two current y-coordinates are sufficiently close for x = -2.17 or whether you should continue to zoom and trace to improve the approximation.

The solutions of the system of two equations $y = x^3 + 3x^2 - 2x - 1$ and $y = x^2 - 3x - 4$ correspond to the solutions of the single equation $x^3 + 3x^2 - 2x - 1 = x^2 - 3x - 4$, which simplifies to $x^3 + 2x^2 + x + 3 = 0$. So you may also graph $y = x^3 + 2x^2 + x + 3$ and find its x-intercepts to solve the system.

3.3.4 Solving Inequalities by Graphing: Consider the inequality $1-\frac{3x}{2} \geq x-4$. To solve it with your TI-85, graph the two functions $y=1-\frac{3x}{2}$ and $y=x-4$ (Figure 3.49). First locate their point of intersection, at $x = 2$. The inequality is true when the graph of $y=1-\frac{3x}{2}$ lies *above* the graph of $y=x-4$, and that occurs for $x < 2$. So the solution is the half-line $x \leq 2$, or $(-\infty, 2]$.

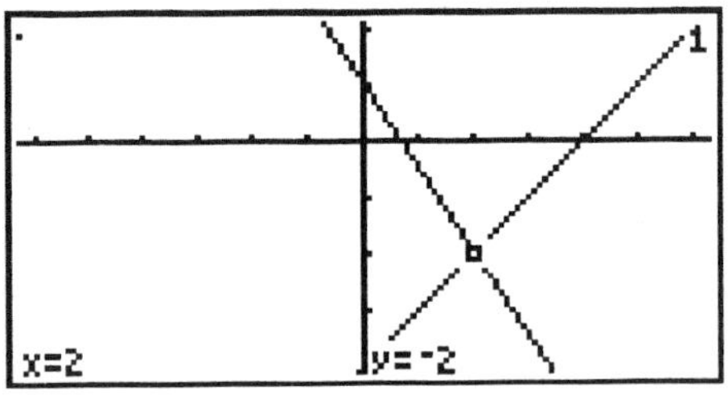

Figure 3.49: Solving $1-\frac{3x}{2} \geq x-4$

The TI-85 is capable of shading the region above or below a graph or between two graphs. For example, to graph $y \geq x^2-1$, first enter the function $y=x^2-1$ as y1 in the GRAPH y(x)= screen. Then press GRAPH MORE F2 *[DRAW]* F1 *[Shade]* 2nd VARS MORE F3 *[EQU]*, move the cursor to y1, and press ENTER , 100) (see Figure 3.50) and again ENTER. These keystrokes instruct the TI-85 to shade the region *above* $y=x^2-1$ and *below* y = 100 (chosen because this is a sufficiently large y-value). The result is shown in Figure 3.51.

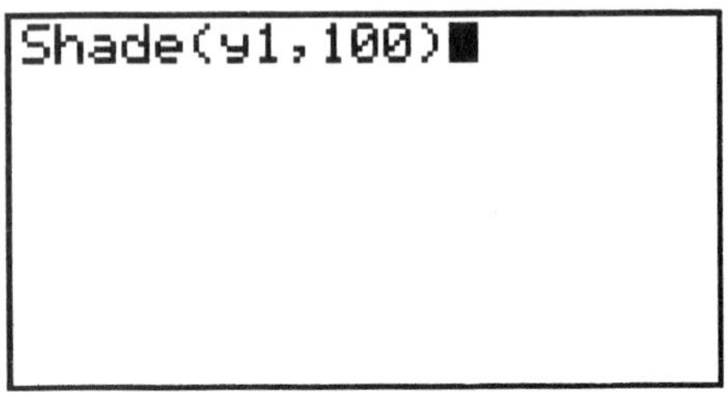

Figure 3.50: DRAW Shade

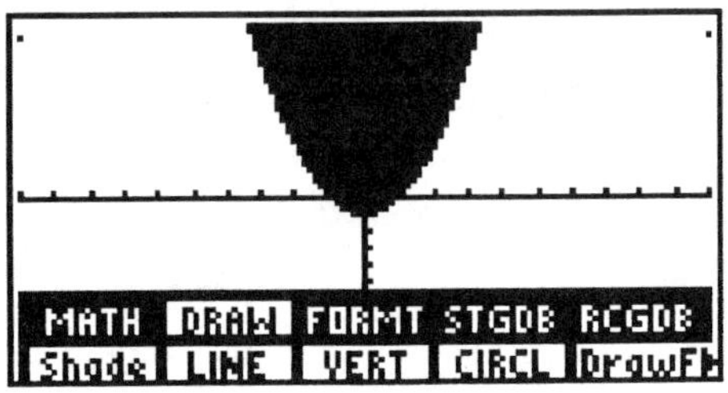

Figure 3.51: Graph of $y \geq x^2-1$

To clear the shading, when you are already in the DRAW menu, press MORE F5 *[CLDRW]*.

Now use shading to solve the previous inequality, $1-\frac{3x}{2} \geq x-4$. The function whose graph forms the lower boundary is named *first* in the SHADE command. To enter this in your TI-85 (see Figure 3.52), press these keys: GRAPH MORE F2 F1 x-VAR - 4 , 1 - 3 x-VAR ÷ 2) ENTER. The shading (see Figure 3.53) extends left from $x = 2$, hence the solution to $1-\frac{3x}{2} \geq x-4$ is the half-line $x \leq 2$, or $(-\infty, 2]$.

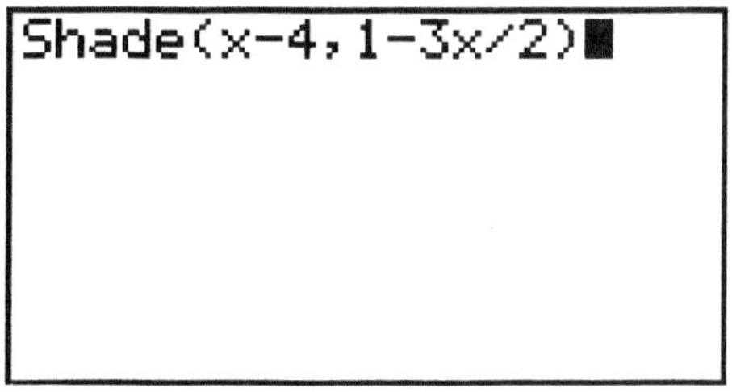

Figure 3.52: DRAW Shade command

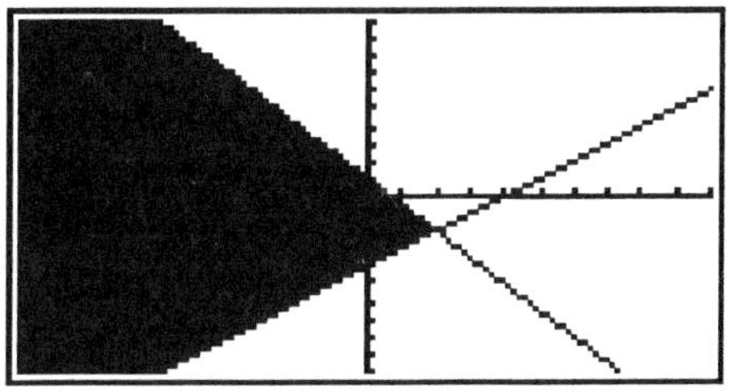

Figure 3.53: Graph of $1-\frac{3x}{2} \geq x-4$

More information about the DRAW menu is in the TI-85 manual.

3.4 Trigonometry

3.4.1 Degrees and Radians: The trigonometric functions can be applied to angles measured either in radians or degrees, but you should take care that the TI-85 is configured for whichever measure you need. Press 2nd MODE to see the current settings. Press ▼ twice and move down to the third line of the mode menu where angle measure is selected. Then press ◀ or ▶ to move between the displayed options. When the blinking cursor is on the measure you want, press ENTER to select it. Then press EXIT or 2nd QUIT to leave the mode menu.

It's a good idea to check the angle measure setting before executing a calculation that depends on a particu lar measure. You may change a mode setting at any time and not interfere with pending calculations. Try the following keystrokes to see this in action.

Expression	*Keystrokes*	*Display*
$\sin 45^\circ$	2nd MODE ▼ ▼ ▶ ENTER	
	EXIT SIN 45 ENTER	.707106781187
$\sin \pi^\circ$	SIN 2nd π ENTER	.054803665149
$\sin \pi$	SIN 2nd π 2nd MODE ▼ ▼	
	ENTER EXIT ENTER	0
$\sin 45$	SIN 45 ENTER	.850903524534
$\sin \frac{\pi}{6}$	SIN (2nd π ÷ 6) ENTER	.5

The first line of keystrokes sets the TI-85 in degree mode and calculates the sine of 45 *degrees*. While the calculator is still in degree mode, the second line of keystrokes calculates the sine of π *degrees*, 3.1415°. The third line changes to radian mode just before calculating the sine of π *radians*. The fourth line calculates the sine of 45 *radians* (the calculator is already in radian mode).

Figure 3.54: Angle measure

The TI-85 makes it possible to mix degrees and radians in a calculation. Execute these keystrokes to calculate $\tan 45^\circ + \sin \frac{\pi}{6}$ as shown in Figure 3.54: TAN 45 2nd MATH F3 *[ANGLE]* F1 *[°]* + SIN (2nd π ÷ 6) F2 *[r]* ENTER. Do you get 1.5 whether your calculator is set *either* in degree mode *or* in radian mode?

3.4.2 Graphs of Trigonometric Functions: When you graph a trigonometric function, you need to pay careful attention to the choice of graph window. For example, graph $y = \dfrac{\sin 30x}{30}$ in the standard viewing rectangle. Trace along the curve to see where it is. Zoom in to a better window, or use the period and amplitude to establish better RANGE values.

Technology Tip: Since $\pi \approx 3.1$, set xMin = 0 and xMax = 6.3 to cover the interval from 0 to 2π in steps of 0.05.

Next graph $y = \tan x$ in the standard window. The TI-85 plots consecutive points and then connects them with a segment, so the graph is not exactly what you should expect. You may wish to change from DrawLine to DrawDot graph (see Section 3.2.3) when you plot the tangent function.

3.5 Differentiation

3.5.1 Limits: Suppose you need to find this limit: $\lim\limits_{x \to 0} \dfrac{\sin 4x}{x}$. Plot the graph of $f(x) = \dfrac{\sin 4x}{x}$ in a convenient viewing rectangle that contains the point where the function appears to intersect the line $x = 0$ (because you want the limit as $x \to 0$). Your graph should lend support to the conclusion that $\lim\limits_{x \to 0} \dfrac{\sin 4x}{x} = 4$.

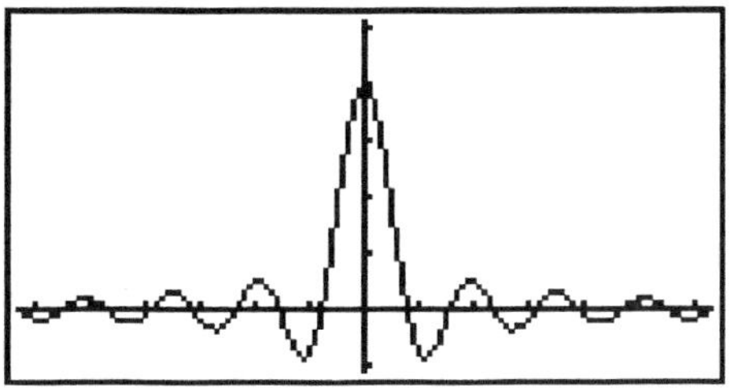

Figure 3.55: Checking $\lim_{x\to 0}\frac{\sin 4x}{x}=4$

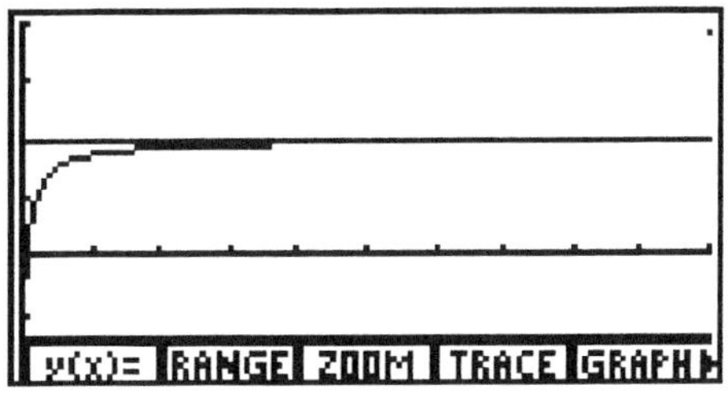

Figure 3.56: Checking $\lim_{x\to\infty}\frac{2x-1}{x+1}=2$

To test the reasonableness of the conclusion that $\lim_{x\to\infty}\frac{2x-1}{x+1}=2$, evaluate the function $f(x)=\frac{2x-1}{x+1}$ for several large positive values of x (since you want the limit as $x\to\infty$). For example, evaluate *f*(100), *f*(1000), and *f*(10,000). Another way to test the reasonableness of this result is to examine the graph of $f(x)=\frac{2x-1}{x+1}$ in a viewing rectangle that extends over large values of *x*. See, as in Figure 3.56 (where the viewing rectangle extends horizontally from 0 to 100), whether the graph is asymptotic to the horizontal line *y* = 2 (enter $\frac{2x-1}{x+1}$ for y1 and 2 for y2) .

3.5.2 Numerical Derivatives: The derivative of a function *f* at *x* can be defined as the limit of the slopes of secant lines, so $f'(x)=\lim_{\Delta x\to 0}\frac{f(x+\Delta x)-f(x-\Delta x)}{2\Delta x}$. And for small values of Δx, the expression $\frac{f(x+\Delta x)-f(x-\Delta x)}{2\Delta x}$ gives a good approximation to the limit.

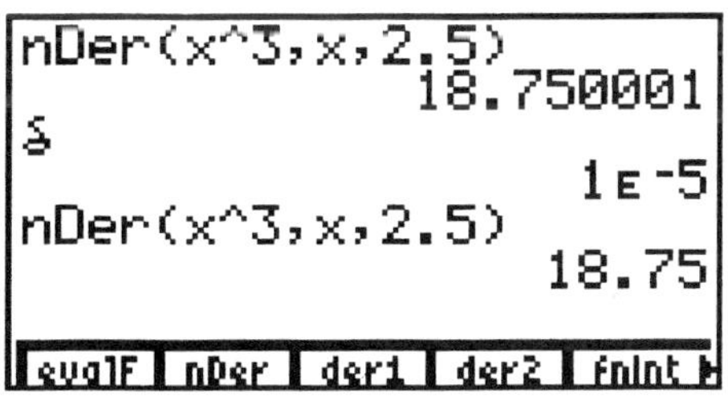

Figure 3.57: Using nDer

Figure 3.58: TOLER menu

The TI-85 has a function nDer in the CALC menu to calculate the *symmetric difference*, $\frac{f(x+\Delta x)-f(x-\Delta x)}{2\Delta x}$. This calculator uses a value for step size Δx that has been stored in the variable δ. For most purposes, δ = 0.001 gives a very good approximation to the derivative and is the TI-85's default (see Figure 3.58). So to find a numerical approximation to $f'(2.5)$ when $f(x) = x^3$ and with Δx = 0.001, press 2nd CALC F2 x-VAR ^ 3 , x-VAR , 2.5) ENTER as shown in the top line of Figure 3.57. The format of this command is nDer(*expression, variable, value*). If you are evaluating for the *current* stored value of the variable, write just nDer(*expression, variable*). Figure 3.57 shows the same derivative approximated again after pressing 2nd TOLER and changing δ to 0.00001.

Note that the function nDer calculates an approximate numerical derivative whose accuracy depends on the choice of δ. For a calculation that employs the rules of differentiation to yield a value as accurate as the TI-85 can be, use the special functions der1 for a first derivative and der2 for a second derivative (both are in the CALC menu). These commands use the same format as nDer, so you would write der1(*expression, variable, value*).

Technology Tip: In general, you may use der1 and der2 with expressions involving the basic calculator operations and functions (for example, $\sin x$ and x^2) or built up from them with simple arithmetic (for example, $\sin x^2$ or $\sin x + x^2$). Refer to the TI-85 manual for more details about restrictions on expressions that can be used with der1 and der2.

You may *not* use nDer or der1 or der2 in the expression for a der1 or der2 command. However, you *can* use der1 and der2 in the expression for an nDer command. So to approximate the *third* derivative of $\sin x^2$ at $x = 2$, you may press 2nd CALC F2 F4 SIN x-VAR x² , x-VAR) , x-VAR , 2).

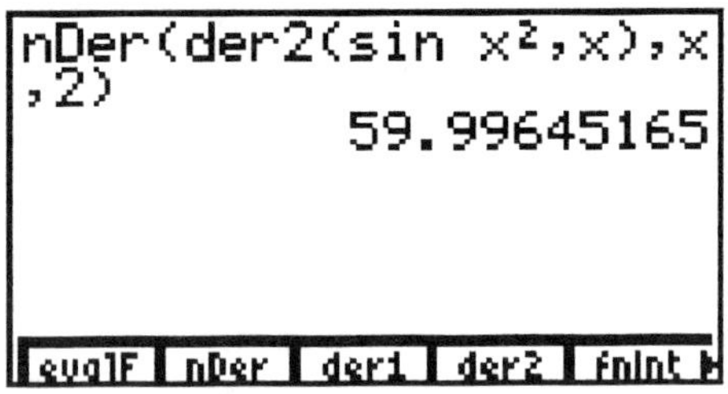

Figure 3.59: $f'''(2)$ for $f(x) = \sin x^2$

Technology Tip: It is sometimes helpful to plot both a function and its derivative together. In Figure 3.61, the function $f(x) = \dfrac{5x-2}{x^2+1}$ and its numerical derivative are graphed. You can duplicate this graph by first entering $\dfrac{5x-2}{x^2+1}$ for y1 and then entering its numerical derivative for y2 by pressing 2nd CALC F3 2nd M2 1 , 2nd M1), as you see in Figure 3.60.

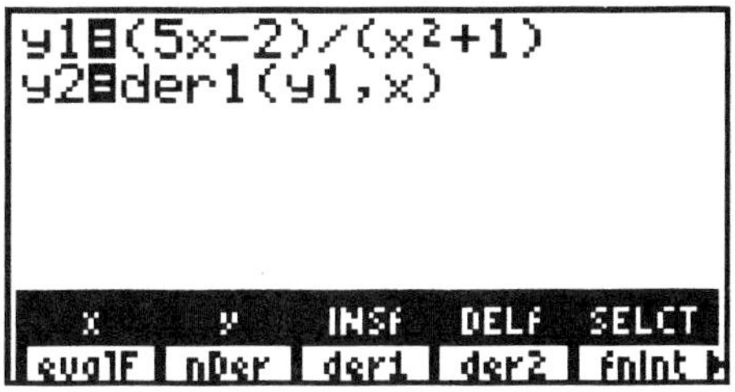

Figure 3.60: Entering $f(x)$ and $f'(x)$

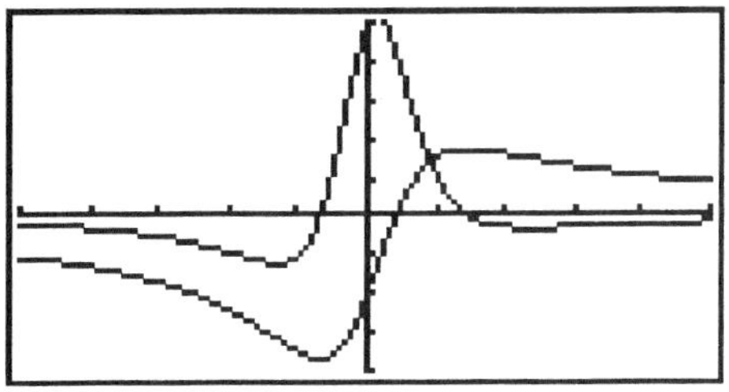

Figure 3.61: Graphs of $f(x)$ and $f'(x)$

You may also approximate a derivative while you are examining the graph of a function. When you are in a graph window, press GRAPH MORE F1 *[MATH]* F4, then use the arrow keys to trace along the curve to a point where you want the derivative (see Figure 3.62 for the graph of $f(x)=\dfrac{5x-2}{x^2+1}$ at x = -2.3) and press ENTER. The TI-85 uses the current value of the variable δ for this approximation.

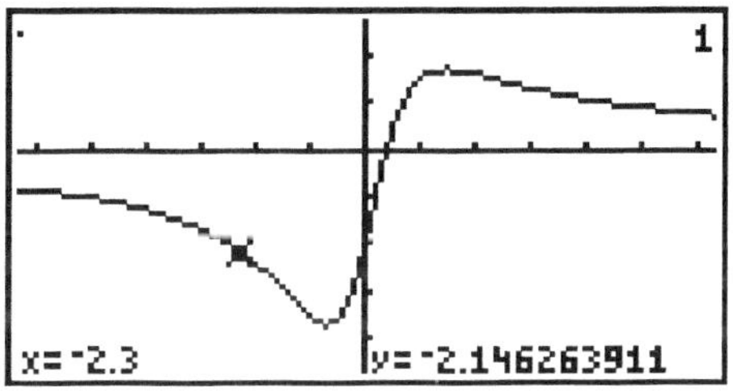

Figure 3.62: $f(x)=\dfrac{5x-2}{x^2+1}$ at x = -2.3

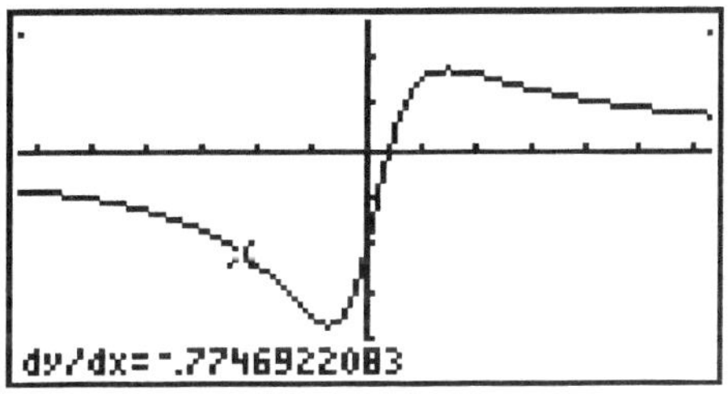

Figure 3.63: dy/dx

Technology Tip: With the TI-85, you can graph a function and the tangent line at one of its points. So graph the function $f(x)=\dfrac{5x-2}{x^2+1}$ once again. Then press GRAPH MORE F1 MORE MORE F3, trace with the cursor to a point of interest, and press ENTER. You may continue to draw more tangent lines, or clear them by pressing GRAPH MORE F2 MORE F5.

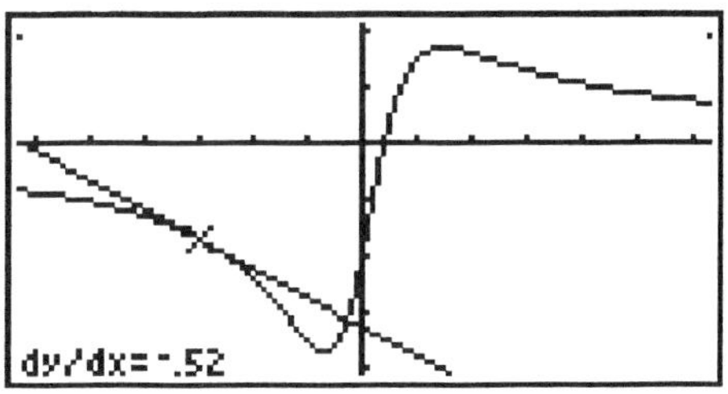

Figure 3.64: Tangent line

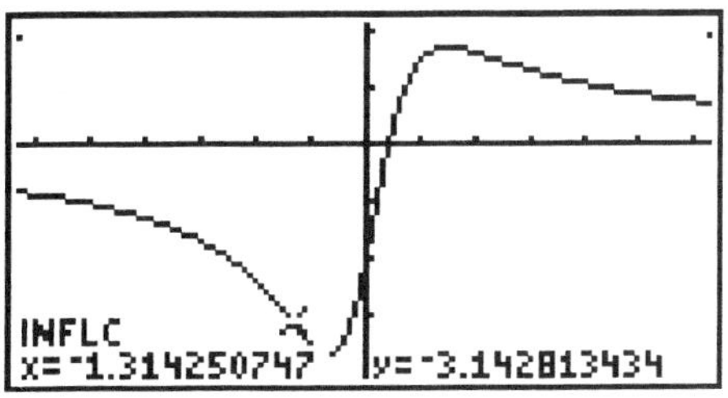

Figure 3.65: Point of inflection

In a similar way, the TI-85 locates a point of inflection. Graph the function, press GRAPH MORE F1 MORE F3, trace with the cursor near a point of inflection, and press ENTER.

You may choose the method of differentiation used by the TI-85 for graphing tangent lines and for locating points of inflection. In the MODE menu (Figure 3.1), move the cursor down to the last line and select either dxDer1 (exact differentiation) to use der1 or dxNDer (numeric differentiation) to use nDer. Recall that der1 is more accurate but also more restrictive, since it applies only to certain functions.

3.5.3 Newton's Method: With your TI-85, you may iterate using Newton's Method to find the zeros of a function. Recall that Newton's Method determines each successive approximation by the formula $x_{n+1} = x_n - \frac{f(x_n)}{f'(x_n)}$.

As an example of the technique, consider $f(x) = 2x^3 + x^2 - x + 1$. Enter this function as y1. A look at its graph suggests that it has a zero near x = -1, so start the iteration by storing -1 as x (see Figure 3.66). Then press these keystrokes: x-VAR - 2nd VARS MORE F3, select y1, keep on by pressing ÷ 2nd CALC F3 2nd VARS MORE F3, again select y1, and conclude by pressing , x-VAR ,) STO▸ x-VAR. Press ENTER repeatedly until two successive approximations differ by less than some predetermined value, say 0.0001. Note that each time you press ENTER, the TI-85 will use its *current* value of x, and that value is changing as you continue the iteration.

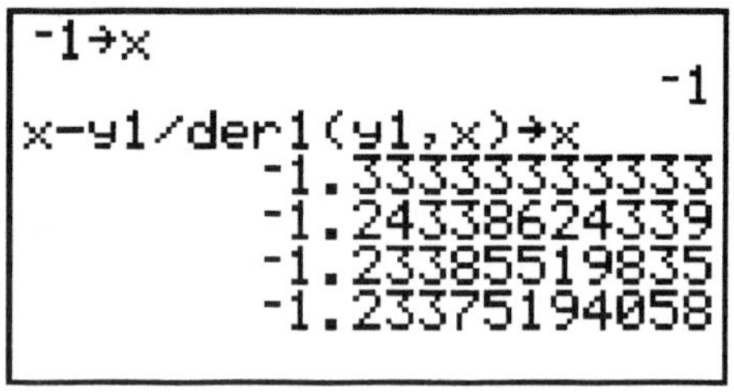

Figure 3.66: Newton's Method

Technology Tip: Newton's Method is sensitive to your seed value for x, so look carefully at the function's graph to make a good first estimate. Also, remember that the method sometimes fails to converge!

You may want to save the Newton's Method formula as a short program. See Section 3.9 or your calculator's manual for further information on programming the TI-85.

3.6 Sequences

3.6.1 Iteration: The ANS feature enables you to perform iterations to evaluate a function repeatedly. As an example, calculate $\frac{n-1}{3}$ for $n = 27$. Then calculate $\frac{n-1}{3}$ for n = the answer to the previous calculation.

Continue to use each answer as *n* in the *next* calculation. Here are keystrokes to accomplish this iteration on the TI-85 (see the results in Figure 3.67). Notice that when you use ANS in place of *n* in a formula, it is sufficient to press ENTER to continue an iteration.

Iteration	*Keystrokes*	*Display*
1	27 ENTER	27
2	(2nd ANS - 1) ÷ 3 ENTER	8.66666666667
3	ENTER	2.55555555556
4	ENTER	.518518518519
5	ENTER	-.16049382716

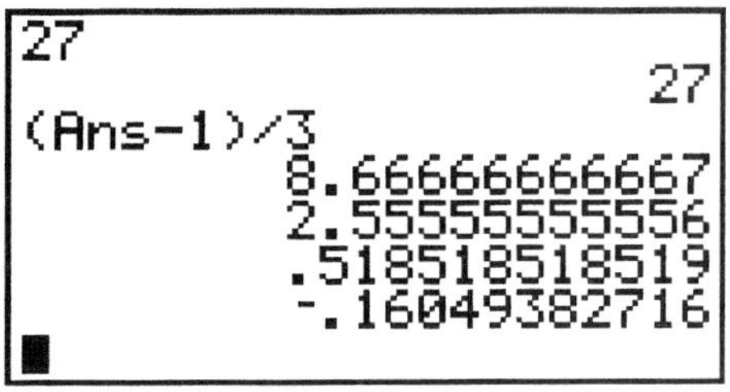

Figure 3.67: Iteration

Press ENTER several more times and see what happens with this iteration. You may wish to try it again with a different starting value.

3.6.2 Arithmetic and Geometric Sequences: Use iteration with the ANS variable to determine the *n*-th term of a sequence. For example, find the 18th term of an *arithmetic* sequence whose first term is 7 and whose common difference is 4. Enter the first term 7, then start the progression with the recursion formula, 2nd ANS + 4 ENTER. This yields the 2nd term, so press ENTER sixteen more times to find the 18th term. For a *geometric* sequence whose common ratio is 4, start the progression with 2nd ANS × 4 ENTER.

Of course, you could also use the *explicit* formula for the *n*-th term of an arithmetic sequence, $t_n = a + (n-1)d$. First enter values for the variables *a*, *d*, and *n*, then evaluate the formula by pressing 2nd alpha a + (2nd alpha n - 1) 2nd alpha d ENTER. For a geometric sequence whose *n*-th term is given by $t_n = a \cdot r^{n-1}$, enter values for the variables *a*, *r*, and *n*, then evaluate the formula by pressing 2nd alpha a 2nd alpha r ^ (2nd alpha n - 1) ENTER.

3.7 Integration

3.7.1 Approximating Definite Integrals: The TI-85 has the function fnInt in the CALC menu to approximate an integral. So to find a numerical approximation to $\int_0^1 \cos x^2 dx$, press 2nd CALC F5 COS x-VAR x² , x-VAR , 0 , 1) ENTER as shown in Figure 3.68. The format of this command is fnInt(*expression, variable, lower limit, upper limit*). In this example, the tolerance tol (which controls the accuracy of the approximation) is 0.00001, the TI-85's default. You may reset the tolerance by pressing 2nd TOLER (refer back to Figure 3.58) or by assigning a value to the variable tol.

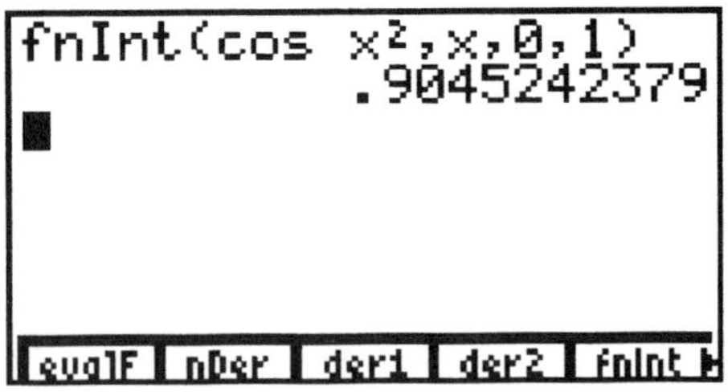

Figure 3.68: fnInt

3.7.2 Areas: You may approximate the area under the graph of a function $y = f(x)$ between $x = A$ and $x = B$ with your TI-85. For example, here are keystrokes for finding the area under the graph of the function $y = \cos x^2$ between $x = 0$ and $x = 1$. This area is represented by the definite integral $\int_0^1 \cos x^2 dx$. So graph $f(x) = \cos x^2$ and press GRAPH MORE F1 F5. Use the arrow keys to trace along the curve to the lower limit and press ENTER; then trace again to the upper limit (see Figure 3.69) and press ENTER. The region under the graph between the lower limit and the upper limit is marked and its area is displayed as in Figure 3.70. The TI-85 uses fnInt with the default tolerance tol = 10^{-5} in this calculation.

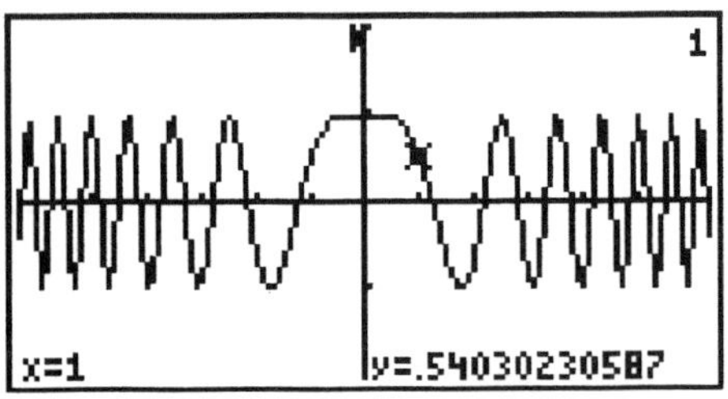

Figure 3.69: Setting the upper limit

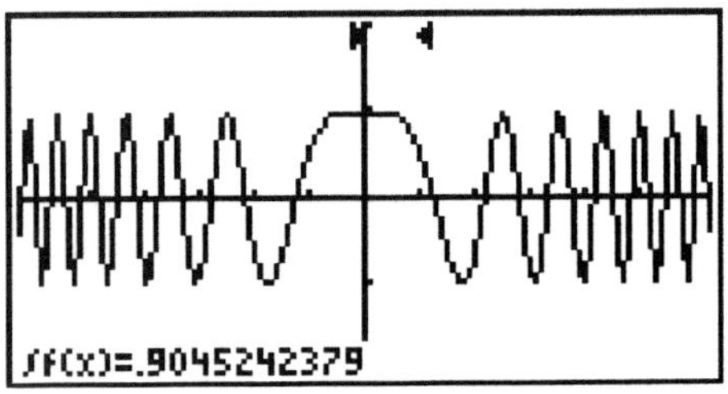

Figure 3.70: ∫f(x)dx

Technology Tip: When approximating the area under $f(x) = \cos x^2$ between $x = 0$ and $x = 1$, both limit points must be visible in the current viewing rectangle. Also, you must trace along the curve to *exactly* where $x = 0$ and $x = 1$. Now to trace along the curve to $x = a$, the viewing rectangle must be chosen so that the function is evaluated at $x = a$. The window shown in Figure 3.69 was made first by pressing ZOOM MORE F4 *[ZDECM]*, then by changing its vertical dimensions to appropriate values. By contrast, find the area under $f(x) = \cos x^2$ between $x = 0$ and $x = 1$ in the ZOOM MORE F3 *[ZTRIG]* window.

Technology Tip: Suppose that you want to find the area between two functions, $y = f(x)$ and $y = g(x)$, from $x = A$ to $x = B$. If $f(x) \geq g(x)$ for $A \leq x \leq B$, then enter the expression $f(x) - g(x)$ for y1 and proceed as before to find the required area.

See Section 2.9 for a sample TI-85 program that uses left and right Riemann Sums as well as the Midpoint Rule, the Trapezoid Rule, and Simpson's Rule to approximate definite integrals.

3.8 Parametric and Polar Graphs

3.8.1 Graphing Parametric Equations: The TI-85 plots parametric equations as easily as it plots functions. Just use the MODE menu (Figure 3.1), go to the fifth line from the top, and change the setting from Func for function graphs to Param for parametric graphs. Be sure, if the independent parameter is an angle measure, that MODE is set to whichever you need, Radian or Degree.

For example, here are the keystrokes needed to graph the parametric equations $x = \cos^3 t$ and $y = \sin^3 t$. First check that angles are currently being measured in radians. Change to parametric mode and press GRAPH F1 to examine the new parametric equation menu E(t)= (Figure 3.70). Enter the two parametric equations by pressing (COS F1) ^ 3 ENTER (SIN F1) ^ 3 ENTER.

Figure 3.71: Parametric E(t)= menu

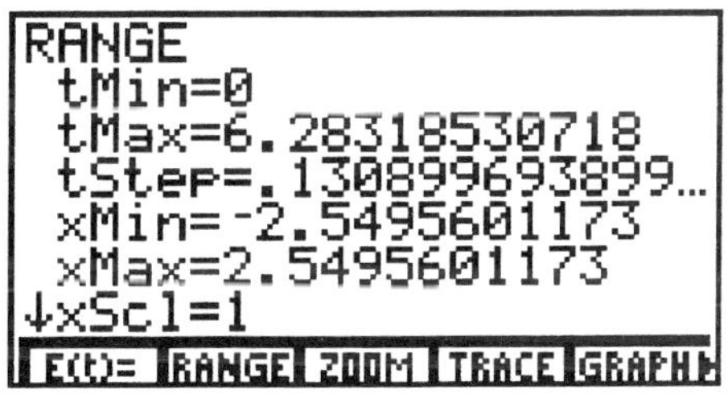

Figure 3.72: Parametric RANGE menu

Also look at the new parametric RANGE menu (Figure 3.72). In the standard viewing rectangle, the values of t go from 0 to 2π in steps of $\frac{\pi}{24} = .1309$. Press GRAPH to see the parametric graph (Figure 3.73).

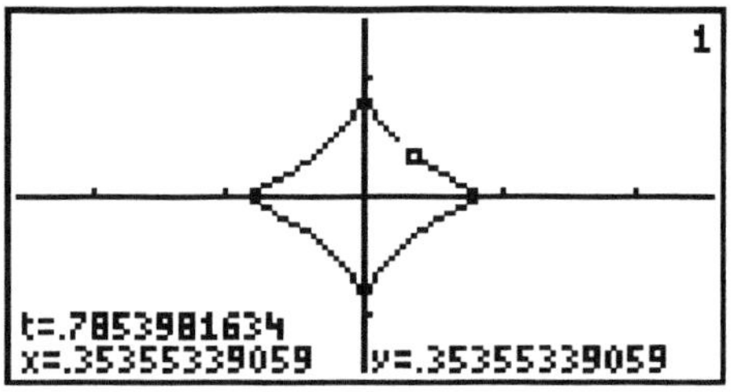

Figure 3.73: Parametric graph of $x = \cos^3 t$ and $y = \sin^3 t$

You may ZOOM and TRACE along parametric graphs just as you did with function graphs. As you trace along this graph, notice that the cursor moves in the *counterclockwise* direction as t increases.

3.8.2 Rectangular-Polar Coordinate Conversion: The CPLX menu (Figure 3.74) provides functions for converting between rectangular and polar coordinate systems.

Given rectangular coordinates $(x, y) = (4, -3)$, convert *from* these rectangular coordinates *to* polar coordinates (r, θ) by pressing 2nd CPLX MORE (4 , (-) 3) F2 ENTER. We see that $r = 5$ and $\theta = -.6435$. The measure of angle θ is displayed in radians, because that is the current default angle measure chosen in the MODE menu.

Suppose $(r, \theta) = (3, \pi)$. To convert *from* these polar coordinates *to* rectangular coordinates (x, y), press 2nd CPLX MORE (3 2nd ∠ π) F1 ENTER. Then $x = -3$ and $y = 0$.

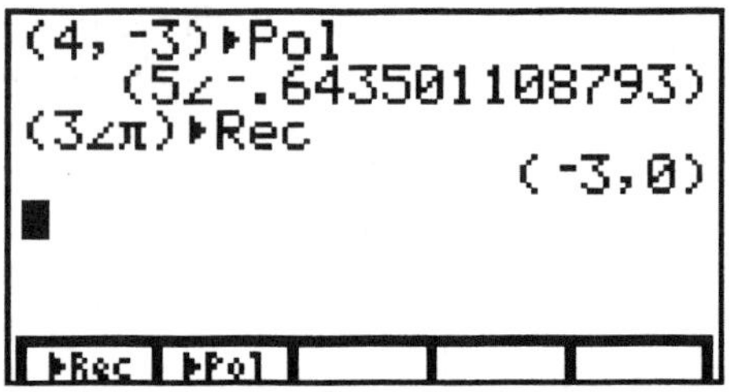

Figure 3.74: Coordinate conversions

3.8.3 Graphing Polar Equations: The TI-85 graphs a polar function in the form $r = f(\theta)$. In the fifth line of the MODE menu, select POL for polar graphs.

For example, to graph $r = 4\sin\theta$, press GRAPH F1 for the r(θ)= menu. Then enter the expression $4\sin\theta$ for r1. Choose a good viewing rectangle and an appropriate interval and increment for θ. In Figure 3.75, the viewing rectangle is roughly "square" and extends from -6.5 to 6.5 horizontally and from -4 to 4 vertically.

Figure 3.75 shows *rectangular* coordinates of the cursor's location on the graph. You may sometimes wish to trace along the curve and see *polar* coordinates of the cursor's location. The first line of the GRAPH FORMT menu (Figure 3.16) has options for displaying the cursor's position in rectangular RectGC or polar PolarGC form.

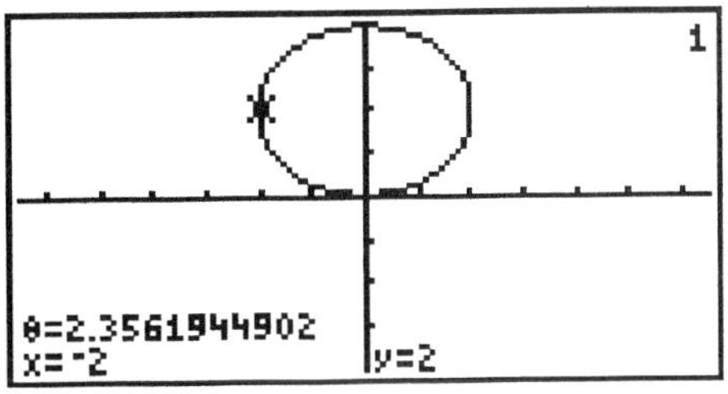

Figure 3.75: Polar graph of $r = 4\sin\theta$

3.10 Programming

3.10.1 Entering a Program: The TI-85 is a programmable calculator that can store sequences of commands for later replay. Here's an example to show you how to enter a useful program that performs numerical integration by several methods: left and right Riemann Sums as well as the Midpoint Rule, the Trapezoid Rule, and Simpson's Rule.

Press PRGM to access the programming menu. The TI-85 has space for many programs, each identified by a name that is up to eight characters long. The names of all your programs are listed alphabetically in the PRGM NAMES menu.

To create a new program, press PRGM F2 *[EDIT]* and enter its name. The cursor is now a blinking **A**, indicating the calculator is set to receive upper case alphabetic characters. Call this program INTEGRAL and press ENTER when you have finished.

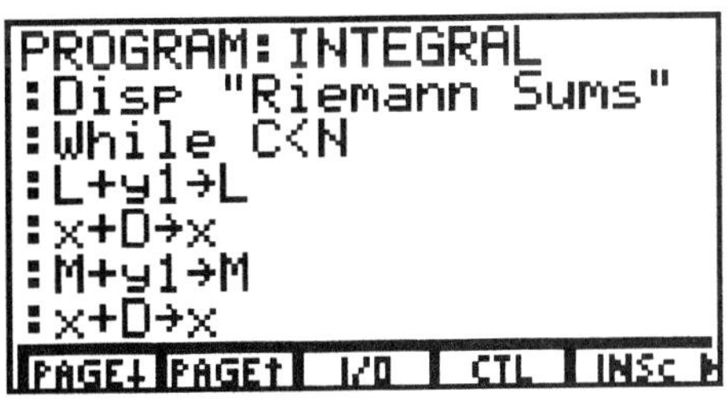

Figure 3.76: Part of program INTEGRAL

Within the program itself, each line begins with a colon : supplied automatically by the calculator after you press ENTER. Any command you could enter directly in the TI-85's home screen can be entered as a line in a program. There are also special programming commands.

Note that the TI-85 calculator checks for program errors as it *runs* a program, not while you enter or edit it.

Enter the program INTEGRAL by pressing the given keystrokes.

Program Line	*Keystrokes*
: Disp "Lower Limit"	F3 F3 MORE F5 ALPHA L 2nd alpha ALPHA O W E R ␣ L I M I T F5 ENTER
displays the words *Lower Limit* on the TI-81 screen	
: Input A	MORE F1 ALPHA A ENTER
waits for you to input a value that will be assigned to the variable *A*	
: Disp "Upper Limit"	F3 MORE F5 ALPHA U 2nd alpha ALPHA P P E R ␣ L I M I T F5 ENTER
: Input B	MORE F1 ALPHA B ENTER
: Disp "Subdivisions"	F3 MORE F5 ALPHA S 2nd alpha ALPHA U B D I V I S I O N S F5 ENTER
: Input N	MORE F1 ALPHA N ENTER
: (B - A)/N → D	(ALPHA B - ALPHA A) ÷ ALPHA N STO▸ D ENTER
calculates Δx and stores its value as *D*	
: 0 → L	0 STO▸ L ENTER
uses the variable *L* with the left Riemann Sum	
: 0 → M	0 STO▸ M ENTER
uses the variable *M* with the Midpoint Rule	
: 0 → C	0 STO▸ C ENTER
uses the variable *C* to keep track of the subdivisions	
: A → x	ALPHA A STO▸ x-VAR ENTER
starts off at the lower limit	
: Disp "Riemann Sums"	F3 MORE F5 ALPHA R 2nd alpha ALPHA I E M A N N ␣ ALPHA S 2nd alpha U M S F5 ENTER
: While C<N	2nd M4 MORE F1 ALPHA C 2nd TEST F2 ALPHA N ENTER
initiates a conditional loop	

: L + y1 → L	ALPHA L + 2nd alpha Y 1 STO▸ L ENTER

adds the value of the function at the *left* endpoint of the current subdivision

: x + D → x	x-VAR + ALPHA D STO▸ x-VAR ENTER

increments by $\frac{1}{2}\Delta x$ to the *midpoint* of the subdivision

: M + y1 → M	ALPHA M + 2nd alpha Y 1 STO▸ M ENTER

adds the value of the function at the *midpoint* of the current subdivision

: x + D → x	x-VAR + ALPHA D STO▸ x-VAR ENTER

increments by another $\frac{1}{2}\Delta x$ to the left endpoint of the *next* subdivision

: C + 1 → C	ALPHA C + 1 STO▸ C ENTER

counts up one subdivision

: End	EXIT MORE MORE F5 ENTER

terminates the While loop

: Disp " left"	2nd M3 F3 MORE F5 2nd alpha ALPHA ␣ L E F T F5 ENTER
: 2D∗L → L	2 ALPHA D × ALPHA L STO▸ L ENTER

calculates left Riemann Sum

: Disp L	MORE F3 ALPHA L ENTER
: Pause	2nd M4 MORE MORE F3 ENTER

during program execution, waits for you to press ENTER

: Disp " right"	2nd M3 F3 MORE F5 2nd alpha ALPHA ␣ R I G H T F5 ENTER
: L + 2D∗y1 → R	ALPHA L + 2 ALPHA D × 2nd alpha Y 1 STO▸ R ENTER
: A → X	ALPHA A STO▸ X ENTER
: R - 2D∗y1 → R	ALPHA R - 2 ALPHA D × 2nd alpha Y 1 STO▸ R ENTER

calculates right Riemann Sum

: Disp R	MORE F3 ALPHA R ENTER
: Pause	2nd M4 MORE MORE F3 ENTER
: Disp "Midpoint Rule"	2nd M3 F3 MORE F5 ALPHA M 2nd alpha ALPHA I D P O I N T ␣ ALPHA R 2nd alpha U L E F5 ENTER

: 2D*M → M	2 ALPHA D × ALPHA M STO▸ M ENTER

calculates numerical integral by Midpoint Rule

: Disp M	MORE F3 ALPHA M ENTER
: Pause	2nd M4 MORE MORE F3 ENTER
: Disp "Trapezoid Rule"	2nd M3 F3 MORE F5 ALPHA T 2nd alpha ALPHA R A P E Z O I D ␣ ALPHA R 2nd alpha U L E " ENTER
: (L + R)/2 → T	(ALPHA L + ALPHA R) ÷ 2 STO▸ T ENTER

calculates numerical integral by Trapezoid Rule (average left and right Riemann Sums)

: Disp T	MORE F3 ALPHA T ENTER
: Pause	2nd M4 MORE MORE F3 ENTER
: Disp "Simpsons Rule"	2nd M3 F3 MORE F5 ALPHA S 2nd alpha ALPHA I M P S O N S ␣ ALPHA R 2nd alpha U L E " ENTER
: (2M + T)/3 → S	(2 ALPHA M + ALPHA T) ÷ 3 STO▸ S ENTER

calculates numerical integral by Simpson's Rule ($\frac{2}{3}$ Midpoint and $\frac{1}{3}$ Trapezoid)

: Disp S	MORE F3 3 ALPHA S ENTER

When you have finished, press 2nd QUIT to leave the program editor.

3.10.2 Executing a Program: To execute the program just entered, press PRGM NAMES and look for INTEGRAL. The names of programs are listed alphabetically; press MORE to advance through the listing. Press the function key above INTEGRAL to select this program, then press ENTER to execute it.

The program INTEGRAL has been written to calculate $\int_A^B f(x)\,dx$ for N subdivisions of the interval $[A, B]$. You must enter the expression $f(x)$ as y1 before running this program. The program itself will prompt you for A, B, and N.

The program has been written to prompt you for values of the coefficients a, b, and c in a quadratic equation $ax^2 + bx + c = 0$. Input a value, then press ENTER to continue the program.

If you need to interrupt a program during execution, press ON.

The instruction manual for your TI-85 gives detailed information about programming. Refer to it to learn more about programming and how to use other features of your calculator.

CHAPTER 4

Hewlett-Packard HP 48G Series Calculator

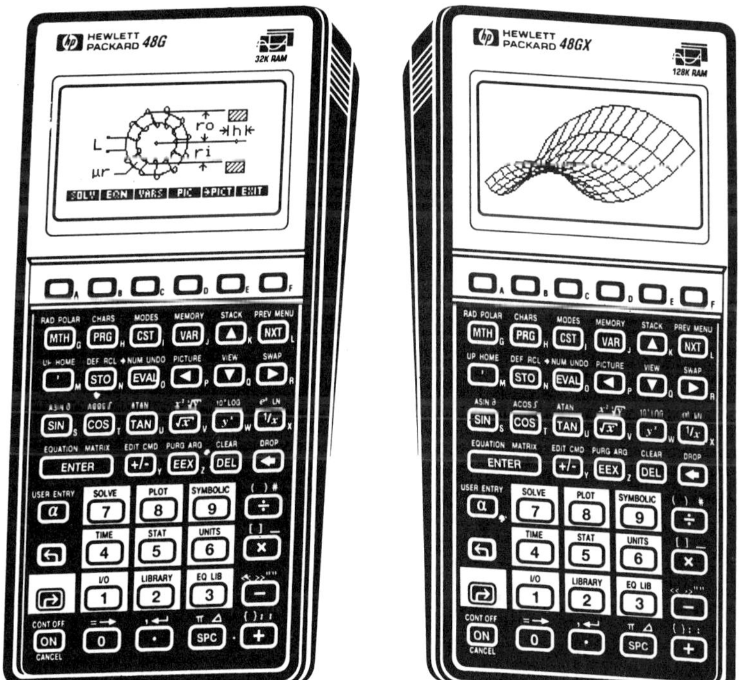

4.1 Getting started with the HP-48G

4.1.1 Basics: Press the ON key to begin using your HP-48G calculator. If you need to adjust the display contrast, first press and hold ON, then press + to darken the display or - to lighten the display. When you have finished with the calculator, turn it off to conserve battery power by pressing the green ↱ key and then OFF.

Check the HP-48G's settings by pressing ↱ and then MODES. At the bottom of the screen is a menu line of options, each corresponding to the white function key below it (see Figure 4.1).

Throughout this chapter of the Guide, we write *[COMMAND]* to represent the white function key directly below the menu item COMMAND. For example, *[OK]* will represent the far-right function key, below OK in the menu line of Figure 4.1.

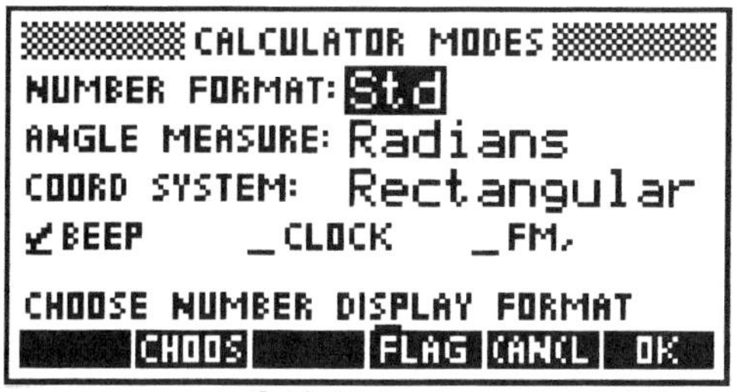

Figure 4.1: CALCULATOR MODES

Use the arrow keys, ▲ ▼ ◀ and ▶, to move the highlight to a mode you want to change. A prompt is displayed at the bottom of the window, just above the menu options. To change the number format, for example, move the highlight to the top of the window and press the function key *[CHOOS]*. Then move the highlight to Standard and press the function key *[OK]* to choose the standard display mode. Change other modes as necessary to configure your calculator for number format, angle measure, and coordinate system as illustrated in Figure 4.1. Details on alternative options will be given later in this guide.

Another way to change a mode setting is to highlight what you wish to change and press the +/- key to cycle among alternatives until the setting you want is displayed.

Accept the displayed settings by pressing *[OK]*. Cancel any changes and return to the home screen by pressing *[CANCL]*.

The four numbered lines in the home screen (Figure 4.2) correspond to the first four *cards* in the HP-48G's *stack*. Mathematical objects - numbers, expressions, equations, matrices - are stored in this stack, which may contain a very large number of cards. New cards are entered at the front of the stack, and existing cards are renumbered. The stack level of a card increases by one as each new card is created. The reverse occurs when you use values from the stack.

Press these keys to observe stack entry: 5.1 ENTER 6.2 ENTER 7.3 ENTER 8.4 ENTER 9.5 ENTER. Now 5.1 has been pushed up to stack level 5; to see it again, press the purple ↰ key and then DROP to drop every card one level (see Figure 4.2). The number 9.5 that was at stack level 1 is now discarded. (When there is no command line displayed, it is sufficient to press just the DROP key without the ↰ key before it.)

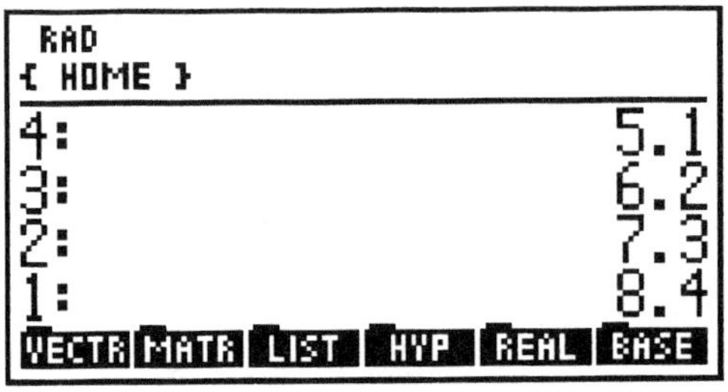

Figure 4.2: The card stack

Clear the entire stack by pressing ↰ CLEAR or just CLEAR. (Since there is no command line displayed, it is sufficient to press CLEAR without the preliminary ↰.) It's a good idea to clear the stack before each new sequence of calculations.

The HP-48G offers two ways of performing arithmetic calculations. The *stack method* is useful for quick calculations. Arguments, or numbers, are entered into the stack first, followed by an operation. For example, to compute $\sqrt{16}$, press 16. The stack moves up to make room for a *command line*. Next press $\sqrt{x}$ and the answer 4 is put in stack level 1. To calculate 12 + 34, press 12 ENTER 34 ENTER +. Actually, the second ENTER, after 34, is not really necessary, because mathematical keys like the + key automatically cause an ENTER before performing the indicated mathematical operation. For example, press 126 ENTER 6 ÷ and get 21.

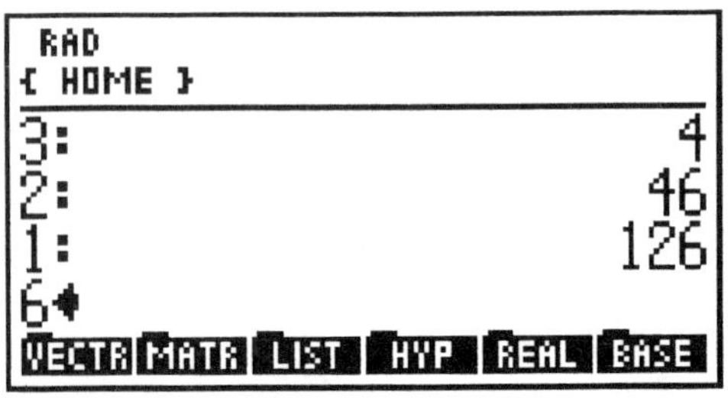

Figure 4.3: Arithmetic by the stack method

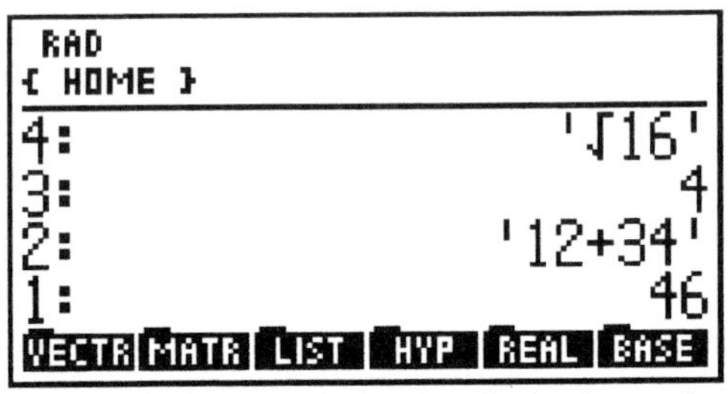

Figure 4.4: Arithmetic by the algebraic method

In the *algebraic method*, you enter an expression first and then you evaluate it. Begin by pressing ' because algebraic expressions must be surrounded by "tick marks." For example, calculate $\sqrt{16}$ again by pressing CLEAR ' $\sqrt{x}$ 16 ENTER. Press ENTER once more to duplicate the expression into stack level 2. Finally, press EVAL to evaluate the expression in stack level 1 and get $\sqrt{16}$ = 4 (see Figure 4.4). Next, to calculate 12 + 34, press ' 12 + 34 ENTER ENTER EVAL.

The HP-48G provides an EquationWriter application to simplify the creation of algebraic expressions. To access the EquationWriter, press ↰ EQUATION. Use the following keystrokes to input $\sqrt{3^2+4^2}$: √x 3 y^x 2 ▶ + 4 y^x 2 ENTER (see Figure 4.5). The right arrow ▶ key is used to advance the cursor and conclude exponents, roots, fractions, and others. The HP-48G User's Guide provides detailed examples to illustrate its EquationWriter.

The expression is now properly formatted with tick marks and entered in stack level 1. So press EVAL to evaluate it.

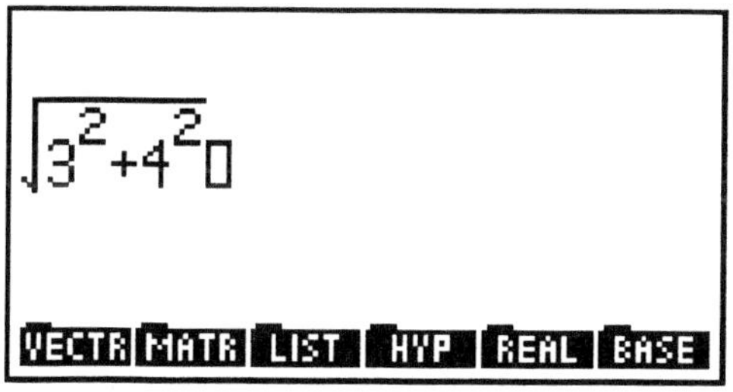

Figure 4.5: EquationWriter

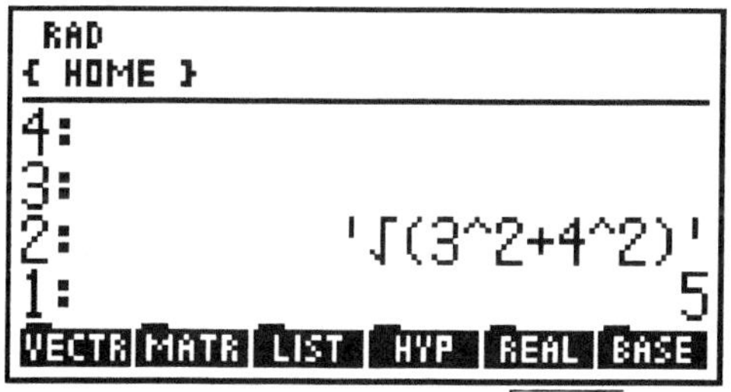

Figure 4.6: Calculating $\sqrt{3^2+4^2}$

Technology Tip: Erase a command line or cancel any command by pressing ON, which serves as the HP-48G's general-purpose CANCEL key.

4.1.2 Editing: Often we do not notice a mistake until we see how unreasonable an answer is. The HP-48G permits you to re-display an entire calculation, edit it easily, then execute the *corrected* calculation.

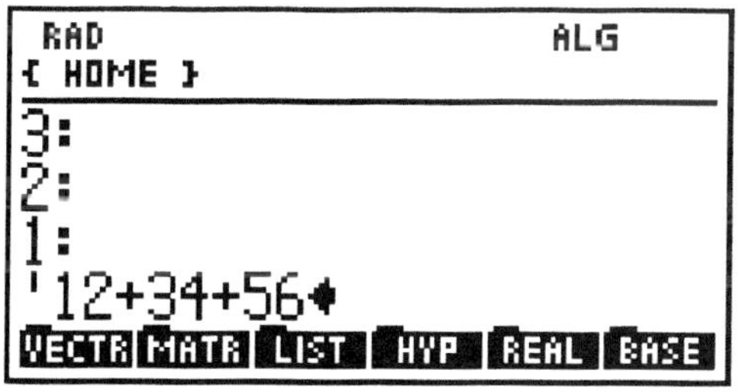

Figure 4.7: Editing the command line

Suppose you had typed 12 + 34 + 56 as in Figure 4.7 but had *not* yet pressed ENTER, when you realize that 34 should have been 74. Simply press ◀ (the *left* arrow key) as many times as necessary to move the blinking cursor left to 3, then press DEL 7 to delete the 3 and insert 7. You might also move the cursor to just right of 3, press ⬅ to backspace over it, then press 7. On the other hand, if 34 should have been 384, move the cursor back to 4 and type 8 (inserts at the cursor position and other characters are pushed to the right). If the 34 should have been 3 only, move the cursor to 4 and press DEL to delete it.

You may edit an expression so long as it remains in the stack. Press ON to clear the command line and ↰

EDIT to edit the expression currently in stack level 1. Use the left and right arrow keys to move through the expression; press DEL or ⬅ to delete unwanted characters; directly enter new characters as required. While editing, you may press ↱ ◀ to jump to the *left* end of an expression; press ↱ ▶ to jump to the *right* end.

When your editing is completed, press ENTER to put the edited expression into stack level 1; otherwise, press CANCEL to quit without saving any changes.

To restore the stack to its state before the last command was executed, press ↱ UNDO.

If the line you wish to edit is higher up in the stack, press DROP (if there is no command line, otherwise press ↰ DROP) as many times as necessary to move the line down the stack until it is at level 1; then press ↰ EDIT as before. Another technique is to press ON (to clear the command line) and ▲ as many times as needed to move the cursor up to the stack level you want; then press ↰ EDIT. When you have completed editing, press ENTER to put the edited expression in the stack level from which you began.

You may prefer to move an expression from the stack into EquationWriter for editing. Consult the User's Guide for instructions on how to edit in EquationWriter.

Technology Tip: When you need to evaluate a formula for different values of a variable, use the editing feature to simplify the process. For example, suppose you want to find the balance in an investment account if there is now \$5000 in the account and interest is compounded annually at the rate of 8.5%. The formula for the balance is $P\left(1+\frac{r}{n}\right)^{nt}$, where P = principal, r = rate of interest (expressed as a decimal), n = number of times interest is compounded each year, and t = number of years. In our example, this becomes $5000(1+.085)^t$. Here are the keystrokes for finding the balance after t = 3, 5, and 10 years.

Years	*Keystrokes*	*Balance*
	' 5000 × ↰ () 1 + .085 ▶ y^x 3 ENTER ENTER ENTER ENTER ▲ ▲ ↰ EDIT ↱ ▶ ◀ ⬅ 5 ENTER ▲ ↰ EDIT ↱ ▶ ◀ ⬅ 10 ENTER	
3	ENTER EVAL	\$6386.45
5	DROP EVAL	\$7518.28
10	DROP EVAL	\$11,304.92

Then to find the balance from the same initial investment but after 5 years when the annual interest rate is 7.5%, press these keys after the last calculation above: DROP ↰ EDIT ↱ ▶ ◀ ⬅ 5 ◀ ◀ ◀ ◀ ⬅ 7 ENTER EVAL. The balance you get should be \$7178.15.

Figure 4.8: Editing expressions

4.1.3 Key Functions: Most keys on the HP-48G offer access to more than one function, just as the keys on a computer keyboard can produce more than one letter ("g" and "G") or even quite different characters ("5" and "%"). The primary function of a key is indicated on the key itself, and you access that function by a simple press on the key. For example, to calculate $\sqrt{25}$ by the stack method, press 25 $\sqrt{x}$.

To access the *purple* function indicated to the *left* above a key, first press ↰ (the ↰ annunciator appears at the top of the window) and *then* press the key. For example, to calculate 10^3, press 3 ↰ 10^x.

For the *green* function indicated to the *right* above a key, first press ↱ (now the ↱ annunciator appears at the top of the window) and *then* press the key. For example, to calculate log 1000, press 1000 ↱ LOG.

When you want to use an uppercase letter printed *below* a key, first press α (the α annunciator appears at the top of the window) and then the key. For example, to use the letter *K* in a formula, press α K. For a lowercase letter, press α ↰ before you press the letter key. So press α ↰ K for the letter *k*. If you need several uppercase letters in a row, press α α, which is like CAPS LOCK on a computer keyboard, and then press all the letters you want. You may also *press and hold* the α key and then press as many letter keys as you wish. To lock in lowercase alpha mode, press α α ↰ α. Remember to press α when you are finished with uppercase lock or α ↰ α when you are finished with lowercase lock and want to restore the keys to their primary functions; ENTER and CANCEL also terminate alpha lock.

4.1.4 Order of Operations: When you put mathematical objects directly into the stack, the operations follow the order of entry. For example, press 3 ENTER 4 ENTER 5 + × and get 27, because you are calculating $3 \cdot (4 + 5)$. Next press 3 ENTER 4 ENTER 5 × + and get 23, because this time you are computing $3 + (4 \cdot 5)$.

When you use algebraic editing, the HP-48G performs calculations according to the standard algebraic rules. Working outwards from inner parentheses, calculations are performed from left to right. Powers and roots are evaluated first, followed by multiplications and divisions, and then additions and subtractions.

Note that the HP-48G distinguishes between *subtraction* and the *negative sign*. If you wish to enter a negative number, it is necessary to use the +/- key. Press +/- to change the sign *after* the number is entered. For example, you would evaluate $-5-(4\cdot -3)$ by pressing ' 5 +/- - ↰ () 4 × 3 +/- EVAL to get 7.

Enter these expressions to practice using your HP-48G.

Expression	*Keystrokes*	*Display*
$7-5\cdot 3$	' 7 - 5 × 3 EVAL	-8
$(7-5)\cdot 3$	' ↰ () 7 - 5 ▶ × 3 EVAL	6
$120-10^2$	' 120 - 10 y^x 2 EVAL	20
$(120-10)^2$	' ↰ () 120 - 10 ▶ y^x 2 EVAL	12100
$\frac{24}{2^3}$	' 24 ÷ 2 y^x 3 EVAL	3
$\left(\frac{24}{2}\right)^3$	' ↰ () 24 ÷ 2 ▶ y^x 3 EVAL	1728
$(7--5)\cdot -3$	' ↰ () 7 - 5 +/- ▶ × 3 +/- EVAL	-36

4.1.5 Algebraic Expressions and Memory: Your calculator can evaluate expressions such as $\frac{N(N+1)}{2}$ *after* you have entered a value for N. Suppose you want $N = 200$. Press ' α N ↰ = 200 ↰ DEF to store the value 200 in memory location N. Whenever you use N in an expression, the calculator will substitute the value 200 until you make a change by storing *another* number in N. Next enter the expression $\frac{N(N+1)}{2}$ by typing ' α N × ↰ () α N + 1 ▶ ÷ 2 EVAL. For $N = 200$, you will find that $\frac{N(N+1)}{2} = 20100$.

The contents of any memory location may be revealed by typing just its letter name and then ENTER. And the HP-48G retains memorized values even when it is turned off, so long as its batteries are good.

4.1.6 Repeated Operations: The result of your *last* calculation is always stored in stack level 1. This makes it easy to use the answer from one computation in another computation. For example, press 30 ENTER 15 + so that 45 is the last result displayed. Then press 9 ÷ and get 5 because $\frac{45}{9} = 5$.

Here is a situation where this is especially useful. Suppose a person makes \$5.85 per hour and you are asked to calculate earnings for a day, a week, and a year. Execute the given keystrokes to find the person's incomes during these periods.

Pay period	*Keystrokes*	*Earnings*
8-hour day	5.85 ENTER 8 ×	\$46.80
5-day week	5 ×	\$234
52-week year	52 ×	\$12,168

*4.1.7 The **MATH** Menu:* Operators and functions associated with a scientific calculator are available either immediately from the keys of the HP-48G or by the purple ↰ or green ↱ shift keys. You have direct key access to common arithmetic operations ($\sqrt{x}$, ↰ x^2, y^x, $1/x$), trigonometric functions (SIN, COS, TAN) and their inverses (ASIN, ACOS, ATAN), exponential and logarithmic functions (↱ LOG, ↰ 10^x, ↱ LN, ↰ e^x), and a famous constant (↰ π).

A significant difference between the HP-48G and many scientific calculators is that the HP-48G's algebraic calculation method requires the argument of a function *after* the function, as you would see a formula written in your textbook. For example, on the HP-48G you calculate $\sqrt{16}$ by pressing the keys ' $\sqrt{x}$ 16 in that order.

Here are keystrokes for basic mathematical operations. Try them for practice on your HP-48G.

Expression	*Keystrokes*	*Display*
$\sqrt{3^2+4^2}$	' $\sqrt{x}$ ↰ () 3 y^x 2 + 4 y^x 2 EVAL	5
$2\frac{1}{3}$	' 2 + 1 ÷ 3 EVAL	2.3333
$\log 200$	' ↱ LOG 200 EVAL	2.3010
$2.34 \cdot 10^5$	' 2.34 × 10 y^x 5 EVAL	234000

Additional mathematical operations and functions are available from the math menu (Figure 4.8). Press MTH to see the various options. You will learn in your mathematics textbook how to apply many of them. As an example, calculate $|-5|$ by pressing 5 +/- MTH *[REAL]* NXT *[ABS]* to see 5.

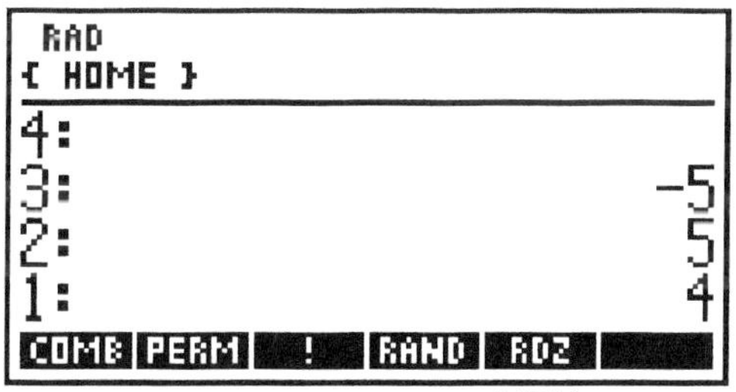

Figure 4.9: Factorial in the MTH menu

The *factorial* of a non-negative integer is the *product* of *all* the integers from 1 up to the given integer. The symbol for factorial is the exclamation point. So 4! (pronounced *four factorial*) is $1 \cdot 2 \cdot 3 \cdot 4 = 24$. You will learn more about applications of factorials in your textbook, but for now use the HP-48G to calculate 4! Press these keystrokes: 4 MTH NXT *[PROB]* *[!]*.

Hyperbolic functions (sinh, cosh, and tanh) and their inverses are available from another sub-menu of the math menu. For example, here are the keystrokes to calculate sinh 3: MTH *[HYP]* 3 *[SINH]* ENTER.

4.2.1 Evaluating Functions: Suppose you receive a monthly salary of $1975 plus a commission of 10% of sales. Let x = your sales in dollars; then your wages W in dollars are given by the equation $W = 1975 + .10x$. If your January sales were $2230 and your February sales were $1865, what was your income during those months?

Here's how to use your HP-48G to perform this task. Input the equation $W = 1975 + .10x$ by pressing these keys: ' α W ↰ = 1975 + .10 × α ↰ X ↰ DEF (see Figure 4.10).

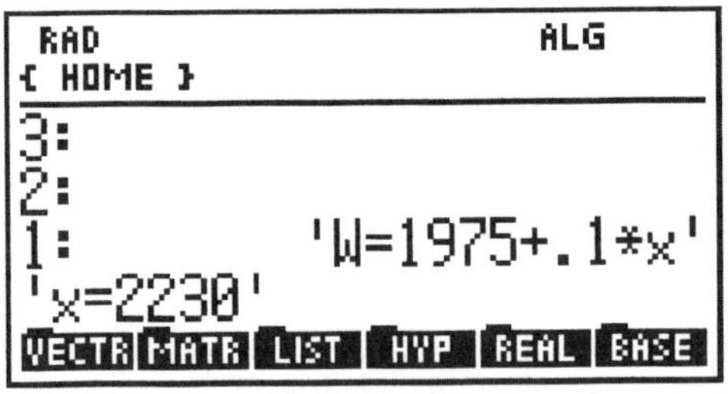

Figure 4.10: Entering a formula

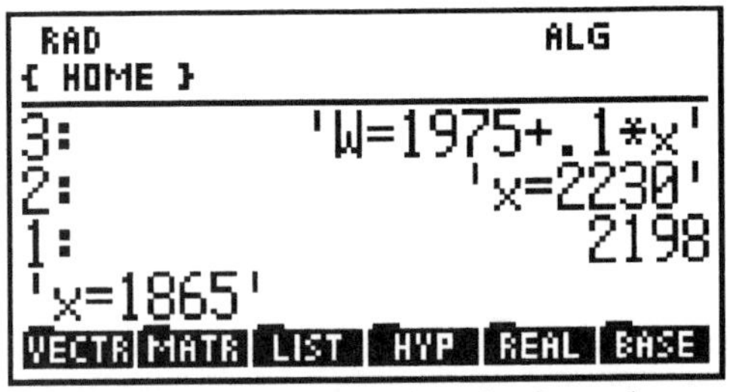

Figure 4.11: Evaluating the formula

Assign the value 2230 to the variable x by these keystrokes: ' α ↰ X ↰ = 2230 ↰ DEF. Next press α W EVAL and find January's wages (see Figure 4.11). Repeat these steps to find the February wages. Each time the HP-48G evaluates W, it uses the *current* value of x.

Another way to accomplish this is to define the function $W(x) = 1975 + .10x$ by pressing ' α W ↰ () α ↰ X ▶ ↰ = 1975 + .10 × α ↰ X ↰ DEF (see Figure 4.12). Then press ' α W ↰ () 2230 EVAL to evaluate $W(2230)$. Repeat for $W(1865)$.

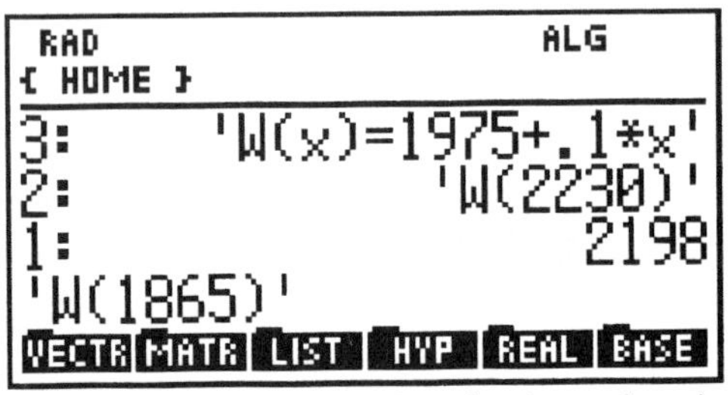

Figure 4.12: Defining and evaluating a function

Technology Tip: The HP-48G allows variable names to be longer than a single letter. You may define such variables, for example, as *length* and *width*. For this reason, the HP-48G requires multiplication to be expressed, so $3x$ must be input as $3 \cdot x$. The calculator would interpret xxx as a three-letter variable name, not as x^3.

4.2.2 *Functions in a Graph Window:* On the HP-48G, once you have entered a function, you can easily generate its graph. The ability to draw a graph contributes substantially to our ability to solve problems.

For example, here is how to graph $y = -x^3 + 4x$. First press ↱ PLOT. If the plot type is not Function, then move the highlight to the TYPE: field, press *[CHOOS]*, move to Function, and press *[OK]*. The independent variable is set for *X* by default; you may change it if you wish. You can get the independent variable quickly by pressing a function key. Move the highlight, if necessary, to EQ: and enter the function (as in Figure 4.13) by pressing ' - *[X]* y^x 3 + 4 × *[X]* *[OK]*. Now press NXT *[ERASE]* *[DRAW]* and the HP-48G switches to a window with the graph of $y = -x^3 + 4x$.

While the HP-48G is calculating coordinates for a plot, it displays a busy indicator at the top of the graph window.

Your graph window may look like the one in Figure 4.14 or it may be different. Since the graph of $y = -x^3 + 4x$ extends infinitely far left and right and also infinitely far up and down, the HP-48G can display only a piece of the actual graph. This displayed rectangular part is called a *viewing rectangle*. You can easily change the viewing rectangle to enhance your investigation of a graph.

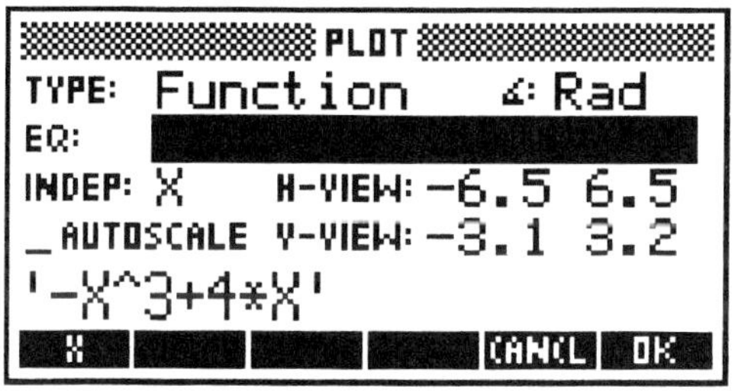

Figure 4.13: PLOT screen

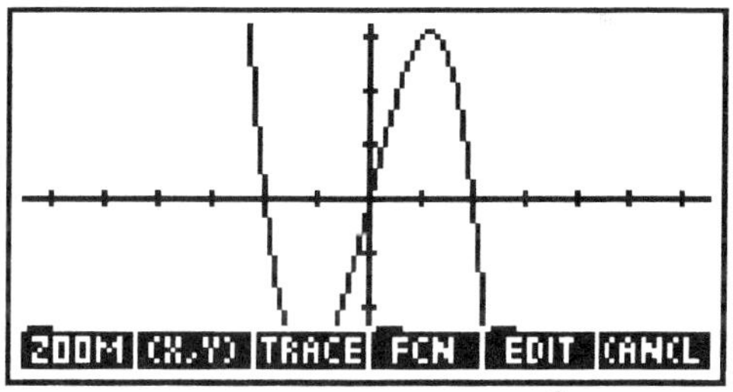

Figure 4.14: Graph of $y = -x^3 + 4x$

The viewing rectangle in Figure 4.14 shows the part of the graph that extends horizontally from x_{min} = -6.5 to x_{max} = 6.5 and vertically from y_{min} = -3.1 to y_{max} = 3.2. This is the *default* viewing rectangle for the HP-48G. The PLOT screen has information about your viewing rectangle.

Use the arrow keys to move around the PLOT menu and enter new values for the horizontal dimensions x_{min} and x_{max} and for the vertical dimensions y_{min} and y_{max}. Remember to use the +/- key, not - (which is subtraction), when you want to enter a negative value. The following figures show different viewing rectangles for the same function, $y = -x^3 + 4x$.

In Figures 4.15 and 4.16, the menu was turned off by pressing *[EDIT]* NXT *[MENU]*. Restore the menu by pressing any function key.

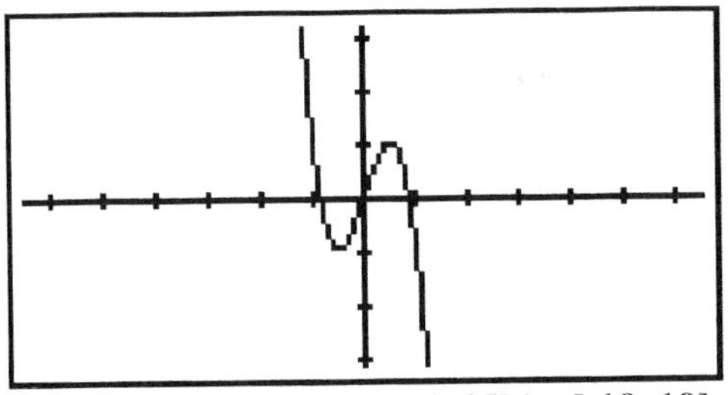

Figure 4.15: Window [-15, 15] by [-10, 10]

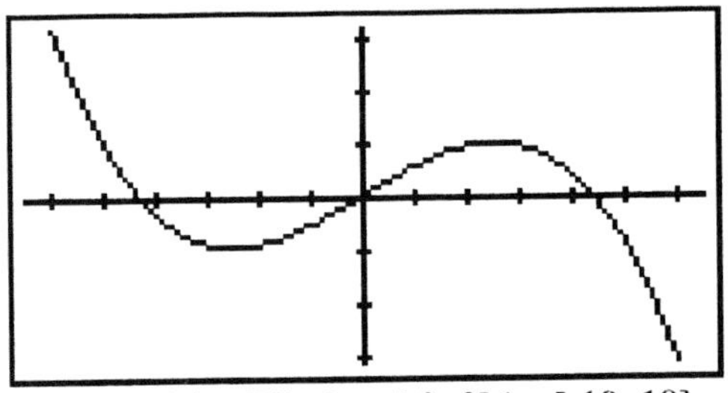

Figure 4.16: Window [-3, 3] by [-10, 10]

To set the plot parameters quickly back to their default values (see Figure 4.13), press *[ZOOM] [ZDFLT]* while in a plot window.

Leave the plot window and return to the home screen by pressing CANCEL.

4.2.3 The Greatest Integer Function: The greatest integer function, written [[x]], gives the greatest *integer* less than or equal to a number x. On the HP-48G, the greatest integer function is called FLOOR and is located under the REAL sub-menu of the MTH menu (see Figure 4.12). So calculate [[6.78]] = 6 by pressing 6.78 MTH *[REAL]* NXT NXT *[FLOOR]*.

To graph y = [[x]], go in the PLOT menu, move beside EQ:, and press ' MTH *[REAL]* NXT NXT *[FLOOR]* α X ENTER. Figure 4.16 shows this graph in a viewing rectangle from -5 to 5 in both directions.

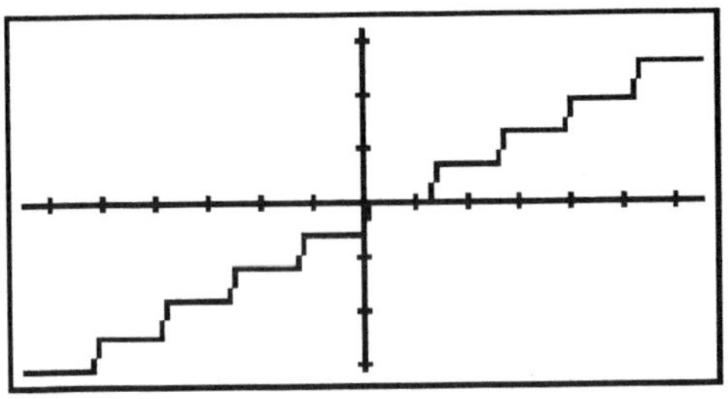

Figure 4.17: Connected graph of y = [[x]]

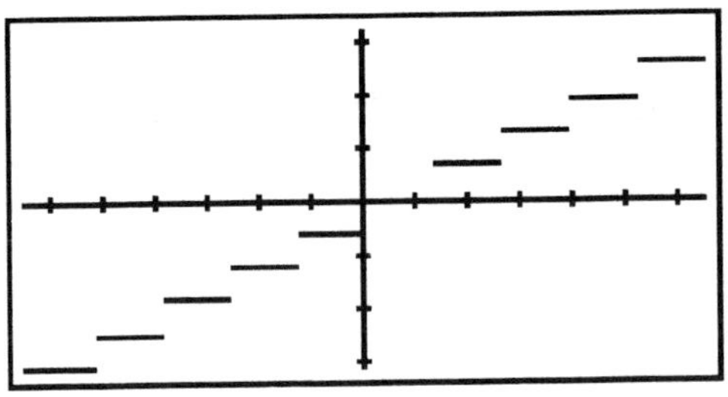

Figure 4.18: Dot graph of y = [[x]]

The true graph of the greatest integer function is a step graph, like the one in Figure 4.18. For the graph of y = [[x]], a segment should *not* be drawn between every pair of successive points. You can change from a connected line graph to a dot graph on the HP-48G from the PLOT menu. Press *[OPTS]* and move to CONNECT; toggle *[✓CHK]* to remove the check mark next to CONNECT; then press *[OK]*. Erase the previous graph and draw a new one.

Usually you want a connected graph, so go back to the plot options menu and toggle CONNECT on again.

4.2.4 Graphing a Circle: Here is a useful technique for graphs that are not functions, but that can be "split" into a top part and a bottom part, or into multiple parts. Suppose you wish to graph the circle whose equation is $x^2 + y^2 = 36$. First solve for y and get an equation for the top semicircle, $y = \sqrt{36 - x^2}$, and for the bottom semicircle, $y = -\sqrt{36 - x^2}$. Then graph the two semicircles simultaneously.

The keystrokes to draw this circle's graph follow. In the PLOT menu, execute these keystrokes to fill the EQ: field with a *list* of the two semicircles: ↰ {} ' √x ↰ () 36 - *[X]* y^x 2 ▶ ▶ SPC ' - √x ↰ () 36 - *[X]* y^x 2 *[OK]*. Then press *[ERASE] [DRAW]* to draw them both.

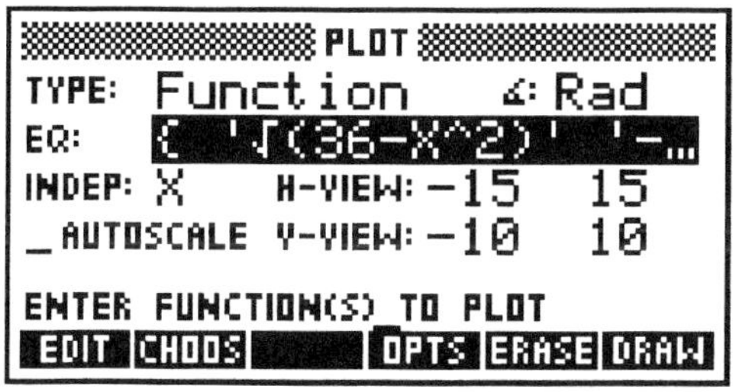

Figure 4.19: Two semicircles

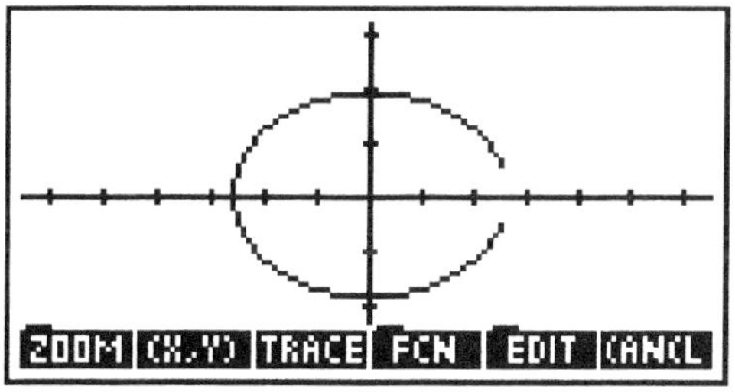

Figure 4.20: Circle: [-15, 15] by [-10, 10]

In the viewing rectangle of Figure 4.20, the graph does *not* look like a circle, because the units along the axes are not the same. Change the window so that the value of y_{max} - y_{min} is $\frac{1}{2}$ times x_{max} - x_{min}. For example, see Figure 4.21 and the corresponding graph in Figure 4.22. The method works because the dimensions of the HP-48G's display are such that the ratio of vertical to horizontal is approximately $\frac{1}{2}$.

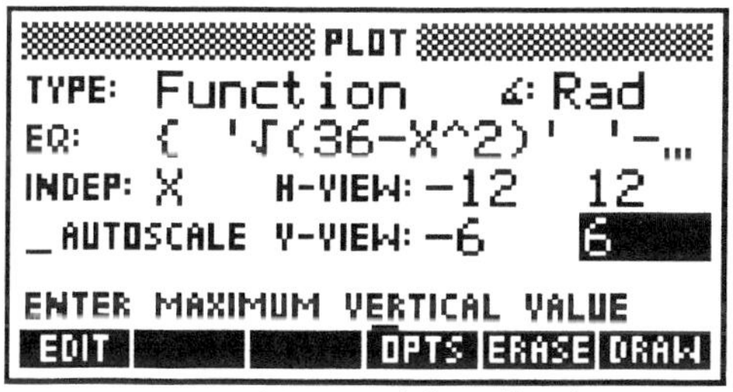

Figure 4.21: $\frac{\text{vertical}}{\text{horizontal}} = \frac{12}{24} = \frac{1}{2}$

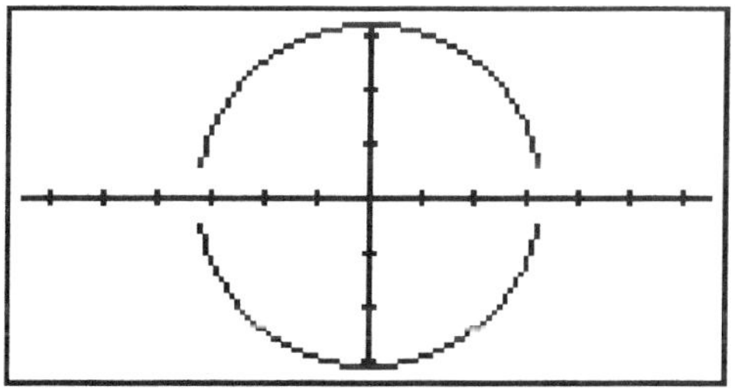

Figure 4.22: A "square" circle

The two semicircles in Figure 4.22 do not meet because of an idiosyncrasy in the way the HP-48G plots a graph.

Technology Tip: A square viewing rectangle, in which units along both axes are the same, is also important when you want to judge whether two lines are perpendicular. The intersection of perpendicular lines will always *look* like a right angle in a square viewing rectangle.

Now if it's just a circle or other conic you wish to graph, the HP-48G has a special Conic PLOT format. So to graph the circle $x^2 + y^2 = 36$, press ↱ PLOT, choose Type: to be Conic, and press *[OK]*. Move the highlight to EQ: and enter the *equation* (as in Figure 4.23) by pressing ' α X y^x 2 + α Y y^x 2 ↰ = 36 pressing ' α X y^x 2 + α Y y^x 2 ↰ = 36 *[OK]*. A good viewing rectangle for this graph extends from -12 to 12 horizontally and from -6 to 6 vertically. Now press *[ERASE] [DRAW]* and achieve a graph identical to that in Figure 4.22. The HP-48G is actually plotting two branches, just as we were doing before.

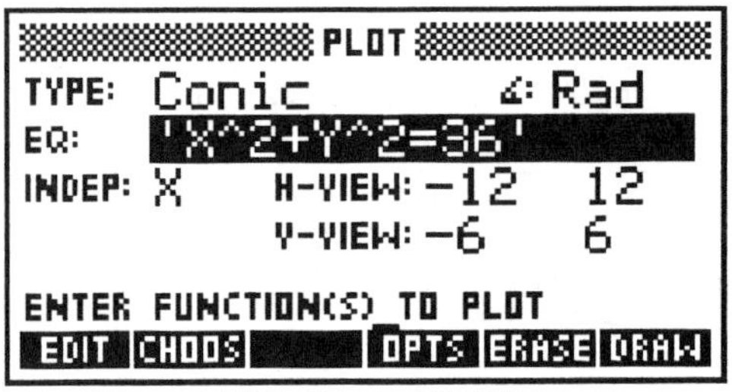

Figure 4.23: Conic PLOT format

4.2.5 ***TRACE:*** Graph $y = -x^3 + 4x$ in the default viewing rectangle. Press any of the arrow keys ▲ ▼ ◄ ► and see the cursor move from the center of the viewing rectangle. Press *[(X,Y)]* so that the coordinates of the cursor's location are displayed at the bottom of the screen, as in Figure 4.24, in floating decimal format. This cursor is called a *free-moving cursor* because it can move from dot to dot *anywhere* in the graph window.

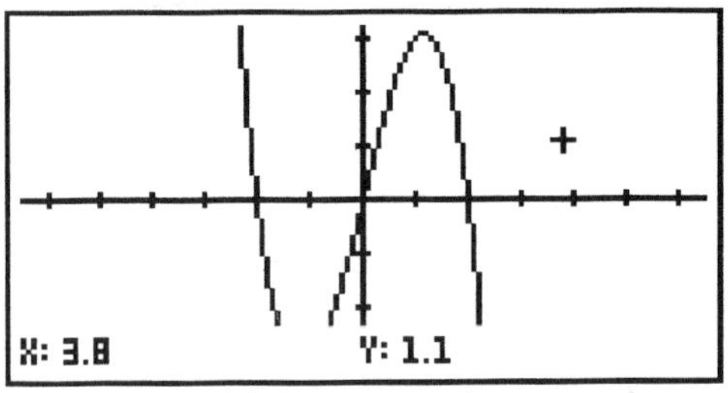

Figure 4.24: Free-moving cursor

Remove the cursor's coordinates and restore the menu by pressing NXT.

Toggle *[TRACE]* on (a white square replaces the "E") to enable the left ◄ and right ► arrow keys to move the cursor along the function. Also press *[(X,Y)]* to display the cursor's coordinates. The cursor is no longer free-moving, but is now constrained to the function. The coordinates that are displayed belong to points on the function's graph, so the y-coordinate is the calculated value of the function at the corresponding x-coordinate.

Now plot a second function, $y = -.25x$, along with $y = -x^3 + 4x$. In the PLOT menu's EQ: field, press the following keys: ↰ {} ' - *[X]* y^x 3 + 4 × *[X]* ► SPC ' .25 +/- × *[X]* (see Figure 4.26). Their graphs are plotted together in Figure 4.27.

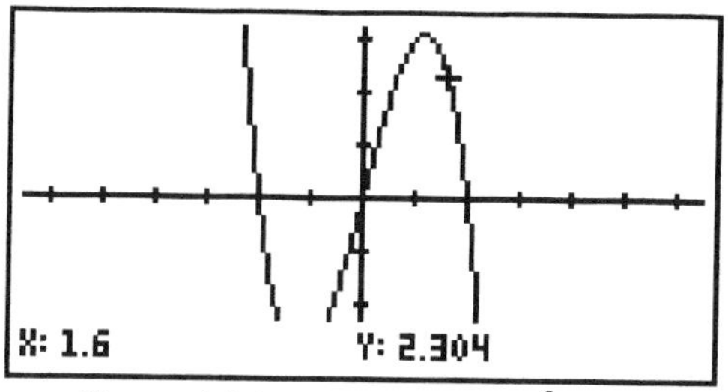

Figure 4.25: Trace on $y = -x^3 + 4x$

Toggle TRACE on, with the cursor's coordinates displayed. The cursor appears first on the graph of $y = -x^3 + 4x$ because it is defined first in the list. Press the up ▲ or down ▼ arrow key to move the cursor vertically to the graph of $y = -.25x$. Next press the right and left arrow keys to trace along the graph of $y = -.25x$. When more than one function is plotted, you can move the trace cursor vertically from one graph to another in this way.

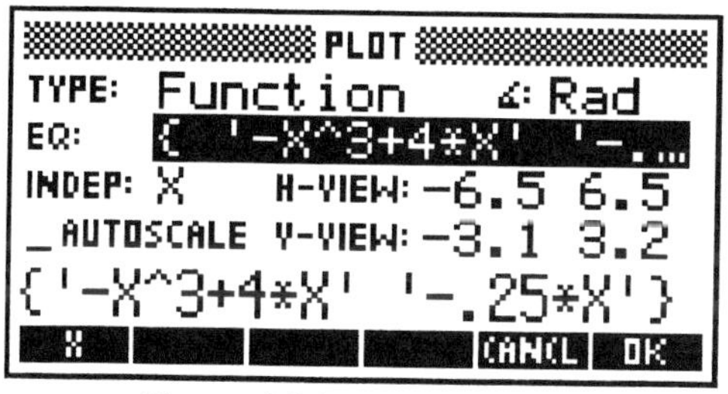

Figure 4.25: Two functions

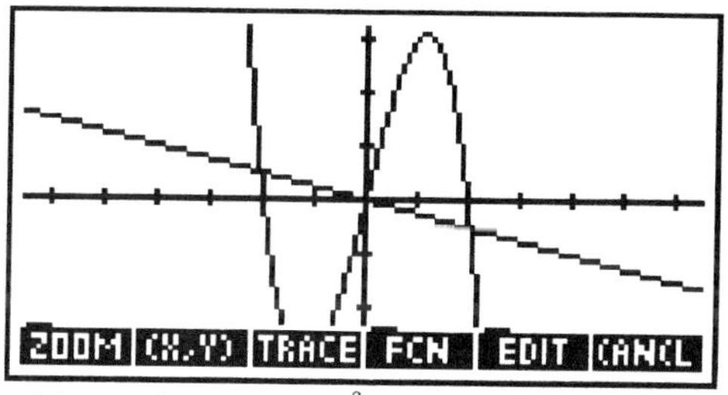

Figure 4.26: $y = -x^3 + 4x$ and $y = -.25x$

Technology Tip: By the way, to remind you of the function being graphed, press ↰ and hold VIEW. This is especially helpful when you are tracing along two or more graphs.

The HP-48G's display has 131 horizontal columns of pixels and 64 vertical rows. So when you trace a curve across a graph window, you are actually moving from Xmin to Xmax in 130 equal jumps, each called Δx. You would calculate the size of each jump to be $\Delta x = \frac{\text{Xmax} - \text{Xmin}}{130}$. Sometimes you may want the jumps to be friendly numbers like .1 or .25 so that, when you trace along the curve, the x-coordinates will be incremented by such a convenient amount. Just set your viewing rectangle for a particular increment Δx by making Xmax = Xmin + 130·Δx. For example, if you want Xmin = -5 and Δx = .3, set Xmax = -5 + 130·.3 = 34. Likewise, set Ymax = Ymin + 63·Δy if you want the vertical increment to be some special Δy.

To center your window around a particular point, say (h, k), and also have a certain Δx, set Xmin = h - 65·Δx and Xmax = h + 65·Δx. Likewise, make Ymin = k - 31·Δy and Ymax = k + 32·Δy. For example, to center a window around the origin, (0, 0), with both horizontal and vertical increments of .25, set the range so that Xmin = 0 - 65·.25 = -16.25, Xmax = 0 + 65·.25 = 16.25, Ymin = 0 - 31·.25 = -7.75, and Ymax = 0 +

$32 \cdot .25 = 8$.

The HP-48G's default window is already a friendly viewing rectangle, centered at the origin (0, 0) with $\Delta x = \Delta y = 0.1$.

See the benefit by first plotting $y = x^2 + 2x + 1$ in a graphing window extending from -10 to 10 in both directions. Trace near its y-intercept, which is (0, 1), and move towards its x-intercept, which is (-1, 0). Then change to the default viewing rectangle, and trace again near the intercepts.

4.2.6 ZOOM: Plot again the two graphs, for $y = -x^3 + 4x$ and for $y = -.25x$. There appears to be an intersection near x = 2. The HP-48G provides several ways to enlarge the view around this point. You can change the viewing rectangle directly by changing the horizontal and vertical view parameters in the PLOT menu. Figure 4.29 shows a new viewing rectangle for the parameters displayed in Figure 4.28. Trace has been turned on and the coordinates of a point on $y = -x^3 + 4x$ that is close to the intersection are displayed.

A more efficient method for enlarging the view is to draw a new viewing rectangle with the cursor. Start again with a graph of the two functions $y = -x^3 + 4x$ and $y = -.25x$ in a default viewing rectangle (press *[ZOOM] [ZDFLT]* for the default window).

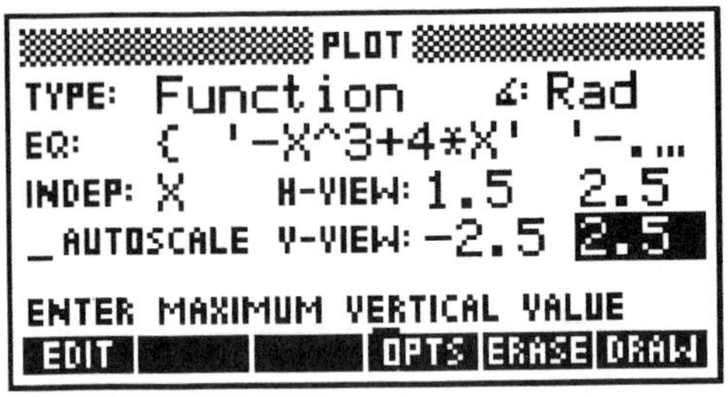

Figure 4.28: New view parameters

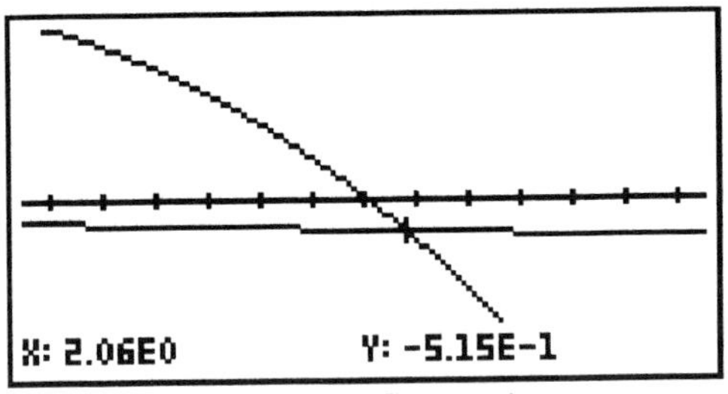

Figure 4.29: Closer view

Now imagine a small rectangular box around the intersection point, near x = 2. First move the cursor to one corner of the new viewing rectangle you imagine. Then press *[ZOOM] [BOXZ]* (Figure 4.30) to draw a box to define this new viewing rectangle. Use the arrow keys to move the cursor to the diagonally opposite corner of the new rectangle (Figure 4.31). If this box looks all right to you, press *[ZOOM]*. The rectangular area you have enclosed will now enlarge to fill the graph window (Figure 4.32).

You may cancel the zoom at any time by pressing *[CANCL]*.

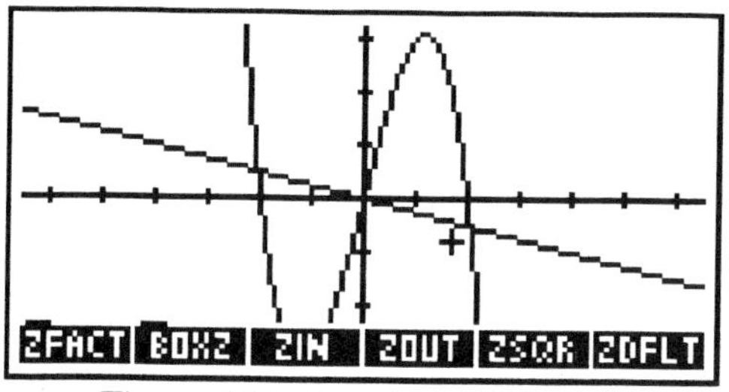

Figure 4.30: One corner selected

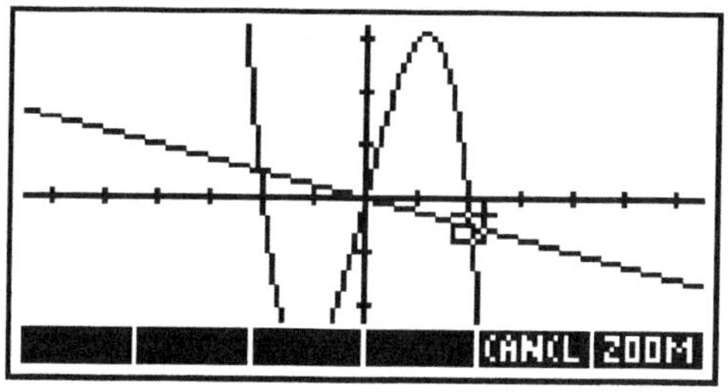

Figure 4.31: Box drawn

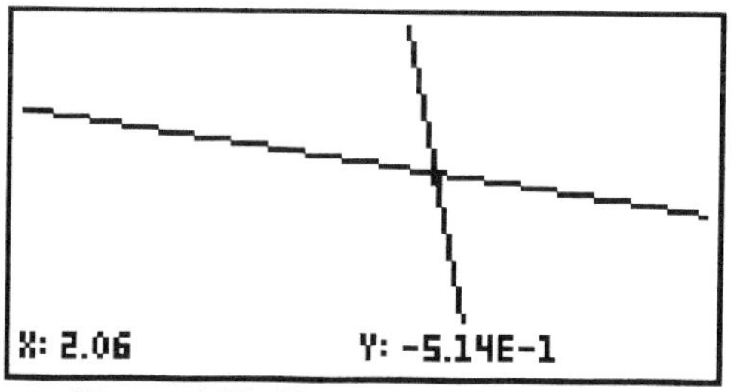

Figure 4.32: New viewing rectangle

You can also gain a quick magnification of the graph around the cursor's location. Return once more to the standard range for the graph of the two functions $y = -x^3 + 4x$ and $y = -.25x$. Use arrow keys to move the cursor as close as you can to the point of intersection near $x = 2$ (see Figure 4.33). Then press *[ZOOM] [ZIN]* and the calculator draws a magnified graph, centered at the cursor's position (Figure 4.34). The view variables are changed to reflect this new viewing rectangle. Look in the PLOT menu to check.

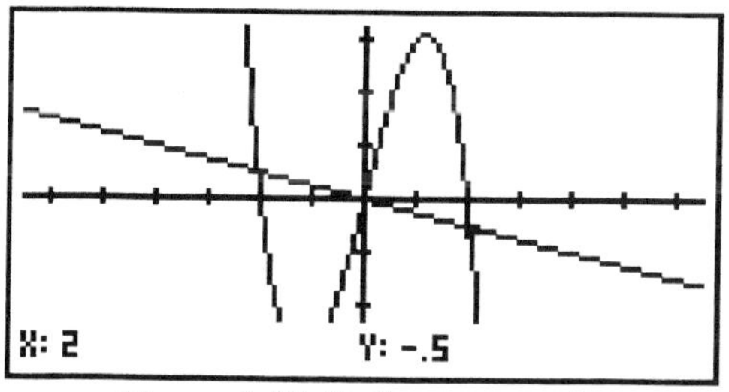

Figure 4.33: Before a zoom in

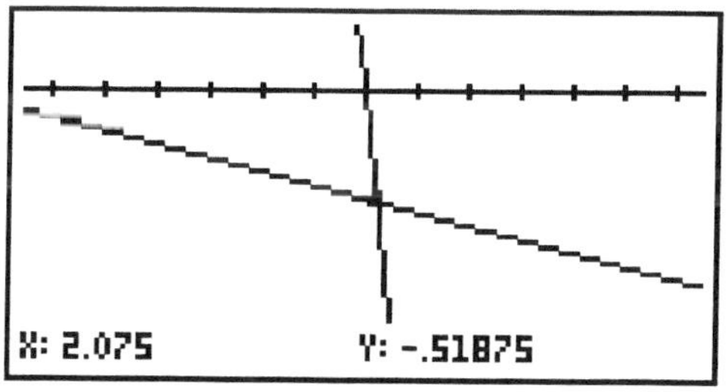

Figure 4.34: After a zoom in

As you see in the ZOOM menu (Figure 4.30), the HP-48G can zoom in (press *[ZOOM] [ZIN]*) or zoom out (press *[ZOOM] [ZOUT]*). Zoom out to see a larger view of the graph, centered at the cursor position. You can change the horizontal and vertical scale of the magnification by pressing *[ZOOM] [ZFACT]* (see Figure 4.34) and editing X-FACTOR and Y-FACTOR, the horizontal and vertical magnification factors.

The default zoom factor is 4 in both directions. It is not necessary for X-FACTOR and Y-FACTOR to be equal. Sometimes, you may prefer to zoom in one direction only, so the other factor should be set to 1. As usual, press [OK] or [CANCL] to leave the ZOOM FACTORS menu.

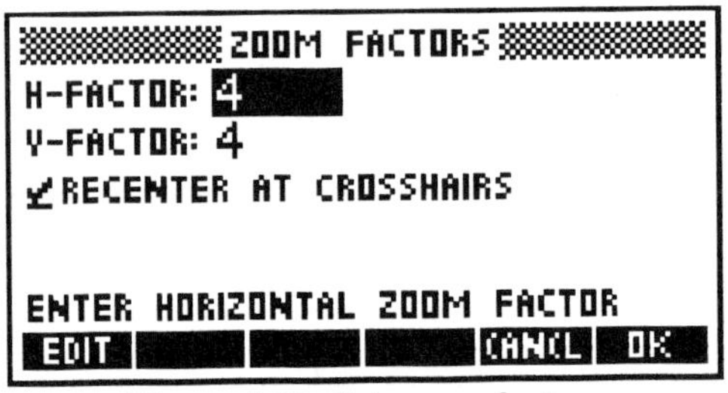

Figure 4.35: Set zoom factors

Technology Tip: If you should zoom in too much and lose the curve, zoom back to the default viewing rectangle and start over. Also, you may wish to use *[ZOOM] [ZSQR]* to make a viewing rectangle in which the vertical scale matches the horizontal scale. This would be helpful if you want to graph the two halfs of a circle, as in Section 4.2.4.

4.2.7 Relative Minimums and Maximums: Graph $y = -x^3 + 4x$ once again in the standard viewing rectangle (Figure 4.9). This function appears to have a relative minimum near x = -1 and a relative maximum near x = 1. You may zoom and trace to approximate these extreme values.

First trace along the curve near the local minimum. Notice by how much the x-values and y-values change as you move from point to point. Trace along the curve until the y-coordinate is as *small* as you can get it, so that you are as close as possible to the local minimum, and zoom in (press *[ZOOM] [ZIN]* or use a zoom box). Now trace again along the curve and, as you move from point to point, see that the coordinates change by smaller amounts than before. Keep zooming and tracing until you find the coordinates of the local minimum point as accurately as you need them, approximately (-1.15, -3.08).

Follow a similar procedure to find the local maximum. Trace along the curve until the y-coordinate is as *great* as you can get it, so that you are as close as possible to the local maximum, and zoom in. The local maximum point on the graph of $y = -x^3 + 4x$ is approximately (1.15, 3.08).

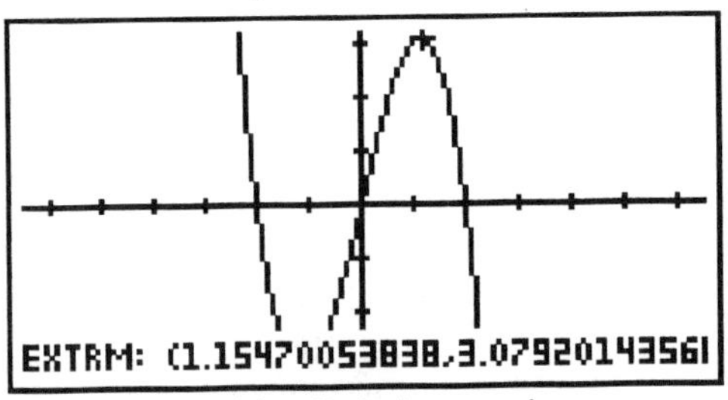

Figure 4.36: Relative maximum

The HP-48G automates the search for relative minimum and relative maximum points. Trace along the curve until the cursor is near a local extreme point. Then press *[FCN] [EXTR]*. The calculator searches for the nearest relative minimum or maximum (actually, it searches for the nearest "critical point" of the graph) and displays the coordinates of the local extreme point it finds (see Figure 4.36).

4.3 Solving Equations and Inequalities

4.3.1 Intercepts and Intersections: Tracing and zooming are also used to locate an x-intercept of a graph, where a curve crosses the x-axis. For example, the graph of $y = x^3 - 8x$ crosses the x-axis three times (see Figure 4.37). After tracing over to the x-intercept point that is furthest to the left, zoom in (Figure 4.38). Continue this process until you have located all three intercepts with as much accuracy as you need. The three x-intercepts of $y = x^3 - 8x$ are approximately -2.828, 0, and 2.828.

Technology Tip: As you zoom in, you may also wish to change the spacing between tick marks on the x-axis so that the viewing rectangle shows scale marks near the intercept point. Then the accuracy of your approximation will be such that the error is less than the distance between two tick marks. Go to the PLOT OPTIONS sub-menu (press *[OPTS]* in the PLOT menu). Move the cursor down and enter an appropriate spacing for the ticks.

An x-intercept of a function's graph is a *root* of the equation $f(x) = 0$. So these techniques for locating x-intercepts also serve to find the roots of an equation.

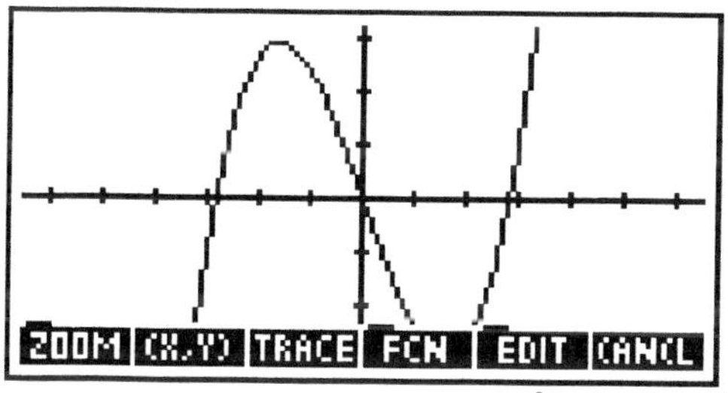

Figure 4.37: Graph of $y = x^3 - 8x$

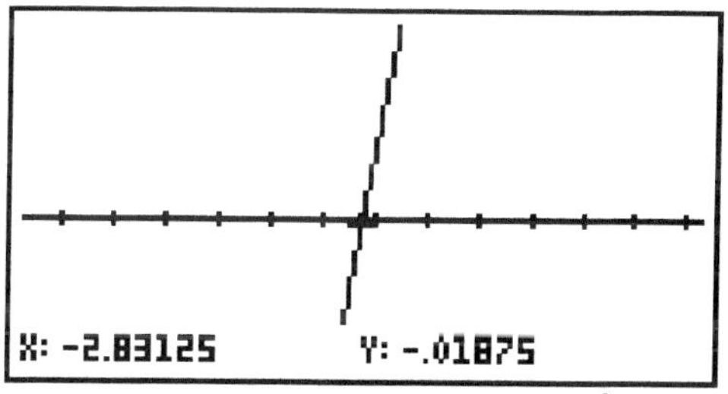

Figure 4.38: An x-intercept of $y = x^3 - 8x$

Once more, the HP-48G automates the search for x-intercepts. First trace along the graph until the cursor is close to an x-intercept. Press *[FCN] [ROOT]* to find the nearest x-intercept of this function. Repeat until you have located all x-intercepts of this graph.

TRACE and ZOOM are especially important for locating the intersection points of two graphs, say the graphs of $y = -x^3 + 4x$ and $y = -.25x$. Trace along one of the graphs until you arrive close to an intersection point. Then press ▲ or ▼ to jump to the other graph. Notice that the x-coordinate does not change, but the y-coordinate is likely to be different (see Figures 4.39 and 4.40).

When the two y-coordinates are as close as they can get, you have come as close as you now can to the point of intersection. So zoom in around the intersection point, then trace again until the two y-coordinates are as close as possible. Continue this process until you have located the point of intersection with as much accuracy as necessary.

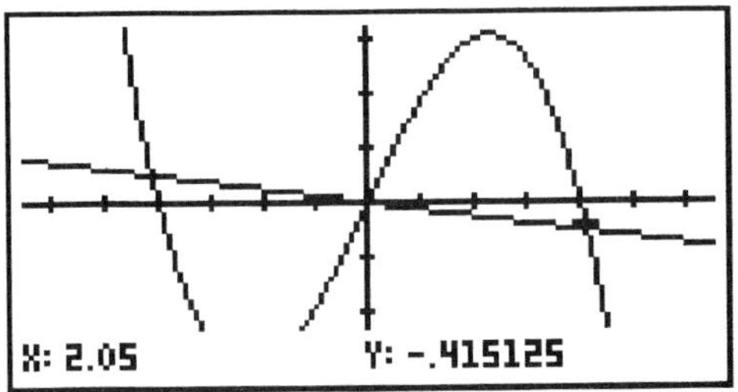

Figure 4.39: Trace on $y=-x^3+4x$

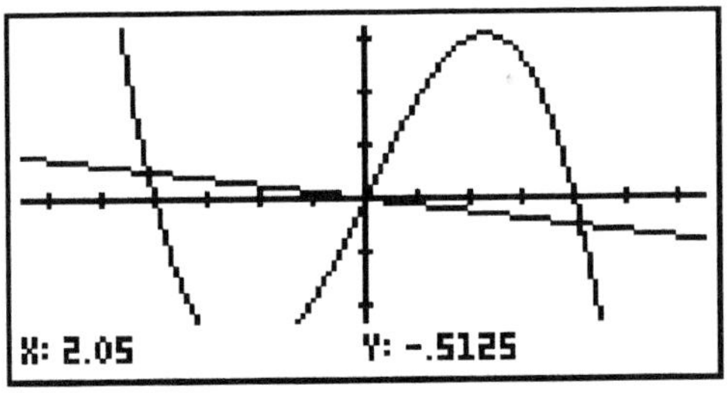

Figure 4.40: Trace on $y=-.25x$

Automate the search for points of intersection by tracing close to an intersection. Then press *[FCN]* *[ISECT]* to locate the nearest intersection point.

4.3.2 Solving Equations by Graphing: Suppose you need to solve the equation $24x^3-36x+17=0$. First graph $y=24x^3-36x+17$ in a window large enough to exhibit *all* its x-intercepts, corresponding to all its roots. Then use trace and zoom to locate each one. In fact, this equation has just one solution, approximately x = -1.414.

Remember that when an equation has more than one x-intercept, it may be necessary to change the viewing rectangle a few times to locate all of them.

Technology Tip: To solve an equation like $24x^3+17=36x$, you may first transform it into standard form, $24x^3-36x+17=0$, and proceed as above. However, you may also graph the *two* functions $y=24x^3+17$ and $y=36x$, then zoom and trace to locate their point of intersection. On the HP-48G, when you enter an equation like $24x^3+17=36x$ in the EQ: field of the PLOT menu, the calculator graphs both sides of the equation.

4.3.3 Solving Systems by Graphing: The solutions to a system of equations correspond to the points of intersection of their graphs. For example, to solve the system $y=x^2-3x-4$ and $y=x^3+3x^2-2x-1$, first graph them together. Then zoom and trace to locate their point of intersection, approximately (-2.17, 7.25).

You must judge whether the two current y-coordinates are sufficiently close for x = -2.17 or whether you should continue to zoom and trace to improve the approximation.

The solutions of the system of two equations $y=x^3+3x^2-2x-1$ and $y=x^2-3x-4$ correspond to the solutions of the single equation $x^3+3x^2-2x-1=x^2-3x-4$, which simplifies to $x^3+2x^2+x+3=0$. So you may also graph $y=x^3+2x^2+x+3$ and find its x-intercepts to solve the system.

4.3.4 Solving Inequalities by Graphing: Consider the inequality $1-\frac{3x}{2} \geq x-4$. To solve it with your HP-48G, graph the two functions $y=1-\frac{3x}{2}$ and $y=x-4$ (Figure 4.41). First locate their point of intersection, at $x = 2$. The inequality is true when the graph of $y=1-\frac{3x}{2}$ lies *above* the graph of $y=x-4$, and that occurs for $x < 2$. So the solution is the half-line $x \leq 2$, or $(-\infty, 2]$.

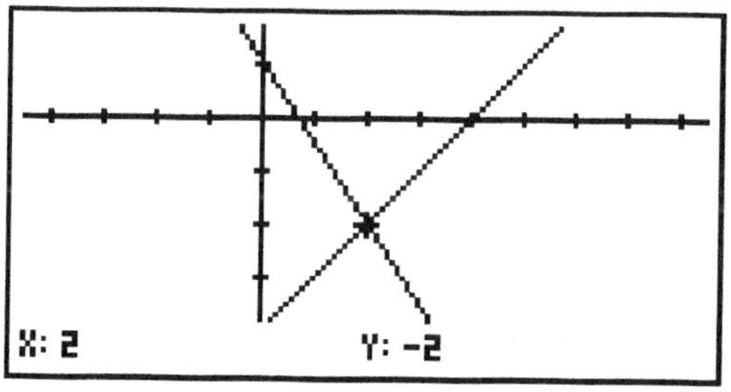

Figure 4.41: Solving $1-\frac{3x}{2} \geq x-4$

You can solve an inequality or a system of inequalities on the HP-48G by using its Truth PLOT (see Figure 4.42). For example, to graph $y \geq x^2 - 1$, choose Truth for TYPE: of plot and use these keystrokes to place the inequality in the EQ: field: ' α Y PRG *[TEST]* *[≥]* α X y^x 2 - 1 ↰ ENTER.

Figure 4.42: Truth PLOT type

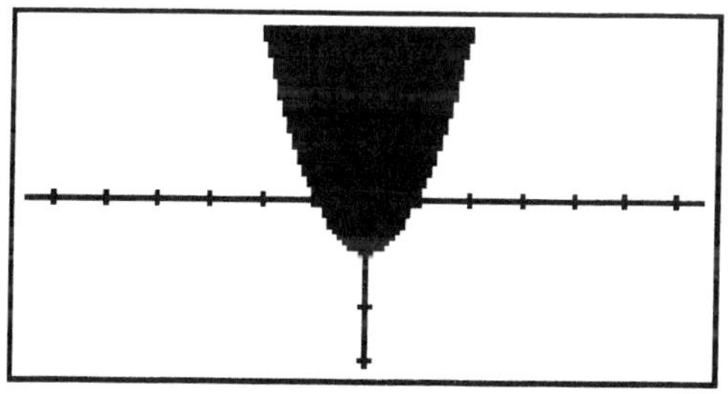

Figure 4.43: Graph of $y \geq x^2 - 1$

Technology Tip: The default step size for a Truth PLOT is an interval of one pixel, which means the calculator tests values corresponding to all 8384 points of its display. So it takes quite a while to produce Figure 4.43! You can speed things up by pressing *[OPTS]* from the PLOT menu and increasing the STEP: value.

4.4 Trigonometry

4.4.1 Degrees and Radians: The trigonometric functions can be applied to angles measured either in radians or degrees, but you should take care that the HP-48G is configured for whichever measure you need. If your calculator is currently set for radian measure, the RAD annunciator is displayed at the top left of the home screen. If the calculator is set for degree measure, there is no annunciator. You may change the default in the MODES menu (see Section 4.1.1). Or toggle quickly between radians and degrees by pressing ↰ RAD.

It's a good idea to check the angle measure setting before executing a calculation that depends on a particular measure. You may change a mode setting at any time and not interfere with pending calculations. Try the following keystrokes to see this in action.

Expression	*Keystrokes*	*Display*
$\sin 45^\circ$	↱ MODES ▼ *press* +/- *until* Degrees *is displayed, then [OK]* 45 SIN	 0.7071
$\sin \pi^\circ$	↰ π SIN ↰ →NUM	0.0548
$\sin \pi$	↰ RAD ↰ π SIN	0.0000
$\sin 45$	45 SIN	0.8509
$\sin \frac{\pi}{6}$	↰ π 6 ÷ SIN ↰ →NUM	0.5000

The first line of keystrokes sets the HP-48G in degree mode and calculates the sine of 45 *degrees*. While the calculator is still in degree mode, the second line of keystrokes calculates the sine of π *degrees*, 3.1415°. The third line toggles to radian mode just before calculating the sine of π *radians*. The fourth line calculates the sine of 45 *radians* (the calculator is already in radian mode).

Technology Tip: Here's how to mix degrees and radians in a calculation. For example, calculate $\tan 45^\circ + \sin \frac{\pi}{6}$. First evaluate $\tan 45^\circ$ in degree mode, then press ENTER to place this value in the stack. Next toggle to radian mode, evaluate $\sin \frac{\pi}{6}$, and enter its value in the stack. Finally, press + to add the two latest stack entries and get 1.5.

4.4.2 Graphs of Trigonometric Functions: When you graph a trigonometric function, you need to pay careful attention to the choice of graph window. For example, graph $y = \dfrac{\sin 30x}{30}$ in the default viewing rectangle. Trace along the curve to see where it is. Zoom in to a better window, or use the period and amplitude to establish a better view.

Technology Tip: The HP-48G has a quick way to make a good window for graphing trigonometric functions. Press *[ZOOM]* NXT NXT *[ZTRIG]* for a window in which $\Delta x = \frac{\pi}{20}$ and $\Delta y = 0.1$.

Next graph $y = \tan x$ in the default window. The HP-48G plots consecutive points and then connects them with a segment, so the graph is not exactly what you should expect. You may wish to change from connected line to dot graph (see Section 4.2.3) when you plot the tangent function.

4.5 Differentiation

4.5.1 Limits: Suppose you need to find this limit: $\lim\limits_{x \to 0} \frac{\sin 4x}{x}$. Plot the graph of $f(x) = \frac{\sin 4x}{x}$ in a convenient viewing rectangle that contains the point where the function appears to intersect the line $x = 0$ (because you want the limit as $x \to 0$). Your graph should lend support to the conclusion that $\lim\limits_{x \to 0} \frac{\sin 4x}{x} = 4$.

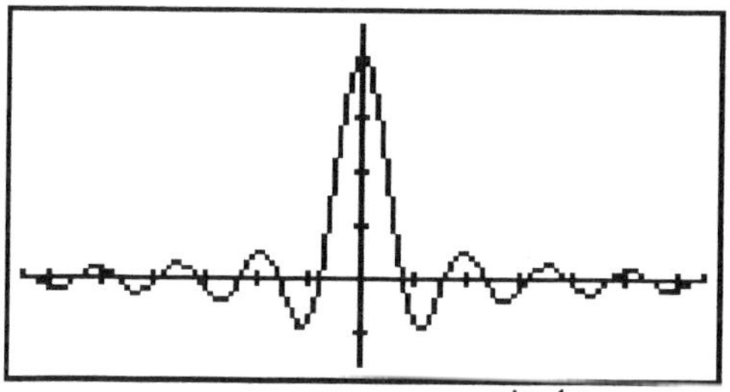

Figure 4.44: Checking $\lim\limits_{x \to 0} \frac{\sin 4x}{x} = 4$

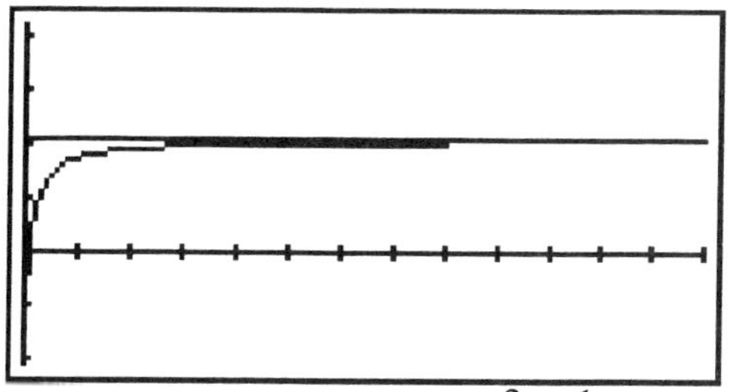

Figure 4.45: Checking $\lim\limits_{x \to \infty} \frac{2x-1}{x+1} = 2$

To test the reasonableness of the conclusion that $\lim\limits_{x \to \infty} \frac{2x-1}{x+1} = 2$, evaluate the function $f(x) - \frac{2x-1}{x+1}$ for several large positive values of x (since you want the limit as $x \to \infty$). For example, evaluate *f*(100), *f*(1000), and *f*(10,000) Another way to test the reasonableness of this result is to examine the graph of $f(x) = \frac{2x-1}{x+1}$ in a viewing rectangle that extends over large values of *x*. See, as in Figure 4.45 (where the viewing rectangle extends horizontally from 0 to 100), whether the graph is asymptotic to the horizontal line *y* = 2 (plot both $y = \frac{2x-1}{x+1}$ and *y* = 2).

4.5.2 Numerical Derivatives: The HP-48G calculates derivatives numerically as well as symbolically. For example, to find a numerical approximation to $f'(2.5)$ when $f(x) = x^3$, first press ↱ SYMBOLIC and select Differentiate. Enter x^3 as the expression and specify *x* as the variable with respect to which you want to differentiate. Press the +/- key to cycle among alternatives until the Numeric result type is displayed and enter 2.5 as the value of *x* for which you want to find the derivative (see Figure 4.46). Finally, press *[OK]* for the answer (Figure 4.47).

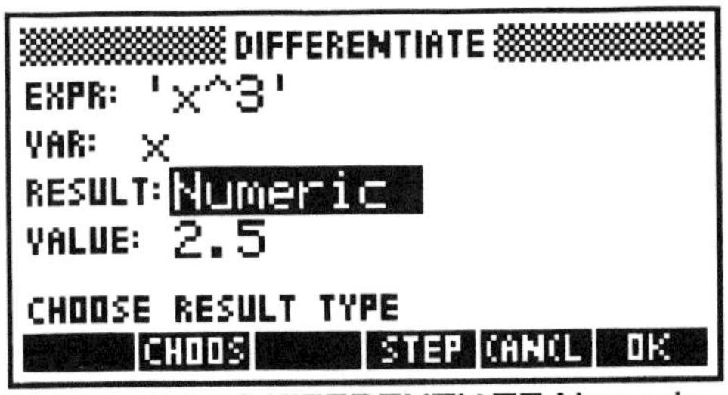

Figure 4.46: DIFFERENTIATE Numeric

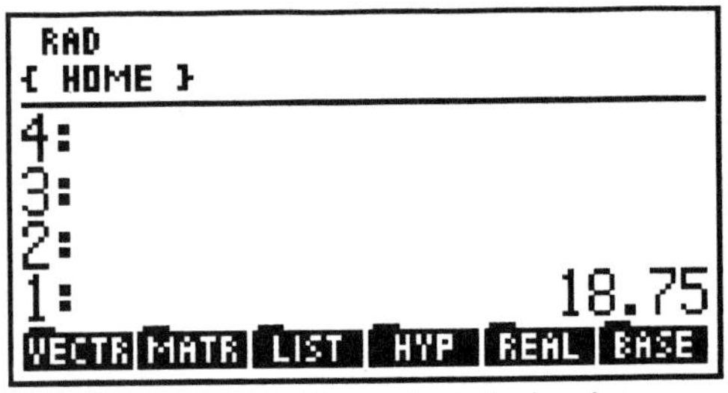

Figure 4.47: Numerical derivative

If you need to differentiate symbolically, first purge your variable from memory by recalling the variable to the stack and pressing ↰ PURG. Next follow the preceding steps except choose the Symbolic result type (Figure 4.48). Then press *[OK]* for the symbolic derivative (Figure 4.49). If you would like to see the intermediate steps taken by the HP-48G as it performs a differentiation, press *[STEP]* to place in the stack the result of the first step. Then press EVAL for subsequent steps in the process of symbolically differentiating the expression.

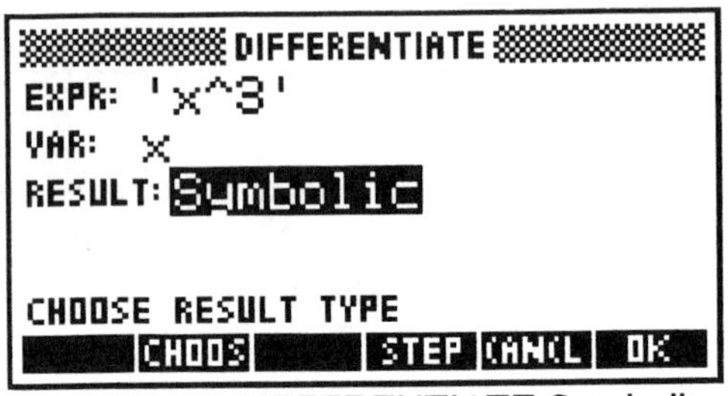

Figure 4.48: DIFFERENTIATE Symbolic

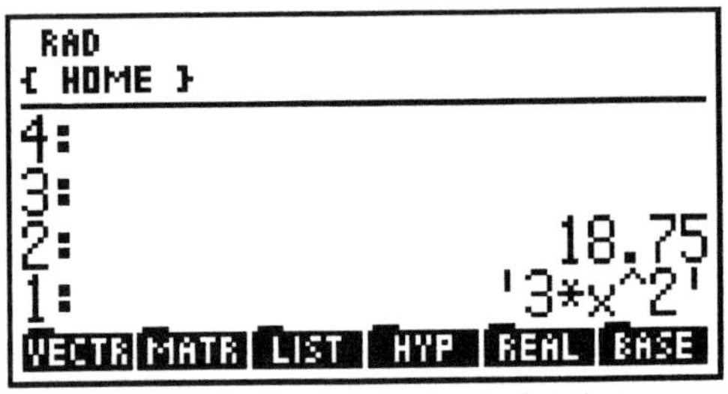

Figure 4.49: Symbolic derivative

To find a derivative in EquationWriter, press ↱ ∂ and enter x (be sure you have already purged the variable x from memory) as the variable of differentiation (see Figure 4.50). Press ▶ and enter the expression x^3, then press ENTER to place this in the stack. Now press EVAL a couple of times for the result (Figure 4.51).

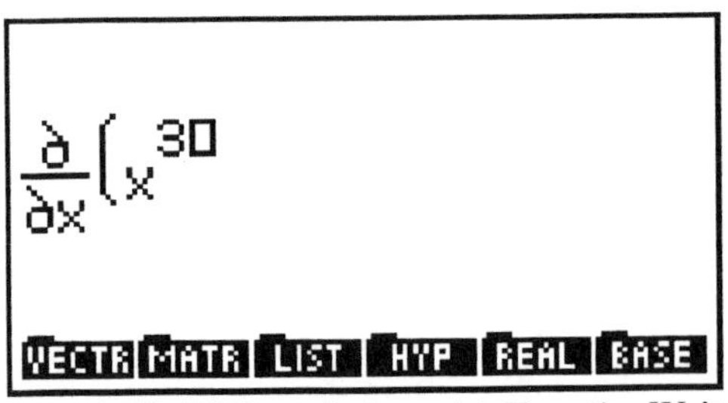

Figure 4.50: Differentiation with EquationWriter

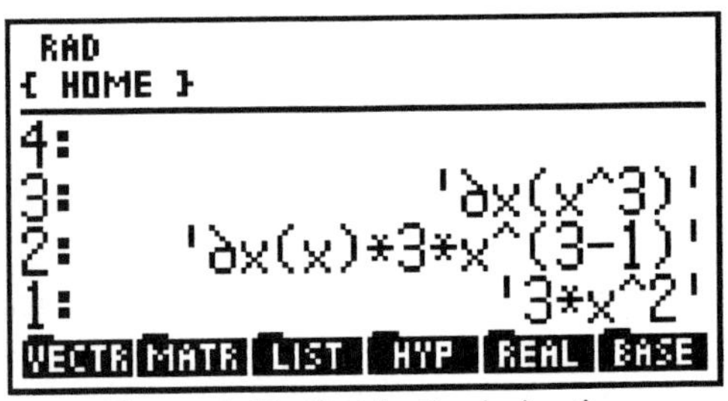

Figure 4.51: Symbolic derivative

Technology Tip: It is sometimes helpful to plot a function and its derivative together. In Figure 4.52, the function $f(x)=\dfrac{5x-2}{x^2+1}$ and its numerical derivative are both graphed.

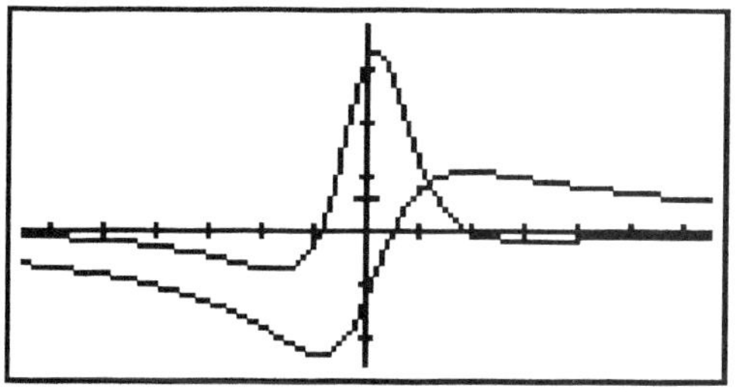

Figure 4.52: Graphs of $f(x)$ and $f'(x)$

You can duplicate this graph by first creating the equation $f(x)=\dfrac{5x-2}{x^2+1}$ (Figure 4.53) with these keystrokes: ' α ↰ F ↰ () α ↰ X ▶ ↰ = ↰ () 5 × α ↰ X - 2 ▶ ÷ ↰ () α ↰ X y^x 2 + 1 ENTER. Then press ↰ DEF to make this equation the definition of a new function.

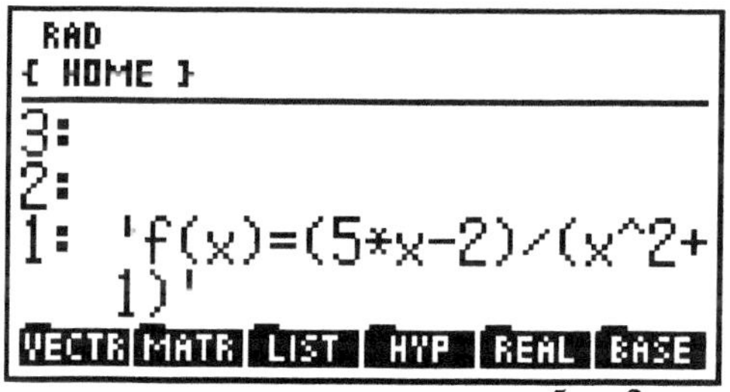

Figure 4.53: Defining $f(x)=\dfrac{5x-2}{x^2+1}$

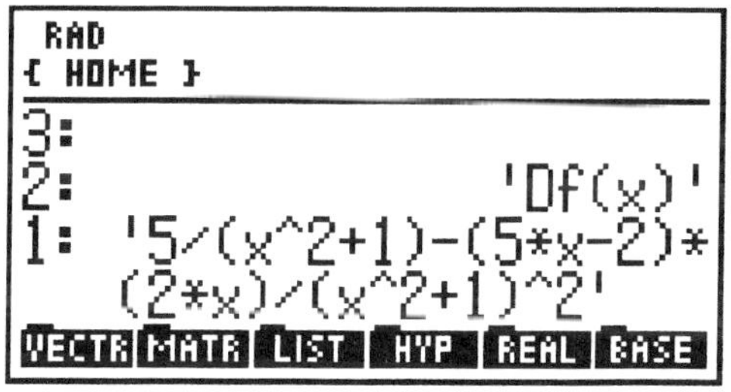

Figure 4.54: Defining $Df(x)=f'(x)$

Next create the equation $Df(x)=f'(x)$ by entering ' α D α ↰ F ↰ () α ↰ X directly into the stack. Be sure to purge the variable x from memory. Use EquationWriter to create the expression $\dfrac{\partial}{\partial x}f(x)$ and put it in the stack. Press EVAL several times until the derivative is fully simplified (Figure 4.54). Then press ↰ = ↰ DEF to make an equation and define a new function.

The final step is to plot the function and its derivative simultaneously. Go into the PLOT menu, move beside EQ:, and press ↰ {} ' α ↰ F ↰ () α ↰ X ▶ ▶ SPC ' α D α ↰ F ↰ () α ↰ X *[OK]*. Also enter α ↰ X beside INDEP: to establish x as the independent variable. Figure 4.52 shows the result after you press *[ERASE] [DRAW]*.

You may also approximate a derivative while you are examining the graph of a function. When you are in a graph window, trace along the curve to a point where you want the derivative (see Figure 4.55 for the graph of $f(x)=\dfrac{5x-2}{x^2+1}$ at x = -2.3) and press *[FCN] [SLOPE]*. The value of the derivative is displayed at the bottom of the graph window (as in Figure 4.56) and also entered in the stack.

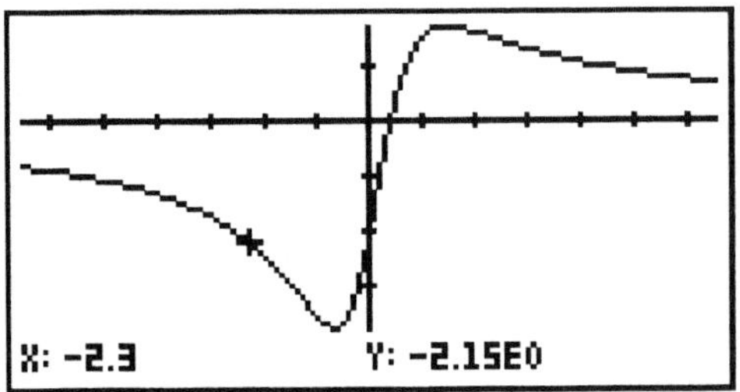

Figure 4.55: $f(x)=\dfrac{5x-2}{x^2+1}$ at x = -2.3

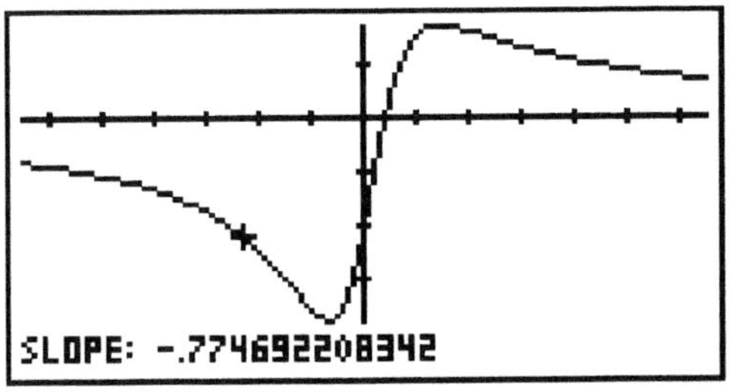

Figure 4.56: $f'(-2.3)$

Technology Tip: With the HP-48G, you can graph a function along with the tangent line at one of its points. So plot the function $f(x)=\dfrac{5x-2}{x^2+1}$ once again. Then trace with the cursor to a point of interest and press *[FCN]* NXT *[TANL]*. The equation of the tangent line is displayed in the graph window and also entered into the stack. You may continue to draw more tangent lines.

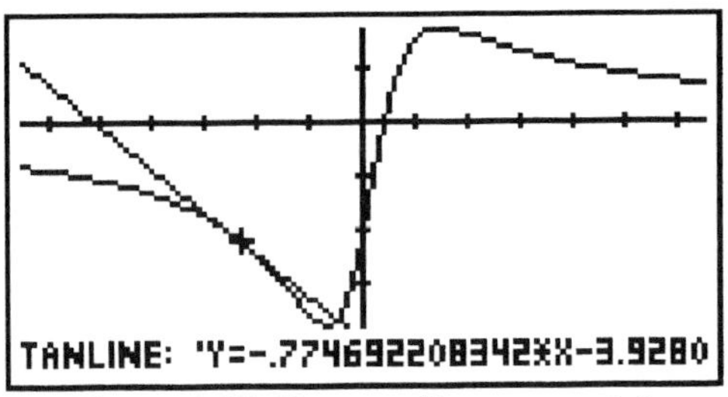

Figure 4.57: Tangent line at x = -2.3

4.5.3 Newton's Method: With your HP-48G, you may iterate using Newton's Method to find the zeros of a function. Recall that Newton's Method determines each successive approximation by the formula $x_{n+1}=x_n-\dfrac{f(x_n)}{f'(x_n)}$.

As an example of the technique, consider $f(x)=2x^3+x^2-x+1$. First define this function and also define its derivative as *Df* (see Figure 4.58). A look at the graph of the function suggests that it has a zero near x = -1, so start the iteration by storing -1 as the variable x. Enter the Newton's Method formula

$y = x - \dfrac{f(x)}{f'(x)} = x - \dfrac{f(x)}{Df(x)}$ as shown in stack level 4 of Figure 4.59. Then press these keys: α Y EVAL ENTER ' α X STO. Execute this sequence of keystrokes repeatedly until two successive approximations differ by less than some predetermined value, say 0.0001. Note that each time you execute these keystrokes, the HP-48G will use its *current* value of x, and that value is changing as you continue the iteration.

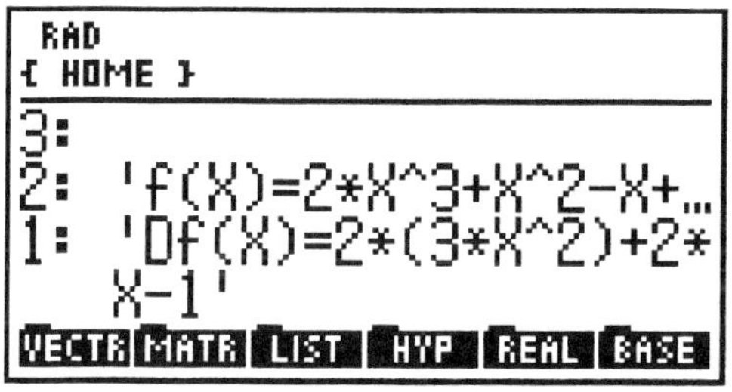

Figure 4.58: Defining $f(x)$ and $Df(x)$

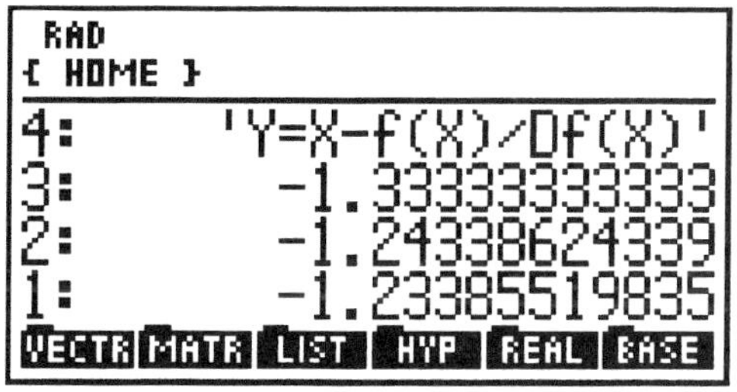

Figure 4.59: Newton's Method

Technology Tip: Newton's Method is sensitive to your seed value for x, so look carefully at the function's graph to make a good first estimate. Also, remember that the method sometimes fails to converge!

You may want to save the Newton's Method formula as a short program. See Section 3.9 or your calculator's manual for further information on programming the HP-48G.

4.6 Sequences

4.6.1 Iteration: Iteration is the process of evaluating a function repeatedly. As an example, calculate $\dfrac{n-1}{3}$ for $n = 27$. Then calculate $\dfrac{n-1}{3}$ for n = the answer to the previous calculation. Continue to use each answer as n in the *next* calculation. Here are keystrokes to accomplish this iteration on the HP-48G calculator (see the results in Figure 4.58).

Iteration	*Keystrokes*	*Display*
	' α Y ↰ = ↰ () α N - 1 ▶ ÷ 3 ↰ DEF	
1	27 ENTER ENTER ' α N STO	27
2	α Y EVAL ENTER ' α N STO	8.66666666667
3	α Y EVAL ENTER ' α N STO	2.55555555556
4	α Y EVAL ENTER ' α N STO	.51851851852
5	α Y EVAL ENTER ' α N STO	-.16049382716

Continue several more times and see what happens with this iteration. You may wish to try it again with a different starting value.

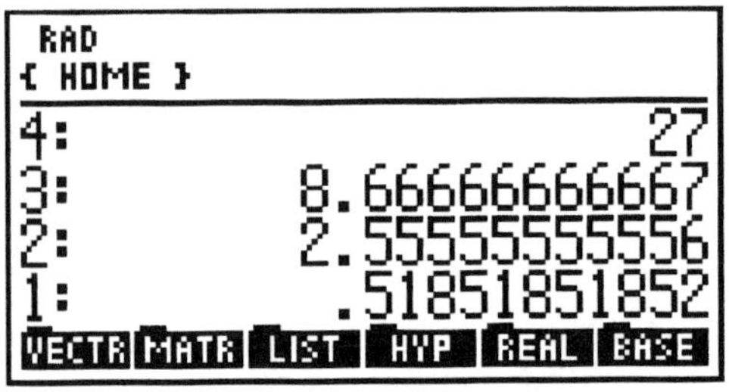

Figure 4.60: Iteration

4.6.2 Arithmetic and Geometric Sequences: It is easy to use direct stack input to determine the n-th term of a sequence. For example, find the 18th term of an *arithmetic* sequence whose first term is 7 and whose common difference is 4. Enter the first term 7 in the stack, then start the progression by pressing 4 +. This yields the 2nd term, so repeat 4 + sixteen more times to find the 18th term. For a *geometric* sequence whose common ratio is 4, start the progression with 4 ×.

Of course, you could also use the *explicit* formula for the n-th term of an arithmetic sequence, $t_n = a + (n-1)d$. First store values for the variables a, d, and n, then evaluate the formula by pressing ' α ↰ A + ↰ () α ↰ N - 1 ▶ × α ↰ D EVAL. For a geometric sequence whose n-th term is given by $t_n = a \cdot r^{n-1}$, enter values for the variables a, r, and n, then evaluate the formula by pressing ' α ↰ A × α ↰ R y^x ↰ () α ↰ N - 1 EVAL.

4.7 Integration

4.7.1 Approximating Definite Integrals: The HP-48G approximates derivatives numerically and also evaluates them symbolically. For example, to find $\int_0^1 \cos x \, dx$, first press ↱ SYMBOLIC and select Integrate. Enter $\cos x$ as the expression and specify x as the variable for this integration.

Figure 4.61: INTEGRATE Numeric

Set 0 as the lower limit and 1 as the upper limit. Press the +/- key to cycle among alternatives until the Numeric result type is displayed (see Figure 4.61). Finally, press *[OK]* for the answer (stack level 3 in Figure 4.63).

If you need to integrate symbolically, first purge your variable from memory by recalling the variable to the stack and pressing ↰ PURG. Next follow the preceding steps except choose the Symbolic result type. Then press *[OK]* for the symbolic integral (stack level 1 in Figure 4.62) and EVAL to evaluate it (stack level 1 in Figure 4.63).

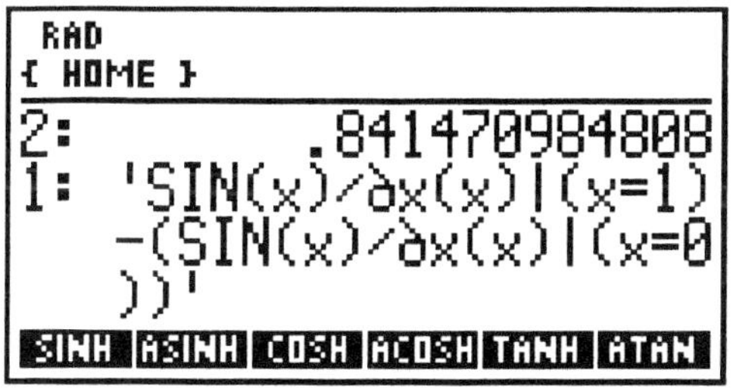

Figure 4.62: INTEGRATE Symbolic

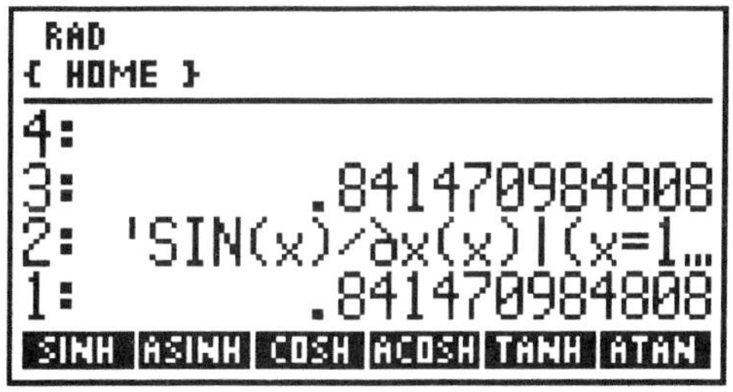

Figure 4.63: $\int_0^1 \cos x\, dx$

Technology Tip: Suppose you want to find an indefinite integral, say $\int \cos x\, dx$. Purge the variable x from memory and integrate symbolically. Enter 0 for the lower limit and the variable x for the upper limit. Press *[OK]* to compute a closed-form expression and place it on stack level 1 (Figure 4.64). Now press PRG *[TYPE] [OBJ→]* 3 ↰ STACK NXT *[DRPN]* to discard the lower limits and press EVAL to evaluate the result for the upper limit and obtain the indefinite integral (Figure 4.65).

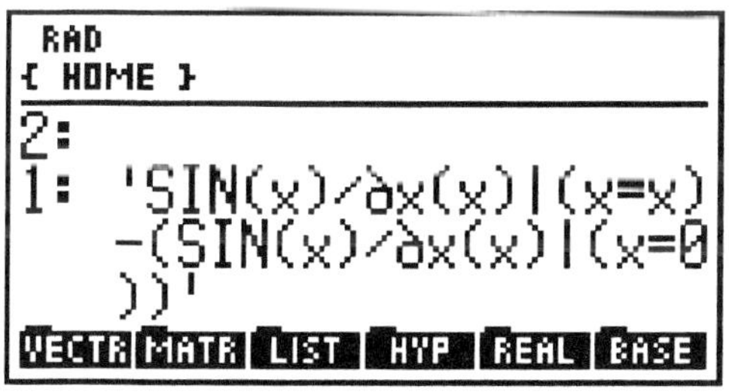

Figure 4.64: Indefinite integral

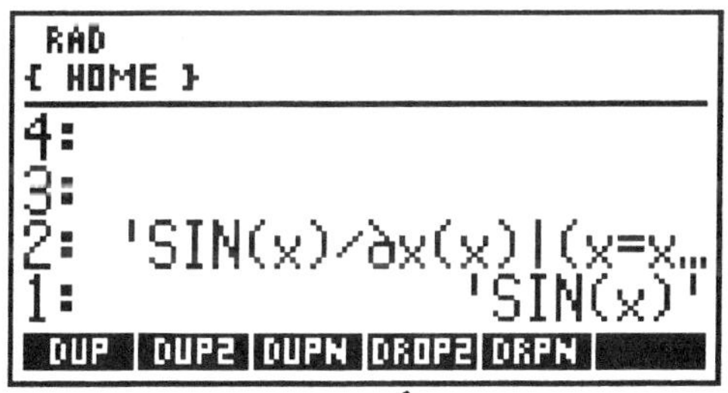

Figure 4.65: $\int \cos x\, dx$

To find a definite integal in EquationWriter, press ↱ ∫ and then enter the lower limit followed by ▶, the upper limit followed by ▶, and the integrand followed by ▶. Next enter the variable of integration (see Figure 4.66 for $\int_0^1 \cos x\, dx$) and press ENTER to place this integral in the stack. Now press EVAL a couple of times for the result (Figure 4.67).

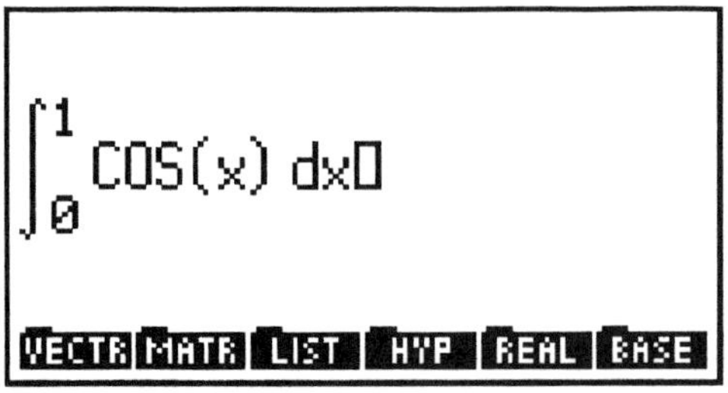

Figure 4.66: Integration with EquationWriter

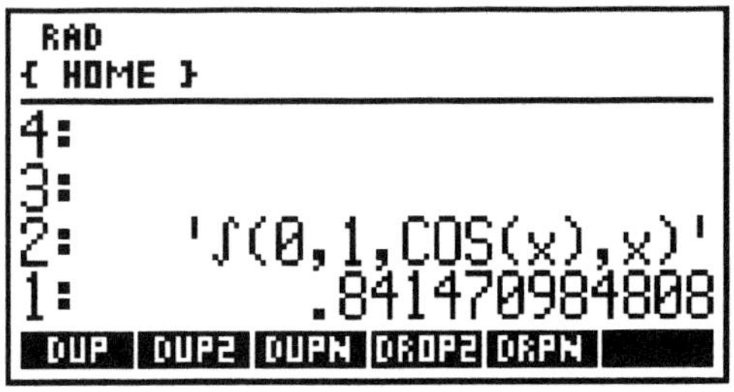

Figure 4.67: Symbolic integration

4.7.2 Areas: You may approximate the area under the graph of a function $y = f(x)$ between $x = A$ and $x = B$ with your HP-48G. For example, here are keystrokes for finding the area under the graph of the function $y = \cos x^2$ between $x = 0$ and $x = 1$. This area is represented by the definite integral $\int_0^1 \cos x^2 dx$. So graph $f(x) = \cos x^2$ and trace along the curve to where $x = 0$, the lower limit. Press the multiplication key × to mark this place (see Figure 4.68). Now trace again to the upper limit, where $x = 1$, and press NXT *[FCN]* *[AREA]*. The area of region under the graph between the lower limit and the upper limit is calculated and displayed.

Technology Tip: When approximating the area under $f(x) = \cos x^2$ between $x = 0$ and $x = 1$, you must trace along the curve to *exactly* where $x = 0$ and $x = 1$. Now to trace along the curve to $x = a$, the viewing rectangle must be chosen so that the function is evaluated at $x = a$. The window shown in Figure 4.68 was made first by zooming to a decimal window, and then changing its vertical dimensions to appropriate values. By contrast, find the area under $f(x) = \cos x^2$ between $x = 0$ and $x = 1$ in a window that extends horizontally from -4 to 4.

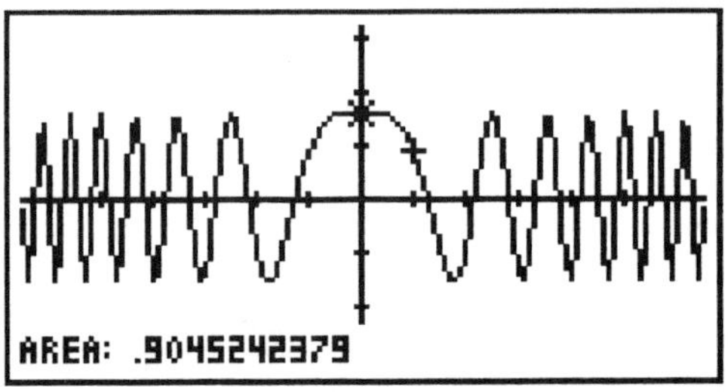

Figure 4.68: Area under a curve

Technology Tip: Suppose that you want to find the area between two functions, $y = f(x)$ and $y = g(x)$, from $x = A$ to $x = B$. If $f(x) \geq g(x)$ for $A \leq x \leq B$, then use $f(x) - g(x)$ for the integrand and proceed as before to find the required area.

4.8 Parametric and Polar Graphs

4.8.1 Graphing Parametric Equations: The HP-48G plots parametric equations as easily as it plots functions. Just go to the PLOT menu (Figure 4.70) and change the type setting to Parametric. Be sure, if the independent parameter is an angle measure, that your calculator is set to whichever you need, radians or degrees.

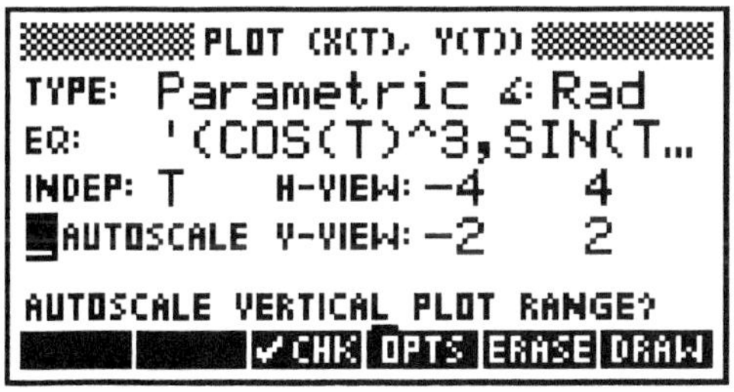

Figure 4.69: Parametric PLOT menu

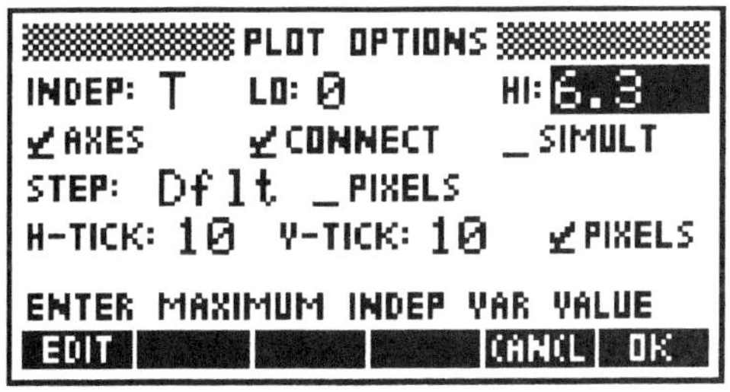

Figure 4.70: Parametric plot options

For example, here are the keystrokes needed to graph the parametric equations $x = \cos^3 t$ and $y = \sin^3 t$. First check that angles are currently being measured in radians. After setting plot type to parametric, change the independent variable to T. Also change the view to extend horizontally from -4 to 4 and vertically from -2 to 2. Press *[OPTS]* so that you may change LO: and HI: values for T so that T ranges from 0 to 6.3 (approximately 2π). Press *[OK]* to accept these changes and return to the main PLOT menu.

Move the cursor to EQ: (Figure 4.69) and enter the two parametric equations in the form $(x(t), y(t))$ by pressing ' ↰ () COS α T ▶ y^x 3 ↰ , ↰ () SIN α T ▶ y^x 3 ENTER. Press *[ERASE] [DRAW]* to see Figure 4.71.

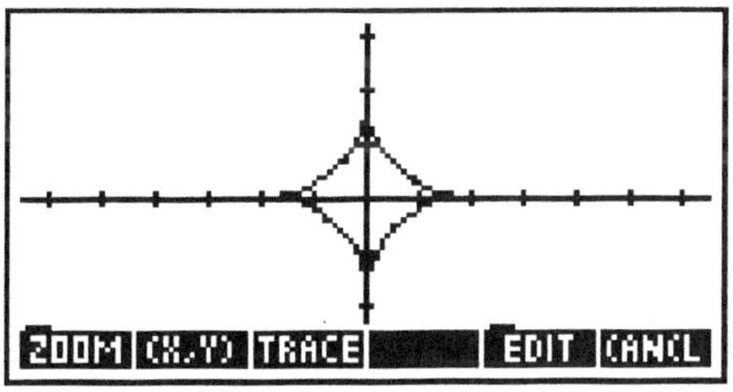

Figure 4.71: Parametric graph of $x = \cos^3 t$ and $y = \sin^3 t$

You may ZOOM and TRACE along parametric graphs just as you did with function graphs. As you trace along this graph, notice that the cursor moves in the *counterclockwise* direction as T increases.

4.8.2 Rectangular-Polar Coordinate Conversion: The HP-48G converts easily between rectangular and polar coordinate systems. Since the conversion uses the current MODES settings, it is a good idea to check the default angle measure beforehand. Of course, you may press ↰ RAD to change the current angle measure setting at any time, as explained in Section 4.4.1. For the following examples, the HP-48G is first set to *degree* measure and *rectangular* coordinates.

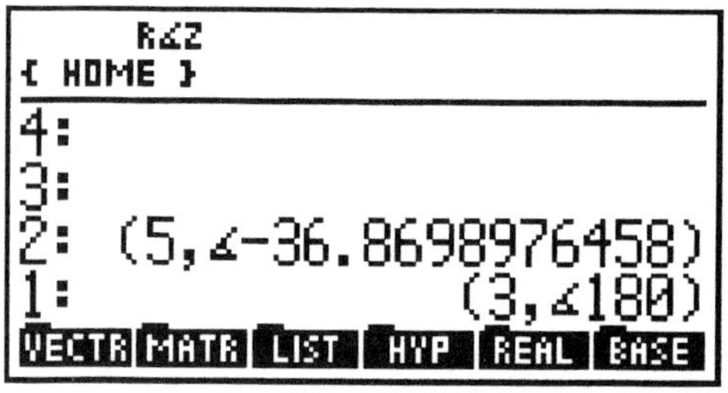

Figure 4.72: Polar coordinates

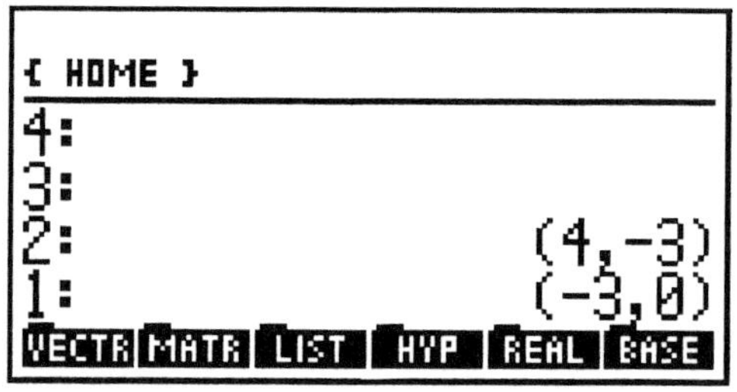

Figure 4.73: Rectangular coordinates

Given rectangular coordinates $(x, y) = (4, -3)$, convert *from* these rectangular coordinates *to* polar coordinates (r, θ) by pressing ↰ () 4 ↰ , 3 +/- ENTER to input (4, -3). Then press ↱ POLAR to toggle the calculator into polar display mode. Notice the polar display annunciator at the top left of the screen (Figure 4.72).

Suppose $(r, \theta) = (3, 180°)$. To convert *from* these polar coordinates *to* rectangular coordinates (x, y), press ↰ () 3 ↰ , ↱ ∠ 180 ENTER to input (3, 180°). Once again, press ↱ POLAR to toggle the HP-48G *off* polar display mode. There should no longer be a polar display annunciator at the top left of the screen (see Figure 4.73).

4.8.3 Graphing Polar Equations: The HP-48G graphs a polar function in a polar plot. To graph $r = 4\sin\theta$, go to the PLOT menu and change plot type to Polar. Make θ the independent variable by pressing α ↱ F in the INDEP: field. Choose a good viewing rectangle and appropriate options LO: and HI: for the parameter θ. In Figure 4.74, the graphing window extends horizontally from -6.5 to 6.5 and vertically from -1.1 to 5.2.

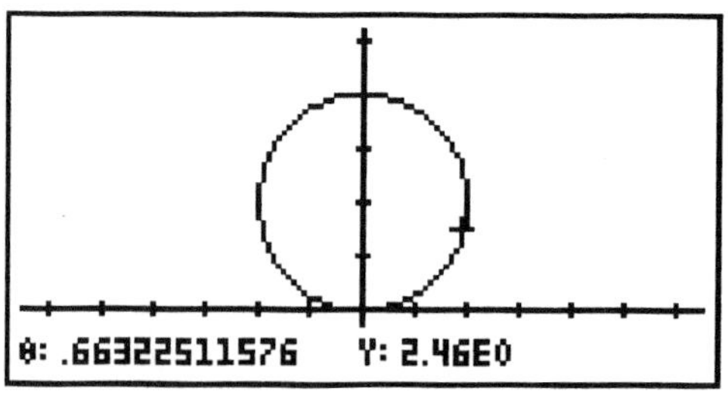

Figure 4.74: Polar graph of $r = 4\sin\theta$

4.10 Programming

4.10.1 Entering a Program: The HP-48G is a programmable calculator that can store sequences of commands for later replay. Its programming language is structured, like other modern computer programming languages you may know. Here's an example to show you how to enter a useful program that performs numerical integration by several methods: left and right Riemann Sums as well as the Midpoint Rule, the Trapezoid Rule, and Simpson's Rule.

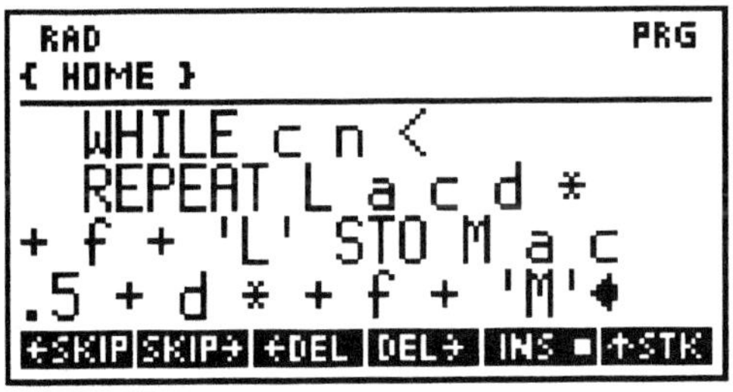

Figure 2.75: Part of program Integrate

An HP-48G program is an object in the stack and can be stored in a variable. Programs are sequences of commands and numbers, the same as you would enter directly in the calculator. The elements of a program are contained between double angle brackets, which you get by pressing ↰ « », and they are separated by spaces, using the SPC key. In the listing below, for readability, commands are presented on separate lines, though the keystrokes should be pressed consecutively.

Write the program Integrate by pressing the keystrokes given in this listing.

Commands	*Keystrokes*
« 0 0 0 'c' STO 'L' STO 'M' STO	↰ « » 0 SPC 0 SPC 0 SPC ' α ↰ C ▶ STO ' α L ▶ STO ' α M ▶ STO

initializes three variables: *L* for the left Riemann Sum, *M* for the Midpoint Rule, and *c* to keep track of subdivisions

'n' STO 'b' STO 'a' STO	' α ↰ N ▶ STO ' α ↰ b ▶ STO ' α ↰ a ▶ STO

stores values for *a*, *b*, and *n* that were placed in the stack beforehand

'f(X)' SWAP = DEFINE	' α ↰ F ↰ () α X ▶ ▶ ↰ SWAP ↰ = ↰ DEF

defines the integrand

b a - n / 'd' STO α ↰ B SPC α ↰ A - α ↰ N ÷ ' α ↰ D ▶ STO

calculates the width *d* of the subdivisions

WHILE c n < PRG *[BRCH] [WHILE] [WHILE]* α ↰ C SPC α ↰ N
PRG *[TEST] [<]*

initiates a conditional loop

REPEAT PRG *[BRCH] [WHILE] [REPEA]*

while the condition above is true, the following commands are executed

L a c d * + f + 'L' STO α L SPC α ↰ A SPC α ↰ C SPC α ↰ D × + α ↰ F +
' α L ▶ STO

adds the value of the function at the *left* endpoint of the current subdivision

M a c .5 + d * + f + 'M' α M SPC α ↰ A SPC α ↰ C SPC .5 + α ↰ D × +
α ↰ F + ' α M ▶ STO

adds the value of the function at the *midpoint* of the current subdivision

c 1 + 'c' STO α ↰ C SPC 1 + ' α ↰ C ▶ STO

counts up one subdivision

End PRG *[BRCH] [WHILE] [END]*

terminates the While loop

L d * 'L' STO α L SPC α ↰ D × ' α L ▶ STO

calculates left Riemann Sum

L d b f * d a f * - + 'R' STO
α L SPC α ↰ D SPC α ↰ B SPC α ↰ F ×
α ↰ D SPC α ↰ A SPC α ↰ F × - + ' α R ▶ STO

calculates right Riemann Sum

M d * 'M' STO α M SPC α ↰ D × ' α M ▶ STO

calculates numerical integral by Midpoint Rule

L R + 2 / 'T' STO α L SPC α R + 2 ÷ ' α T ▶ STO

calculates numerical integral by Trapezoid Rule (average left and right Riemann Sums)

2 M * T + 3 / 'S' STO 2 SPC α M × α T + 3 ÷ ' α S ▶ STO

calculates numerical integral by Simpson's Rule ($\frac{2}{3}$ Midpoint and $\frac{1}{3}$ Trapezoid)

CLEAR ↰ CLEAR

for tidiness, clears the stack

S “Simpsons rule” →TAG

α S SPC ↱ "" α S α α ↰ α I M P S O N S SPC R U L E
α ↰ α ▶ PRG *[TYPE] [▸TAG]*

displays the value with a descriptive label

T “Trapezoid rule” →TAG

α T SPC ↱ "" α T α α ↰ α R A P E Z O I D SPC R U L E
α ↰ α *[▸TAG]*

M “Midpoint rule” →TAG

α M SPC ↱ "" α M α α ↰ α I D P O I N T SPC R U L E
α ↰ α *[▸TAG]*

“Riemann sums” ↱ "" α R α α ↰ α I E M A N N SPC S U M S α ↰ α ▶ SPC

R “right” →TAG α R SPC ↱ "" α α ↰ α R I G H T α ↰ α *[▸TAG]*

L “left” →TAG » α L SPC ↱ "" α α ↰ α L E F T α ↰ α *[▸TAG]* ENTER

After entering these commands in the stack, store the program under the name Integrate by pressing ' α I α α ↰ α N T E G R A T E α ↰ α STO.

The HP-48G has a collection of sample programs that you can see and use and even modify. To get them from the calculator's memory, enter the word TEACH in the command line, then press ENTER. This loads the EXAMPLES directory. There is a listing of the sample programs in your User's Guide. To view any program, enter its name into stack level 1 and press ↰ EDIT.

4.10.2 Executing a Program: To execute the program just entered, put its name in stack level 1 and press ENTER. If you have forgotten its name, press VAR (and, if necessary, NXT) until the first five letters of Integrate appear above a function key. Then press that function key *[INTEG]* to execute this program.

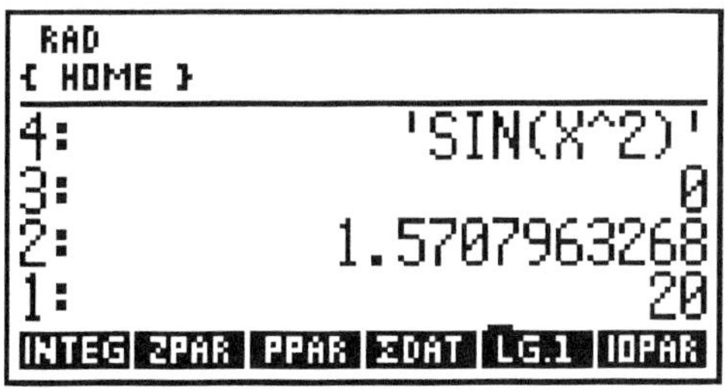

Figure 2.76: Preparing for program Integrate

The program Integrate has been written to calculate $\int_a^b f(X)\,dX$ for n subdivisions of the interval $[a, b]$. You must put in the stack an expression $f(X)$ (using uppercase X for the independent variable), limits a and b, and an integer n (as shown in Figure 2.76 for $\int_0^{\frac{\pi}{2}} \sin(X^2)\,dX$ with 20 subdivisions) before running this program.

After Integrate finishes, the approximation to the definite integral by left Riemann Sums is in stack level 1; the approximation by right Riemann Sums is in stack level 2. The Midpoint Rule approximation is in stack level 4. Use the ▲ key to move up to stack level 5 for the Trapezoid Rule approximation and to stack level 6 for the Simpson's Rule approximation. You may also press ↰ DROP repeatedly to drop objects down the stack one level at a time.

The instruction manual for your HP-48G gives detailed information about programming. Refer to it to learn more about programming and how to use other features of your calculator.

CHAPTER 5

Casio *fx*-7700GB Power Graphic Calculator

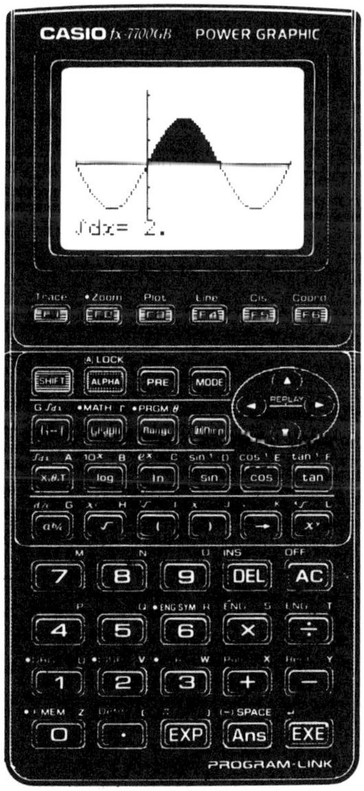

5.1 Getting started with the Casio 7700

5.1.1 Basics: Press the ON key to begin using your Casio 7700 calculator. If you need to adjust the display contrast, first press MODE, then press ▶ (the *right* arrow key) to increase the contrast or ◀ (the *left* arrow key) to decrease the contrast. Press MODE again a couple of times to clear the screen. When you have finished with the calculator, turn it off to conserve battery power by pressing SHIFT and then OFF.

Check the Casio 7700's settings by pressing and holding [M]Disp. To start with, here are the keystrokes to configure your calculator as illustrated in Figure 5.1: MODE 1 MODE + MODE MODE + MODE MODE 5 SHIFT DRG F2 EXE SHIFT DISP F3 EXE. The settings are for running programs and standard arithmetic computations, rectangular coordinates and connected graphs, radian angle measure, and normal display format. Details on alternative options will be given later in this guide. For now, remove any menu that remains by pressing PRE until the screen is clear.

```
    RUN / COMP
G-type : REC/CON
angle  : Rad
display:Nrm1



    Step    0
```

Figure 5.1: [M]Disp screen

```
1+2+3+4+5+6+7+8+
9+10+11+12+13+14
+15+16+17+18+19+
20
                 210

12+34+56
```

Figure 5.2: Home screen

5.1.2 Editing: One advantage of the Casio 7700 is that up to seven lines are visible at one time, so you can *see* a long calculation. For example, type this sum (see Figure 5.2):

$$1 + 2 + 3 + 4 + 5 + 6 + 7 + 8 + 9 + 10 + 11 + 12 + 13 + 14 + 15 + 16 + 17 + 18 + 19 + 20$$

Then press EXE to see the answer, too.

Often we do not notice a mistake until we see how unreasonable an answer is. The Casio 7700 permits you to re-display an entire calculation, edit it easily, then execute the *corrected* calculation.

Suppose you had typed 12 + 34 + 56 as in Figure 5.2 but had *not* yet pressed EXE, when you realize that 34 should have been 74. Simply press ◀ (the *left* arrow key) as many times as necessary to move the blinking cursor left to 3, then type 7 to write over it. On the other hand, if 34 should have been 384, move the cursor back to 4, press SHIFT INS (the cursor changes to a blinking frame) and then type 8 (inserts at the cursor position and other characters are pushed to the right). If the 34 should have been 3 only, move the cursor to 4 and press DEL to delete it.

Technology Tip: To move quickly to the *beginning* of an expression you are currently editing, press ▲

(the *up* arrow key); to jump to the *end* of that expression, press ▼ (the *down* arrow key).

Even if you had pressed EXE, you may still edit the previous expression. Press the *left* or *right* arrow key to *redisplay* the last expression that was entered. Now you can change it. If you press ◀, the cursor will be at the *end* of the previous expression; if you press ▶, the cursor will appear at the *beginning*. Even if you have already pressed some keys since the last EXE, but *not* EXE again, you can still recall the previous expression by first pressing AC to clear the screen and then pressing ◀ or ▶.

Technology Tip: When you need to evaluate a formula for different values of a variable, use the editing feature to simplify the process. For example, suppose you want to find the balance in an investment account if there is now $5000 in the account and interest is compounded annually at the rate of 8.5%. The formula for the balance is $P\left(1+\frac{r}{n}\right)^{nt}$, where P = principal, r = rate of interest (expressed as a decimal), n = number of times interest is compounded each year, and t = number of years. In our example, this becomes $5000(1+.085)^t$. Here are the keystrokes for finding the balance after t = 3, 5, and 10 years.

Years	*Keystrokes*	*Balance*
3	5000 (1 + .085) x^y 3 EXE	$6386.45
5	◀ ◀ 5 EXE	$7518.28
10	◀ ◀ 10 EXE	$11,304.92

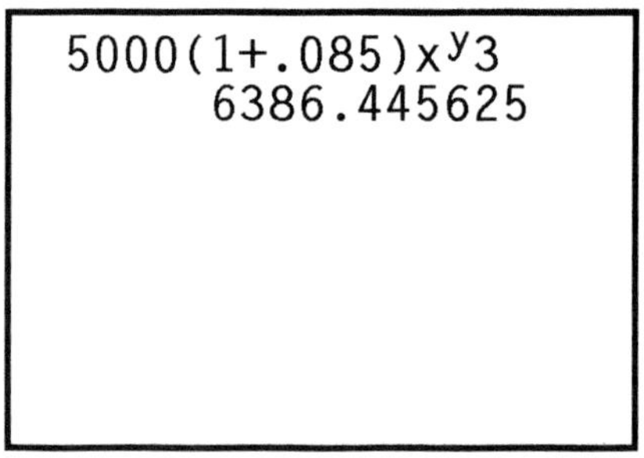

Figure 5.3: Editing expressions

Then to find the balance from the same initial investment but after 5 years when the annual interest rate is 7.5%, press these keys to change the last calculation above: ◀ ◀ DEL ◀ 5 ◀ ◀ ◀ ◀ ◀ 7 EXE.

5.1.3 Key Functions: Most keys on the Casio 7700 offer access to more than one function, just as the keys on a computer keyboard can produce more than one letter ("g" and "G") or even quite different characters ("5" and "%"). The primary function of a key is indicated on the key itself, and you access that function by a simple press on the key.

To access the *second* function indicated to the *left* above a key, first press SHIFT (the cursor changes to a blinking **S** and a menu appears at the bottom of the screen) and *then* press the key. For example, to calculate 25^2, press 25 SHIFT x² EXE.

When you want to use a letter or other character printed to the *right* above a key, first press ALPHA (the cursor changes to a blinking **A** and a menu appears at the bottom of the screen) and then the key. For example, to use the letter K in a formula, press ALPHA K. If you need several letters in a row, press SHIFT A-LOCK, which is like **CAPS LOCK** on a computer keyboard, and then press all the letters you want. Remember to press ALPHA when you are finished and want to restore the keys to their primary functions.

5.1.4 Order of Operations: The Casio 7700 performs calculations according to the standard algebraic rules. Working outwards from inner parentheses, calculations are performed from left to right. Powers and roots are evaluated first, followed by multiplications and divisions, and then additions and subtractions.

Enter these expressions to practice using your Casio 7700.

Expression	*Keystrokes*	*Display*
$7-5\cdot3$	7 - 5 × 3 EXE	-8
$(7-5)\cdot3$	(7 - 5) × 3 EXE	6
$120-10^2$	120 - 10 SHIFT x² EXE	20
$(120-10)^2$	(120 - 10) SHIFT x² EXE	12100
$\frac{24}{2^3}$	24 ÷ 2 x^y 3 EXE	3
$\left(\frac{24}{2}\right)^3$	(24 ÷ 2) x^y 3 EXE	1728
$(7--5)\cdot-3$	(7 - - 5) × - 3 EXE	-36

5.1.5 Algebraic Expressions and Memory: Your calculator can evaluate expressions such as $\frac{N(N+1)}{2}$ *after* you have entered a value for N. Suppose you want $N = 200$. Press 200 → ALPHA N EXE to store the value 200 in memory location N. Whenever you use N in an expression, the calculator will substitute the value 200 until you make a change by storing *another* number in N. Next enter the expression $\frac{N(N+1)}{2}$ by typing ALPHA N (ALPHA N + 1) ÷ 2 EXE. For $N = 200$, you will find that $\frac{N(N+1)}{2} = 20100$.

The contents of any memory location may be revealed by typing just its letter name and then EXE. And the Casio 7700 retains memorized values even when it is turned off, so long as its batteries are good.

5.1.6 Repeated Operations with **Ans**: The result of your *last* calculation is always stored in memory location Ans and replaces any previous result. This makes it easy to use the answer from one computation in another computation. For example, press 30 + 15 EXE so that 45 is the last result displayed. Then press Ans ÷ 9 EXE and get 5 because $\frac{45}{9} = 5$.

With a function like division, you press the ÷ key *after* you enter an argument. For such functions, whenever you would start a new calculation with the previous answer followed by pressing the function key, you may press just the function key. So instead of Ans ÷ 9 in the previous example, you could have pressed simply ÷ 9 to achieve the same result. This technique also works for these functions: + - × x^2 x^y x^{-1}.

Here is a situation where this is especially useful. Suppose a person makes $5.85 per hour and you are asked to calculate earnings for a day, a week, and a year. Execute the given keystrokes to find the person's incomes during these periods (results are shown in Figure 5.4):

Pay period	*Keystrokes*	*Earnings*
8-hour day	5.85 × 8 EXE	$46.80
5-day week	Ans × 5 EXE	$234
52-week year	× 52 EXE	$12,168

```
5.85x8
                46.8
Ansx5
                234.
234.x52
              12168.
```

Figure 5.4: Ans key

In general, the Casio 7700 does not distinguish between the negative sign and the subtraction operator. But when you enter -4 as the *first* number in a calculation, you must use the negative key SHIFT (-) rather than the - key. Press these keys for an illustration: 8 EXE - 5 EXE SHIFT (-) 5 EXE. It is just as easy to press 0 - 5 EXE, especially if you cannot remember where the (-) key is.

5.1.7 The **MATH** *Menu:* Operators and functions associated with a scientific calculator are available either immediately from the keys of the Casio 7700 or by SHIFT keys. You have direct key access to common arithmetic operations (SHIFT x^2, $\sqrt{\ }$, SHIFT x^{-1}, x^y), trigonometric functions (sin, cos, tan) and their inverses (SHIFT $\sin^{-1}$, SHIFT $\cos^{-1}$, SHIFT $\tan^{-1}$), exponential and logarithmic functions (log, SHIFT 10^x, ln, SHIFT e^x), and a famous constant (SHIFT π).

A significant difference between the Casio 7700 and many scientific calculators is that the Casio 7700 requires the argument of a function *after* the function, as you would see a formula written in your textbook. For example, on the Casio 7700 you calculate $\sqrt{16}$ by pressing the keys $\sqrt{\ }$ 16 in that order.

The Casio 7700 has a special fraction key $a^b\!/\!_c$ for entering fractions and mixed numbers. To enter a fraction such as $2/5$, press 2 $a^b\!/\!_c$ 5 EXE. To enter a mixed number like $2\frac{3}{4}$, press 2 $a^b\!/\!_c$ 3 $a^b\!/\!_c$ 4 EXE. Press $a^b\!/\!_c$ to toggle between the mixed number and its decimal equivalent; press SHIFT $d\!/\!_c$ and see $2\frac{3}{4}$ as an improper fraction, $\frac{11}{4}$.

Here are keystrokes for basic mathematical operations. Try them for practice on your Casio 7700.

Expression	*Keystrokes*	*Display*
$\sqrt{3^2+4^2}$	$\sqrt{\ }$ (3 SHIFT x^2 + 4 SHIFT x^2) EXE	5
$2\frac{1}{3}$	2 $a^b\!/\!_c$ 1 $a^b\!/\!_c$ 3 EXE $a^b\!/\!_c$	2.333333333
$\log 200$	LOG 200 EXE	2.301029996
$2.34 \cdot 10^5$	2.34 × SHIFT 10^x 5 EXE	234000

Additional mathematical operations and functions are available from the MATH menu. Press SHIFT MATH to see the four categories of mathematical functions. They are listed across the bottom of the Casio 7700 screen and correspond to the first four function keys, F1 to F4. You will learn in your mathematics textbook how to apply many of them. As an example, calculate $|-5|$ by pressing SHIFT MATH F3 (for access to numerical functions) and then F1 -5 EXE. To clear any menu from the screen, press PRE.

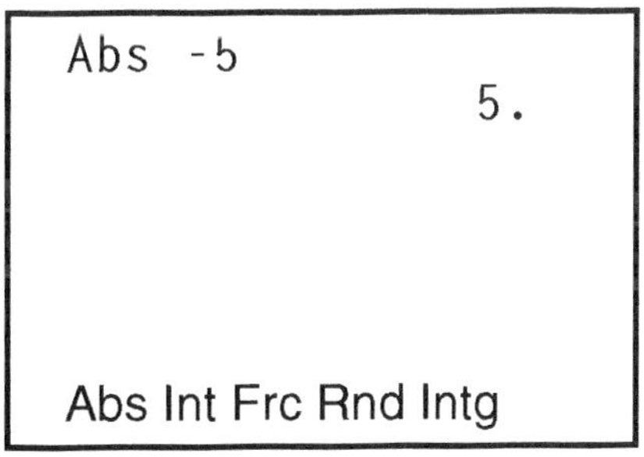

Figure 5.5: MATH NUM menu

The *factorial* of a non-negative integer is the *product* of *all* the integers from 1 up to the given integer. The symbol for factorial is the exclamation point. So 4! (pronounced *four factorial*) is $1\cdot2\cdot3\cdot4 = 24$. You will learn more about applications of factorials in your textbook, but for now use the Casio 7700 to calculate 4! Press these keystrokes: 4 SHIFT MATH F2 F1 EXE.

Hyperbolic functions (sinh, cosh, and tanh) and their inverses are available from the HYP sub-menu of the

MATH menu. For example, here are the keystrokes to calculate sinh 3: SHIFT MATH F1 F1 3 ENTER.

5.2 Functions and Graphs

5.2.1 Evaluating Functions: Suppose you receive a monthly salary of \$1975 plus a commission of 10% of sales. Let x = your sales in dollars; then your wages W in dollars are given by the equation $W = 1975 + .10x$. If your January sales were \$2230 and your February sales were \$1865, what was your income during those months?

```
2230→X
1975+.10X
                2198.
```

Figure 5.6: Evaluating a function

Here's how to use your Casio 7700 to perform this task. First press AC to get a blank home screen. Then set $x = 2230$ by pressing 2230 → X,θ,T. (The X,θ,T key lets you enter a variable x without having to use the ALPHA key.) Then press SHIFT ↵ to allow another expression to be input on a single command line. Finally, enter the expression $1975 + .10x$ by pressing these keys: 1975 + .10 X,θ,T. Now press EXE to calculate the answer (Figure 5.6).

It is not necessary to repeat all these steps to find the February wages. Simply press ▶ to recall the entire previous line, change 2230 to 1865, and press EXE.

Technology Tip: The Casio 7700 does not require multiplication to be expressed between variables, so xxx means x^3. It is often easier to press two or three x's together than to search for the square key or the powers key. Of course, expressed multiplication is also not required between a constant and a variable. Hence to enter $2x^3 + 3x^2 - 4x + 5$ in the Casio 7700, you might save keystrokes and press just these keys: 2 X,θ,T X,θ,T X,θ,T + 3 X,θ,T X,θ,T - 4 X,θ,T + 5.

5.2.2 Functions in a Graph Window: On the Casio 7700, you can easily generate the graph of a function. The ability to draw a graph contributes substantially to our ability to solve problems.

For example, here is how to graph $y = -x^3 + 4x$. First press Graph and then - X,θ,T x^y 3 + 4 X,θ,T to enter the function (as in Figure 5.7). Now press EXE and the Casio 7700 changes to a window with the graph of $y = -x^3 + 4x$.

While the Casio 7700 is busy calculating coordinates for a plot, it displays a solid square at the top right of the graph window. When you see this indicator, even though the screen does not change, you know that the calculator is working.

Switch back and forth between the graph window and the home screen by pressing G↔T.

The graph window on your calculator may look like the one in Figure 5.8 or it may be different. Since the graph of $y = -x^3 + 4x$ extends infinitely far left and right and also infinitely far up and down, the Casio 7700 can display only a piece of the actual graph. This displayed rectangular part is called a *viewing rectangle*.

You can easily change the viewing rectangle to enhance your investigation of a graph. For example, press any of the arrow keys to pan the graph window in the corresponding direction. If you press the down arrow, for example, the window will pan down so that you may look at points below the current window.

```
Graph Y=-Xx^y3+4X
                done
```

Figure 5.7: Graph command

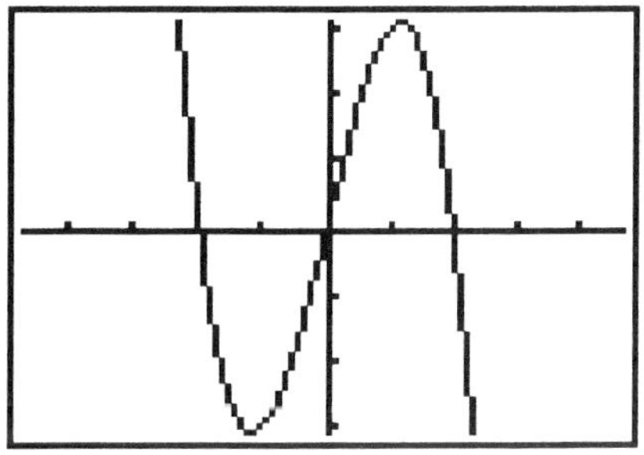

Figure 5.8: Graph of $y = -x^3 + 4x$

The viewing rectangle in Figure 5.8 shows the part of the graph that extends horizontally from -4.7 to 4.7 and vertically from -3.1 to 3.1. Press RANGE to see information about your viewing rectangle. Figure 5.9 shows the RANGE screen that corresponds to the viewing rectangle in Figure 5.8. This is the *standard* viewing rectangle for the Casio 7700.

```
Range
Xmin:-4.7
 max:4.7
 scl:1
Ymin:-3.1
 max:3.1
 scl:1
INIT
```

Figure 5.9: Standard RANGE

The variables Xmin and Xmax are the minimum and maximum x-values of the viewing rectangle; Ymin and Ymax are its minimum and maximum y-values.

Xscl and Yscl set the spacing between tick marks on the axes.

Use the arrow keys ▲ and ▼ to move up and down from one line to another in this list; pressing the EXE key will move down the list. Enter a new value to over-write a previous value. You may also edit the entry as you would edit an expression. To leave the RANGE menu, press the RANGE key once or twice more. Finally, press EXE to redraw the graph. The following figures show different RANGE screens and the corresponding viewing rectangle for each one.

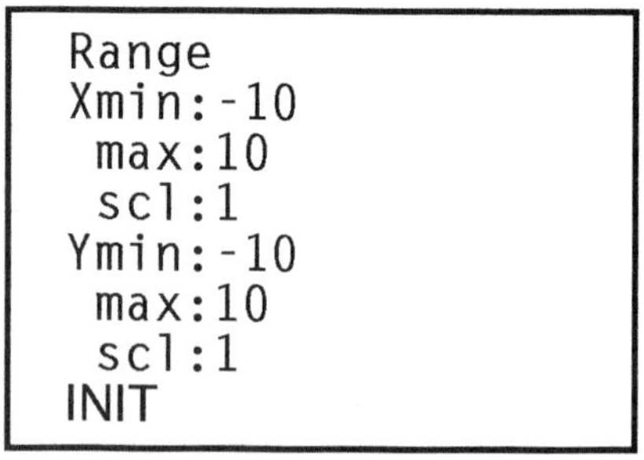

Figure 5.10: -10 to 10 in both directions

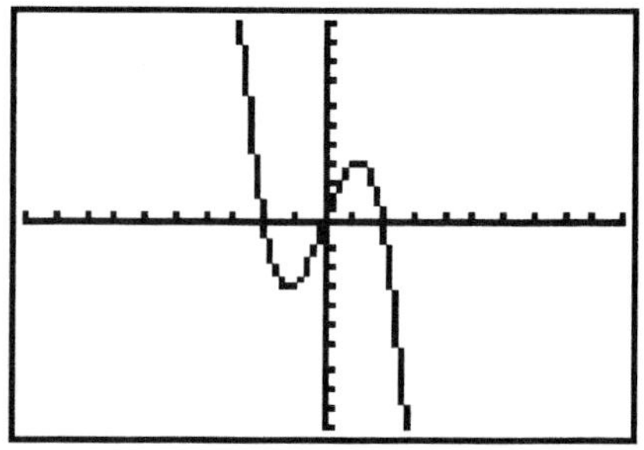

Figure 5.11: Graph of $y=-x^3+4x$

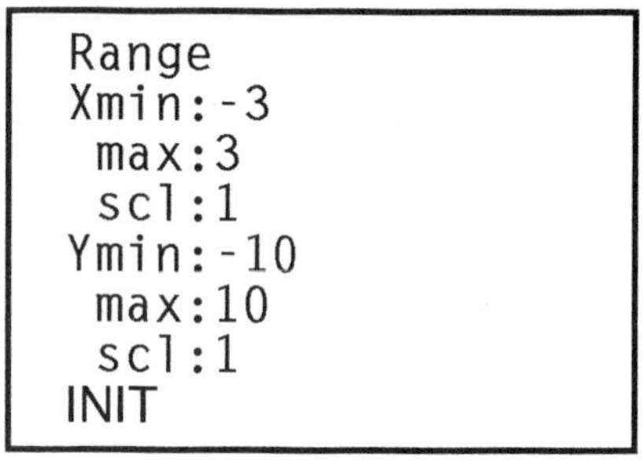

Figure 5.12: Custom window

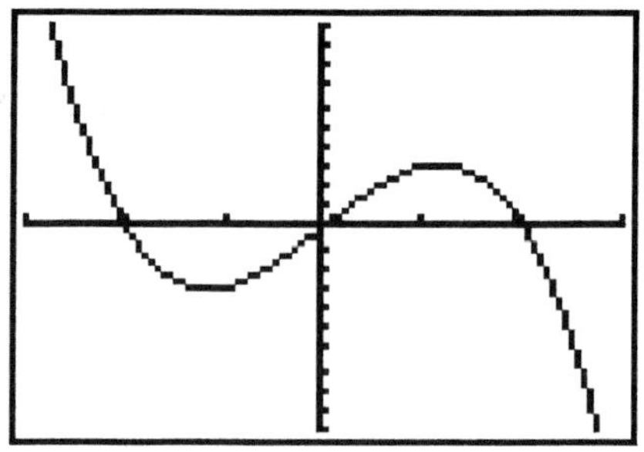

Figure 5.13: Graph of $y=-x^3+4x$

To initialize the viewing rectangle quickly to standard values (see Figure 5.9), press RANGE F1 RANGE RANGE. Then press EXE to redraw the graph.

As you pan over the graph by pressing the arrow keys, the RANGE dimensions are updated automatically. More information about windows is presented later, in Section 5.2.4.

Technology Tip: Clear any graphs by pressing F5 when the Casio 7700 is showing the graph screen or SHIFT F5 when it is displaying the home screen. The CLS command now appears in the home screen; press EXE to implement it.

Another way to clear the graph window is to press RANGE, re-enter the *current* value for Xmin (or make any "change" in a range value), then press RANGE RANGE to exit. This method *keeps* the graph command as the *current* command, so you may edit it as necessary. Also, the Casio 7700 keeps a graph "active" for zooming and tracing only if the graphing instruction is the last command executed.

If you're going to use a function later, or if you need to perform some calculations before returning to its graph, save it in the Casio 7700's FUNCTION MEMORY. Six different functions, expressions, or commands can be stored here. Press SHIFT f-MEM and then F5 for a listing of current contents of function memory. To *store* a function or command, enter it first in the home screen, but do *not* press EXE. Press SHIFT f-MEM F1 and then an integer from 1 to 6, corresponding to a function memory location. To *recall* a function or command from memory to the home screen, press SHIFT f-MEM F2 and the integer corresponding to the function you want.

It's a good idea to reserve at least one function memory location, say f_1, for temporary storage of functions, and use the remaining locations for longer-term storage.

5.2.3 The Greatest Integer Function: The greatest integer function, written $[[x]]$, gives the greatest *integer* less than or equal to a number x. On the Casio 7700, the greatest integer function is called Intg and is located under the NUM sub-menu of the MATH menu (see Figure 5.5). So calculate $[[6.78]] = 6$ by pressing SHIFT MATH F3 F5 6.78 EXE.

To graph $y = [[x]]$, press GRAPH SHIFT MATH F3 F5 X,θ,T EXE. Figure 5.14 shows this graph in a viewing rectangle from −5 to 5 in both directions.

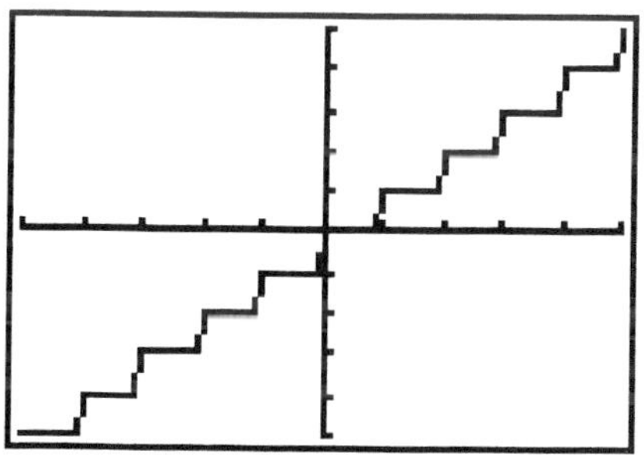

Figure 5.14: Connected graph of $y = [[x]]$

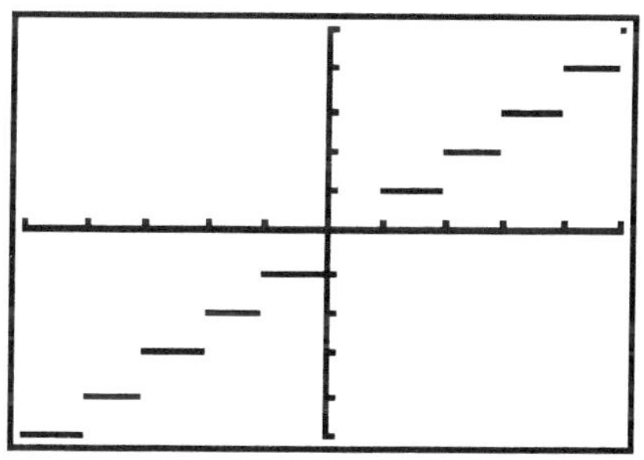

Figure 5.15: Dot graph of $y = [[x]]$

The true graph of the greatest integer function is a step graph, like the one in Figure 5.15. For the graph of $y = [[x]]$, a segment should *not* be drawn between every pair of successive points. You can change from CONNECT line to PLOT graph on the Casio 7700 from the MODE menu. First clear the graph window by pressing RANGE, re-enter the *current* value for Xmin, then press RANGE RANGE to exit. Next press MODE MODE 6 EXE to draw the new graph.

5.2.4 Graphing a Circle: Here is a useful technique for graphs that are not functions, but that can be "split" into a top part and a bottom part, or into multiple parts. Suppose you wish to graph the circle whose equation is $x^2+y^2=36$. First solve for y and get an equation for the top semicircle, $y=\sqrt{36-x^2}$, and for the bottom semicircle, $y=-\sqrt{36-x^2}$. Then graph the two semicircles simultaneously.

The keystrokes to draw this circle's graph follow. Store $\sqrt{36-x^2}$ as f_1 by pressing √ (36 - X,θ,T SHIFT x²) SHIFT ⊞-MEM F1 1. Then press AC GRAPH SHIFT ⊞-MEM F2 1 SHIFT ↵ GRAPH - F2 1 EXE to draw both halves of the circle.

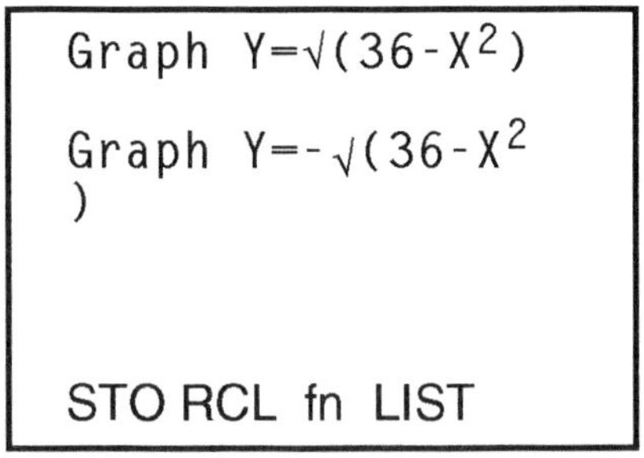

Figure 5.16: Two semicircles

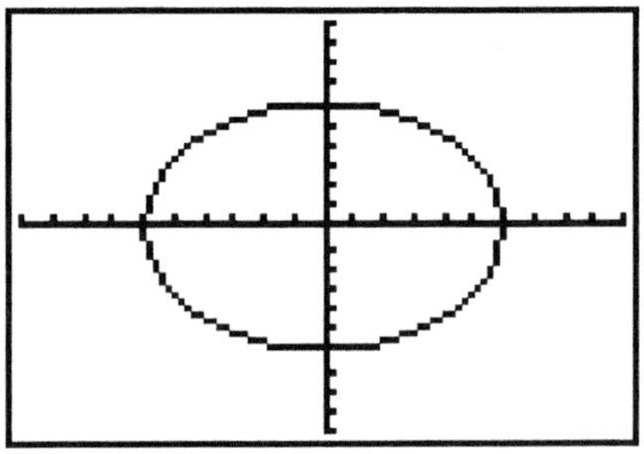

Figure 5.17: Circle's graph - one view

If your range were set to a viewing rectangle extending from -10 to 10 in both directions, your graph would look like Figure 5.17. Now this does *not* look like a circle, because the units along the axes are not the same. You need what is called a "square" viewing rectangle. The Casio 7700's standard viewing rectangle is square, but too small to display a circle of radius 6. So double the dimensions of the standard window and change it to extend horizontally from -9.4 to 9.4 and vertically from -6.2 to 6.2.

Technology Tip: Another way to get a square graph is to change the range variables so that the value of Ymax - Ymin is $\frac{2}{3}$ times Xmax - Xmin. For example, see the RANGE in Figure 5.18 and the corresponding graph in Figure 5.19. The method works because the dimensions of the Casio 7700's display are such that the ratio of vertical to horizontal is $\frac{2}{3}$.

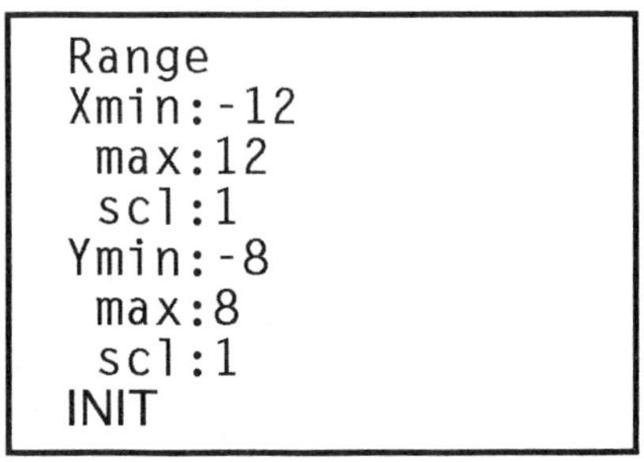

Figure 5.18: $\frac{\text{vertical}}{\text{horizontal}}=\frac{16}{24}=\frac{2}{3}$

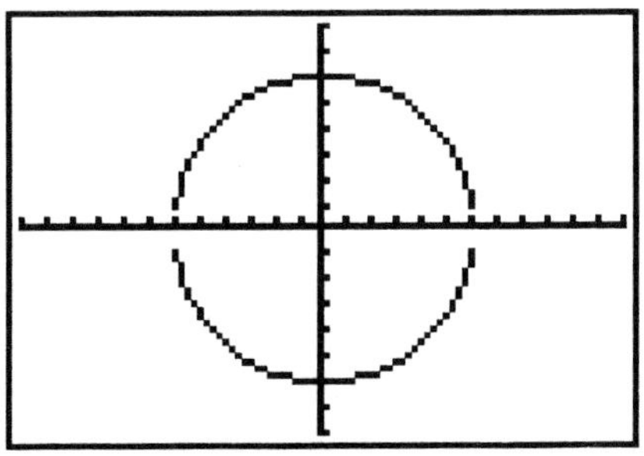

Figure 5.19: A "square" circle

The two semicircles in Figure 5.19 do not meet because of an idiosyncrasy in the way the Casio 7700 plots a graph.

Back when you input the command to draw the graph, you could have entered f_1 and $-f_1$ instead of the corresponding expressions. Try this by pressing AC GRAPH SHIFT ⊞-MEM F3 1 SHIFT ↵ GRAPH - F3 1 EXE. The graph should be just as it was before.

Technology Tip: The square viewing rectangle is also important when you want to judge whether two lines are perpendicular. The intersection of perpendicular lines will always *look* like a right angle in a square viewing rectangle.

5.2.5 TRACE: Graph $y=-x^3+4x$ in the standard viewing rectangle. When the graph window is displayed, press F1 to enable the left ◀ and right ▶ arrow keys to trace along the function. The coordinates that are displayed belong to points on the function's graph, so the y-coordinate is the calculated value of the function at the corresponding x-coordinate.

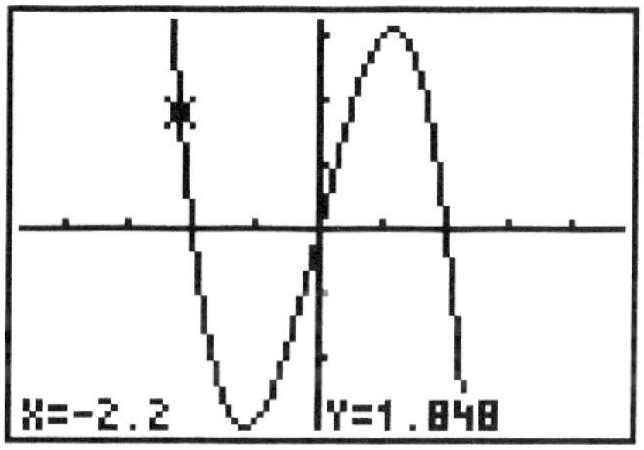

Figure 5.20: Trace on $y=-x^3+4x$

To see more decimal places in the coordinates of the points that are traced, press F6 to cycle between the x-coordinate alone, the y coordinate alone, and both coordinates.

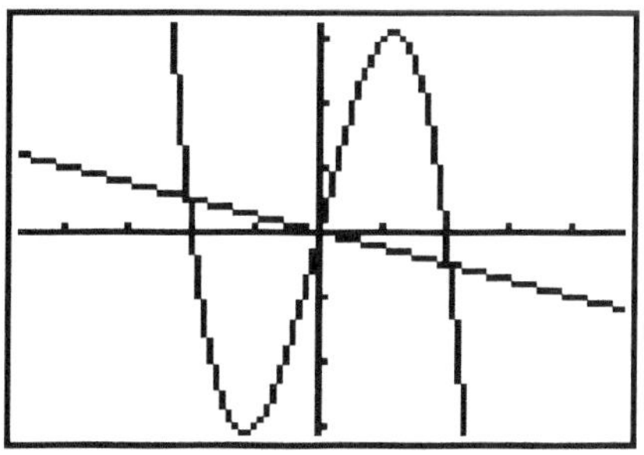
Figure 5.21: $y=-x^3+4x$ and $y=-.25x$

Now plot a second function, $y=-.25x$, along with $y=-x^3+4x$. From the graph window above, press G↔T to return to the home screen, then press ◀ to edit the previous graph command. Add the second graph command to this by pressing SHIFT ↵ GRAPH and the keys for $-.25x$. Finally, press EXE to draw both functions.

Press TRACE and the cursor appears first on the graph of $y=-.25x$ because it is the last function plotted. Press the up ▲ or down ▼ arrow key to move the cursor vertically to the graph of $y=-x^3+4x$. Next press the right and left arrow keys to trace along the graph of $y=-x^3+4x$. When more than one function is plotted, you can move the trace cursor vertically from one graph to another in this way.

Technology Tip: By the way, trace along the graph of $y=-.25x$ and press and hold either ◀ or ▶. Eventually you will reach the left or right edge of the window. Keep pressing the arrow key and the Casio 7700 will allow you to continue the trace by panning the viewing rectangle. Check the RANGE screen to see that Xmin and Xmax are automatically updated.

The Casio 7700's display has 95 horizontal columns of pixels and 63 vertical rows. So when you trace a curve across a graph window, you are actually moving from Xmin to Xmax in 94 equal jumps, each called Δx. You would calculate the size of each jump to be $\Delta x=\frac{\text{Xmax}-\text{Xmin}}{94}$. Sometimes you may want the jumps to be friendly numbers like .1 or .25 so that, when you trace along the curve, the x-coordinates will be incremented by such a convenient amount. Just set your viewing rectangle for a particular increment Δx by making Xmax = Xmin + 94·Δx. For example, if you want Xmin = -5 and Δx = .3, set Xmax = -5 + 94·.3 = 23.2. Likewise, set Ymax = Ymin + 62·Δy if you want the vertical increment to be some special Δy.

To center your window around a particular point, say (h, k), and also have a certain Δx, set Xmin = h - 47·Δx and Xmax = h + 47·Δx. Likewise, make Ymin = k - 31·Δy and Ymax = k + 31·Δy. For example, to center a window around the origin, (0, 0), with both horizontal and vertical increments of .25, set the range so that Xmin = 0 - 47·.25 = -11.75, Xmax = 0 + 47·.25 = 11.75, Ymin = 0 - 31·.25 = -7.75, and Ymax = 0 + 31·.25 = 7.75.

The Casio 7700's standard window is already a friendly viewing rectangle, centered at the origin (0, 0) with $\Delta x = \Delta y = 0.1$.

See the benefit by first plotting $y=x^2+2x+1$ in a window that extends from -10 to 10 in both directions. Trace near its y-intercept, which is (0, 1), and move towards its x-intercept, which is (-1, 0). Then initialize the range to the standard window and trace again near the intercepts.

5.2.6 ZOOM: Plot again the two graphs, for $y=-x^3+4x$ and for $y=-.25x$. There appears to be an intersection near x = 2. The Casio 7700 provides several ways to enlarge the view around this point. You can change the viewing rectangle directly by pressing RANGE and editing the values of Xmin, Xmax, Ymin, and Ymax. Figure 5.22 shows a new viewing rectangle for the range extending from 1.5 to 2.5 horizontally and from -2.5 to 2.5 vertically.

Trace along the graphs until coordinates of a point that is close to the intersection are displayed.

A more efficient method for enlarging the view is to draw a new viewing rectangle with the cursor. Start again with a graph of the two functions $y=-x^3+4x$ and $y=-.25x$ in a standard viewing rectangle.

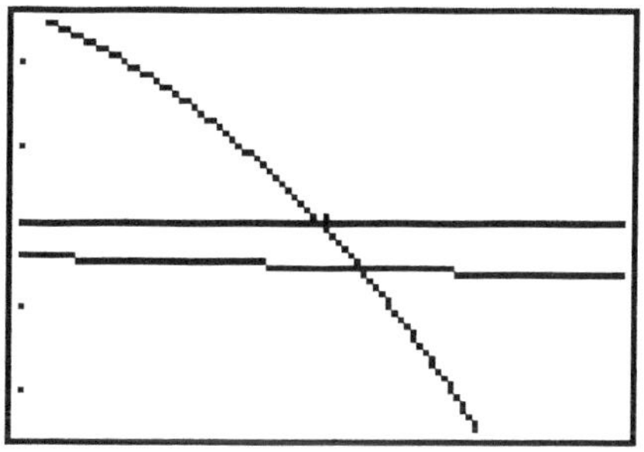

Figure 5.22: Closer view

Now imagine a small rectangular box around the intersection point, near x = 2. Press ZOOM F1 (Figure 5.23) to draw a box to define this new viewing rectangle. Use the arrow keys to move the cursor, which is now free-moving and whose coordinates are displayed at the bottom of the window, to one corner of the new viewing rectangle you imagine.

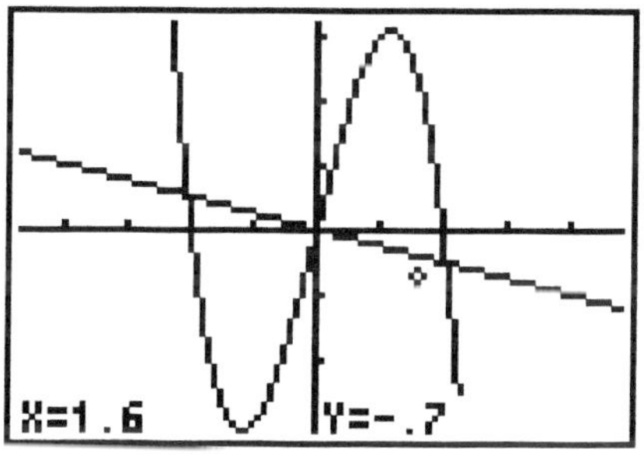

Figure 5.23: One corner selected

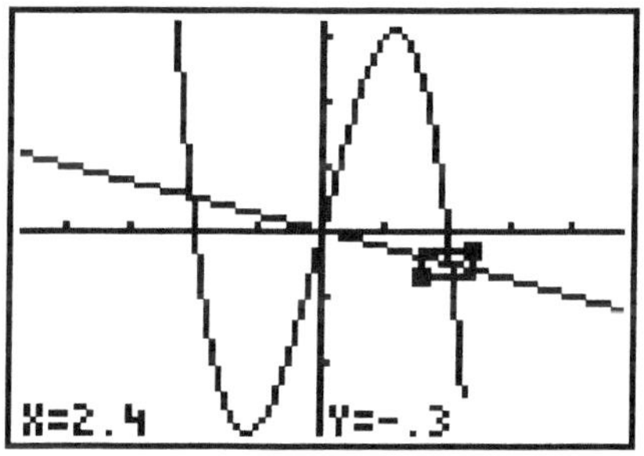

Figure 5.24: Box drawn

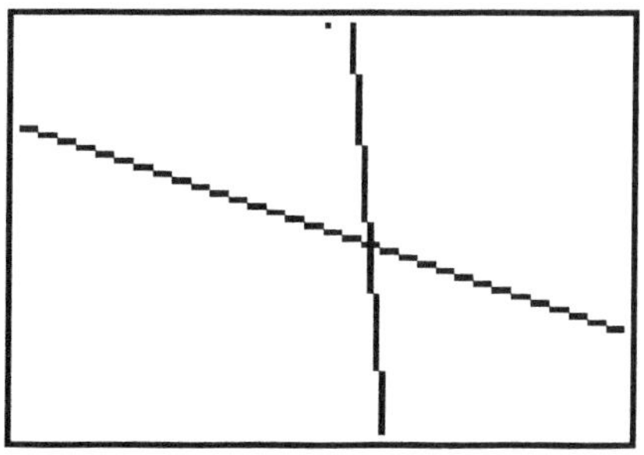

Figure 5.25: New viewing rectangle

Press EXE to fix the corner where you have moved the cursor. Use the arrow keys again to move the cursor to the diagonally opposite corner of the new rectangle (Figure 5.24). If this box looks all right to you, press EXE. The rectangular area you have enclosed will now enlarge to fill the graph window (Figure 5.25).

You may cancel the zoom any time *before* you press this last EXE. Press another function key such as F1 to cancel the zoom and initiate a trace instead, or press F2 to zoom again and start over.

You can also gain a quick magnification of the graph around the cursor's location. Return once more to the standard range for the graph of the two functions $y = -x^3 + 4x$ and $y = -.25x$. Trace along the graphs to move the cursor as close as you can to the point of intersection near $x = 2$ (see Figure 5.26). Then press F2 F3 and the calculator draws a magnified graph, centered at the cursor's position (Figure 5.27). The range values are changed to reflect this new viewing rectangle. Look in the RANGE menu to check.

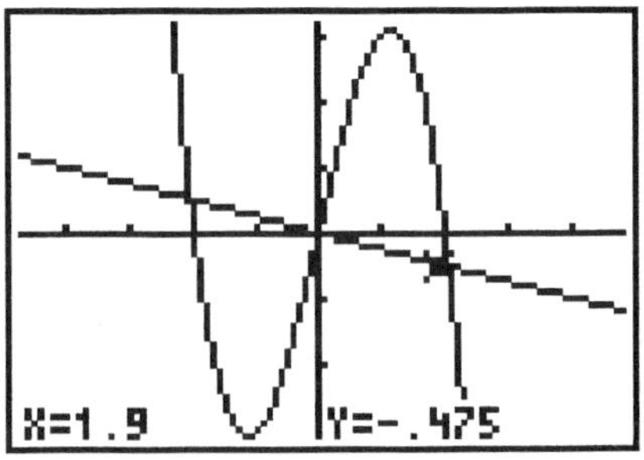

Figure 5.26: Before a zoom in

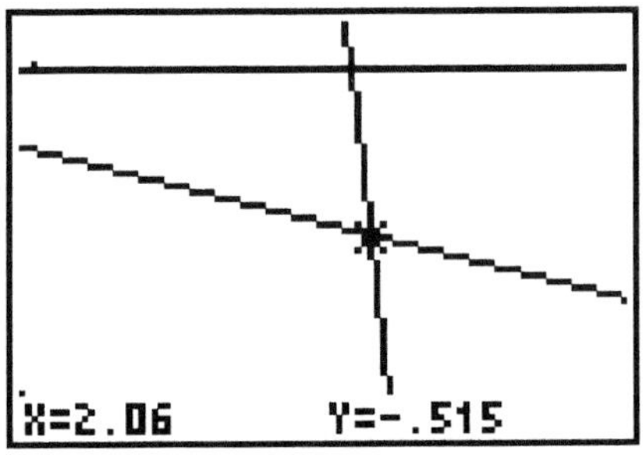

Figure 5.27: After a zoom in

As you see in the Zoom menu (press F2), the Casio 7700 can zoom in (press F2 F3) or zoom out (press F2 F4). Zoom out to see a larger view of the graph, centered at the cursor position. You can change the horizontal and vertical scale of the magnification by pressing F2 F2 and editing Xfct and Yfct, the horizontal and vertical magnification factors.

The default zoom factor is 2 in both directions (press F1 in the Zoom Factor menu). It is not necessary for Xfct and Yfct to be equal. Sometimes, you may prefer to zoom in one direction only, so the other factor should be set to 1. Press EXE as needed to leave the Zoom Factor menu.

Technology Tip: If you should zoom in too much and lose the curve, zoom back to the original viewing rectangle and start over. Press F2 F5 for the viewing rectangle you started with. Or use the arrow keys to pan over if you think the curve is not too far away. You can also just initialize the range to the Casio 7700's standard window.

5.2.7 Relative Minimums and Maximums: Graph $y = -x^3 + 4x$ once again in the standard viewing rectangle (Figure 5.8). This function appears to have a relative minimum near $x = -1$ and a relative maximum near $x = 1$. You may zoom and trace to approximate these extreme values.

First trace along the curve near the local minimum. Notice by how much the x-values and y-values change as you move from point to point. Trace along the curve until the y-coordinate is as *small* as you can get it, so that you are as close as possible to the local minimum, and zoom in (press F2 F3 or use a zoom box). Now trace again along the curve and, as you move from point to point, see that the coordinates change by smaller amounts than before. Keep zooming and tracing until you find the coordinates of the local minimum point as accurately as you need them, approximately (-1.15, -3.08).

Follow a similar procedure to find the local maximum. Trace along the curve until the y-coordinate is as *great* as you can get it, so that you are as close as possible to the local maximum, and zoom in. The local maximum point on the graph of $y = -x^3 + 4x$ is approximately (1.15, 3.08).

Technology Tip: Press F6 a couple of times to display only the y-coordinate. Then while tracing towards a minimum or maximum, it's easier to see where the y-coordinate is least or greatest.

5.3 Solving Equations and Inequalities

5.3.1 Intercepts and Intersections: Tracing and zooming are also used to locate an x-intercept of a graph, where a curve crosses the x-axis. For example, the graph of $y = x^3 - 8x$ crosses the x-axis three times (see Figure 5.28). After tracing over to the x-intercept point that is furthest to the left, zoom in (Figure 5.29). Continue this process until you have located all three intercepts with as much accuracy as you need. The three x-intercepts of $y = x^3 - 8x$ are approximately -2.828, 0, and 2.828.

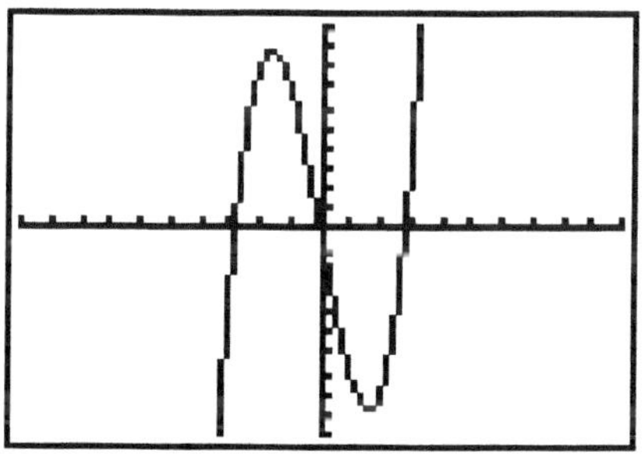

Figure 5.28: Graph of $y = x^3 - 8x$

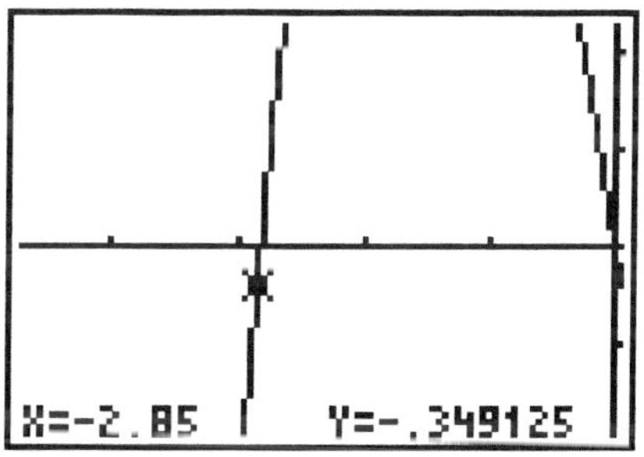

Figure 5.29: An x-intercept of $y = x^3 - 8x$

Technology Tip: As you zoom in, you may also wish to change the spacing between tick marks on the x-axis so that the viewing rectangle shows scale marks near the intercept point. Then the accuracy of your approximation will be such that the error is less than the distance between two tick marks. Change the x-scale on the Casio 7700 from the RANGE menu. Move the cursor down to Xscl and enter an appropriate value.

TRACE and ZOOM are especially important for locating the intersection points of two graphs, say the graphs of $y = -x^3 + 4x$ and $y = -.25x$. Trace along one of the graphs until you arrive close to an intersection point. Then press ▲ or ▼ to jump to the other graph. Notice that the x-coordinate does not change, but the y-coordinate is likely to be different (see Figures 5.31 and 5.32).

When the two y-coordinates are as close as they can get, you have come as close as you now can to the point of intersection. So zoom in around the intersection point, then trace again until the two y-coordinates are as close as possible. Continue this process until you have located the point of intersection with as much accuracy as necessary.

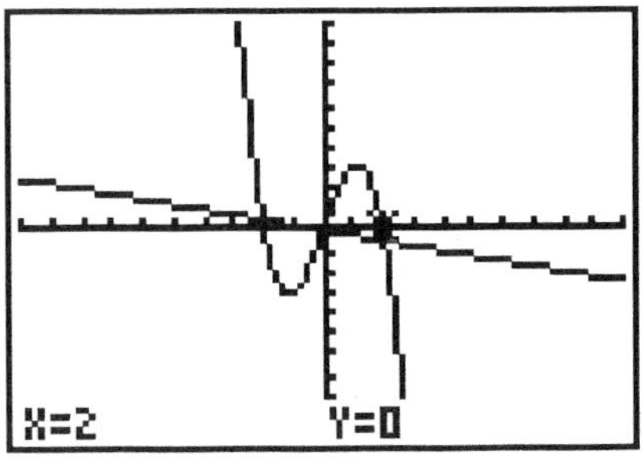

Figure 5.30: Trace on $y = -x^3 + 4x$

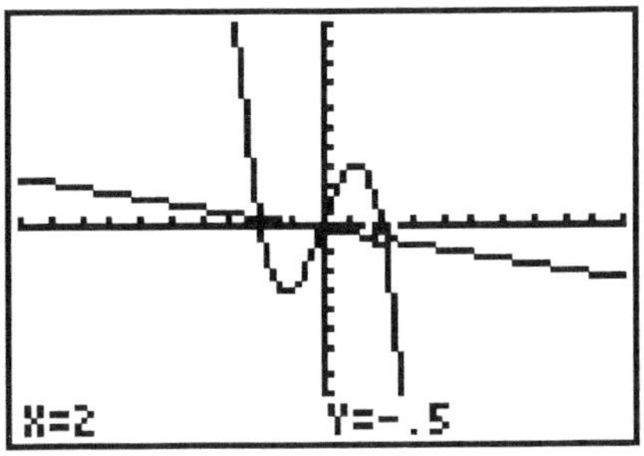

Figure 5.31: Trace on $y = -.25x$

5.3.2 Solving Equations by Graphing: Suppose you need to solve the equation $24x^3 - 36x + 17 = 0$. First graph $y = 24x^3 - 36x + 17$ in a window large enough to exhibit *all* its x-intercepts, corresponding to all its roots. Then use trace and zoom to locate each one. In fact, this equation has just one solution, approximately x = -1.414.

Remember that when an equation has more than one x-intercept, it may be necessary to change the viewing rectangle a few times to locate all of them.

Technology Tip: To solve an equation like $24x^3 + 17 = 36x$, you may first transform it into standard form, $24x^3 - 36x + 17 = 0$, and proceed as above. However, you may also graph the *two* functions $y = 24x^3 + 17$ and $y = 36x$, then zoom and trace to locate their point of intersection.

5.3.3 Solving Systems by Graphing: The solutions to a system of equations correspond to the points of intersection of their graphs (Figure 5.32). For example, to solve the system $y = x^2 - 3x - 4$ and $y = x^3 + 3x^2 - 2x - 1$, first graph them together. Then zoom and trace to locate their point of intersection, approximately (-2.17, 7.25).

You must judge whether the two current y-coordinates are sufficiently close for x = -2.17 or whether you should continue to zoom and trace to improve the approximation.

The solutions of the system of two equations $y = x^3 + 3x^2 - 2x - 1$ and $y = x^2 - 3x - 4$ correspond to the solutions of the single equation $x^3 + 3x^2 - 2x - 1 = x^2 - 3x - 4$, which simplifies to $x^3 + 2x^2 + x + 3 = 0$. So you may also graph $y = x^3 + 2x^2 + x + 3$ and find its x-intercepts to solve the system.

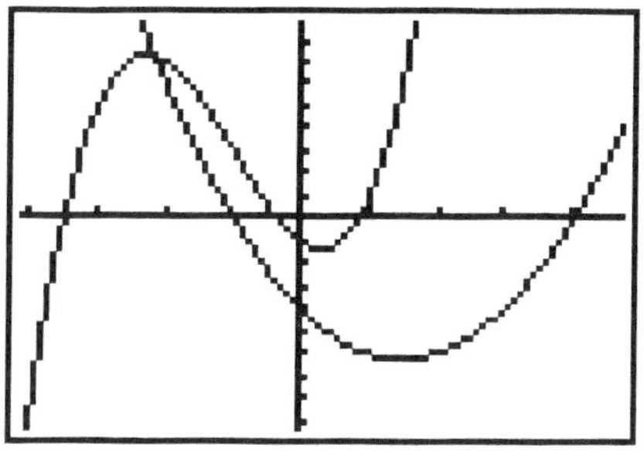

Figure 5.32: Solving a system of equations

5.3.4 Solving Inequalities by Graphing: Consider the inequality $1-\frac{3x}{2} \geq x-4$. To solve it with your Casio 7700, graph the two functions $y=1-\frac{3x}{2}$ and $y=x-4$ (Figure 5.33). First locate their point of intersection, at $x = 2$. The inequality is true when the graph of $y=1-\frac{3x}{2}$ lies *above* the graph of $y=x-4$, and that occurs for $x < 2$. So the solution is the half-line $x \leq 2$, or $(-\infty, 2]$.

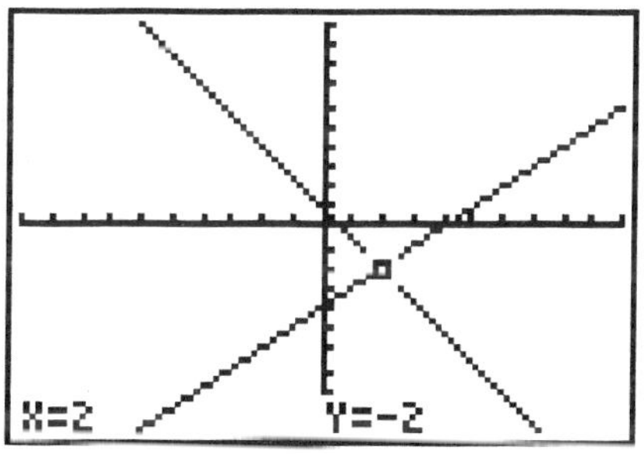

Figure 5.33: Solving $1-\frac{3x}{2} \geq x-4$

The Casio 7700 is capable of graphing inequalities of the form $y \leq x$, $y < x$, $y \geq x$, or $y > x$. For example, to graph $y \geq x^2 - 1$, first change to inequality mode by pressing MODE MODE ÷. Now, after you press GRAPH, a menu of inequalities appears. Next press F3, the keystrokes for $x^2 - 1$, and EXE (see Figure 5.34).

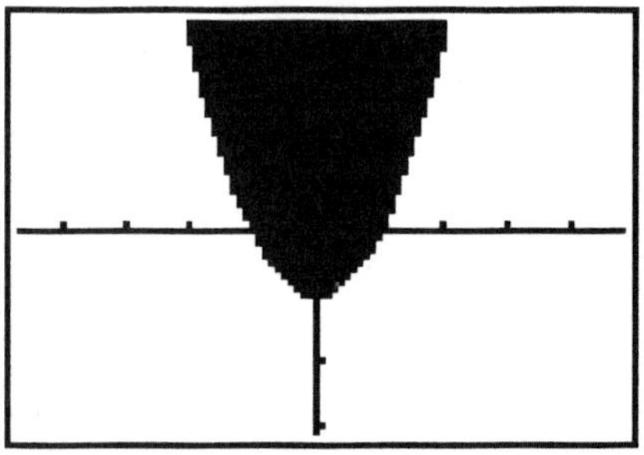

Figure 5.34: Graph of $y \geq x^2 - 1$

Solve a system of inequalities, such as $1-\frac{3x}{2} \geq y$ and $y > x-4$, by plotting the two inequality graphs simultaneously. First, clear the graph window and reset the range to a convenient window. Then, if necessary, change to inequality graphing mode. Press Graph F4 and the keystrokes for $1-\frac{3x}{2}$; press SHIFT ↲ F1 and the keystrokes for $x-4$. After you press EXE, watch the two inequalities as they are drawn.

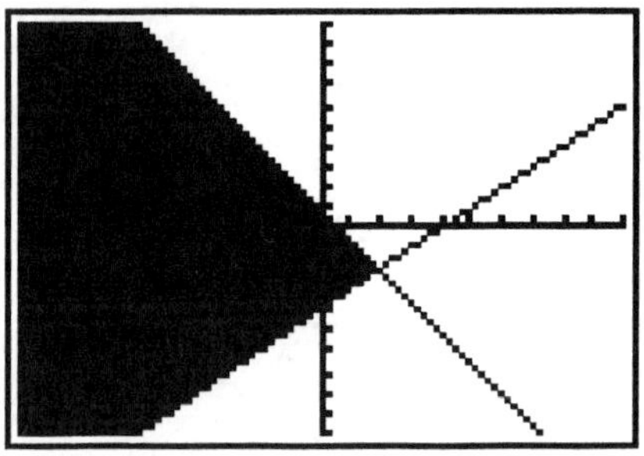

Figure 5.35: Graphs of $1-\frac{3x}{2} \geq y$ and $y > x-4$

Next press F1 to trace along the boundaries of the inequality. Notice that the Casio 7700 displays coordinates appropriately as inequalities. Zooming is also available in inequality graphing mode.

When you have concluded your work with inequality graphs, press MODE MODE + to restore your calculator to rectangular graphing mode.

Technology Tip: Since you can change the mode of the Casio 7700 at any time, you can graph inequalities and functions together at the same time. Simply change to inequality mode (MODE MODE ÷) before entering an inequality; then change to rectangular graphing mode (MODE MODE +) before graphing a function. You can combine them on a single command line with the SHIFT ↲ keys.

5.4 Trigonometry

5.4.1 Degrees and Radians: The trigonometric functions can be applied to angles measured either in radians or degrees, but you should take care that the Casio 7700 is configured for whichever measure you need. Press M Disp to see the current setting. To change the default angle measure, press SHIFT DRG for a menu of options. Press F1 for degree measure or F2 for radian measure, then press EXE to make it so.

It's a good idea to check the angle measure setting before executing a calculation that depends on a particular measure. You may change a mode setting at any time and not interfere with pending calculations. Try the following keystrokes to see this in action.

Expression	*Keystrokes*	*Display*
$\sin 45^\circ$	SHIFT DRG F1 EXE SIN 45 EXE	.7071067812
$\sin \pi^\circ$	SIN SHIFT π EXE	.05480366515
$\sin \pi$	SHIFT DRG F2 EXE SIN SHIFT π EXE	0
$\sin 45$	SIN 45 EXE	.8509035245
$\sin \frac{\pi}{6}$	SIN (SHIFT π $a^b\!/\!_c$ 6) EXE	.5

The first line of keystrokes sets the Casio 7700 in degree mode and calculates the sine of 45 *degrees*. While the calculator is still in degree mode, the second line of keystrokes calculates the sine of π *degrees*, 3.1415°. The third line changes to radian mode just before calculating the sine of π *radians*. The fourth line calculates the sine of 45 *radians* (the calculator is already in radian mode).

The Casio 7700 makes it possible to mix degrees and radians in a calculation. Execute these keystrokes to calculate $\tan 45^\circ + \sin \frac{\pi}{6}$ as shown in Figure 5.36: TAN 45 SHIFT DRG F1 + SIN (SHIFT π ÷ 6) F2 EXE. Do you get 1.5 whether your calculator is set *either* in degree mode *or* in radian mode?

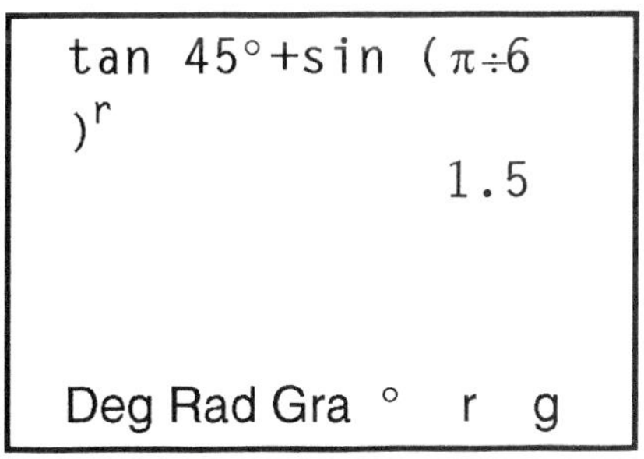

Figure 5.36: Angle measure

5.4.2 Graphs of Trigonometric Functions: When you graph a trigonometric function, you need to pay careful attention to the choice of graph window. For example, graph $y=\frac{\sin 30x}{30}$ in the standard viewing rectangle. Trace along the curve to see where it is. Zoom in to a better window, or use the period and amplitude to establish better RANGE values.

Technology Tip: Since $\pi \approx 3.1$, set Xmin = 0 and Xmax = 6.3 to cover the interval from 0 to 2π.

5.5 Differentiation

5.5.1 Limits: Suppose you need to find this limit: $\lim_{x\to 0}\frac{\sin 4x}{x}$. Plot the graph of $f(x)=\frac{\sin 4x}{x}$ in a convenient viewing rectangle that contains the point where the function appears to intersect the line $x=0$ (because you want the limit as $x\to 0$). Your graph should lend support to the conclusion that $\lim_{x\to 0}\frac{\sin 4x}{x}=4$.

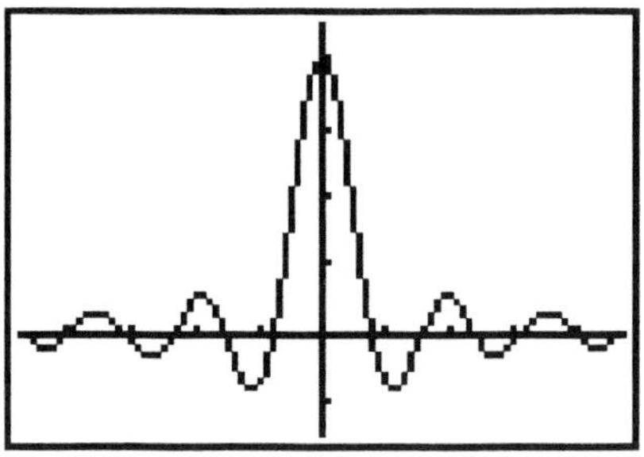

Figure 5.37: Checking $\lim_{x\to 0}\frac{\sin 4x}{x}=4$

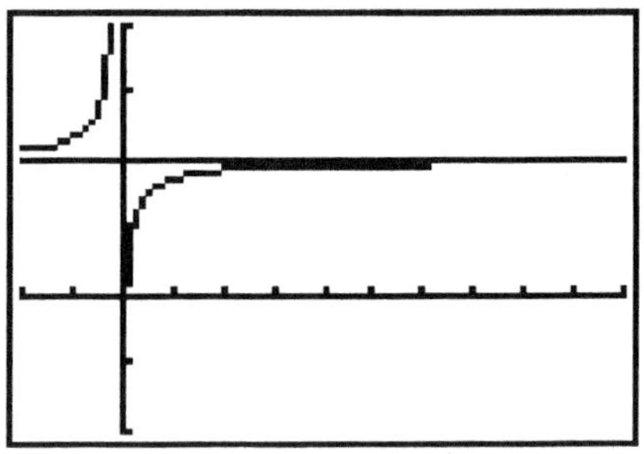

Figure 5.38: Checking $\lim_{x\to \infty}\frac{2x-1}{x+1}=2$

To test the reasonableness of the conclusion that $\lim_{x\to \infty}\frac{2x-1}{x+1}=2$, evaluate the function $f(x)=\frac{2x-1}{x+1}$ for several large positive values of x (since you want the limit as $x\to\infty$). For example, evaluate $f(100)$, $f(1000)$, and $f(10{,}000)$. Another way to test the reasonableness of this result is to examine the graph of $f(x)=\frac{2x-1}{x+1}$ in a viewing rectangle that extends over large values of x. See, as in Figure 5.38 (where the viewing rectangle extends horizontally from -20 to 100), whether the graph is asymptotic to the horizontal line y = 2 (both $y=\frac{2x-1}{x+1}$ and y = 2 are graphed together).

5.5.2 Numerical Derivatives: The derivative of a function *f* at *x* can be defined as the limit of the slopes of secant lines, so $f'(x) = \lim_{\Delta x \to 0} \frac{f(x+\Delta x) - f(x-\Delta x)}{2\Delta x}$. And for small values of Δx, the expression $\frac{f(x+\Delta x) - f(x-\Delta x)}{2\Delta x}$ gives a good approximation to the limit.

As an example, approximate the derivative $f'(2.5)$ of the function $f(x) = x^3$ with Δx = 0.001. First store x^3 in the function memory as f_1 (press X,θ,T x^y 3 SHIFT ⊞-MEM F1 1 EXE) and set D, for the increment Δx, as 0.001 (press .001 → ALPHA D EXE). Also, make x = 2.5. Then execute these keystrokes: X,θ,T + ALPHA D → X,θ,T SHIFT ↵ SHIFT ⊞-MEM F3 1 → ALPHA B SHIFT ↵ X,θ,T - 2 ALPHA D → X,θ,T SHIFT ↵ F3 1 → ALPHA C SHIFT ↵ (ALPHA B - ALPHA C) ÷ 2 ALPHA D. Finally, press EXE to calculate $f'(2.5)$ for $f(x) = x^3$.

Right now, you should save all this so that you may use it again with other functions. Press ◀ SHIFT ⊞-MEM F3 6 to save it as f_6. In the future, store an expression as f_1, set D to be 0.001 and x to be some value, and approximate the numerical derivative $f'(x)$ simply by recalling f_6.

You may also want to save these commands as a short program. See Section 5.9 or your calculator's manual for further information on programming the Casio 7700. Section 5.9 also contains a useful program that plots both a function and its first derivative together.

5.5.3 Newton's Method: With your Casio 7700, you may iterate using Newton's Method to find the zeros of a function. Recall that Newton's Method determines each successive approximation by the formula $x_{n+1} = x_n - \frac{f(x_n)}{f'(x_n)}$.

As an example of the technique, consider $f(x) = 2x^3 + x^2 - x + 1$. Store this expression in the function memory as f_1. A look at its graph suggests that it has a zero near x = -1, so start the iteration by storing -1 for x. Now press these keystrokes to modify the series of commands that were stored above as f_6: AC SHIFT ⊞-MEM F2 6 → ALPHA N. And store these new commands back as f_6. Then execute these keystrokes for Newton's Method: AC SHIFT ⊞-MEM F2 6 SHIFT ↵ X,θ,T - F3 1 ÷ ALPHA N → X,θ,T. You may also wish to store these commands in the function memory as f_5. Press ENTER repeatedly until two successive approximations differ by less than some predetermined value, say 0.0001. Note that each time you press ENTER, the Casio 7700 will use its *current* value of x, and that value is changing as you continue the iteration. By the way, Newton's Method finds a root of $f(x) = 2x^3 + x^2 - x + 1$ at $x \approx$ -1.23375.

Technology Tip: Newton's Method is sensitive to your seed value for x, so look carefully at the function's graph to make a good first estimate. Also, remember that the method sometimes fails to converge!

You may want to save the Newton's Method formula as a short program. See Section 5.9 or your calculator's manual for further information on programming the Casio 7700.

5.6 Sequences

5.6.1 Iteration: The Ans feature enables you to perform iterations to evaluate a function repeatedly. As an example, calculate $\frac{n-1}{3}$ for $n = 27$. Then calculate $\frac{n-1}{3}$ for n = the answer to the previous calculation. Continue to use each answer as n in the *next* calculation. Here are keystrokes to accomplish this iteration on the Casio 7700 calculator (see the results in Figure 5.39). Notice that when you use Ans in place of n in a formula, it is sufficient to press EXE to continue an iteration.

Iteration	*Keystrokes*	*Display*
1	27 EXE	27
2	(Ans - 1) ÷ 3 EXE	8.666666667
3	EXE	2.555555556
4	EXE	.5185185185
5	EXE	-.1604938272

Press EXE several more times and see what happens with this iteration. You may wish to try it again with a different starting value.

```
27
                27
(Ans-1)/3
       8.666666667
       2.555555556
       .5185185185
      -.1604938272
```

Figure 5.39: Iteration

5.6.2 Arithmetic and Geometric Sequences: Use iteration with the Ans variable to determine the n-th term of a sequence. For example, find the 18th term of an *arithmetic* sequence whose first term is 7 and whose common difference is 4. Enter the first term 7, then start the progression with the recursion formula, Ans + 4 EXE. This yields the 2nd term, so press EXE sixteen more times to find the 18th term. For a *geometric* sequence whose common ratio is 4, start the progression with Ans × 4 EXE.

Of course, you could also use the *explicit* formula for the n-th term of an arithmetic sequence, $t_n = a + (n-1)d$. First enter values for the variables a, d, and n, then evaluate the formula by pressing ALPHA A + (ALPHA N - 1) ALPHA D EXE. For a geometric sequence whose n-th term is given by

$t_n = a \cdot r^{n-1}$, enter values for the variables a, r, and n, then evaluate the formula by pressing ALPHA A ALPHA R ^ (ALPHA N - 1) EXE.

5.7 Integration

5.7.1 Approximating Definite Integrals: The Casio 7700 has the function SHIFT $\int dx$ that uses Simpson's Rule with 2^n subdivisions (where n is an integer from 1 through 9) to approximate an integral. So to find a numerical approximation to $\int_0^1 \cos x^2 dx$ with $n = 5$ (that is, with $2^5 = 32$ subdivisions), press SHIFT $\int dx$ COS X,T,θ SHIFT x² SHIFT , 0 SHIFT , 1 SHIFT , 5) ENTER. The format here is ∫(*expression, lower limit, upper limit, integer*).

See Section 5.9 for a sample program that uses left and right Riemann Sums as well as the Midpoint Rule, the Trapezoid Rule, and Simpson's Rule to enable the Casio 7700 to approximate definite integrals.

5.7.2 Areas: You may approximate the area under the graph of a function $y = f(x)$ between $x = A$ and $x = B$ with your Casio 7700. For example, here are keystrokes for finding the area under the graph of the function $y = \cos x^2$ between $x = 0$ and $x = 1$. This area is represented by the definite integral $\int_0^1 \cos x^2 dx$. Since the Casio 7700 employs Simpson's Rule with 2^n subdivisions , it is also necessary to specify some integer n from 1 through 9; in this example, we'll take $n = 6$ for $2^6 = 64$ subdivisions. So store $\cos x^2$ in function memory f_1, clear the graph window with SHIFT F5 EXE, and execute these keystrokes: SHIFT G-∫dx SHIFT ⊞-MEM F3 1 SHIFT , 0 SHIFT , 1 SHIFT , 6 EXE. The region under the graph between the lower limit and the upper limit is shaded and the area is displayed as in Figure 5.40.

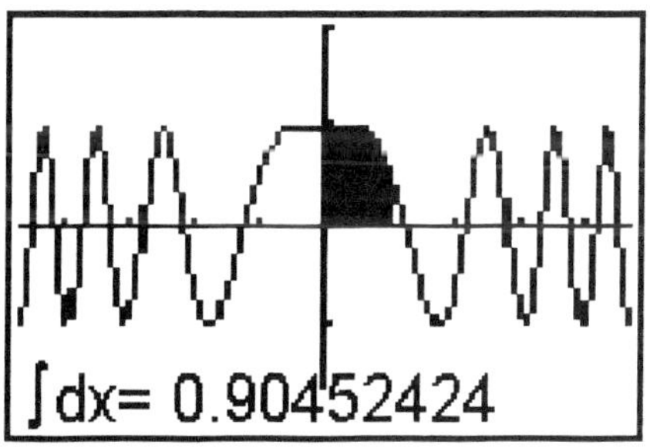

Figure 5.40: G-∫dx

Technology Tip: Suppose that you want to find the area between two functions, $y = f(x)$ and $y = g(x)$, from $x = A$ to $x = B$. If $f(x) \geq g(x)$ for $A \leq x \leq B$, then store the expression $f(x) - g(x)$ as f_1 and proceed as before to find the required area.

5.8 Parametric and Polar Graphs

5.8.1 Graphing Parametric Equations: The Casio 7700 plots parametric equations as easily as it plots functions. Just press MODE MODE × to set the calculator in parametric mode. Be sure, if the independent parameter is an angle measure, that angle measure has been set to whichever you need, Rad or Deg.

For example, here are the keystrokes needed to graph the parametric equations $x = \cos^3 t$ and $y = \sin^3 t$. First check that angles are currently being measured in radians. Change to parametric mode and press GRAPH (COS X,θ,T) x^y 3 SHIFT , (SIN X,θ,T) x^y 3) EXE. Now, when you press the variable key X,θ,T, you get a T because the calculator is in parametric mode.

Press RANGE RANGE to see that, in the standard window, the values of T go from 0 to 2π in steps of $\frac{2\pi}{100}$=.0628, with the view from -4.7 to 4.7 in the horizontal direction and -3.1 to 3.1 in the vertical. But here in Figure 5.41, the viewing rectangle has been changed to extend from -2 to 2 in both directions.

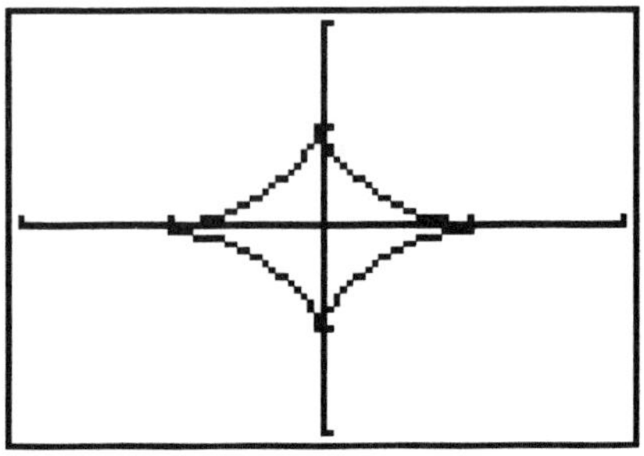

Figure 5.41: Parametric graph of $x = \cos^3 t$ and $y = \sin^3 t$

You may ZOOM and TRACE along parametric graphs just as you did with function graphs. As you trace along this graph, notice that the cursor moves in the *counterclockwise* direction as T increases.

When you are done working with parametric graphs, press MODE MODE + to restore your calculator to its rectangular graphing mode.

Technology Tip: Since you can change the mode of the Casio 7700 at any time, you can combine parametric graphs with function and inequality graphs on a single command line with the SHIFT ↵ keys.

5.8.2 Rectangular-Polar Coordinate Conversion: Convertion between rectangular and polar coordinate systems is accomplished directly through keystrokes on the Casio 7700. These functions use the current angle measure setting, so it is a good idea to check the default angle measure before any conversion. Of course, you may override the current angle measure setting, as explained in Section 5.4.1. For the following examples, the Casio 7700 is set to radian measure.

The Casio 7700 uses I and J to store the results of a conversion. So going *from* rectangular *to* polar coordinates, you get $(r,\theta)=(\mathrm{I},\mathrm{J})$. Going the other way, *from* polar *to* rectangular coordinates, you get $(x,y)=(\mathrm{I},\mathrm{J})$.

Given rectangular coordinates $(x, y)=(4,-3)$, convert *from* these rectangular coordinates *to* polar coordinates (r,θ) by pressing SHIFT Pol(4 SHIFT , - 3) EXE. The value of r is displayed; press ALPHA J EXE to display the value of θ. The polar coordinates are (5, -.6435).

Suppose $(r,\theta)=(3,\pi)$. To convert *from* these polar coordinates *to* rectangular coordinates (x, y), press SHIFT Rec(3 SHIFT , SHIFT π) EXE. The x-coordinate is displayed; press ALPHA J EXE to display the y-coordinate. The rectangular coordinates are (-3, 0).

```
Pol(4,-3)
                   5
J
     -0.6435011088
Rec(3,π)
                  -3
J
```

Figure 5.42: Coordinate conversions

5.8.3 Graphing Polar Equations: The Casio 7700 graphs a polar function when you write it in polar form. For example, to graph $r=4\sin\theta$, first change to polar mode by pressing MODE MODE -. Choose a good viewing rectangle and an appropriate range for the parameter θ.

Press RANGE RANGE to see that, in the standard window, the values of θ go from 0 to 2π in steps of $\frac{2\pi}{100}=0628$, with the view from -4.7 to 4.7 in the horizontal direction and -3.1 to 3.1 in the vertical. But for the graph in Figure 5.43, the viewing rectangle has been changed to extend from -6 to 6 horizontally and from -4 to 4 vertically.

Trace along this graph to see the polar coordinates of the cursor's location displayed at the bottom of the window. Zooming works just the same as before.

When you have concluded your work with polar graphs, press MODE MODE + to restore your calculator to its rectangular graphing mode.

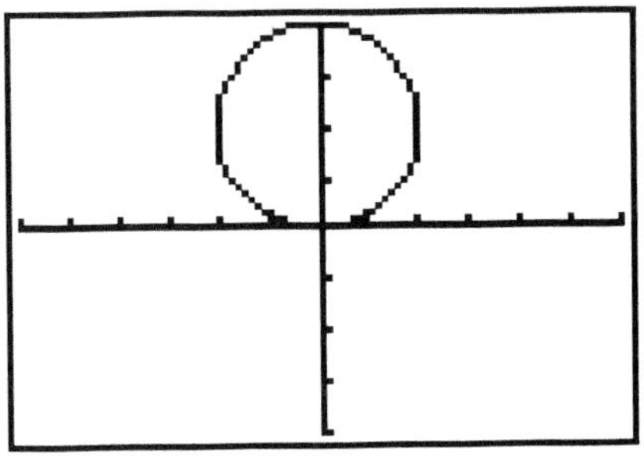

Figure 5.43: Polar graph of $r = 4\sin\theta$

Technology Tip: As with parametric and inequality graphs, you can combine polar graphs with other graphs on a single command line by using the SHIFT ↵ keys.

5.10 Programming

5.10.1 Entering a Program: The Casio 7700 is a programmable calculator that can store sequences of commands for later replay. Here are two examples to show you how to enter useful programs. One program performs numerical integration by several methods: left and right Riemann Sums as well as the Midpoint Rule, the Trapezoid Rule, and Simpson's Rule. The second program plots a function together with its derivative.

Press MODE 2 to write a program. You start with the program list. The Casio 7700 has space for up to 38 programs, each named by a number or letter. If a program location is not used, the word *empty* appears to the right of its name in the list. Press the up or down arrow keys to move the cursor to an empty program area; you may also press the key corresponding to a program's name and jump directly there. For example, to go to program 5, press 5; to edit program B, press ALPHA B.

When the cursor is blinking next to the program area you've chosen, press EXE to edit that program.

Now enter a descriptive title, so press SHIFT A-LOCK and name this program INTEGRAL. Press ALPHA to cancel the alpha lock. Then press EXE to begin writing the actual program. If you do not enter a title, the first line of the program appears in the program list.

Any command you could enter directly in the Casio 7700's home screen can be entered as a line in a program. There are also special programming commands.

Write the program INTEGRAL by pressing the keystrokes given in the listing below.

Program Line	*Keystrokes*
"Lower Limit"? → A	SHIFT A-LOCK F2 L O W E R SPACE L I M I T F2 ALPHA SHIFT PRGM F4 → ALPHA A EXE

displays *Lower Limit?* on the Casio 7700 screen and
waits for you to input a value that will be assigned to the variable A

"Upper Limit"? → B	SHIFT A-LOCK F2 U P P E R SPACE L I M I T F2 ALPHA F4 → ALPHA B EXE
"Subdivisions"? → N	SHIFT A-LOCK F2 S U B D I V I S I O N S F2 ALPHA F4 → ALPHA N EXE
(B - A)/2N → D	(ALPHA B - ALPHA A) ÷ 2 ALPHA N → ALPHA D EXE

calculates $\frac{1}{2}\Delta x$ and stores its value as D

0 → L	0 → ALPHA L EXE

uses the variable L with the left Riemann Sum

0 → M	0 → ALPHA M EXE

uses the variable M with the Midpoint Rule

0 → C	0 → ALPHA C EXE

uses the variable C to keep track of the subdivisions

A → X	ALPHA A → X,θ,T EXE

starts off at the lower limit

"Riemann Sums"	SHIFT A-LOCK F2 R I E M A N N SPACE S U M S F2 ALPHA EXE
Lbl 1	F1 F3 1 EXE

jumping point for the Goto command below

L + f1 → L	ALPHA L + SHIFT F-MEM F3 1 → ALPHA L EXE

adds the value of the function at the *left* endpoint of the current subdivision

X + D → X	X,θ,T + ALPHA D → X,θ,T EXE

increments by $\frac{1}{2}\Delta x$ to the *midpoint* of the subdivision

M + f1 → M	ALPHA M + SHIFT F-MEM F3 1 → ALPHA M EXE

adds the value of the function at the *midpoint* of the current subdivision

X + D → X   x,θ,T + ALPHA D → x,θ,T EXE

increments by another $\frac{1}{2}\Delta x$ to the left endpoint of the *next* subdivision

C + 1 → C   ALPHA C + 1 → ALPHA C EXE

counts up one subdivision

C < N ⇒ Goto 1   ALPHA C SHIFT PRGM F2 F4 ALPHA N PRE F1 F1 F2 1 EXE

tests whether the *last* subdivision has been reached:

in case not, then go back to the line Lbl 1 above and calculate another rectangular area; if yes, continue on to the next line

" Left"   SHIFT A-LOCK F2 SPACE L E F T F2 ALPHA EXE

2DL → L   2 ALPHA D ALPHA L → ALPHA L EXE

calculates left Riemann Sum

L◢   ALPHA L PRE F5

during program execution, waits for you to press EXE

" Right"   SHIFT A-LOCK F2 SPACE R I G H T F2 ALPHA EXE

L + 2Df_1 → R   ALPHA L + 2 ALPHA D SHIFT F-MEM F3 1 → ALPHA R EXE

A → X   ALPHA A → x,θ,T EXE

R - 2Df_1 → R   ALPHA R - 2 ALPHA D F3 1 → ALPHA R EXE

calculates right Riemann Sum

R◢   ALPHA R SHIFT PRGM F5

"Midpoint Rule"   SHIFT A-LOCK F2 M I D P O I N T SPACE R U L E F2 ALPHA EXE

2DM → M   2 ALPHA D ALPHA M → ALPHA M EXE

calculates numerical integral by Midpoint Rule

M◢   ALPHA M F5

"Trapezoid Rule"   SHIFT A-LOCK F2 T R A P E Z O I D SPACE R U L E F2 ALPHA EXE

(L + R)/2 → T   (ALPHA L + ALPHA R) ÷ 2 → ALPHA T EXE

calculates numerical integral by Trapezoid Rule (average left and right Riemann Sums)

T◢	ALPHA T F5
"Simpsons Rule"	SHIFT Ⓐ-LOCK F2 S I M P S O N S SPACE R U L E F2 ALPHA EXE
(2M + T)/3 → S	(2 ALPHA M + ALPHA T) ÷ 3 → ALPHA S EXE

calculates numerical integral by Simpson's Rule ($\frac{2}{3}$ Midpoint and $\frac{1}{3}$ Trapezoid)

S	ALPHA S EXE

When you have finished, press MODE 1 to leave the program editor and restore the calculator to RUN mode for calculations and program execution.

Here is a short program that enables the Casio 7700 to plot both a function and its derivative together. Name this program GDERIV and enter it into your calculator's memory by pressing the keystrokes in the listing below.

Program Line	*Keystrokes*
Range -4.7, 4.7, 1, -3.1, 3.1, 1	Range -4.7 SHIFT , 4.7 SHIFT , 1 SHIFT , -3.1 SHIFT , 3.1 SHIFT , 1 EXE

sets up the standard graphing window

.001 → D	.001 → ALPHA D EXE

uses $\Delta x = 0.001$ for approximating derivatives

Graph Y = f_1	Graph SHIFT Ⓕ-MEM F3 1 EXE

graphs the function stored as f_1

-4.7 → A	-4.7 → ALPHA A EXE

starts off at the left edge of the standard graphing window

Lbl 1	SHIFT PRGM F1 F3 1 EXE
Line	SHIFT F4 EXE

draws a segment between the last two plotted points

A + D → X	ALPHA A + ALPHA D → X,θ,T EXE
f_1 → B	SHIFT Ⓕ-MEM F3 1 → ALPHA B EXE
A - D → X	ALPHA A - ALPHA D → X,θ,T EXE
f_1 → C	F3 1 → ALPHA C EXE

(B - C)/2D → Y (ALPHA B - ALPHA C) ÷ 2 ALPHA D → ALPHA Y EXE

the preceding five commands approximate the derivative as in Section 5.5.2

Plot A,Y SHIFT F3 ALPHA A SHIFT , ALPHA Y EXE

plots a point on the graph of the derivative

A + .1 → A ALPHA A + .1 → ALPHA A EXE

moves on to the next point

A ≤ 4.7 ⇒ Goto 1 ALPHA A SHIFT PRGM F2 F6 4.7 PRE F1 F1 F2 1 EXE

tests whether the right edge of the standard graphing window has been reached

Line SHIFT F4

If you want to clear a program, press MODE 3. Move to the program you want to delete, and when the cursor is blinking next to its name, press AC to remove it from the calculator's memory.

5.10.2 Executing a Program: To execute one of the programs just entered, press SHIFT PRGM F3 and then the number or letter that it was named; finally, press EXE to run it. If you have forgotten its name, you must go back to program writing mode to find it.

The program INTEGRAL has been written to calculate $\int_A^B f(x)\,dx$ for N subdivisions of the interval $[A, B]$. You must store the expression $f(x)$ as f_1 before running this program. The program itself will prompt you for A, B, and N.

The program GDERIV plots a function and its derivative together in the standard Casio 7700 graph window. It expects that you stored the expression $f(x)$ as f_1 beforehand. After the program has run, press G↔T to view the graphs.

If you need to interrupt a program during execution, press AC.

The instruction manual for your Casio 7700 gives detailed information about programming. Refer to it to learn more about programming and how to use other features of your calculator.

CHAPTER 6

Sharp EL-9200/9300 Graphing Scientific Calculator

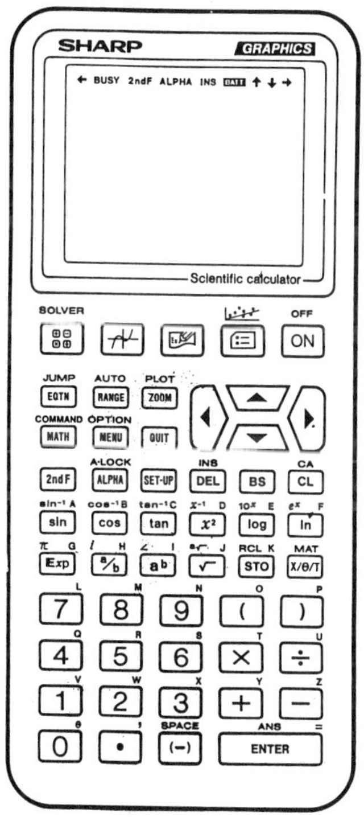

6.1 Getting started with the Sharp EL-9200/9300

6.1.1 Basics: Press the ON key to begin using your Sharp EL-9200/9300 calculator. If you need to adjust the display contrast, first press 2ndF and then press OPTION. Next press + (the *plus* key) to increase the contrast or - (the *minus* key) to decrease the contrast. Leave this menu by pressing QUIT. When you have finished with the calculator, turn it off to conserve battery power by pressing 2ndF and then OFF.

Figure 6.1: Operation mode keys

The four keys left of ON are used to set the Sharp EL-9200/9300's operation mode: for calculations, graphs, programming, statistics, statistical graphs, and solving equations (EL-9300 only). Press the first mode key, the one with arithmetic operators, for *calculation* mode. You need to press the calculation mode key before performing computations or evaluations.

Check the Sharp EL-9200/9300's settings by pressing SETUP. If necessary, use ▲ (the *up* arrow key) or ▼ (the *down* arrow key) to highlight a setting you want to change; you may also jump to a setting by pressing its letter. Next press ENTER or ▶ (the *right* arrow key) to move to a sub-menu of options; use an arrow key to move to your choice and press ENTER to put it into effect. Once again, you may just jump to an option by pressing its number. To start with, select these options as illustrated in Figure 6.2 by pressing the indicated keys: radian measure, press B 2; floating decimal point, press C 1; rectangular coordinates, E 1; one-line editing, F 2; decimal answers, G 1. Details on alternative options will be given later in this guide. For now, leave the SETUP menu by pressing QUIT. You may return to this menu at any time.

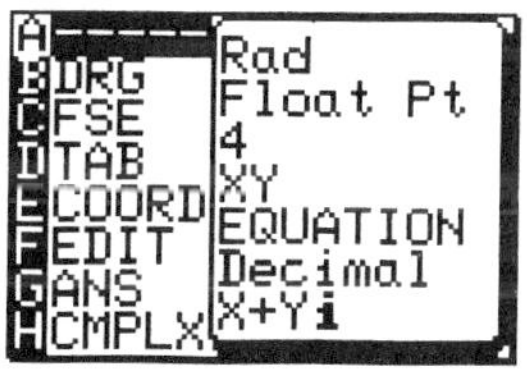

Figure 6.2: SETUP menu

Now press MENU 1 for real-number calculation mode.

6.1.2 Editing: One advantage of one-line editing on the Sharp EL-9200/9300 is that up to 8 lines are visible at a time , so you can *see* a long calculation. For example, type this sum (see Figure 6.3):

$$1 + 2 + 3 + 4 + 5 + 6 + 7 + 8 + 9 + 10 + 11 + 12 + 13 + 14 + 15 + 16 + 17 + 18 + 19 + 20$$

Then press ENTER to see the answer, too.

Often we do not notice a mistake until we see how unreasonable an answer is. The Sharp EL-9200/9300 permits you to re-display an entire calculation, edit it easily, then execute the *corrected* calculation.

Suppose you had typed 12 + 34 + 56 as in Figure 6.3 but had *not* yet pressed ENTER, when you realize that 34 should have been 74. Simply press ◀ (the *left* arrow key) as many times as necessary to move the blinking cursor left to 3, then type 7 to write over it. On the other hand, if 34 should have been 384, move the cursor back to 4, press 2ndF INS (the cursor changes to a blinking arrow) and then type 8 (inserts at the cursor position and other characters are pushed to the right). Press 2ndF INS again to cancel insert mode. If the 34 should have been 3 only, either move the cursor *onto* 4 and press DEL to delete it, or move the cursor just *after* the 4 and press BS to back space over it.

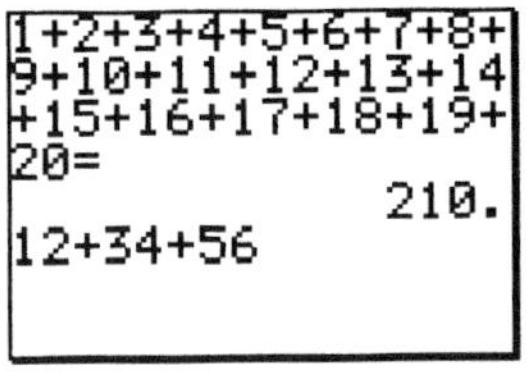

Figure 6.3: Editing expressions

Technology Tip: To move quickly to the *beginning* of an expression you are currently editing, press 2ndF ◀; to jump to the *end* of that expression, press 2ndF ▶.

Even if you had pressed ENTER, you may still edit the previous expression. Press CL and then any arrow key to *recall* the last expression that was entered. Pressing the *up* or *left* arrow key restores the previous expression with the cursor at the *end* of the line; pressing the *down* or *right* arrow key restores the last expression with the cursor at the *beginning* of the line. Now you can change it. In fact, the Sharp EL-9200/9300 retains many prior entries in a "last entry" storage area. Press 2ndF and an arrow key repeatedly to cycle through previous command lines that the calculator has remembered.

Technology Tip: When you need to evaluate a formula for different values of a variable, use the editing feature to simplify the process. For example, suppose you want to find the balance in an investment account if there is now \$5000 in the account and interest is compounded annually at the rate of 8.5%. The formula for the balance is $P(1+\frac{r}{n})^{nt}$, where P = principal, r = rate of interest (expressed as a decimal), n = number of times interest is compounded each year, and t = number of years. In our example, this becomes $5000(1+.085)^t$. Here are the keystrokes for finding the balance after t = 3, 5, and 10 years.

Years	*Keystrokes*	*Balance*
3	CL 5000 (1 + .085) a^b 3 ENTER	\$6386.45
5	◀ ◀ 5 ENTER	\$7518.28

10	◄ ◄ 10 ENTER	$11,304.92

Then to find the balance from the same initial investment but after 5 years when the annual interest rate is 7.5%, press these keys to change the last calculation above: ◄ ◄ DEL ◄ 5 ◄ ◄ ◄ ◄ ◄ 7 ENTER.

6.1.3 Key Functions: Most keys on the Sharp EL-9200/9300 offer access to more than one function, just as the keys on a computer keyboard can produce more than one letter ("g" and "G") or even quite different characters ("5" and "%"). The primary function of a key is indicated on the key itself, and you access that function by a simple press on the key.

To access the *second* function indicated in *yellow* above a key, first press 2ndF (an indicator appears at the top of the screen) and *then* press the key. For example, to calculate 5^{-1}, press 5 2ndF x^{-1} ENTER.

When you want to use a letter or other character printed in *blue* above a key, first press ALPHA (another indicator appears at the top of the screen) and then the key. For example, to use the letter K in a formula, press ALPHA K. If you need several letters in a row, press 2ndF A-LOCK, which is like CAPS LOCK on a computer keyboard, and then press all the letters you want. Remember to press ALPHA when you are finished and want to restore the keys to their primary functions.

6.1.4 Order of Operations: The Sharp EL-9200/9300 performs calculations according to the standard algebraic rules. Working outwards from inner parentheses, calculations are performed from left to right. Powers and roots are evaluated first, followed by multiplications and divisions, and then additions and subtractions.

Note that the Sharp EL-9200/9300 distinguishes between *subtraction* and the *negative sign*. If you wish to enter a negative number, it is necessary to use the (-) key. For example, you would evaluate $-5-(4\cdot-3)$ by pressing (-) 5 - (4 × (-) 3) ENTER to get 7.

Enter these expressions to practice using your Sharp EL-9200/9300.

Expression	*Keystrokes*	*Display*
$7-5\cdot3$	7 - 5 × 3 ENTER	-8
$(7-5)\cdot3$	(7 - 5) × 3 ENTER	6
$120-10^2$	120 - 10 x^2 ENTER	20
$(120-10)^2$	(120 - 10) x^2 ENTER	12100
$\frac{24}{2^3}$	24 ÷ 2 a^b 3 ENTER	3
$\left(\frac{24}{2}\right)^3$	(24 ÷ 2) a^b 3 ENTER	1728
$(7--5)\cdot-3$	(7 - (-) 5) × (-) 3 ENTER	-36

6.1.5 Algebraic Expressions and Memory: Your calculator can evaluate expressions such as $\frac{N(N+1)}{2}$ *after* you have entered a value for N. Suppose you want $N = 200$. Press 200 STO N to store the value 200 in memory location N. (The STO key prepares the Sharp EL-9200/9300 for an alphabetical entry, so it is *not* necessary to press ALPHA also. And there is no need to press ENTER at the end.) Whenever you use N in an expression, the calculator will substitute the value 200 until you make a change by storing *another* number in N. Next enter the expression $\frac{N(N+1)}{2}$ by typing ALPHA N (ALPHA N + 1) ÷ 2 ENTER. For $N = 200$, you will find that $\frac{N(N+1)}{2} = 20100$.

The contents of any memory location may be revealed by typing just its letter name and then ENTER. Another way to recall the value of N is to press 2ndF RCL N. And the Sharp EL-9200/9300 retains memorized values even when it is turned off, so long as its batteries are good.

6.1.6 Repeated Operations with ANS: The result of your *last* calculation is always stored in memory location ANS and replaces any previous result. This makes it easy to use the answer from one computation in another computation. For example, press 30 + 15 ENTER so that 45 is the last result displayed. Then press 2ndF ANS ÷ 9 ENTER and get 5 because $\frac{45}{9} = 5$.

With a function like division, you press the ÷ key *after* you enter an argument. For such functions, whenever you would start a new calculation with the previous answer followed by pressing the function key, you may press just the function key. So instead of 2ndF ANS ÷ 9 in the previous example, you could have pressed simply ÷ 9 to achieve the same result. This technique also works for these functions: + - × x^2 a^b $^a\!/_b$ 2ndF x^{-1}.

Here is a situation where this is especially useful. Suppose a person makes $5.85 per hour and you are asked to calculate earnings for a day, a week, and a year. Execute the given keystrokes to find the person's incomes during these periods (results are shown in Figure 6.4):

Pay period	*Keystrokes*	*Earnings*
8-hour day	5.85 × 8 ENTER	$46.80
5-day week	× 5 ENTER	$234
52-week year	× 52 ENTER	$12,168

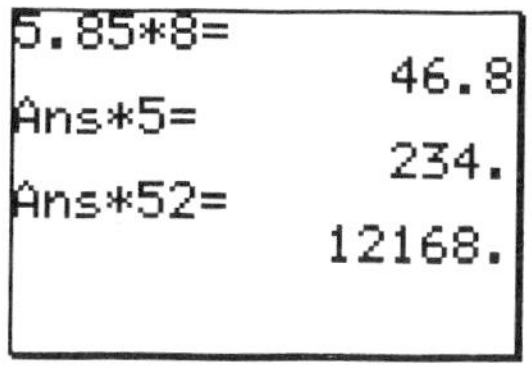

Figure 6.4: ANS variable

6.1.7 The* MATH *Menu: Operators and functions associated with a scientific calculator are available either immediately from the keys of the Sharp EL-9200/9300 or by 2ndF keys. You have direct key access to common arithmetic operations (x^2, $\sqrt{\ }$, 2ndF x^{-1}, a^b, 2ndF $\sqrt[a]{\ }$), trigonometric functions (sin, cos, tan) and their inverses (2ndF $\sin^{-1}$, 2ndF $\cos^{-1}$, 2ndF $\tan^{-1}$), exponential and logarithmic functions (log, 2ndF 10^x, ln, 2ndF e^x), and a famous constant (2ndF π).

A significant difference between the Sharp EL-9200/9300 and many scientific calculators is that the Sharp EL-9200/9300 requires the argument of a function *after* the function, as you would see a formula written in your textbook. For example, on the Sharp EL-9200/9300 you calculate $\sqrt{16}$ by pressing the keys $\sqrt{\ }$ 16 in that order.

Here are keystrokes for basic mathematical operations. Try them for practice on your Sharp EL-9200/9300.

Expression	*Keystrokes*	*Display*
$\sqrt{3^2+4^2}$	$\sqrt{\ }$ (3 x^2 + 4 x^2) ENTER	5
$2\frac{1}{3}$	2 + 3 2ndF x^{-1} ENTER	2.333333333
$\log 200$	LOG 200 ENTER	2.301029996
$2.34 \cdot 10^5$	2.34 × 2ndF 10^x 5 ENTER	234000
$\sqrt[3]{125}$	3 2ndF $\sqrt[a]{\ }$ 125 ENTER	5

Back in Section 6.1.1, you used the SETUP menu to select *one-line* editing. The Sharp EL-9200/9300 calculator also supports *equation* editing, so that mathematical expressions appear on the screen as they do in your textbook (see Figure 6.5 and Figure 6.6 for a comparison). Press SETUP F 1 ENTER to enable equation editing and once again execute the keystrokes listed above.

The equation editor displays "built-up" expressions and reduces the need for parentheses, but the calculator's response to keystrokes can be slower.

In equation editing, you terminate the scope of some functions by pressing ▶, instead of adding extra parentheses. For example, evaluate $\sqrt{3^2+4^2}+5^2$ with the following keystrokes in one-line editing: $\sqrt{\ }$ (3 x^2 + 4 x^2) + 5 x^2 ENTER. The answer is 50. Try these keystrokes again in equation editing and the answer is different because you are evaluating $\sqrt{(3^2+4^2)+5^2}$ and not $\sqrt{3^2+4^2}+5^2$ here. Now press these keys in the equation editor: √ 3 x² + 4 x² ► + 5 x² ENTER to get 50 again. In practice, simply watch the screen and the cursor to see when ► is needed during equation editing.

Additional mathematical operations and functions are available from the MATH menu (Figure 6.7). Press MATH to see the various options. You will learn in your mathematics textbook how to apply many of them. As an example, calculate $|-5|$ by pressing MATH A 1 (-) 5 ENTER. To leave the MATH menu and take no other action, press QUIT.

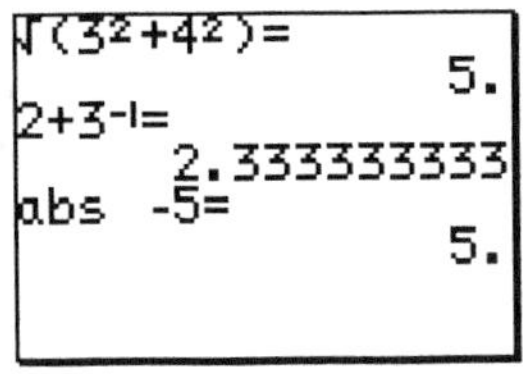

Figure 6.5: One-line editing

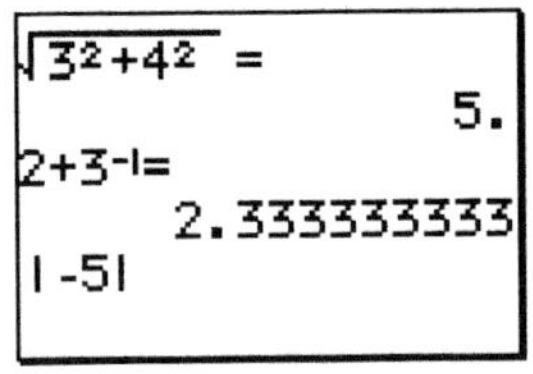

Figure 6.6: Equation editing

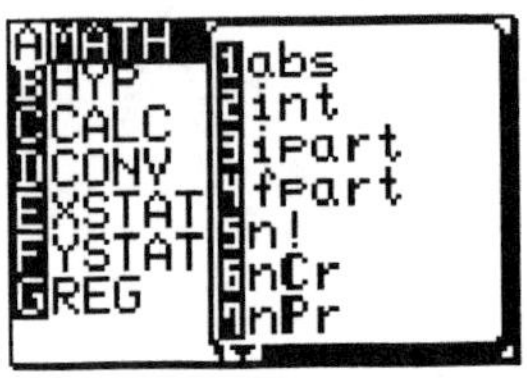

Figure 6.7: MATH menu

The *factorial* of a non-negative integer is the *product* of *all* the integers from 1 up to the given integer. The symbol for factorial is the exclamation point. So 4! (pronounced *four factorial*) is $1 \cdot 2 \cdot 3 \cdot 4 = 24$. You will learn more about applications of factorials in your textbook, but for now use the Sharp EL-9200/9300 to calculate 4! Press these keystrokes: 4 MATH A 5 ENTER.

Hyperbolic functions (sinh, cosh, and tanh) and their inverses are available from the HYP sub-menu of the MATH menu. For example, here are the keystrokes to calculate sinh 3: MATH B 1 3 ENTER.

6.2 Functions and Graphs

6.2.1 Evaluating Functions: Suppose you receive a monthly salary of \$1975 plus a commission of 10% of sales. Let x = your sales in dollars; then your wages W in dollars are given by the equation $W = 1975 + .10x$. If your January sales were \$2230 and your February sales were \$1865, what was your income during those months?

Here's how to use your Sharp EL-9200/9300 to perform this task. Let $x = 2230$ by pressing CL 2230 STO X/θ/T. (The X/θ/T key lets you enter the variable x easily without having to use the ALPHA key.) Then evaluate the expression $1975 + .10x$ for January's wages by pressing these keys: 1975 + .10 X/θ/T ENTER. Now set $x = 1865$ by pressing 1865 STO X/θ/T. These steps are shown in Figure 6.8. Recall the expression $1975 + .10x$ by pressing 2ndF ▲ *twice*, then press ENTER (see Figure 6.9) to find the February wages.

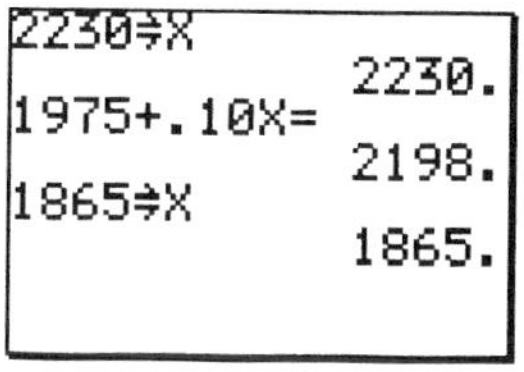

Figure 6.8: Evaluating a function

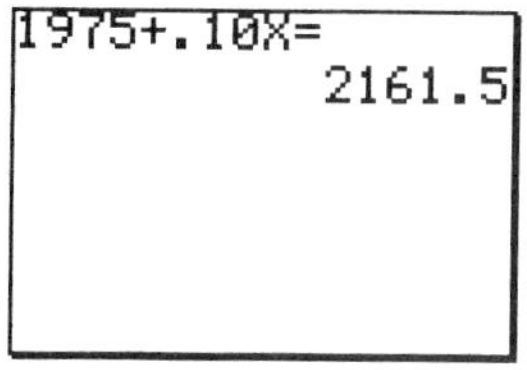

Figure 6.9: February's wages

Each time the Sharp EL-9200/9300 evaluates the function $1975 + .10x$, it uses the *current* value of x.

Technology Tip: The Sharp EL-9200/9300 does not require multiplication to be expressed between variables, so xxx means x^3. It is often easier to press two or three x's together than to search for the square key or the power key. Of course, expressed multiplication is also not required between a constant and a variable. Hence to enter $2x^3+3x^2-4x+5$ in the Sharp EL-9200/9300, you might save keystrokes and press just these keys: 2 X/θ/T X/θ/T X/θ/T + 3 X/θ/T X/θ/T - 4 X/θ/T + 5.

6.2.2 Functions in a Graph Window: Enter the graph mode of the Sharp EL-9200/9300 by pressing the second key in the top row. The ability to draw a graph contributes substantially to our ability to solve problems.

For example, here is how to graph $y=-x^3+4x$. First press the graph mode key and delete anything that may be there by moving with the up or down arrow key (in equation editing, press 2ndF and then the arrow key) to Y1 or to any of the other functions and pressing CL wherever necessary. Then, with the cursor on the top line Y1, press (-) X/θ/T a^b 3 + 4 X/θ/T to enter the function (as in Figure 6.10 for one-line editing and Figure 6.11 for equation editing).

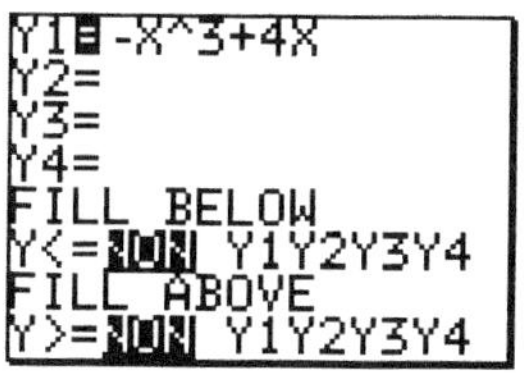

Figure 6.10: Graph entry - one-line editing

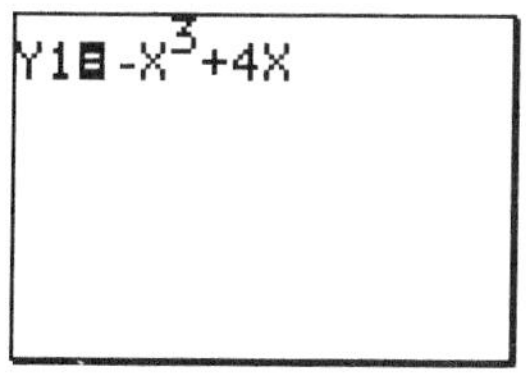

Figure 6.11: Graph entry - equation editing

Now press the graph mode key again and the Sharp EL-9200/9300 changes to a window with the graph of

$y=-x^3+4x$. You may return to edit the function by pressing either EQTN or MENU A and a number.

Your graph window may look like the one in Figure 6.12 or it may be different. Since the graph of $y=-x^3+4x$ extends infinitely far left and right and also infinitely far up and down, the Sharp EL-9200/9300 can display only a piece of the actual graph. This displayed rectangular part is called a *viewing rectangle*. You can easily change the viewing rectangle to enhance your investigation of a graph.

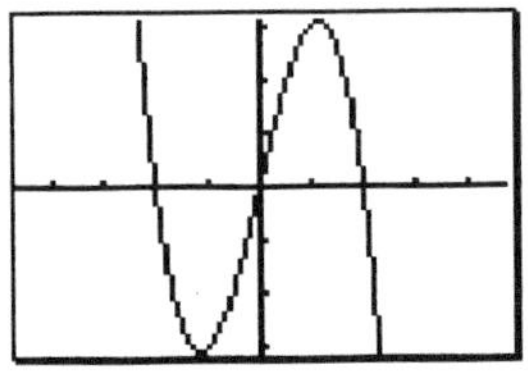

Figure 6.12: Graph of $y=-x^3+4x$

The viewing rectangle in Figure 6.12 shows the part of the graph that extends horizontally from -4.7 to 4.7 and vertically from -3.1 to 3.1. Press RANGE to see information about your viewing rectangle; press arrow keys to move between the X RANGE and the Y RANGE screens. Figures 6.13 and 6.14 show the RANGE screens that correspond to the viewing rectangle in Figure 6.12. This is the *default* viewing rectangle for the Sharp EL-9200/9300.

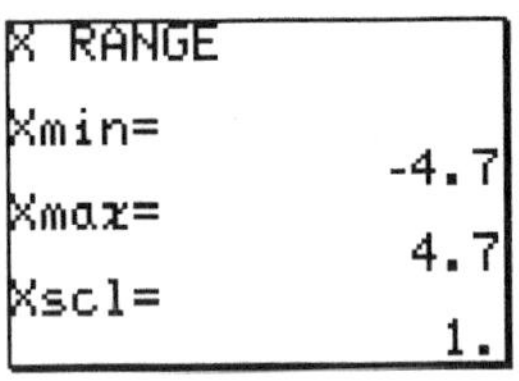

Figure 6.13: Default X RANGE

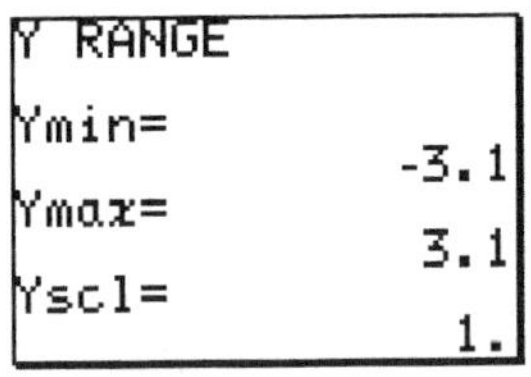

Figure 6.14: Default Y RANGE

The variables Xmin and Xmax are the minimum and maximum x-values of the viewing rectangle; Ymin and Ymax are its minimum and maximum y-values. Xscl and Yscl set the spacing between tick marks on the axes.

Use the arrow keys ▲ and ▼ to move up and down from one line to another in these lists; pressing the ENTER key will move down the list. Input a new value. The Sharp EL-9200/9300 will *not* permit a maximum that is *less* than the corresponding minimum. Also, remember to use the (-) key, not - (which is subtraction), when you want to enter a negative value. The following figures show different viewing rectangles with their ranges.

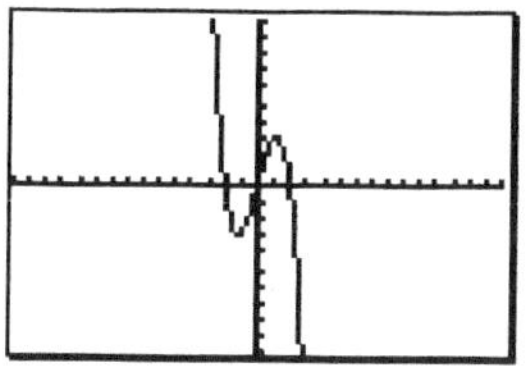

Figure 6.15: Window [-15, 15] by [-10, 10]

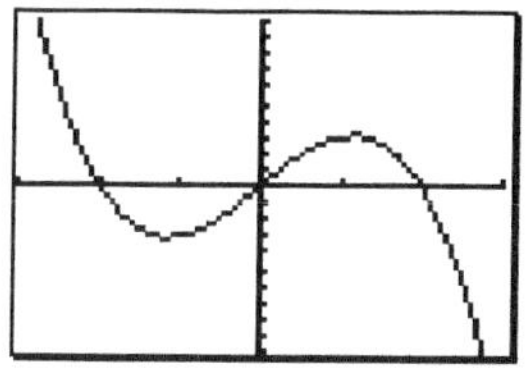

Figure 6.16: Window [-3, 3] by [-10, 10]

To set the range quickly to default values (see Figures 6.13 and 6.14), press RANGE MENU A ENTER. You may also set range values suitable for graphing particular functions, such as power and root functions (RANGE MENU B), exponential and logarithmic functions (RANGE MENU C), and trigonometric functions (RANGE MENU D).

Technology Tip: After you input a function, press 2ndF AUTO to draw the graph in a window with the current X RANGE values but automatically scaled in the vertical direction. This is an advantage when you are not sure how tall a viewing rectangle to set.

6.2.3 The Greatest Integer Function: The greatest integer function, written [[x]], gives the greatest *integer* less than or equal to a number x. On the Sharp EL-9200/9300, the greatest integer function is called int and is located by pressing MATH A 2 (see Figure 6.7). So calculate [[6.78]] = 6 by pressing the calculation mode key and then MATH A 2 6.78 ENTER.

To graph y = [[x]], press the graph mode key, move beside Y1, and press CLEAR MATH A 2 x/θ/T. Then press the graph mode key again to draw the graph. Figure 6.17 shows this graph in a viewing rectangle from -5 to 5 in both directions.

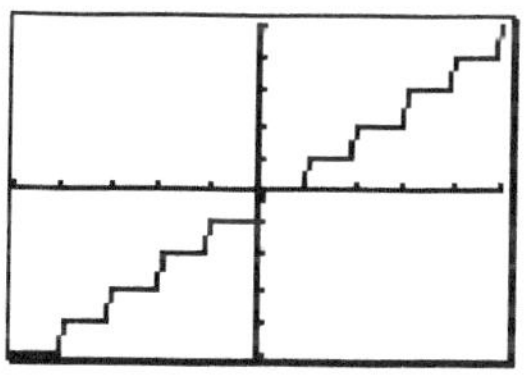

Figure 6.17: Connected graph of y = [[x]]

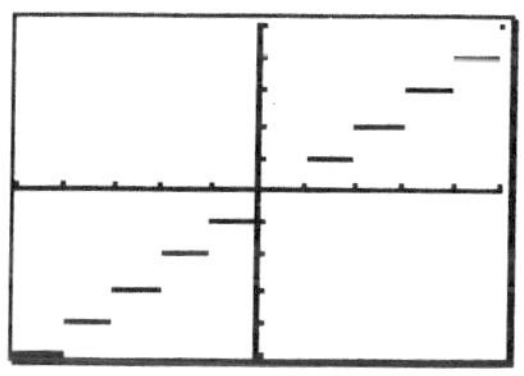

Figure 6.18: Dot graph of y = [[x]]

The true graph of the greatest integer function is a step graph, like the one in Figure 6.18. For the graph of y = [[x]], a segment should *not* be drawn between every pair of successive points. You can change from Connected line to Dot graph on the Sharp EL-9200/9300 by pressing MENU C 2. Restore the calculator to Connected by pressing MENU C 1.

6.2.4 Graphing a Circle: Here is a useful technique for graphs that are not functions, but that can be "split" into a top part and a bottom part, or into multiple parts. Suppose you wish to graph the circle whose equation is $x^2 + y^2 = 36$. First solve for y and get an equation for the top semicircle, $y = \sqrt{36 - x^2}$, and for the

bottom semicircle, $y = -\sqrt{36 - x^2}$. Then graph the two semicircles simultaneously.

The keystrokes to draw this circle's graph follow. Enter $\sqrt{36 - x^2}$ as Y1 and $-\sqrt{36 - x^2}$ as Y2 (see Figure 6.19) by pressing the graph mode key and then √ (36 - X/θ/T x^2) ENTER (-) √ (36 - X/θ/T x^2). Press the graph mode key again to draw them both.

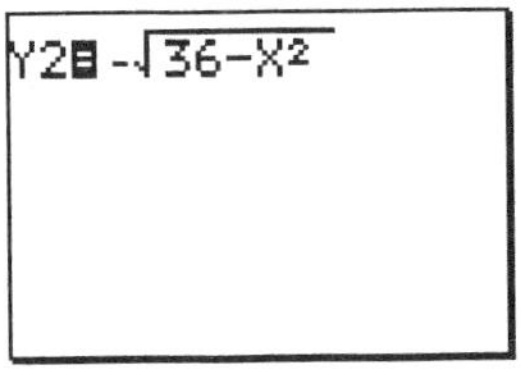

Figure 6.19: Bottom semicircle

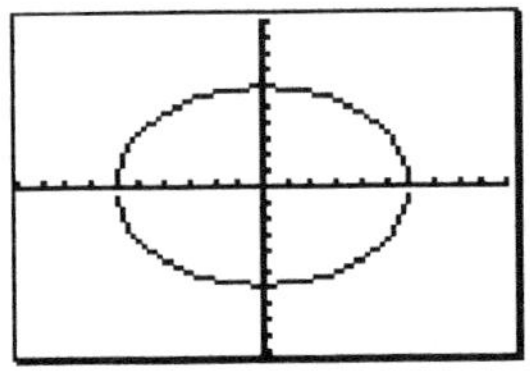

Figure 6.20: Circle's graph

If your range were set so that the viewing rectangle extends from -10 to 10 in both directions, your graph would look like Figure 6.20. Now this does *not* look like a circle, because the units along the axes are not the same. Press RANGE and change the viewing rectangle to extend from -12 to 12 in the horizontal direction and from -8 to 8 in the vertical direction and see a graph (Figure 6.21) that appears more circular.

Technology Tip: The way to get a circle's graph to look circular is to change the range variables so that the value of Ymax - Ymin is $\frac{2}{3}$ times Xmax - Xmin. The method works because the dimensions of the Sharp EL-9200/9300's display are such that the ratio of vertical to horizontal is approximately $\frac{2}{3}$.

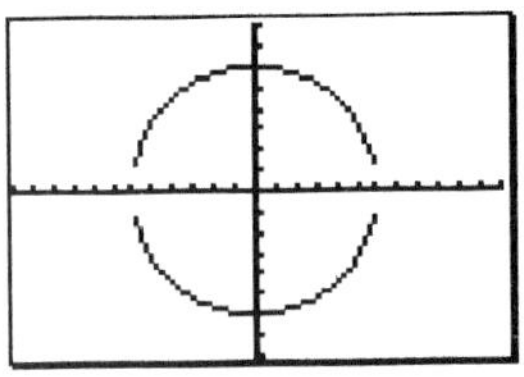

Figure 6.21: A circle

The two semicircles in Figure 6.21 do not meet because of an idiosyncrasy in the way the Sharp EL-9200/9300 plots a graph.

Technology Tip: A square viewing rectangle, in which units along both axes are the same, is also important when you want to judge whether two lines are perpendicular. The intersection of perpendicular lines will always *look* like a right angle in a square viewing rectangle.

6.2.5 TRACE: Graph $y = -x^3 + 4x$ in the default viewing rectangle. Press either of the arrow keys ◀ or ▶ and see the cursor move along the graph. The coordinates of the cursor's location are displayed at the bottom of the screen, as in Figure 6.22, in floating decimal format. The cursor is constrained to the function.

The coordinates that are displayed belong to points on the function's graph, so the y-coordinate is the calculated value of the function at the corresponding x-coordinate.

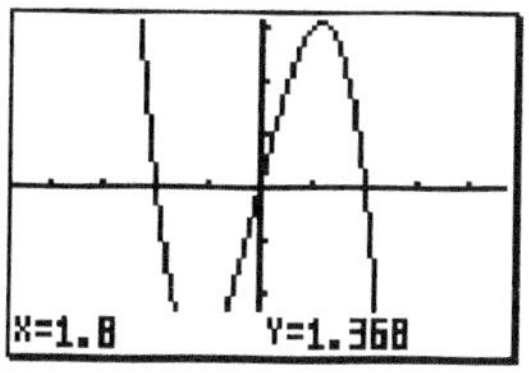

Figure 6.22: Trace on $y=-x^3+4x$

Press 2ndF ◀ or 2ndF ▶ to jump to the endpoints of the part of the graph that is displayed in a window. Remove the trace cursor and its coordinates from the graph window by pressing CL.

Now plot a second function, $y=-.25x$, along with $y=-x^3+4x$. Press MENU A 2 and enter $-.25x$ for Y2, then press the graphing mode key.

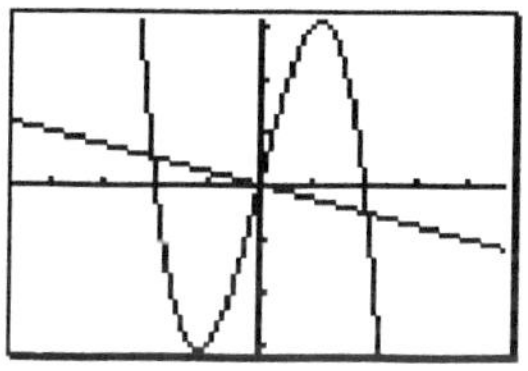

Figure 6.23: $y=-x^3+4x$ and $y=-.25x$

Note that the equal signs next to Y1 and Y2 are *both* highlighted. This means *both* functions will be graphed. Press MENU A 1, move the cursor directly on top of the equal sign next to Y1 and press ENTER. This equal sign should no longer be highlighted. Now press the graph mode key and see that only Y2 is plotted.

So up to 4 different functions may be stored in the Y= list and any combination of them may be graphed simultaneously. You can make a function active or inactive for graphing by pressing ENTER on its equal sign to highlight (activate) or remove the highlight (deactivate). Go back and do what is needed in order to graph Y1 but not Y2.

Now activate Y2 again so that both graphs are plotted. Press ◀ or ▶ and the cursor appears first on the graph of $y=-x^3+4x$ because it is Y1. Press ▲ to move the cursor vertically to the graph of $y=-.25x$; move the cursor back to $y=-x^3+4x$ by pressing ▼. Next press the right and left arrow keys to trace along the graph of $y=-.25x$. When more than one function is plotted, you can move the trace cursor vertically from one graph to another in this way.

Technology Tip: By the way, trace along the graph of $y=-.25x$ and press and hold either ◀ or ▶.

Eventually you will reach the left or right edge of the window. Keep pressing the arrow key and the Sharp EL-9200/9300 will allow you to continue the trace by panning the viewing rectangle. Check the RANGE screen to see that Xmin and Xmax are automatically updated.

The Sharp EL-9200/9300's display has 95 horizontal columns of pixels and 63 vertical rows. So when you trace a curve across a graph window, you are actually moving from Xmin to Xmax in 94 equal jumps, each called Δx. You would calculate the size of each jump to be $\Delta x = \frac{\text{Xmax} - \text{Xmin}}{94}$. Sometimes you may want the jumps to be friendly numbers like .1 or .25 so that, when you trace along the curve, the x-coordinates will be incremented by such a convenient amount. Just set your viewing rectangle for a particular increment Δx by making Xmax = Xmin + 94·Δx. For example, if you want Xmin = -5 and Δx = .3, set Xmax = -5 + 94·.3 = 23.2. Likewise, set Ymax = Ymin + 62·Δy if you want the vertical increment to be some special Δy.

To center your window around a particular point, say (h, k), and also have a certain Δx, set Xmin = h - 47·Δx and Xmax = h + 47·Δx. Likewise, make Ymin = k - 31·Δy and Ymax = k + 31·Δy. For example, to center a window around the origin, (0, 0), with both horizontal and vertical increments of .25, set the range so that Xmin = 0 - 47·.25 = -11.75, Xmax = 0 + 47·.25 = 11.75, Ymin = 0 - 31·.25 = -7.75, and Ymax = 0 + 31·.25 = 7.75.

The Sharp EL-9200/9300's standard window is already a friendly viewing rectangle, centered at the origin (0, 0) with $\Delta x = \Delta y = 0.1$.

See the benefit by first plotting $y = x^2 + 2x + 1$ in a graphing window extending from -5 to 5 in both directions. Trace near its y-intercept, which is (0, 1), and move towards its x-intercept, which is (-1, 0). Then initialize the range to the default window and trace again near the intercepts.

6.2.6 ZOOM: Plot again the two graphs, for $y = -x^3 + 4x$ and for $y = -.25x$. There appears to be an intersection near x = 2. The Sharp EL-9200/9300 provides several ways to enlarge the view around this point. You can change the viewing rectangle directly by pressing RANGE and editing the values of Xmin, Xmax, Ymin, and Ymax. Figure 6.24 shows a new window extending from 1 to 3 horizontally and from -2 to 1 vertically. Trace has been turned on and the coordinates of a point on $y = -x^3 + 4x$ that is close to the intersection are displayed.

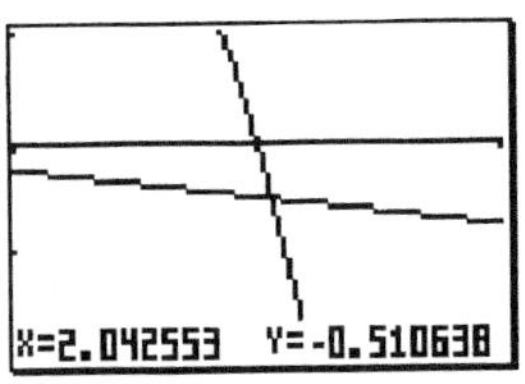

Figure 6.24: Closer view

A more efficient method for enlarging the view is to draw a new viewing rectangle with the cursor. Start again with a graph of the two functions $y = -x^3 + 4x$ and $y = -.25x$ in a default viewing rectangle (press

RANGE MENU ENTER for the default window, from -4.7 to 4.7 along the x-axis and from -3.1 to 3.1 along the y-axis).

Now imagine a small rectangular box around the intersection point, near $x = 2$. Press ZOOM 1 (Figure 6.25) to draw a box to define this new viewing rectangle. Use the arrow keys to move the cursor, whose coordinates are displayed at the bottom of the window, to one corner of the new viewing rectangle you imagine.

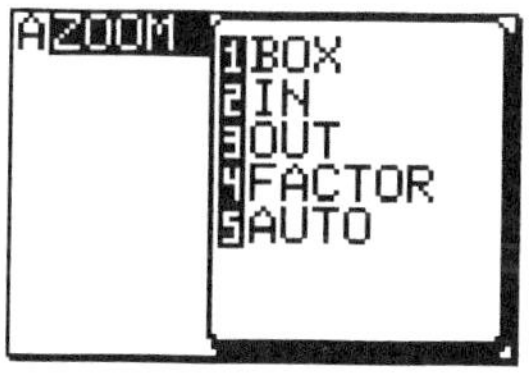

Figure 6.25: ZOOM menu

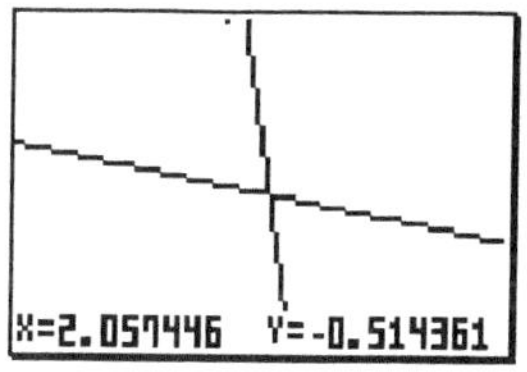

Figure 6.26: New viewing rectangle

Press ENTER to fix the corner where you have moved the cursor. Use the arrow keys again to move the cursor to the diagonally opposite corner of the new rectangle. If this box looks all right to you, press ENTER. The rectangular area you have enclosed will now enlarge to fill the graph window (Figure 6.26).

You may cancel the zoom any time *before* this last ENTER by pressing CL.

You can also gain a quick magnification of the graph around the cursor's location. Return once more to the default range for the graph of the two functions $y = -x^3 + 4x$ and $y = -.25x$. Trace as close as you can to the point of intersection near $x = 2$ (see Figure 6.23). Then press ZOOM 2 and the calculator draws a magnified graph, centered at the cursor's position (Figure 6.27). The range variables are changed to reflect this new viewing rectangle. Look in the RANGE menu to check.

As you see in the ZOOM menu (Figure 6.25), the Sharp EL-9200/9300 can zoom in (press ZOOM 2) or zoom out (press ZOOM 3). Zoom out to see a larger view of the graph, centered at the cursor position. You can change the horizontal and vertical scale of the magnification by pressing ZOOM 4 and editing X-FACTOR and Y-FACTOR, the horizontal and vertical magnification factors.

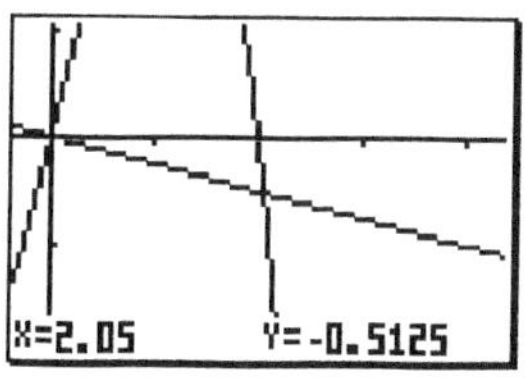

Figure 6.27: After a zoom in

It is not necessary for X-FACTOR and Y-FACTOR to be equal. Sometimes, you may prefer to zoom in one direction only, so the other factor should be set to 1. As usual, press QUIT to leave the ZOOM menu.

Technology Tip: If you should zoom in too much and lose the curve, press ZOOM 5 for auto scaling and start again.

An advantage of zooming in from the default viewing rectangle or from a friendly viewing rectangle is that subsequent windows will also be friendly.

6.2.7 Relative Minimums and Maximums: Graph $y = -x^3 + 4x$ once again in the default viewing rectangle (Figure 6.12). This function appears to have a relative minimum near x = -1 and a relative maximum near x = 1. You may zoom and trace to approximate these extreme values.

First trace along the curve near the local minimum. Notice by how much the x-values and y-values change as you move from point to point. Trace along the curve until the y-coordinate is as *small* as you can get it, so that you are as close as possible to the local minimum, and zoom in (press ZOOM 2 or use a zoom box). Now trace again along the curve and, as you move from point to point, see that the coordinates change by smaller amounts than before. Keep zooming and tracing until you find the coordinates of the local minimum point as accurately as you need them, approximately (-1.15, -3.08).

Follow a similar procedure to find the local maximum. Trace along the curve until the y-coordinate is as *great* as you can get it, so that you are as close as possible to the local maximum, and zoom in. The local maximum point on the graph of $y = -x^3 + 4x$ is approximately (1.15, 3.08).

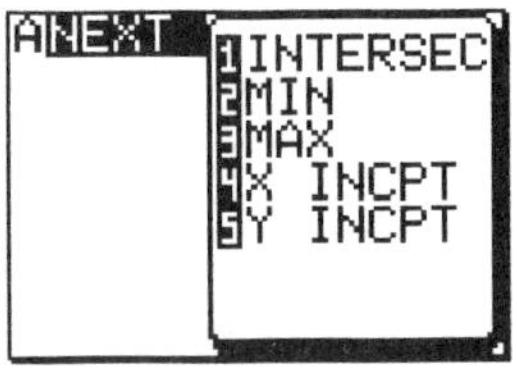

Figure 6.28: JUMP menu

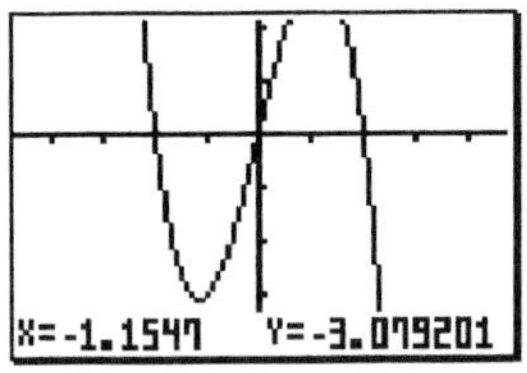

Figure 6.29: Relative minimum on $y = -x^3 + 4x$

The Sharp EL-9200/9300 automates the search for relative minimum and relative maximum points. Trace along the curve until the cursor is to the *left* of a local extreme point. Then press 2ndF JUMP (Figure 6.28) and choose 2 for a minimum value of the function or 3 for a maximum value. The calculator searches from left to right for the next relative minimum or maximum and displays the *approximate* coordinates of the relative minimum/maximum point (see Figure 6.29).

6.3 Solving Equations and Inequalities

6.3.1 Intercepts and Intersections: Tracing and zooming are also used to locate an x-intercept of a graph, where a curve crosses the x-axis. For example, the graph of $y = x^3 - 8x$ crosses the x-axis three times (see Figure 6.30). After tracing over to the x-intercept point that is furthest to the left, zoom in (Figure 6.31). Continue this process until you have located all three intercepts with as much accuracy as you need. The three x-intercepts of $y = x^3 - 8x$ are approximately -2.828, 0, and 2.828.

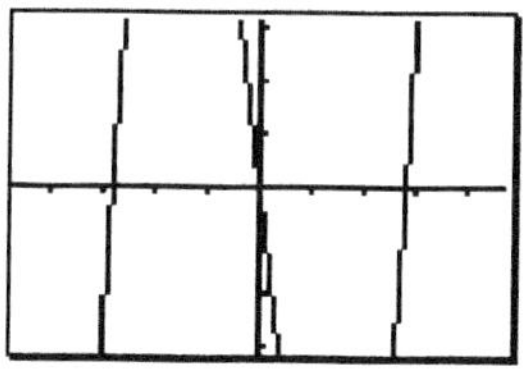

Figure 6.30: Graph of $y = x^3 - 8x$

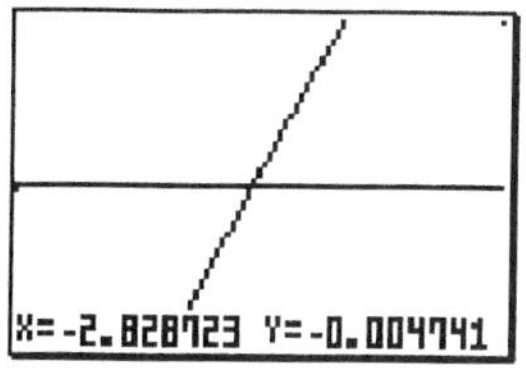

Figure 6.31: An x-intercept of $y = x^3 - 8x$

Technology Tip: As you zoom in, you may also wish to change the spacing between tick marks on the x-axis so that the viewing rectangle shows scale marks near the intercept point. Then the accuracy of your approximation will be such that the error is less than the distance between two tick marks. Change the x-scale on the Sharp EL-9200/9300 from the RANGE menu. Move the cursor down to Xscl and enter an appropriate value.

Once more, the Sharp EL-9200/9300 automates the search for x-intercepts. First trace along the graph until the cursor is just left of an x-intercept. Press 2ndF JUMP (Figure 6.28) and choose 4 to find the next x-intercept of this function. Repeat until you have located all x-intercepts of this graph.

An x-intercept of a function's graph is a *root* of the equation $f(x) = 0$. So these techniques for locating x-intercepts also serve to find the roots of an equation.

TRACE and ZOOM are especially important for locating the intersection points of two graphs, say the graphs of $y = -x^3 + 4x$ and $y = -.25x$. Trace along one of the graphs until you arrive close to an intersection point. Then press ▲ or ▼ to jump to the other graph. Notice that the x-coordinate does not change, but the y-coordinate is likely to be different (see Figures 6.32 and 6.33).

When the two y-coordinates are as close as they can get, you have come as close as you now can to the point of intersection. So zoom in around the intersection point, then trace again until the two y-coordinates are as close as possible. Continue this process until you have located the point of intersection with as much accuracy as necessary.

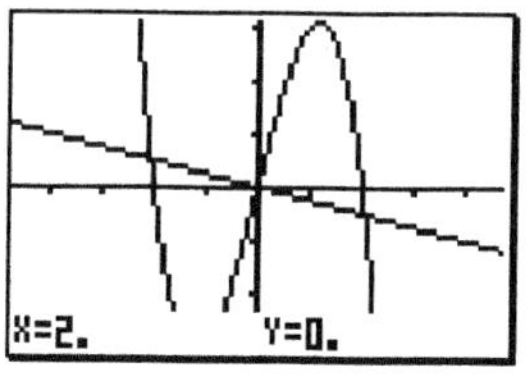

Figure 6.32: Trace on $y = -x^3 + 4x$

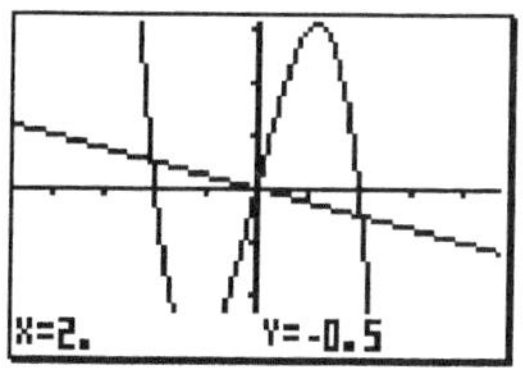

Figure 6.33: Trace on $y = -.25x$

Automate the search for points of intersection by tracing along one curve until you are left of an intersection. Then press 2ndF JUMP 1 to locate the next intersection point. The calculator displays *approximate* coordinates; zoom in to improve the approximation.

6.3.2 Solving Equations by Graphing: Suppose you need to solve the equation $24x^3 - 36x + 17 = 0$. First graph $y = 24x^3 - 36x + 17$ in a window large enough to exhibit *all* its x-intercepts, corresponding to all its roots. Then use trace and zoom to locate each one. In fact, this equation has just one solution, approximately x = -1.414.

Remember that when an equation has more than one x-intercept, it may be necessary to change the viewing rectangle a few times to locate all of them.

Technology Tip: To solve an equation like $24x^3 + 17 = 36x$, you may first transform it into standard form, $24x^3 - 36x + 17 = 0$, and proceed as above. However, you may also graph the *two* functions $y = 24x^3 + 17$ and $y = 36x$, then zoom and trace to locate their point of intersection.

6.3.3 Solving Systems by Graphing: The solutions to a system of equations correspond to the points of intersection of their graphs (Figure 6.34). For example, to solve the system $y = x^2 - 3x - 4$ and $y = x^3 + 3x^2 - 2x - 1$, first graph them together. Then zoom and trace to locate their point of intersection, approximately (-2.17, 7.25).

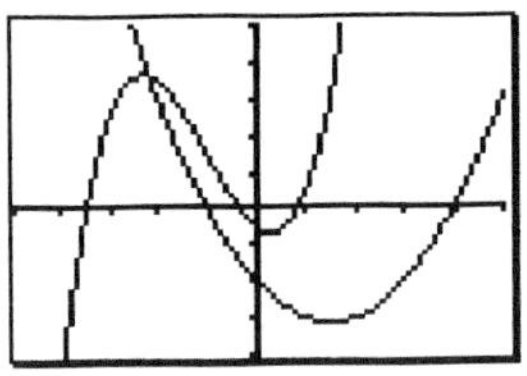

Figure 6.34: Solving a system of equations

You must judge whether the two current y-coordinates are sufficiently close for x = -2.17 or whether you should continue to zoom and trace to improve the approximation.

The solutions of the system of two equations $y = x^3 + 3x^2 - 2x - 1$ and $y = x^2 - 3x - 4$ correspond to the solutions of the single equation $x^3 + 3x^2 - 2x - 1 = x^2 - 3x - 4$, which simplifies to $x^3 + 2x^2 + x + 3 = 0$. So you may also graph $y = x^3 + 2x^2 + x + 3$ and find its x-intercepts to solve the system.

6.3.4 Solving Inequalities by Graphing: Consider the inequality $1 - \frac{3x}{2} \geq x - 4$. To solve it with your Sharp EL-9200/9300, graph the two functions $y = 1 - \frac{3x}{2}$ and $y = x - 4$ (Figure 6.35). First locate their point of intersection, at x = 2. The inequality is true when the graph of $y = 1 - \frac{3x}{2}$ lies *above* the graph of $y = x - 4$, and that occurs for $x < 2$. So the solution is the half-line $x \le 2$, or $(-\infty, 2]$.

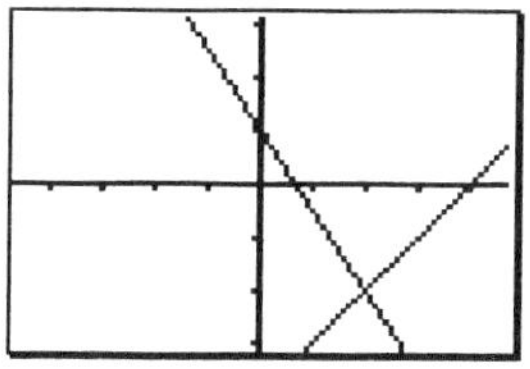

Figure 6.35: Solving $1-\frac{3x}{2} \ge x-4$

The Sharp EL-9200/9300 is capable of shading the region above or below a graph or between two graphs. For example, to graph $y \ge x^2-1$, first input the function $y = x^2-1$ as Y1. Then press MENU 5 (see Figure 6.36). Move the cursor to Y1 in the FILL ABOVE part and press ENTER to highlight it. These keystrokes instruct the calculator to shade the region *above* $y = x^2-1$. The result is shown in Figure 6.37.

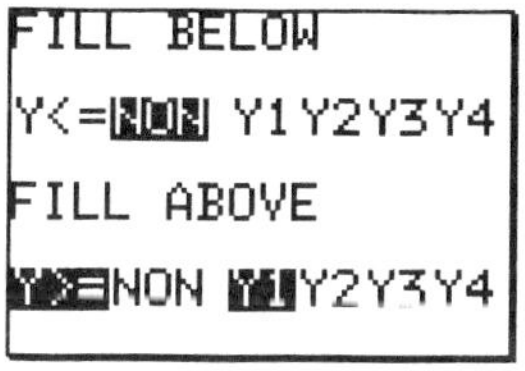

Figure 6.36: FILL menu

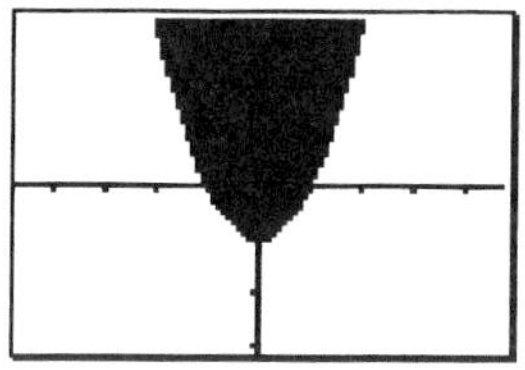

Figure 6.37: Graph of $y \ge x^2-1$

To clear the shading, press MENU 5 and highlight NON for both FILL BELOW and FILL ABOVE.

Now use shading to solve the previous inequality, $1-\frac{3x}{2} \ge x-4$. Input $y = 1-\frac{3x}{2}$ as Y1 and $y = x-4$ as Y2. Then press MENU 5 and highlight Y1 for FILL BELOW and Y2 for FILL ABOVE. The shading extends left from $x = 2$, hence the solution to $1-\frac{3x}{2} \ge x-4$ is the half-line $x \le 2$, or $(-\infty, 2]$.

Figure 6.38: FILL menu

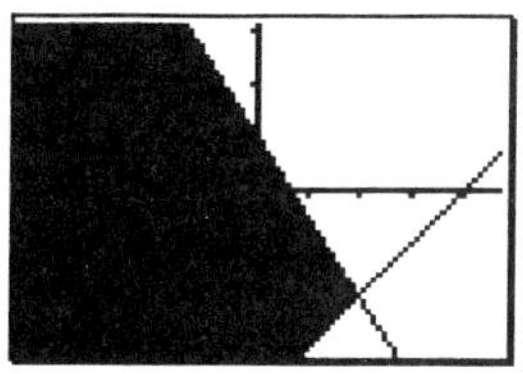

Figure 6.39: Graph of $1-\frac{3x}{2} \ge x-4$

6.4 Trigonometry

6.4.1 Degrees and Radians: The trigonometric functions can be applied to angles measured either in radians or degrees, but you should take care that the Sharp EL-9200/9300 is configured for whichever measure you need. Back in calculation mode (press the calculation mode key first), press SETUP to see the current settings. Next press B and then 1 for degrees or 2 for radians. To leave the SETUP menu, press QUIT.

It's a good idea to check the angle measure setting before executing a calculation that depends on a particular measure. You may change a mode setting at any time and not interfere with pending calculations. Try the following keystrokes to see this in action.

Expression	*Keystrokes*	*Display*
$\sin 45^\circ$	SETUP B 1 ENTER sin 45 ENTER	 0.707106781
$\sin \pi^\circ$	sin 2ndF π ENTER	0.054803665
$\sin \pi$	sin 2ndF π SETUP B 2 ENTER ENTER	 0.
$\sin 45$	sin 45 ENTER	0.850903524
$\sin \frac{\pi}{6}$	sin 2ndF π a/b 6 ENTER	0.5

The first line of keystrokes sets the Sharp EL-9200/9300 in degree mode and calculates the sine of 45 *degrees*. While the calculator is still in degree mode, the second line of keystrokes calculates the sine of π *degrees*, 3.1415°. The third line changes to radian mode just before calculating the sine of π *radians*. The fourth line calculates the sine of 45 *radians* (the calculator is already in radian mode).

Technology Tip: Here's how to mix degrees and radians in a calculation. Execute these keystrokes to calculate $\tan 45^\circ + \sin \frac{\pi}{6}$ as shown in Figure 6.40: tan 45 SETUP B 1 ENTER ENTER + sin 2ndF π a/b 6 SETUP B 2 ENTER ENTER. Do you get 1.5 whether your calculator began *either* in degree mode *or* in radian mode?

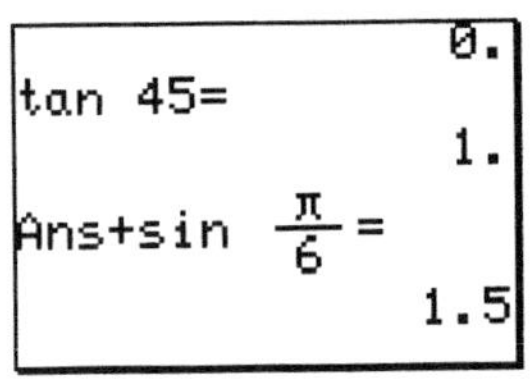

Figure 6.40: Angle measure

6.4.2 Graphs of Trigonometric Functions: When you graph a trigonometric function, you need to pay careful attention to the choice of graph window. For example, graph $y = \frac{\sin 30x}{30}$ in the default viewing rectangle. Trace along the curve to see where it is. Zoom in to a better window, or use the period and amplitude to establish better RANGE values.

Technology Tip: Create a good viewing rectangle for a trigonometric graph by pressing RANGE MENU D and selecting from the list of trigonometric functions.

6.5 Differentiation

6.5.1 Limits: Suppose you need to find this limit: $\lim_{x \to 0} \frac{\sin 4x}{x}$. Plot the graph of $f(x) = \frac{\sin 4x}{x}$ in a convenient viewing rectangle that contains the point where the function appears to intersect the line $x = 0$ (because you want the limit as $x \to 0$). Your graph should lend support to the conclusion that $\lim_{x \to 0} \frac{\sin 4x}{x} = 4$.

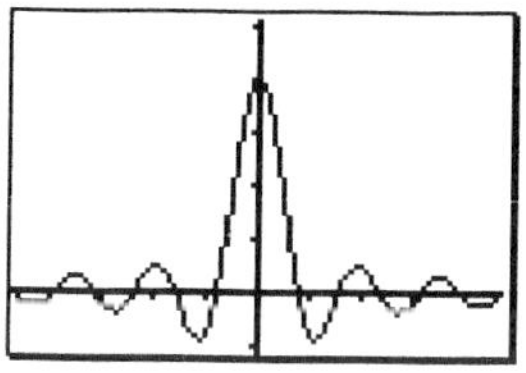

Figure 6.41: Checking $\lim_{x \to 0} \frac{\sin 4x}{x} = 4$

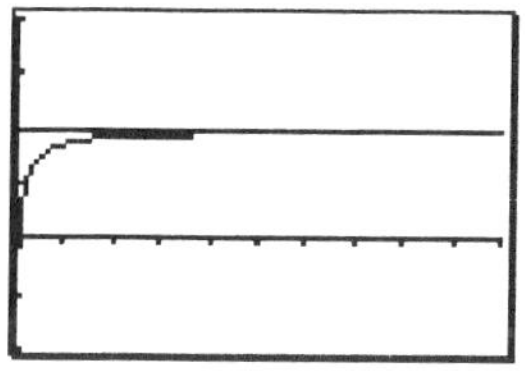

Figure 6.42: Checking $\lim_{x \to \infty} \frac{2x-1}{x+1} = 2$

To test the reasonableness of the conclusion that $\lim_{x \to \infty} \frac{2x-1}{x+1} = 2$, evaluate the function $f(x) = \frac{2x-1}{x+1}$ for several large positive values of x (since you want the limit as $x \to \infty$). For example, evaluate *f*(100), *f*(1000), and *f*(10,000). Another way to test the reasonableness of this result is to examine the graph of $f(x) = \frac{2x-1}{x+1}$ in a viewing rectangle that extends over large values of *x*. See, as in Figure 6.42 (where the viewing rectangle extends horizontally from 0 to 100), whether the graph is asymptotic to the horizontal line *y* = 2 (enter $\frac{2x-1}{x+1}$ for Y1 and 2 for Y2).

6.5.2 Numerical Derivatives: The derivative of a function *f* at *x* can be defined as the limit of the slopes of secant lines through the point $(x, f(x))$, so $f'(x) = \lim_{\Delta x \to 0} \frac{f(x+\Delta x) - f(x)}{\Delta x}$. And for small values of Δx, the expression $\frac{f(x+\Delta x) - f(x)}{\Delta x}$ gives a good approximation to the limit.

The Sharp EL-9200/9300 has a function d/dx(in the MATH CALC menu (Figure 6.43) to calculate the *difference quotient*, $\frac{f(x+\Delta x)-f(x)}{\Delta x}$. So to find a numerical approximation to $f'(2.5)$ when $f(x)=x^3$ and with $\Delta x = 0.001$, press (for one-line editing) MATH C 8 X/θ/T ^ 3 ALPHA , 2.5 ALPHA , .001) ENTER as shown in Figure 6.44. The format of this command is d/dx(*expression*, *value*, Δ*x*). The same derivative is also approximated in Figure 6.43 using $\Delta x = 0.00001$. For most purposes, $\Delta x = 0.00001$ gives a very good approximation to the derivative and is the Sharp EL-9200/9300 calculator's default. So if you do use this value, just enter d/dx(*expression*, *value*), as in the final calculation of Figure 6.44.

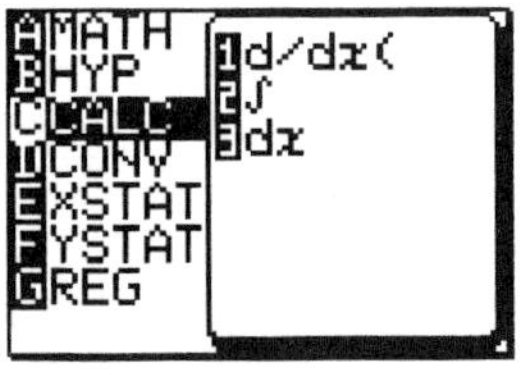

Figure 6.43: MATH CALC menu

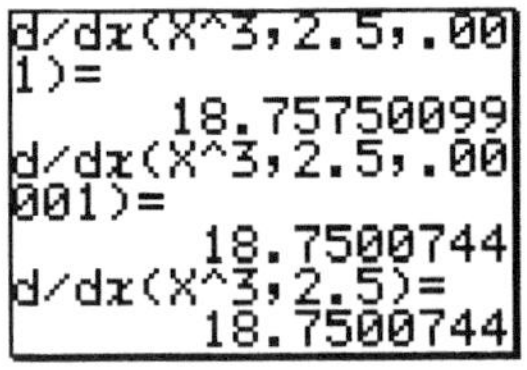

Figure 6.44: Using d/dx(

Technology Tip: It is sometimes helpful to plot both a function and its derivative together. In Figure 6.46, the function $f(x)=\frac{5x-2}{x^2+1}$ and its numerical derivative (actually, an approximation to the derivative given by the difference quotient) are graphed. You can duplicate this graph by first entering $\frac{5x-2}{x^2+1}$ for Y1. Then enter its numerical derivative for Y2 by pressing MATH C 1, the keystrokes for $\frac{5x-2}{x^2+1}$ again, and finally ALPHA , X/θ/T) as you see in Figure 6.45.

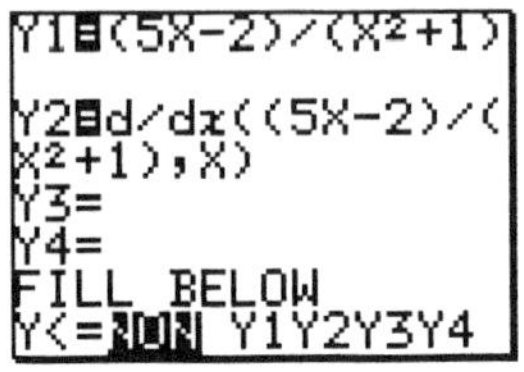

Figure 6.45: Entering $f(x)$ and $f'(x)$

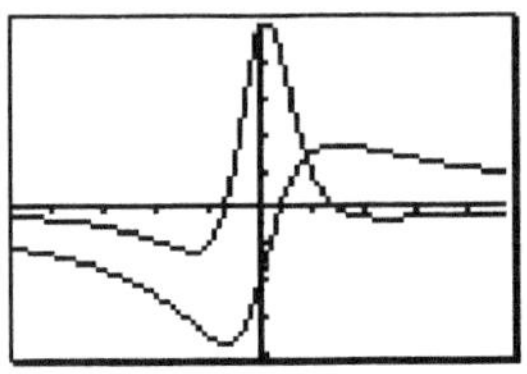

Figure 6.46: Graphs of $f(x)$ and $f'(x)$

6.5.3 Newton's Method: With your Sharp EL-9200/9300, you may iterate using Newton's Method to find the zeros of a function. Recall that Newton's Method determines each successive approximation by the formula $x_{n+1}=x_n-\frac{f(x_n)}{f'(x_n)}$.

As an example of the technique, consider $f(x)=2x^3+x^2-x+1$. A look at its graph suggests that it has a zero near x = -1, so start the iteration by storing -1 as x (see Figure 6.47). Then execute these keystrokes:

X/θ/T - (followed by the keystrokes for $2x^3+x^2-x+1$; next press) ÷ MATH C 1 again followed by the keystrokes for $2x^3+x^2-x+1$; and finally press ALPHA , X/θ/T) STO X/θ/T. Press ENTER repeatedly until two successive approximations differ by less than some predetermined value, say 0.0001. Note that each time you press ENTER, the Sharp EL-9200/9300 will use its *current* value of *x*, and that value is changing as you continue the iteration.

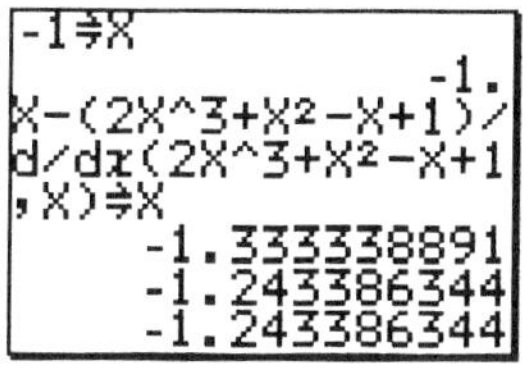

Figure 6.47: Newton's Method

Technology Tip: Newton's Method is sensitive to your seed value for *x*, so look carefully at the function's graph to make a good first estimate. Also, remember that the method sometimes fails to converge!

You may want to save the Newton's Method formula as a short program. See Section 2.9 or your calculator's manual for further information on programming the Sharp EL-9200/9300.

6.6 Sequences

6.6.1 Iteration: The 2ndF ANS feature enables you to perform iterations to evaluate a function repeatedly. As an example, calculate $\frac{n-1}{3}$ for $n=27$. Then calculate $\frac{n-1}{3}$ for n = the answer to the previous calculation. Continue to use each answer as *n* in the *next* calculation. Here are keystrokes to accomplish this iteration on the Sharp EL-9200/9300 calculator (see the results in Figure 6.48). Notice that when you use Ans in place of *n* in a formula, it is sufficient to press ENTER to continue an iteration.

Assure that you are in the correct mode by pressing the calculation mode key, then MENU 1.

Iteration	*Keystrokes*	*Display*
1	27 ENTER	27.
2	(2ndF ANS - 1) ÷ 3 ENTER	8.666666667
3	ENTER	2.555555556
4	ENTER	0.518518518
5	ENTER	-0.160493827

Press ENTER several more times and see what happens with this iteration. You may wish to try it again with a different starting value.

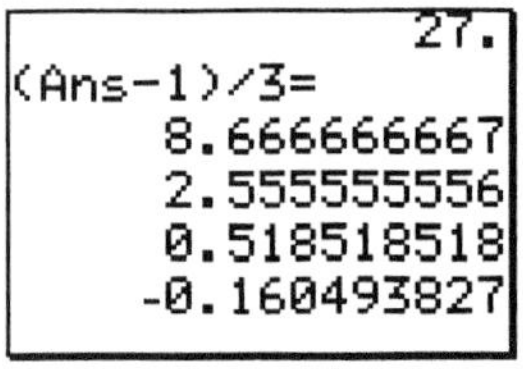

Figure 6.48: Iteration

6.6.2 Arithmetic and Geometric Sequences: Use iteration with the Ans variable to determine the n-th term of a sequence. For example, find the 18th term of an *arithmetic* sequence whose first term is 7 and whose common difference is 4. Enter the first term 7, then start the progression with the recursion formula, 2ndF ANS + 4 ENTER. This yields the 2nd term, so press ENTER sixteen more times to find the 18th term. For a *geometric* sequence whose common ratio is 4, start the progression with 2ndF ANS × 4 ENTER.

Of course, you could also use the *explicit* formula for the n-th term of an arithmetic sequence, $t_n = a + (n-1)d$. First enter values for the variables a, d, and n, then evaluate the formula by pressing ALPHA A + (ALPHA N - 1) ALPHA D ENTER. For a geometric sequence whose n-th term is given by $t_n = a \cdot r^{n-1}$, enter values for the variables a, r, and n, then evaluate the formula by pressing ALPHA A ALPHA R a^b (ALPHA N - 1) ENTER.

6.7 Integration

6.7.1 Approximating Definite Integrals: The Sharp EL-9200/9300 has the function ∫ in the MATH CALC menu to approximate an integral by Simpson's Rule,

$$\int_a^b f(x)\,dx \approx \frac{b-a}{3n}\left[f(x_0)+4f(x_1)+2f(x_2)+4f(x_3)+\ldots+4f(x_{n-1})+f(x_n)\right].$$

So to find a numerical approximation to $\int_0^1 \cos x^2 dx$ with 20 subdivisions (a number that controls the accuracy of the approximation), press these keystrokes for one-line editing: MATH C 2 COS X/θ/T x^2 ALPHA , 0 ALPHA , 1 ALPHA , 10 MATH 3 ENTER as shown in Figure 6.49. For equation editing, press MATH C 2 0 ▲ 1 ▶ COS X/θ/T x^2 ALPHA , 10 MATH 3 ENTER as illustrated in Figure 6.50. The format of this command is ∫ *expression, lower limit, upper limit, ½ the number of subdivisions* dx.

Note that this calculator requires that integration begin with an integral sign and conclude with a dx. Also, since the usual statement of Simpson's Rule requires an *even* number of subdivisions, you enter any integer and the Sharp EL-9200/9300 uses *double* that number of subdivisions. The same integral is also approximated in Figure 6.49 using 100 subdivisions, this calculator's default that is used when no other number is specified.

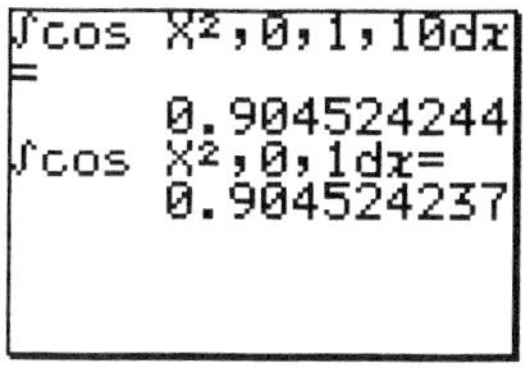

Figure 6.49: One-line editing: ∫ dx

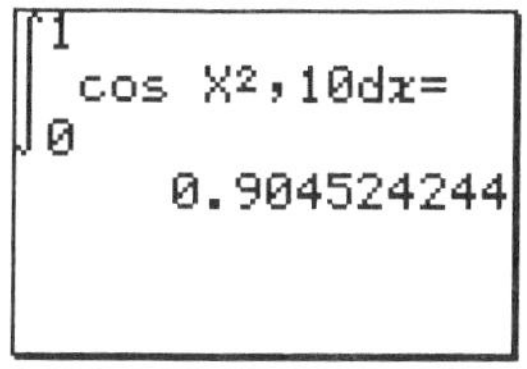

Figure 6.50: Equation editing: ∫ dx

6.7.2 Areas: You may approximate the area under the graph of a function $y = f(x)$ between $x = A$ and $x = B$ with your Sharp EL-9200/9300. For example, the area under the graph of the function $y = \cos x^2$ between $x = 0$ and $x = 1$ is represented by the definite integral $\int_0^1 \cos x^2 dx$, which is approximated as shown above.

Technology Tip: Suppose that you want to find the area between two functions, $y = f(x)$ and $y = g(x)$, from $x = A$ to $x = B$. If $f(x) \geq g(x)$ for $A \leq x \leq B$, then approximate $\int_A^B (f(x) - g(x))\, dx$ to find the required area.

See Section 2.9 for a sample Sharp EL-9200/9300 program that uses left and right Riemann Sums as well as the Midpoint Rule, the Trapezoid Rule, and Simpson's Rule to approximate definite integrals.

6.8 Parametric and Polar Graphs

6.8.1 Graphing Parametric Equations: The Sharp EL-9200/9300 plots parametric equations as easily as it plots functions. Just use the SETUP menu (Figure 6.2), go to COORD, and select XYT (press SETUP E 3). Be sure, if the independent parameter is an angle measure, that DRG is set to whichever you need, Rad or Deg.

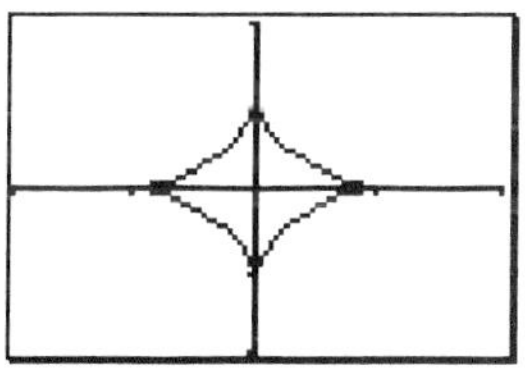

Figure 6.51: Parametric graph of $x = \cos^3 t$ and $y = \sin^3 t$

For example, here are the keystrokes needed to graph the parametric equations $x = \cos^3 t$ and $y = \sin^3 t$. First check that angles are currently being measured in radians. Change to parametric mode and press the graphing mode key. Enter the two parametric equations by pressing (cos X/θ/T) a^b 3 ENTER for X1T and (sin X/θ/T) a^b 3 ENTER for Y1T . Now, when you press the variable key X/θ/T, you get a T because the calculator is in parametric mode.

Also look at the new RANGE menu. Set T to range from 0 to 2π (the step size Tstp is automatically changed to $\frac{2\pi}{94}=.0668$, since the Sharp EL-9200/9300 plots in 94 increments across the screen). And a good viewing rectangle extends from -2 to 2 in both directions. Press the graphing mode key again to see the parametric graph (Figure 6.51).

You may ZOOM and TRACE along parametric graphs just as you did with function graphs. As you trace along this graph, notice that the cursor moves in the *counterclockwise* direction as T increases.

6.8.2 Rectangular-Polar Coordinate Conversion: The MATH menu (Figure 6.7) provides functions for converting between rectangular and polar coordinate systems. These functions use the current settings, so it is a good idea to check the default angle measure before any conversion. For the following examples, the Sharp EL-9200/9300 is set to radian measure; check that it is in calculation mode, too.

Given rectangular coordinates $(x, y) = (4, -3)$, convert *from* these rectangular coordinates *to* polar coordinates (r, θ) by pressing 4 ALPHA , (-) 3 MATH D 3. The value of r is displayed; press ALPHA θ ENTER to display the value of θ.

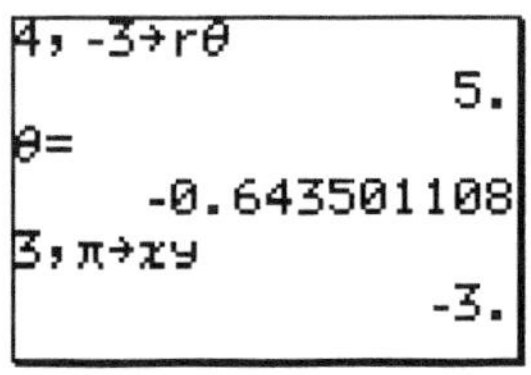

Figure 3.52: Coordinate conversions

Suppose $(r, \theta) = (3, \pi)$. To convert *from* these polar coordinates *to* rectangular coordinates (x, y), press 3 ALPHA , 2ndF π MATH D 4. The x-coordinate is displayed; press ALPHA Y ENTER to display the y-coordinate.

6.8.3 Graphing Polar Equations: The Sharp EL-9200/9300 graphs a polar function after you press SETUP E 2. For example, to graph $r = 4\sin\theta$, press the graphing mode key and input 4 sin ALPHA θ for R1. Now, when you press the variable key X/θ/T, you get a θ because the calculator is in polar mode. Choose a good viewing rectangle and an appropriate range for θ. In Figure 6.53, the graphing window is the default, but with θ ranging from 0 to 2π and the vertical axis extending from -2.1 to 4.1.

You are able to trace along a polar curve and see both *polar* and *rectangular* coordinates of the cursor's location.

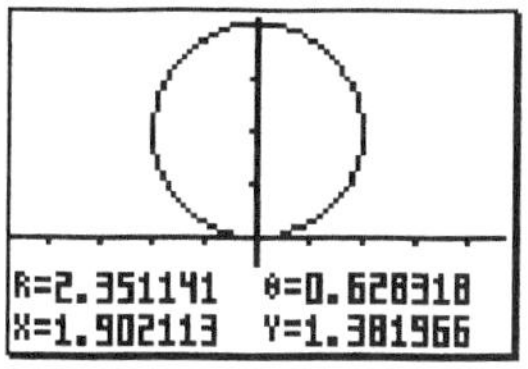

Figure 6.53: Polar graph of $r = 4\sin\theta$

6.10 Programming

6.10.1 Entering a Program: The Sharp EL-9200/9300 is a programmable calculator that can store sequences of commands for later replay. Here's an example to show you how to enter a useful program that performs numerical integration by several methods: left and right Riemann Sums as well as the Midpoint Rule, the Trapezoid Rule, and Simpson's Rule.

Press the programming mode key (in the middle of the top row) to access the programming menu, where you will find a list of programs that were input previously. The Sharp EL-9200 has space for up to 55 programs, and the Sharp EL-9300 has space for up to 99 programs.

To create a new program, press C ENTER, then 1 so this program will run in real mode. The ALPHA indicator is on, so press letter keys to name this program integrate. Then press ▼ to continue.

Notice that the name integrate is in *lowercase* letters. In programming mode, pressing ALPHA or 2ndF A-LOCK allows you to enter a lowercase letter. For uppercase letters, press ALPHA 2ndF or 2ndF A-LOCK 2ndF.

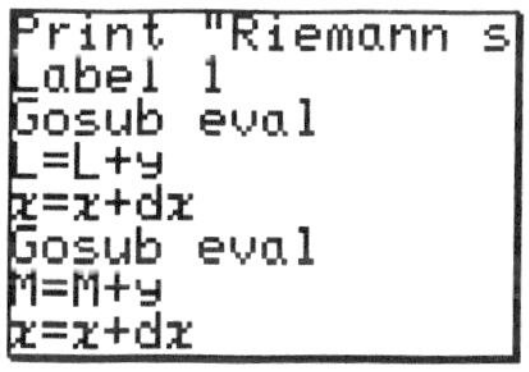

Figure 6.54: Part of program integrate

A single *uppercase* letter, when used for a variable name, refers to a memory location. It is called a *global* variable. For any other program, or even outside programming mode, this memory location retains the value you store there until you store something else. However a *lowercase* letter names a *local* variable that exists only during the current program. Values stored in local variables cannot be passed to another program and are not available outside the program in which they are created.

Lowercase variable names can be longer than one letter. For example, length is a valid local variable name. So multiplication between local variables must be expressed: you must enter length × width for a product.

Any command you could enter directly in the Sharp EL-9200/9300's home screen can be entered as a line in a program. There are also special programming commands.

You *must* press ENTER or ▼ after each line to complete the entry. Press CL to clear a single line; press 2ndF CA to delete an entire program.

Enter the program integrate by pressing the keystrokes given in the listing below. You may interrupt program input at any time by pressing a mode key. To return later for more editing, press the programming mode key, then B, use the arrow keys to locate the program's name in the listing, and press ENTER. Take care, however, that the keystrokes given here assume that you are entering these lines of code sequentially. Frequently, for example, when you press 2ndF A-LOCK to put the calculator in alphabetic entry mode for one line of code, subsequent lines will assume that the calculator is already in that state.

Program Line	*Keystrokes*
: Goto start	2nd COMMAND B 2 2ndF A-LOCK S T A R T

jumps over the next three lines of code, which are placed at the beginning of the program for convenient access when you are changing the integrand

: Label eval	2nd COMMAND 1 E V A L ALPHA ▼

a subroutine to evaluate your function for the current value of x

: y = *f(x)*	ALPHA Y ALPHA = *expression in the local variable x* ▼

enter the integrand here as an expression in the local variable x

: Return	2nd COMMAND 5

continues the main program from the point where this subroutine was called

: Label start	2nd COMMAND 1 2ndF A-LOCK S T A R T ▼

jumping point for the Goto command above

: Print "Lower limit	2ndF COMMAND A 1 2ndF COMMAND 2 2ndF L O W E R SPACE L I M I T ▼

displays the words *Lower limit* on the Sharp EL-9200/9300 screen

: Input llim	2ndF COMMAND 3 L L I M ▼

waits for you to input a value that will be assigned to the local variable *llim*

: Print "Upper limit	2ndF COMMAND 1 2ndF COMMAND 2 2ndF U P P E R SPACE L I M I T ▼
: Input ulim	2ndF COMMAND 3 U L I M ▼
: Print "Subdivisions	2ndF COMMAND 1 2ndF COMMAND 2 2ndF S U B D I V I S I O N S ▼

: Input n	2ndF COMMAND 3 N ▼
: dx = (ulim- llim)/2n	D X = ALPHA (2ndF A-LOCK U L I M ALPHA - 2ndF A-LOCK L L I M ALPHA) ÷ 2 ALPHA N ▼

calculates $\frac{1}{2}\Delta x$ and stores its value as local variable *dx*

: L = 0	ALPHA 2ndF L ALPHA = 0 ▼

uses the global variable *L* with the left Riemann Sum

: M = 0	ALPHA 2ndF M ALPHA = 0 ▼

uses the global variable *M* with the Midpoint Rule

: c = 0	ALPHA C ALPHA = 0 ▼

uses the local variable *c* to keep track of the subdivisions

: x = llim	2ndF A-LOCK X = L L I M ▼

starts off at the lower limit

: Print "Riemann Sums	2ndF COMMAND 1 2ndF COMMAND 2 2ndF R I E M A N N SPACE 2ndF S U M S ALPHA ▼
: Label 1	2ndF COMMAND B 1 1 ▼
: Gosub eval	2ndF COMMAND 4 2ndF A-LOCK E V A L ▼

calls a subroutine named eval to evaluate the function for the current value of *x*

: L = L + y	2ndF L = 2ndF L ALPHA + 2ndF A-LOCK y ▼

adds the value of the function at the *left* endpoint of the current subdivision

: x = x + dx	X = X ALPHA + 2ndF A-LOCK D X ▼

increments by $\frac{1}{2}\Delta x$ to the *midpoint* of the subdivision

: Gosub eval	2ndF COMMAND 4 2ndF A-LOCK E V A L ▼
: M = M + y	2ndF M = 2ndF M ALPHA + 2ndF A-LOCK y ▼

adds the value of the function at the *midpoint* of the current subdivision

: x = x + dx	X = X ALPHA + 2ndF A-LOCK D X ▼

increments by another $\frac{1}{2}\Delta x$ to the left endpoint of the *next* subdivision

: c = c + 1	C = C ALPHA + 1 ▼

counts up one subdivision

: If c < n Goto 1	2ndF COMMAND 3 2ndF A-LOCK C 2ndF COMMAND C 2 N SPACE 2ndF COMMAND B 2 ALPHA 1 ▼

tests whether the *last* subdivision has been reached:

in case not, then go back to Label 1 above and calculate another rectangular area; if yes, continue on to the next line

for readability, inserts a space before the Goto command

: Print " left	2ndF COMMAND A 1 2ndF COMMAND 2 2ndF A-LOCK SPACE L E F T ▼
: L = 2L∗dx	2ndF L = ALPHA 2 ALPHA 2ndF L × 2ndF A-LOCK D X ▼

calculates left Riemann Sum

: Print L	2ndF COMMAND 1 2ndF L ▼
: Wait	2ndF COMMAND 4 ▼

during program execution, waits for you to press ENTER

: Print " right	2ndF COMMAND 1 2ndF COMMAND 2 SPACE R I G H T ▼
: Gosub eval	2ndF COMMAND B 4 E V A L ▼
: R = L + 2y∗dx	2ndF R = 2ndF L ALPHA + 2 ALPHA Y × 2ndF A-LOCK D X ▼
: x = llim	X = L L I M ▼
: Gosub eval	2ndF COMMAND 4 E V A L ▼
: R = R - 2y∗dx	2ndF R = 2ndF R ALPHA - 2 ALPHA Y × 2ndF A-LOCK D X ▼

calculates right Riemann Sum

: Print R	2ndF COMMAND A 1 2ndF R ▼
: Wait	2ndF COMMAND 4 ▼
: Print "Midpoint rule	2ndF COMMAND 1 2ndF COMMAND 2 2ndF M I D P O I N T SPACE R U L E ▼
: M = 2M∗dx	2ndF M = ALPHA 2 ALPHA 2ndF M × 2ndF A-LOCK D X ▼

calculates numerical integral by Midpoint Rule

: Print M	2ndF COMMAND 1 2ndF M ▼
: Wait	2ndF COMMAND 4 ▼

: Print "Trapezoid rule"	2ndF COMMAND 1 2ndF COMMAND 2 2ndF T R A P E Z O I D SPACE R U L E ▼
: T = (L + R)/2	2ndF T = ALPHA (ALPHA 2ndF L + ALPHA 2ndF R) ÷ 2 ▼

calculates numerical integral by Trapezoid Rule (average left and right Riemann Sums)

: Print T	2ndF COMMAND 1 2ndF ALPHA 2ndF T ▼
: Wait	2ndF COMMAND 4 ▼
: Print "Simpsons rule	2ndF COMMAND 1 2ndF COMMAND 2 2ndF S I M P S O N S SPACE R U L E ▼
: S = (2M + T)/3	2ndF S = ALPHA (2 ALPHA 2ndF M + ALPHA 2ndF T) ÷ 3 ▼

calculates numerical integral by Simpson's Rule ($\frac{2}{3}$ Midpoint and $\frac{1}{3}$ Trapezoid)

: Print S	2ndF COMMAND 1 ALPHA 2ndF S ▼
: End	2ndF COMMAND 6 ▼

stops execution at the conclusion of the main program

When you have finished, press any mode key to leave the program editor.

6.10.2 Executing a Program: To execute the program just entered, press the programming mode key and ENTER. Go to its name in the program listing, then press ENTER to select this program and to execute it.

The program integrate has been written to calculate $\int_{llim}^{ulim} f(x)\,dx$ for n subdivisions of the interval [*llim*, *ulim*]. Before running this program, you must first enter the expression $f(x)$ for the integrand once in the third line. The program itself will prompt you for *llim*, *ulim*, and n. Input a value, then press ENTER to continue.

If you need to interrupt a program during execution, press QUIT.

The instruction manual for your Sharp EL-9200/9300 gives detailed information about programming. Refer to it to learn more about programming and how to use other features of your calculator.

CHAPTER 7

BestGrapher for the IBM

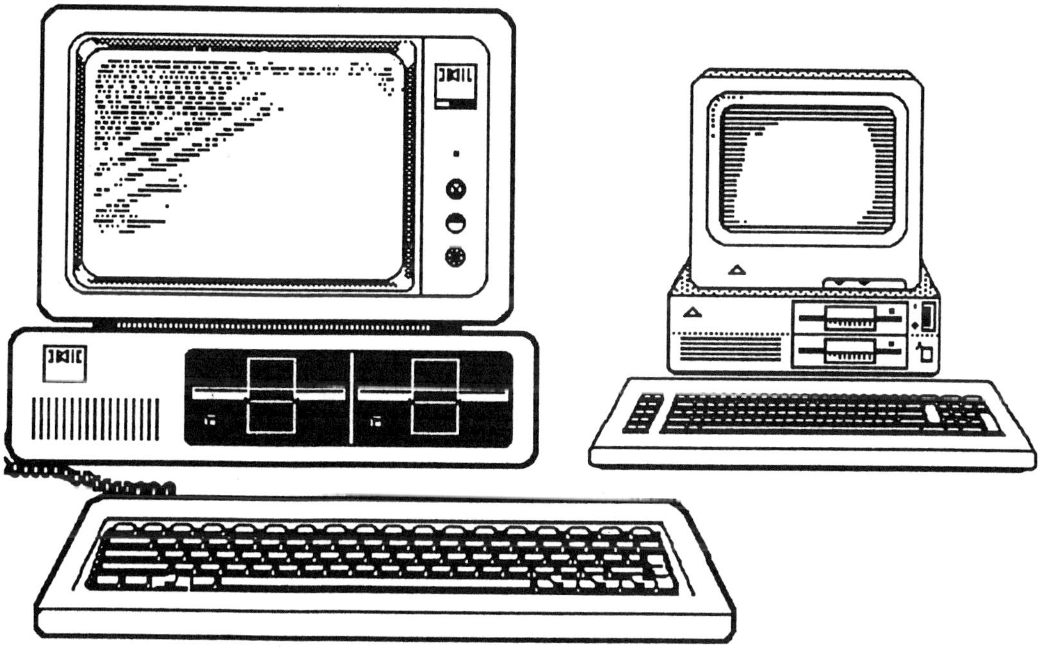

Chapter 7. BestGrapher for the IBM

7.1 Introduction

7.1.1 ***What is BestGrapher:*** BestGrapher is an easy-to-use, surprisingly powerful function graphing program that is designed to clarify the concepts of precalculus and calculus. It can graph functions in rectangular or polar coordinates as well as parameterized functions and conics. Graphs can easily be rescaled or resized. When BestGrapher is in rectangular plotting mode, it can evaluate a function, find zeros and the intersection of curves, draw tangent and secant lines, for example. BestGrapher can print images on the system printer. The images created by BestGrapher can also be copied and included in a document prepared by word-processing software.

This highly accessible program is an excellent teaching tool for both demonstrations and student exploration and experimentation.

7.1.2 Installing BestGrapher: BestGrapher runs on an IBM PC or compatible and requires the following hardware and software:

- At least 256K of memory
- DOS 2.1 or later
- CGA, EGA or VGA video adapter (monochrome monitors or cards will not work with this program).

To install the BestGrapher software, follow these steps:

1. Copy the BestGrapher files.
    - If your PC has a hard drive, create a directory called BG on the hard drive and copy the files from the BestGrapher diskette into the new directory.
    - If your PC has floppy drives, format a blank diskette and copy the BestGrapher files from the original software diskette to the formatted disk.
2. Store the original diskette in a secure place and use the copy as your work disk.

The program disk contains several files. BGrapher.exe is the primary file.

7.1.3 Getting Help: If at any time you need a reminder of the tasks that BestGrapher can perform, press the **F2** key. The following list of commands and corresponding one letter codes will be displayed in the Data window.

Commands:

<N>ew funct
<E>rase
e<V>aluate
find zer<O>
<Z>oom
li<M>it
<S>ecant
<T>angent
norma<L>
<D>ifferen
<I>ntegrate
<R>otate

Toggling the **F2** key will remove the list of BestGrapher commands. For an explanation of each command, read section 7.4.1.

7.2 Using BestGrapher

7.2.1 Getting Started: Turn on and boot your computer in the ordinary way from either a hard drive or a DOS system diskette in drive A.

To start BestGrapher from a hard drive:

1. Change the directory to \BG.

2. Type RUN and press Enter.

To start BestGrapher from a floppy drive:

1. Put the working copy into drive A.

2. Change the drive to A.

3. Type RUN and press Enter.

Whichever method you use to start BestGrapher, there is a short delay while the program loads from the diskette or hard drive. When the loading is complete, four windows will open and you will see the prompt <N>ew function in the Command window at the bottom of the screen. You are ready to begin.

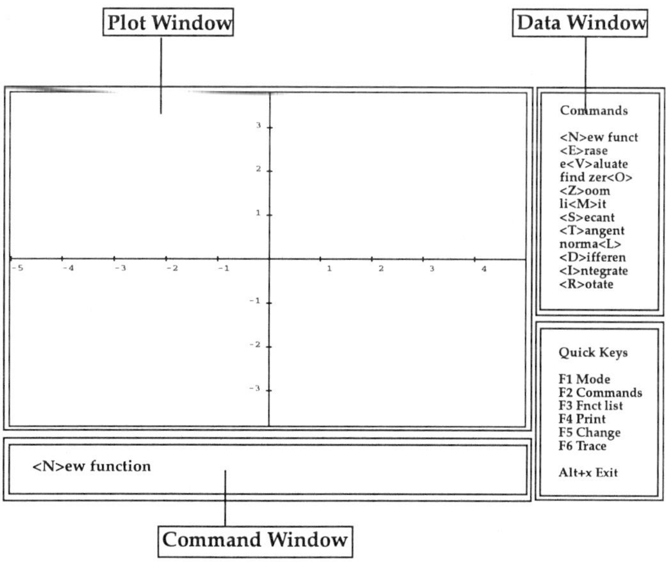

To quickly introduce the capabilities of BestGrapher we will plot and find a zero of a function.

Example: Plot and find the smallest real zero of the function f(**x**) = $\mathbf{x^3 - 2x}$.

- Type the letter **N**; the prompt f(x) = ☐ is displayed in the Command window.
- Type the expression **x^3 – 2x** (the ^ character is shift-6 on the keyboard).
- Press the Enter key; the function will be graphed and a table of values will be displayed in the Data window.

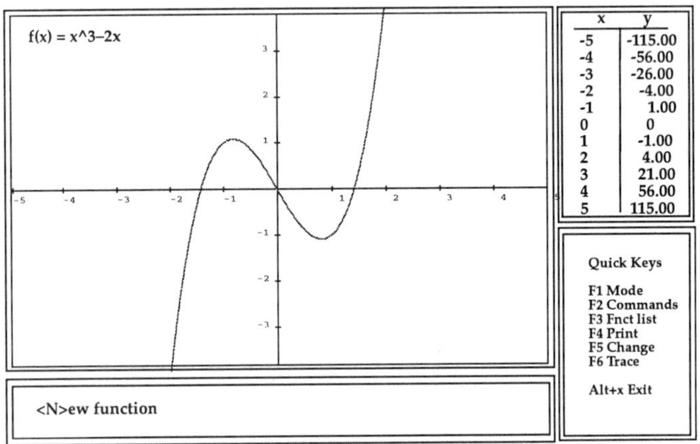

Graph of f(x) = $x^3 - 2x$

To execute a BestGrapher command, all you need to do is type one letter. Each command has its own one letter code so, for example, to find a function zero, type the letter **O**.

- Press the **O** key. You see

Enter an interval [a,b] containing one zero A: ☐

- It appears from the graph that f has a zero in the interval [1, 2]. Type **1** and press the Enter key.

• You now see

B: ☐

• Type **2** and press the Enter key; an approximation of the smallest zero, f(1.41421356) = 0, is displayed in the upper left corner of the plot window.

7.2.2 Entering Functions: Basically, BestGrapher is a function grapher and the first step in using the program is to enter a function. The format for entering a function is very similar to ordinary mathematics notation. Legal functions are, for example:

(x + 2)(x + 3), sin x, cos(2x), xln x and arctan(exp x).

All implied parentheses and multiplication are evaluated correctly. The * sign is not needed in BestGrapher but will be accepted if used.

- For division, use the slash symbol, / .
- If you type pi, BestGrapher will treat it as if you entered an approximation of π to 10 decimal places. For example, sin(pi x) will graph as a sin curve with period 2.
- You may use any type of parentheses, (, [or { .
- To raise something to a power use the caret symbol ^ .
- When using BestGrapher you may type in upper or lower case letters.
- If you make a mistake while typing, press the BACKSPACE key to erase the last character you typed.

Example: Sketch a graph of $\mathbf{f(x) = \pi\cos^2(3x)}$. Evaluate the function f at x = 2.3.

- Type the letter **N** and the prompt f(x) = ☐ is displayed.
- Type the expression **pi(cos(3x))^2**.
- Press the Enter key; the function will be graphed and a table of values will be displayed in the Data window.

• To e(V)aluate the function, type the letter **V** and you will see

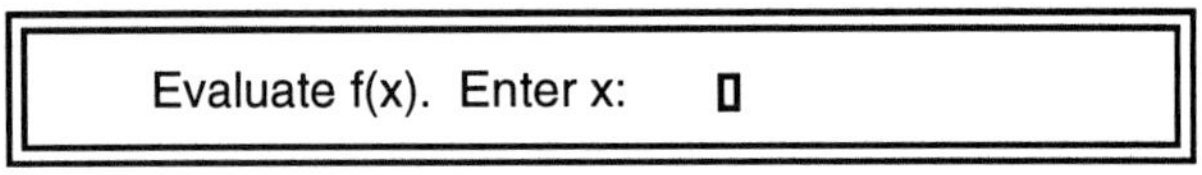

• Type 2.3 and press the Enter key. The value f(2.3) = 2.09043912 is displayed in the Plot window.

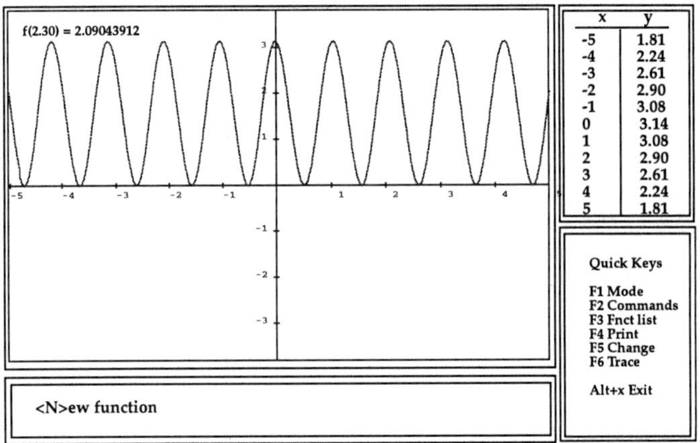

Evaluation of $f(x) = \pi \cos^2(3x)$ at $x = 2.3$

7.2.3 Additional Features for Entering Functions: In addition to entering a function from the keyboard, it is possible to select a function from a list of previously entered functions. Pressing the **F3** key displays a list of saved functions. You (Q)uit the list by pressing the **Q** key and (E)rase the list by pressing the **E** key or, if you enter the number of a desired function, its graph is sketched in the Plot window.

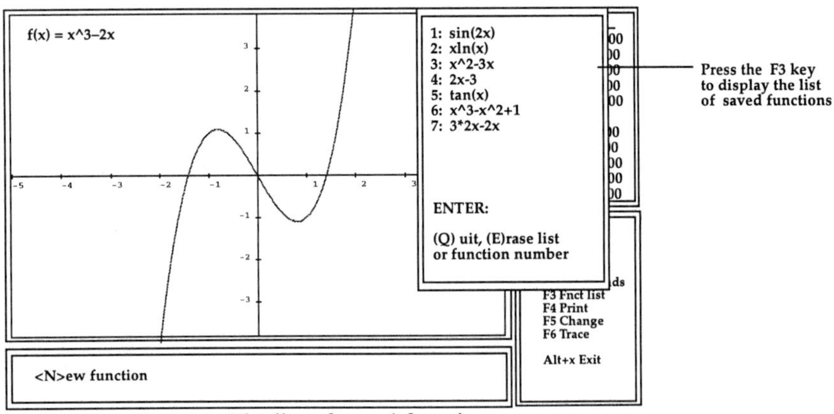

The list of saved functions

7.2.4 The Viewing Rectangle: The coordinate plane is infinite; with a graphing utility like BestGrapher you view one rectangle of the plane at a time. This viewing rectangle, called Plot in BestGrapher, is a lens through which you see a close-up or distant view of a graph by changing the dimensions of the viewing rectangle. The dimensions of the standard or default BestGrapher viewing rectangle are x minimum = -5, x maximum = 5, y minimum = -4 and y maximum = 4.

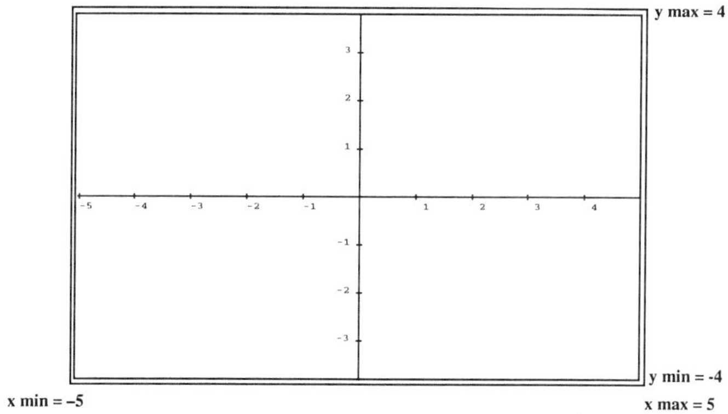

The standard viewing rectangle

If you wish to change the settings of the Plot window, press the **F5** key. The Change menu will appear on the screen and offer 5 choices.

```
You may change:
   1: viewing rectangle
   2: color
   3: speed/accuracy
   4: save configuration data
   5: quit this menu

Type the number of your choice and press ENTER
```

Change menu

If you want to change the dimensions of the viewing rectangle, type the number **1**, and press the Enter key. After deciding if the x- and y-axis should be calibrated in terms of π, a screen appears and there is an opportunity to change the horizontal dimensions of the viewing rectangle.

Now I need the domain [a, b] on which to graph

Enter x minimum A : -10

Enter x maximum B : ☐

Domain screen

The next screen asks for the vertical dimensions of the viewing rectangle.

Now I need the range [a, b] on which to graph

Enter y minimum A : -10

Enter y maximum B : ☐

Range screen

By choosing different viewing rectangles of a graph it is possible to obtain different views of a graph's shape.

Example: Use BestGrapher to graph the function $\mathbf{f(x) = 0.1x^4 - x^3 + 2x^2}$ in the viewing rectangle a) [-5,5] x [-4, 4] and b) [-15,15] x [-15,15].

a) Enter the rule 0.1x^4 – x^3 + 2x^2 and press the Enter key.

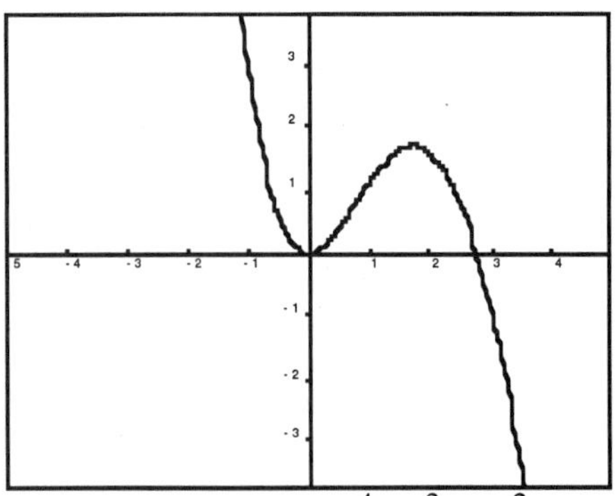

Graph of $f(x) = 0.1x^4 - x^3 + 2x^2$

b) To change the dimensions of the Plot window

- Press the **F5** key and select option **1** from the Change menu.
- After being queried about scaling the x or y axis in terms of π, screens appear in which you can set

x minimum = -15
x maximum = 15
y minimum = -15
y maximum = 15

- Press the [Enter] key and the following graph is sketched in the viewing rectangle [-15,15] x [-15,15].

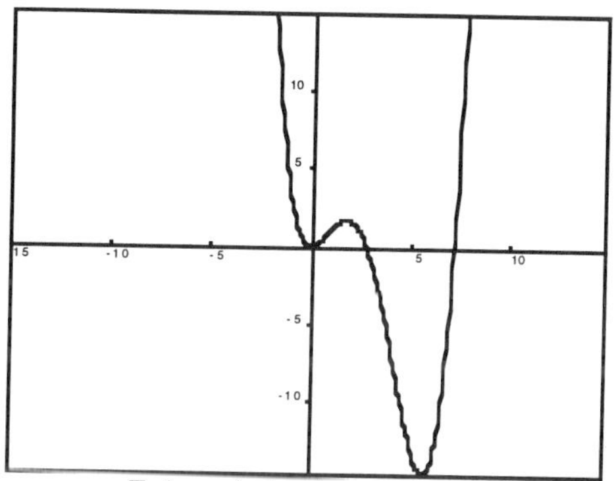

Enlarged viewing rectangle

7.2.5 Zooming: The BestGrapher viewing rectangle can be automatically modified. If you execute the (Z)oom command by pressing the **Z** key, 4 choices are displayed in the Command window.

Zoom: (d)efault, (i)n, (o)ut or (b)ox

- **(d)efault**: redefines the default viewing rectangle, $-5 \leq x \leq 5$ and $-4 \leq y \leq 4$.
- **(i)n**: magnifies the graph in the Plot window.
- **(o)ut:** views more of the graph in the Plot window.
- **(b)ox**: lets you use a cursor to select opposite corners of a box to define a new viewing rectangle.

The following graphs illustrate the effect of zooming in and zooming out.

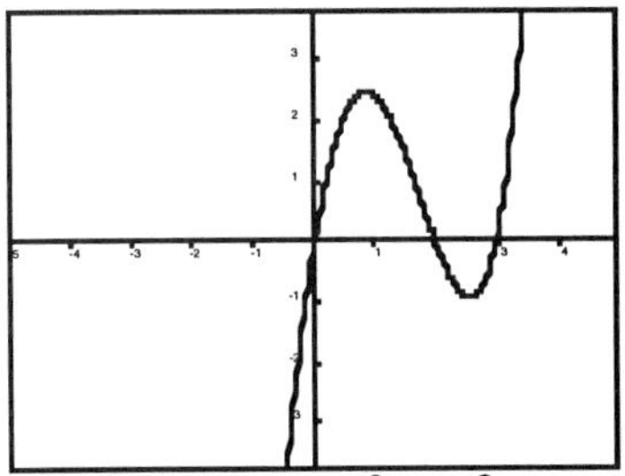

Graph of $f(x) = .2x^2 - 4x^2 + 6x$

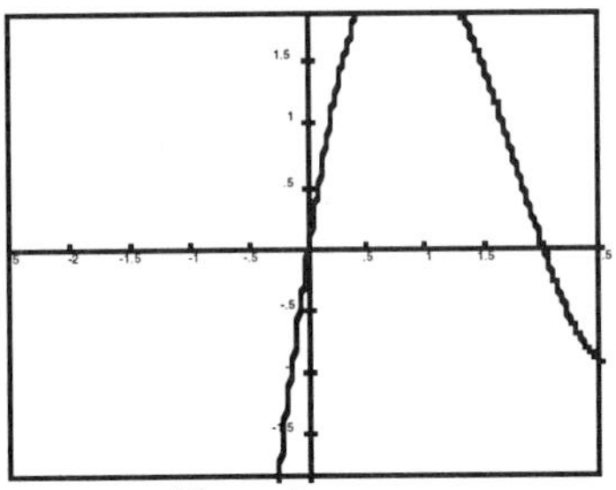

Zoom in

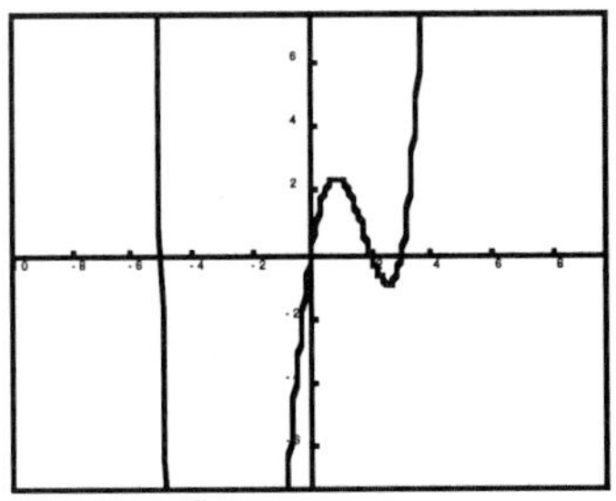

Zoom out

Technology Tip: If you should zoom in or out too much and lose the curve, press the **Z** key and select the (d)efault option to reset the standard viewing rectangle.

The (Z)oom command includes an especially powerful feature of BestGrapher- the ability to put a rectangular box around a piece of a curve and then have that part of the curve magnified to fill the viewing rectangle.

Example: Plot the functions $\mathbf{f(x) = 2cosx}$ and $\mathbf{g(x) = x^3 - 2x}$ on the same coordinate axes and determine the number of times that the graphs intersect.

- Press the **E** key to clear the Plot and Data windows.
- Press the **Z** key and select the (d)efault option to reset the standard viewing rectangle.
- Enter and plot the function $f(x) = 2\cos x$.

- Enter and plot the function $g(x) = x^3 - 2x$.

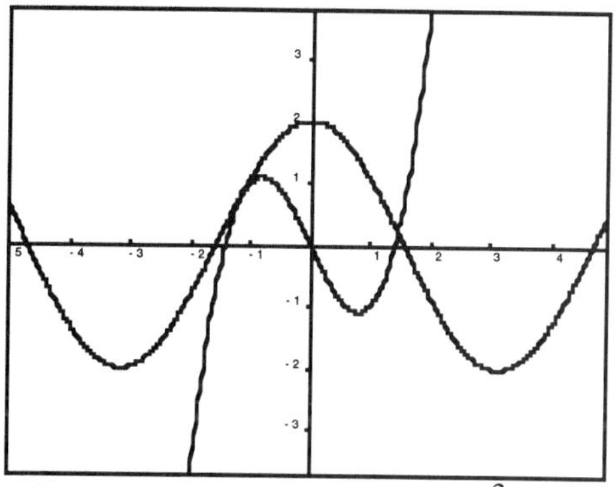

Graphs of $f(x) = 2\cos x$ and $g(x) = x^3 - 2x$

The graphs appear to intersect in two points; there is an intersection point in the first quadrant and a possible intersection point in the second quadrant. We would like to see more detail. Imagine a rectangular box surrounding the portion of the curves that we are interested in.

- Press the **Z** key and select the (b)ox option. You see a cursor positioned at the origin in the Plot window and the following message in the Command window.

> select the first corner (spacebar)

- Using the arrow keys, move the cursor to any corner of the box you want to define and press the space bar. Now you see the following message in the Command window.

> select the other corner (spacebar)

- Move the cursor to the opposite corner of the box you want to define and press the space bar.

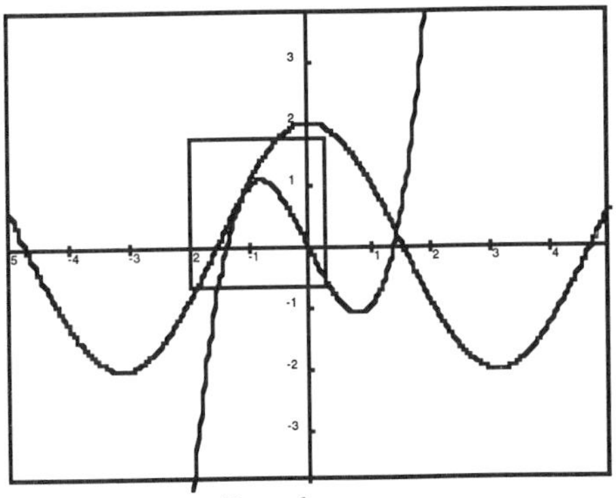

Box drawn

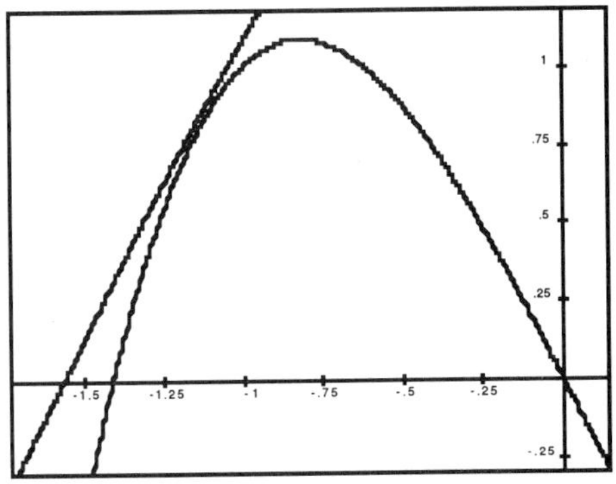

New viewing rectangle

It appears that the graphs intersect only once in the first quadrant.

7.2.6 ***Tracing:*** The Trace command, **F6** in the Quick Keys window, allows you to move a cursor along a graph showing the x and y coordinates of the cursor position in the Command window. When in Trace mode, the left- and right-arrows move the cursor. Pressing the esc key takes you out of Trace mode.

Example: Use the Trace feature to determine the approximate maximum value of the function $\mathbf{f(x) = x^3 sin(2x)}$ on the interval [0,2].

- Press the **F5** key to select the Change menu.
- Set the viewing rectangle so that $-1 \leq x < 3$ and $-1 \leq y \leq 3$.
- Enter the function as x^3sin(2x) and press the Enter key.
- Choose the Trace command by pressing the **F6** key. You see

please enter the initial x-coordinate: ☐

- Enter the number **1**. The cursor is positioned on the graph at the point where x = 1.
- Use the left and right arrow keys to move the cursor and see that the approximate maximum value is y = 1.172 occurring at x = 1.22.

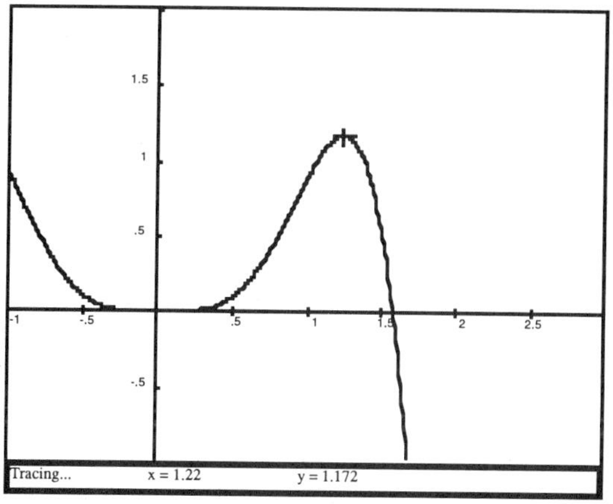

Trace on the graph of $f(x) = x^3 \sin(2x)$

- Press the esc key to exit Trace mode.

7.2.7 Differentiate a function: BestGrapher will differentiate a function symbolically and plot the graph of the derivative function.

Example: Graph the function **f(x) = sin(2x)** and its derivative on the same coordinate axes. Find the x-coordinate of a relative maximum point on the graph of f.

- Press the **E** key to clear the Plot and Data windows.
- Enter and plot the function **f(x) = sin(2x)**.
- Choose the Differentiate Command by pressing the **D** key. BestGrapher plots the derivative function and displays its rule.

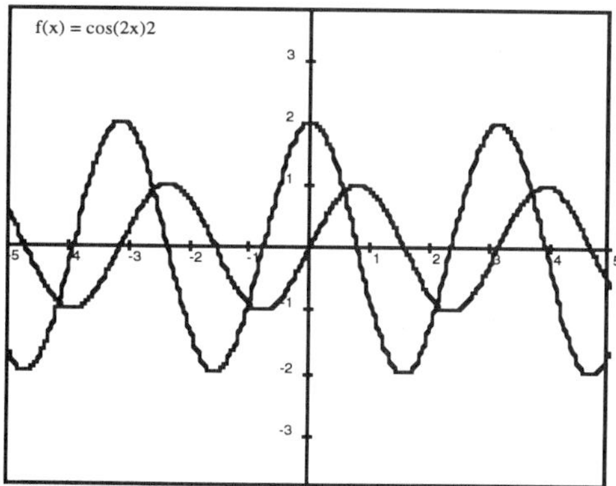

Graph of f(x) = sin(2x) and f'(x) = cos(2x) 2

Notice that the zeros of the derivative correspond to the relative maximum and minimum points on the graph of f(x) = sin(2x).

- Use the **O** key to approximate the zer(O) of **f'(x) = cos(2x)2** in the interval [0, 1].
- A relative maximum of **f(x) = sin(2x)** occurs at approximately x = 0.7854

7.2.8 Integrate a Function: BestGrapher will numerically approximate a definite integral using your choice of method and number of subintervals.

Example: Use the Trapezoid Rule with 10 subdivisions to approximate the $\int_{-1}^{2} (x - \sin x^2)\, dx$.

- Enter and graph the function **f(x) = x – sin(x²).**
- Choose the Integrate Command by pressing the **I** key. A menu appears that offers four methods of approximating the definite integral.

Which Method? (U)pper, (L)ower, (T)rapezoid, (S)impson

- Choose the Trapezoid Rule by pressing the **T** key.
- Now a request for the left endpoint is made in the command window. Enter A = –1.

On what interval? Enter A: ▯

- Next a request for the right endpoint of the interval appears in the command window. Enter B = 2.
- Finally a request for the number of subintervals. Enter n = 10.

Partition into how many equal subintervals? Enter n: ▯

Upon entering the number of subintervals the 10 trapezoids are sketched and the trapezoid approximation is displayed, $\int_{-1}^{2} (x - \sin x^2)\, dx. \approx .397007635$

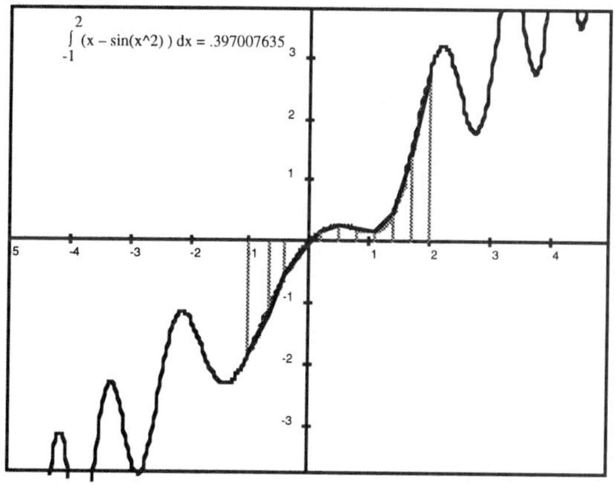

Trapezoid Approximation, 10 subdivisions

7.2.9 Volumes of Solids of Revolution: BestGrapher has a Rotate option that makes it possible to approximate volumes of solids of revolution. If a function f is continuous and nonnegative on the interval [a, b] and R is the region bounded by the graph of f, the x-axis and the lines x = a and x = b, then the volume of the solid obtained by rotating R about

a) the x- axis is $V = \pi \int_a^b [f(x)]^2\, dx$, (disks) b) the y- axis is $V = 2\pi \int_a^b x\, f(x)\, dx$, (shells).

Example: Approximate the volume of the solid that is generated by rotating the first quadrant region bounded by the graph of **f(x) = x lnx** and the line **x = 2** about the y-axis.

- Enter and graph the function **f(x) = x lnx.**
- Choose the Rotate Command by pressing the **R** key. A menu appears that offers the disk or shell method of approximating the volume of the solid.

Horiz. (disks) or vert. (shells) line? Type H or V: ▯

Enter option V for vertical shells.

- Next a request for the equation of the vertical line about which the region is to be rotated.

> Rotate about vertical line x = ▯

Enter x = 0.

- Now a question about the method of approximating the definite integral.

> Which Method? (U)pper, (L)ower, (T)rapezoid, (S)impson

- Choose the Upper sum method by entering the letter U.
- Now a request for the left endpoint is made in the command window. Enter A = 1.

> On what interval? Enter A: ▯

- Next a request for the right endpoint of the interval appears in the command window. Enter B = 2.
- Finally a request for the number of subintervals. Enter n = 10.

> Partition into how many equal subintervals? Enter n: ▯

Upon entering the number of subintervals the 10 shells are sketched and an upper sum approximation of the volume is displayed

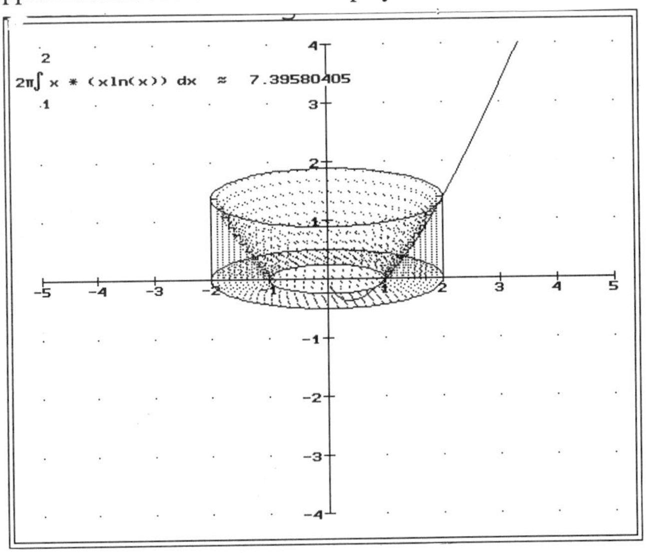

7.2.10 ***Parametric Mode:*** BestGrapher allows you to plot a curve that is expressed parametrically by functions x = f(t) and y = g(t) over the domain $a \le t \le b$. This makes it possible to plot several parametric curves and employ the zoom and trace features. The steps for defining a parametric graph are similar to those for defining a function.

Example: Graph the curve defined by the parametric equations

$$\mathbf{x = t + 1} \text{ and } \mathbf{y = 2 - t^2} \text{ for } -2 \le t \le 2.$$

Approximate the value of t that produces the largest y-coordinate.

- Select the Mode menu by pressing the **F1** key. A menu will appear that offers three choices: (R)ectangular, (P)olar or p(A)rametric.

> Enter function type:
>
> (R)ectangular, (P)olar, or p(A)rametric

- Enter the letter **A**. Pressing **N** for (N)ew function now puts the prompt x(t), y(t) = ▯ in the Command window.

- Enter the right side of each parametric equation: t + 1 , 2 – t^2.

Remember to separate the expressions with a comma.

- Enter the domain $-2 \le t \le 2$ and press the [Enter] key.

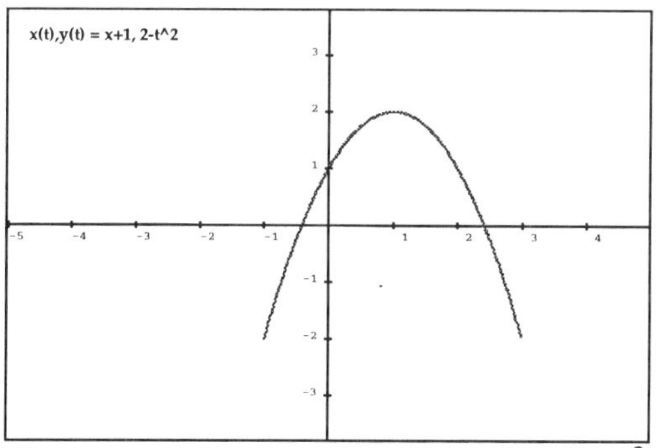

Graph of parametric equations x = t+1 and $y = 2\text{-}t^2$

• Now select Trace mode by pressing the **F6** key and enter an initial t value.

Note that as the cursor is moved along the curve, the values of x, y and t are displayed in the Command window.

• Use the arrow keys to see that the approximate maximum is y = 2 at t = 0.

7.2.11 Polar Curves: If Polar in the Mode menu is selected, all subsequent graphs will be plotted in polar coordinates, that is, an angle coordinate θ and a radius coordinate r, (r, θ).

Example: Plot the polar equation **r = 3cos(2θ)** on the interval $0 \le \theta \le \pi$.

• Select the Mode menu by pressing the **F1** key. A menu will appear that offers three choices: (R)ectangular, (P)olar or p(A)rametric.

Enter function type: (R)ectangular, (P)olar, or p(A)rametric

• Enter the letter **P**. Pressing **N** for (N)ew function now puts the prompt r(θ) = ☐ in the Command window.

• Enter the function as 3cos(2x) and press the [Enter] key.

• Now a request for the range of θ values is made in the Command window. Set A = 0, B = 6.28 and press the [Enter] key.

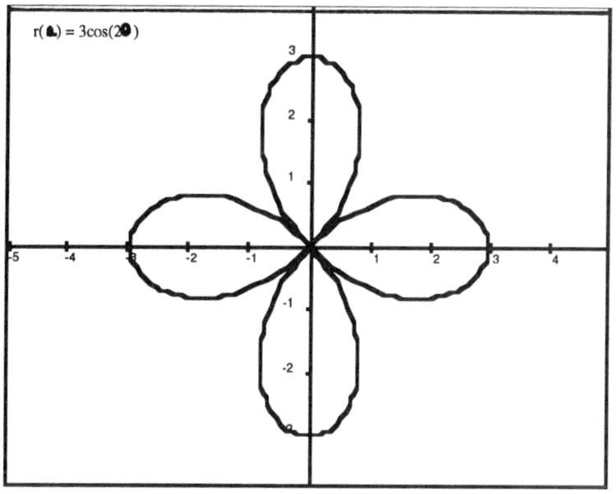

Polar graph of r = 3cos(2θ)

- Now the Trace or Zoom commands may be used to examine the curve.

7.2.12 Saving and Printing Your Work: While you are working in BestGrapher, functions may be saved to, or retrieved from the Function list; however, the Function list is lost when you exit the program. It is possible to save the settings for the viewing rectangle by pressing the **F5 key** and choosing the number 4 option, **4: save configuration data**.

BestGrapher allows you to print the contents of the whole screen or just the contents of the Plot window. Make sure that your printer is on and properly connected; press the **F4 key** and the following screen is displayed.

```
Select a printer:

          1: EpsonMX
          2: EpsonLQ
          3: EpsonFX
          4: ToshibaP
          5: HPLaserPlus
          6: Quit this menu

Type the number of your choice and press ENTER
```

Enter the number of the appropriate printer or select quit and press the Enter key.

7.3 Problem Solving with BestGrapher

This section contains a collection of problems from algebra, precalculus and calculus that demonstrate the problem solving capability of BestGrapher.

7.3.1 Domain and Range of a Function: A mathematical function is a rule, or set of instructions, that assigns an output to each input. The **domain** is the set of possible input values and the **range** is the set of possible output values. Here we will examine the domain and range of a function using BestGrapher.

Example: Plot the function defined by $\mathbf{f(x) = x + 3 + \sqrt{4 - x^2}}$.
Use the graph to approximate the domain and range of f.

Solution:

- Enter the function as x + 3 + sqr(4 – x^2) and press the the Enter key.
- Only a piece of the graph appears on the screen. This indicates that some points of the graph of f do not lie within the standard viewing rectangle. To expand the viewing rectangle, press the **Z** key to display the zoom options; then press the **O** key to obtain the graph below.

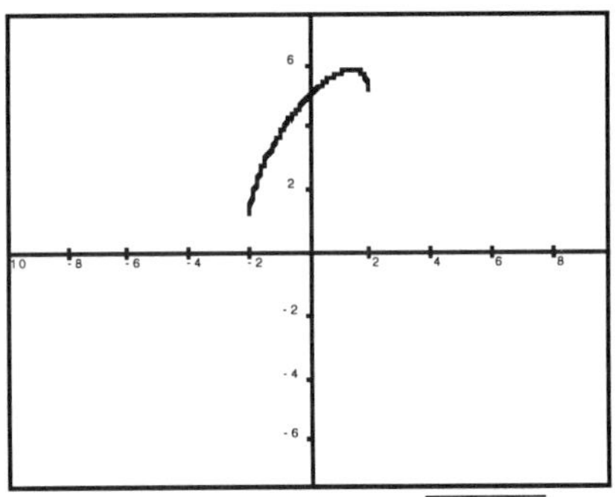

Graph of $f(x) = x + 3 + \sqrt{4 - x^2}$

- You can see from the graph that the domain is the set of real numbers x such that $-2 \le x \le 2$.
- The range appears to be between 1 and a value less than 6. To approximate the maximum range value of f, we trace along the graph to the maximum point and zoom in to get a closer and closer approximation. We estimate that the range of f is all values f(x) such that $1 \le f(x) \le 5.8284$.

Activities and Questions to Explore

1. Use BestGrapher to approximate the range of the following functions.

a) $f(x) = 5x - x^2 - 17$ b) $f(x) = x^3 + x - 15$

c) $f(x) = 3x^4 + 4x^3$ d) $f(x) = (x-2)\sqrt{3-x}$

7.3.2 Equation Solving: Remember that a zero (or root) of the function f refers to a number z in the domain of f such that $f(z) = 0$. Thus finding function zeros means seeking the x coordinate of the points at which the graph intersects the x axis. It is easy to convert any equation-solving problem into a zero-finding problem by simply moving everything nonzero to one side of the equation. For example, solving

$$\sin x = x^2 - x - 6$$

is equivalent to solving

$$\sin x - x^2 + x + 6 = 0,$$

which means seeking zeros for the function $f(x) = \sin x - x^2 + x + 6$. Thus the zero finding capabilities of BestGrapher can be employed to approximate the solutions of an equation.

Example: Use BestGrapher to approximate solutions of $\mathbf{x^2 = 3x + 1}$.

Solution: In standard form, this equation is $x^2 - 3x - 1 = 0$. If we graph $f(x) = x^2 - 3x - 1$, then our task becomes equivalent to finding the zeros of the function f.

- Enter the function as x^2 – 3x – 1 and press the Enter to obtain the graph below.

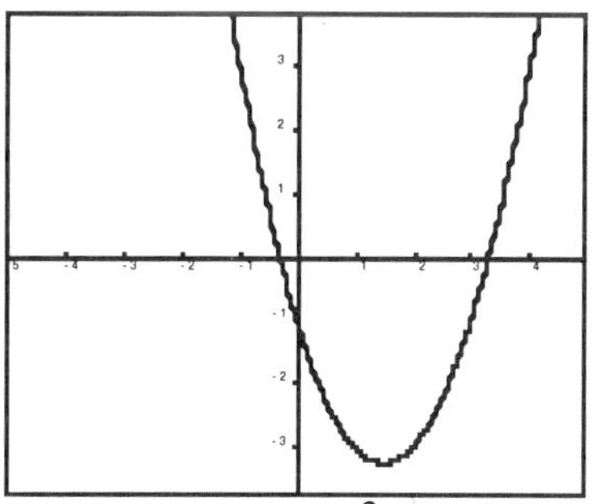

Graph of $f(x) = x^2 - 3x - 1$

- The function f has two zeros, one in the interval [-1, 0] and a second zero in the interval [3, 4]. Press the **O** key and enter a = -1 and b = 0 in order to see that the approximate zero in the interval [-1, 0] is -0.30278
- Press the **O** key again and enter a = 3 and b = 4 in order to see that the approximate zero in the interval [3, 4] is 3.3028.

  Thus the approximate solutions of the equation $x^2 = 3x + 1$ are {-0.30278, 3.3028} .

Activities and Questions to Explore

1. Use BestGrapher to approximate solutions of the following inequalities. Give the answers in interval notation where the endpoints are accurate to two decimal places.

a) $2x - 1 < 4 - 3x$ b) $x^2 + x \leq 6$ c) $|3x - 8| \leq 4$

Technology Tip: BestGrapher employs the Bisection Method to approximate a continuous functions zeros. Briefly, given an initial interval [a,b], the program checks to see if f(a) and f(b) are opposite in sign. If so, the Intermediate Value Theorem guarantees that the continuous function must have a zero in [a,b]. The midpoint m = (a+b)/2 is calculated, and f(m) is compared to f(a) and f(b). If m happens to be a zero, the program displays this information; otherwise, by comparing signs, it learns which half of [a,b] contains the zero to be located. Now the mid-value check is repeated, using the new interval [a,m] or [m,b]. In this way smaller and smaller intervals are defined that contain a zero of f. This iteration process continues until an interval of suitable short length is found or the last midpoint is a zero. Unhappily, the Bisection Method will not always find a function zero. It requires that a function change sign at the zero sought. Thus it will not work with a function like $f(x) = (x - \sqrt{2})^2$.

7.3.3 Graphing Conic Sections: To graph an equation using BestGrapher, you must first write the equation as one or more functions. For example, to graph the circle $x^2 + y^2 = 9$ you can write the upper part of the circle as

$$f(x) = \sqrt{9 - x^2}$$

and the lower half of the circle as

$$f(x) = -\sqrt{9 - x^2} .$$

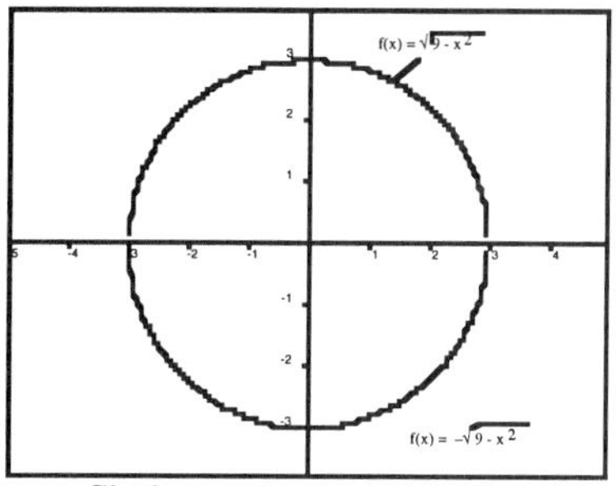

Circle graph - standard view

Example: Graph the parabola $\mathbf{y^2 = x + 4}$ and show that the normal lines to the parabola at the points (-3, 1) and (-3, -1) intersect on the axis of the parabola.

Solution: To graph the parabola $y^2 = x + 4$, we plot two functions

$f(x) = \sqrt{4 + x}$ and $f(x) = -\sqrt{4 + x}$ on the same axes.

- Enter the upper half of the parabola as sqr(4+x) and press the Enter key.
- To draw a normal line to the graph at the point where x = -3, first press the **L** key. Then enter the value -3 when the prompt appears in the Command window and press the Enter key.
- Press the **N** key and enter the lower half of the parabola as -sqr(4+x).
- To draw a normal line to the lower half of the parabola at the point where x = -3, first press the **L** key. Then enter the value -3 when the prompt appears in the Command window and press the Enter key.

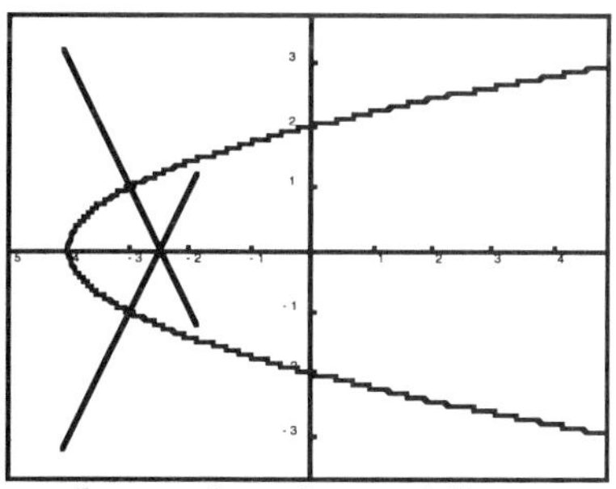

Intersection of normal lines

Activities and Questions to Explore

1. Use BestGrapher to plot and identify the following conic sections.

a) $x^2 + y^2 = 16$ b) $\frac{x^2}{9} + \frac{y^2}{16} = 1$ c) $\frac{x^2}{4} - \frac{y^2}{9} = 1$

7.3.4 Maximum and Minimum Values: Finding a maximum or minimum is often an important part of problem solving. For example, manufacturers want to maximize their profits, contractors want to minimize their costs, and a physician would like to select the smallest dosage of a drug that will cure a disease. Determining the maximum or minimum value of some quantity can often be reduced to finding the largest and smallest value of a function on some interval.

Example: A hiker finds herself in a forest 2 miles from a straight road. She wants to walk to her car which is parked 10 miles down the road. If she can walk 4 mph along the road, but only 3 mph through the forest, toward what point on the road should she walk in order to reach her car in the least time?

Solution: From the figure, the distance to the point P on the road is $\sqrt{x^2 + 4}$ and the distance from P to the car is $10 - x$.

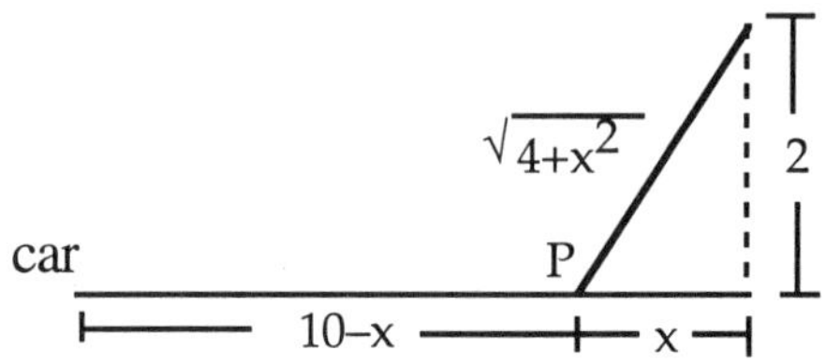

Since time = distance/rate, the total time f(x) to reach the car is

$$\mathbf{f(x)} = \frac{\sqrt{4+x^2}}{3} + \frac{(10 - x)}{4} \quad \text{with } 0 \le x \le 10.$$

- Press the **F5** key and select option **1** from the Change menu; set the dimensions of the viewing rectangle so that $-2 \le x \le 12$ and $-6 \le y \le 6$.
- Enter the function f as sqr(4+x^2)/3 + (10 – x)/4.
- Press the Enter key and see the following graph.

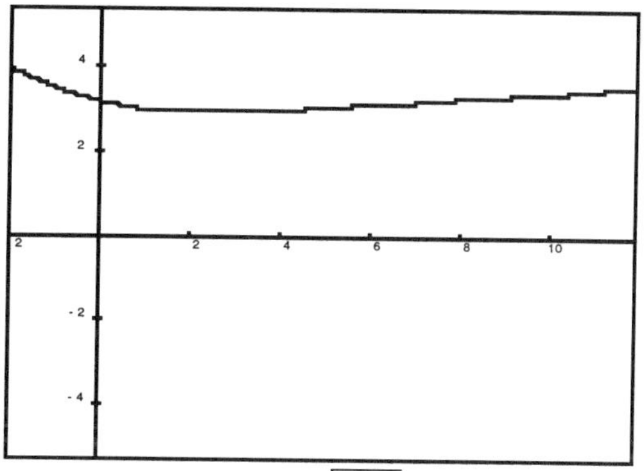

Graph of $f(x) = \frac{\sqrt{4+x^2}}{3} + \frac{(10-x)}{4}$

- To locate the minimum value we first graph the derivative of f(x) by pressing the **D** key. Then to approximate the zero of the derivative that corresponds to the minimum value on the graph of f, press the **O** key and find that the approximate minimum time is 2.941 hours at x = 2.268 miles.

Activities and Questions to Explore

1. Find the maximum and minimum values of the function on the given interval.

   a) $f(x) = x - x^3$ on [0, 1]. b) $f(x) = 3x - x^2$ on [0, 3].

2. A weight oscillates on a spring; its height is given by $f(x) = \sin x + \cos x + 1$.

   a) What are the highest and lowest points?

   b) How large an interval do you need to use in order to determine the largest and smallest points?

*7.3.5 **Area of a Region Between Two Curves*** The definite integral has a wide variety of applications. For example, integrals can be used to measure the area between two curves.

Example: Approximate the area of the region R bounded above by the graph of $\mathbf{f(x) = 2\sin x}$ and and below by the graph of $\mathbf{g(x) = x^2}$.

Solution: The picture below shows the region we are interested in.

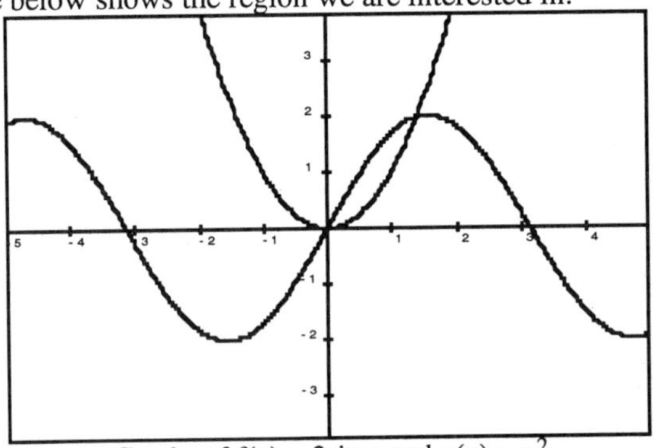

Graphs of $f(x) = 2\sin x$ and $g(x) = x^2$

In this region, $2 \sin x \geq x^2$, so that Area = $\int_a^b (2 \sin x - x^2)\, dx$ where a and b are the x-values of the points of intersection of the curves. The graph of $y = 2 \sin x - x^2$ below indicates that a = 0 and b is a point to the right of the origin in the interval [1, 2].

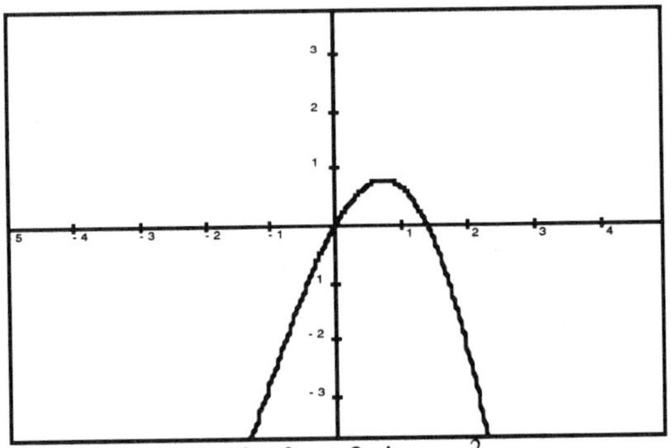

Graph of $y = 2 \sin x - x^2$

To estimate b we apply the zer(O) finding capability of BestGrapher to the function $y = 2 \sin x - x^2$. You should verify that b = 1.4044

To approximate the integral $\int_0^{1.4044} (x^2 - \sin x)\, dx$

press the **I** key and on the interval [0, 1.4044], use Simpson's rule with 20 subdivisions to obtain the approximate area = 0.74542

Note that the area between curves may also be fonund by integrating each function separately and taking the difference of the results, rather than integrating the difference function.

Activities and Questions to Explore

In Exercises 1–2, sketch the region bounded by the graphs of the given functions and find the area of the region.

1. $f(x) = x^2 + 2x + 1$ and $g(x) = 2x + 5$.

2. $f(x) = \arctan x$ and $g(x) = x^2 - 1$.

7.3.6 ***Simulating the Motion of a Particle:*** It is possible to simulate the linear motion of a particle by combining parametric mode and the BestGrapher trace feature.

Example: Let the position (x-coordinate) of a moving particle on the line y = 1 be given by $x(t) = t^2 - 2t$ for $0 \leq t \leq 3$.

Using parametric mode in BestGrapher, simulate the motion of the particle.

Solution: • Select the Mode menu by pressing the **F1** key. A menu will appear that offers three choices: (R)ectangular, (P)olar or p(A)rametric.

Enter function type:
(R)ectangular, (P)olar, or p(A)rametric

• Press the **A** key. Now pressing **N** for (N)ew function puts the prompt x(t), y(t) = ☐ in the Command window.

• Enter the right sides of the parametric equations $x(t) = t^2 - 2t$ and $y(t) = 1$ as t^2 – 2t, 1. Remember to separate the expressions with a comma..

- Enter the domain $0 \leq t \leq 3$ and press the Enter key.

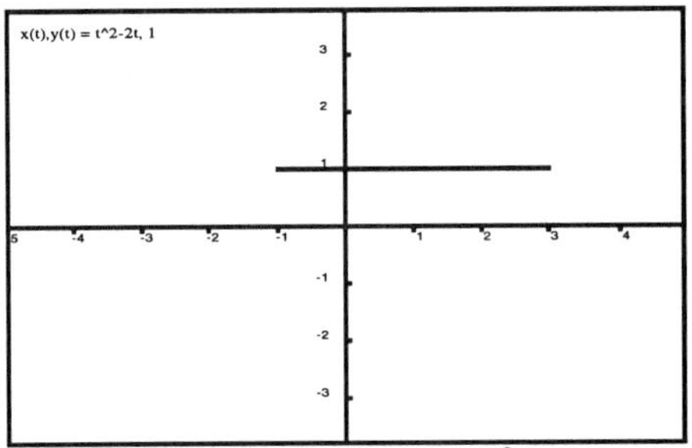

Graphs of parametric equations $x = t^2 - 2t$ and $y = 1$

- Choose Trace by pressing the **F6** key and use the arrow keys to position the cursor at the point where $t = 0$.
- Now hold down the right arrow key and watch the motion of the particle.

Activities and Questions to Explore

1. What is the coordinate of the particle at $t = 0, 1, 2,$ and 3?
2. What is the total distance traveled by the particle for $t = 0$ to $t = 3$?
3. If the parameter t represents time in seconds, what is the average speed of the particle?
4. At what points and at what time is the particle at rest? moving to the right?
5. Does it appear that the particle is moving at a constant speed?

7.4 BestGrapher Commands and Quick Keys

7.4.1 Commands: The following is a brief description of the commands that can be executed in BestGrapher.

•(**N**)ew function: The **N** command tells **BestGrapher** that a new function is being defined.

•(**E**)rase: The **E** command clears the viewing rectangle.

•e(**V**)aluate: The **V** command evaluates the last function graphed at an argument you specify.

•find zer(**O**): Searches for a zero of the last function graphed on an interval you supply.

•(**Z**)oom: <o>ut to see more of the graph; <i>n for greater detail or<b>ox in a portion of the coordinate plane.

•li(**M**)it: The **M** command will make **BestGrapher** search for a delta for any epsilon your supply.

•(**S**)ecant: Draws a secant to a curve.

•(**T**)angent: Draws an exact tangent to the last function graphed.

•(**N**)ormal: Draws a normal to the last function.

•(**D**)ifferentiate: Graphs the derivative of the last function graphed.

•(**I**)ntegrate: Graphically approximates the integral of the last function graphed using upper or lower sums or the trapezoidal rule or Simpson's rule.

•(**R**)otate: Graphically approximates the volume swept out when an interval of the last function graphed is rotated about a horizontal or vertical line.

For calculus students, **BestGrapher** will differentiate and antidifferentiate. Typing a **D** will cause **BestGrapher** to differentiate symbolically. Alternatively, the pseudo-function " deriv " will differentiate symbolically and graph the derivative of whatever is passed to it as an argument. So typing " antideriv (3x^2+5x) " would approximate the antiderivative of its argument. It does this by approximating the indefinite integral from zero to x using Simpson's rule. Since it always starts from zero, you may want to add a constant.

7.4.2 Quick Keys: Since there are a number of menus and tasks that you will be employing again and again we have provided Quick Keys. Notice the window in the lower right corner of the screen, which lists several commands and the keys for invoking them.

Quick Keys

F1 Mode
F2 Commands
F3 Fnct list
F4 Print
F5 Change
F6 Trace

Alt + X Exit

- Press **F2** to display a list of all commands.
- Press **F3** to display a list of previously entered functions.
- Press **F4** to display a menu for printing.
- Press **F5** to display a menu for changing the viewing rectangle
- Press **F6** to invoke tracing mode.
- Press **ALT-X** to exit the program.

CHAPTER 8

BestGrapher for the Macintosh

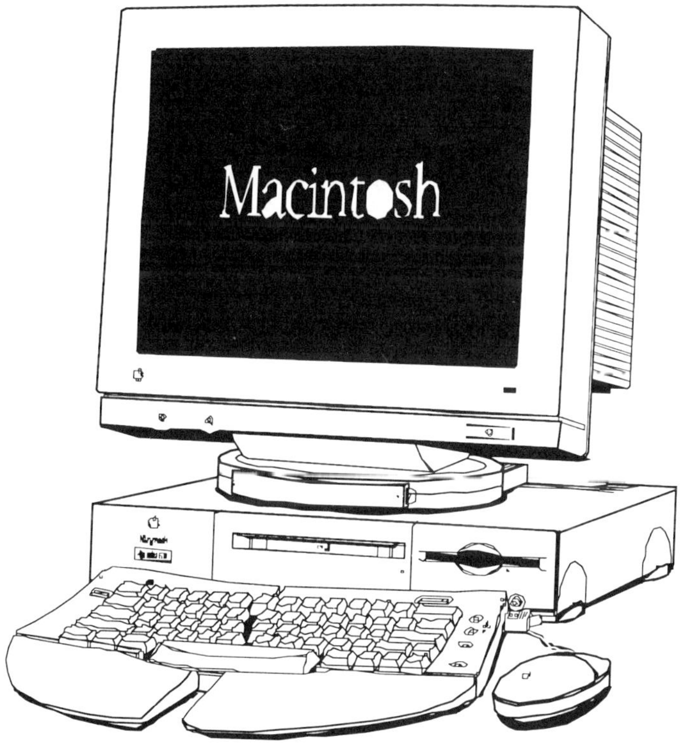

Chapter 8. BestGrapher for the Macintosh

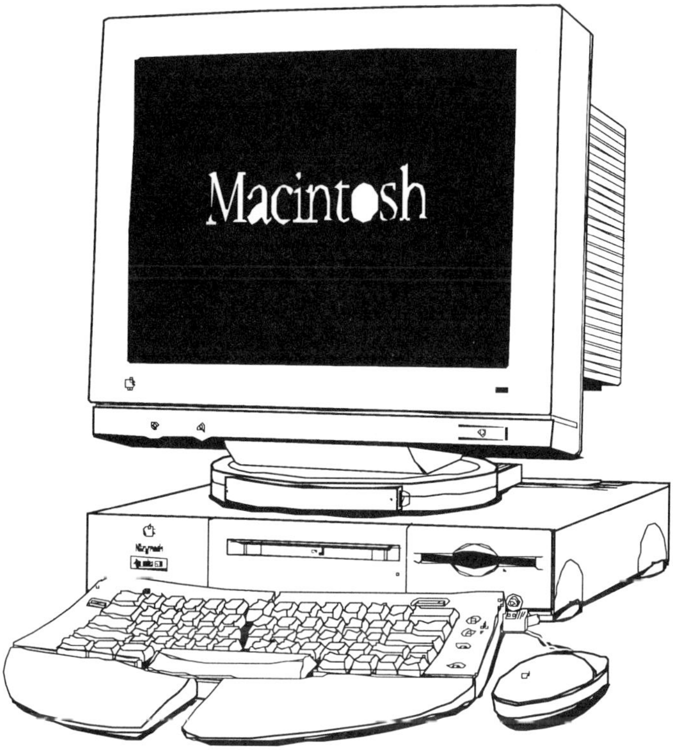

8.1 Introduction

8.1.1 What is BestGrapher: BestGrapher is an easy-to-use, surprisingly powerful function graphing program that is designed to clarify the concepts of precalculus and calculus. It can graph functions in rectangular or polar coordinates as well as parameterized functions and conics. Graphs can easily be rescaled or resized. When BestGrapher is in rectangular plotting mode, it can evaluate a function, find zeros and the intersection of curves, draw tangent and secant lines, for example. BestGrapher can print images on an ImageWriter or Laser printer. The images created by BestGrapher can also be copied to the Clipboard, and included in a document prepared by word-processing software.

This highly accessible program is an excellent teaching tool for both demonstrations and student exploration and experimentation.

8.1.2 Installing BestGrapher: BestGrapher runs on any Macintosh and requires the following hardware and software:

- At least 1 MB of memory (2 MB with MultiFinder)
- System 6.0 or later
- One 800K disk drive and a hard drive or two 800K drives

Insert the BestGrapher disk into a disk drive. The disk will be read by the Macintosh and the BestGrapher disk window will open. To run BestGrapher, double-click on the BestGrapher icon, shown in the figure below.

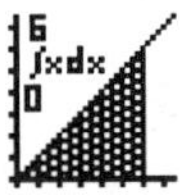

The BestGrapher program icon

The program will start and three windows will open. Use the Quit command under the File menu to exit BestGrapher.

You can copy BestGrapher to your hard drive by dragging the icon to the hard disk icon. If you are using BestGrapher from a floppy disk, be sure to make a backup copy and work with it, keeping the original disk in a safe place.

8.1.3 Getting Help: If you need a description of some BestGrapher feature or shortcut, select BestGrapher Instructions under the Help icon (System 7) or the Apple menu (System 6). The following help window will appear.

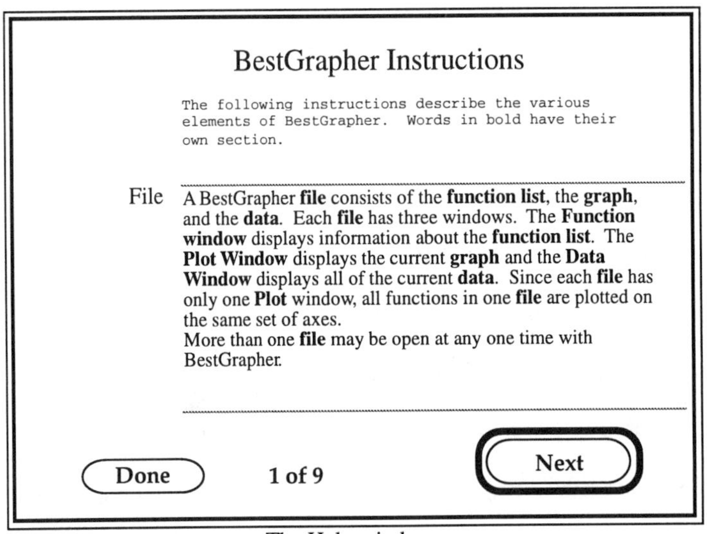

The Help window

8.2 Using BestGrapher

8.2.1 Getting Started: To run BestGrapher, double-click the BestGrapher icon. Three windows will appear on the screen; the Function window at the top, the Data window bottom left, and the Plot window bottom right.

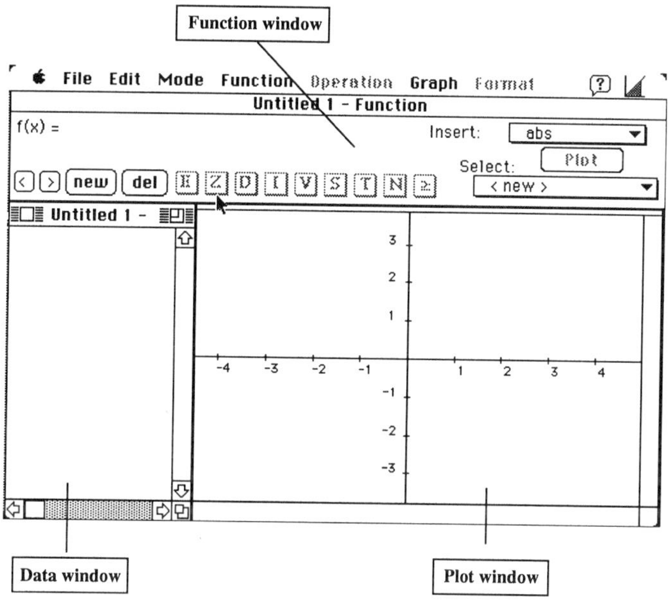

To quickly introduce the capabilities of BestGrapher we will plot and find a zero of a function.

Example: Plot and find the smallest real zero of the function $f(\mathbf{x}) = \mathbf{x}^3 - \mathbf{2x}$.

- Click on the Function window to make it active.
- The blinking cursor in the text function box is ready to receive the function. Type the expression **x^3 – 2x** (the ^ character is shift-6 on the keyboard).
- Click the Plot button (or press the Return key); the function will be graphed and a table of values will be displayed in the Data window.

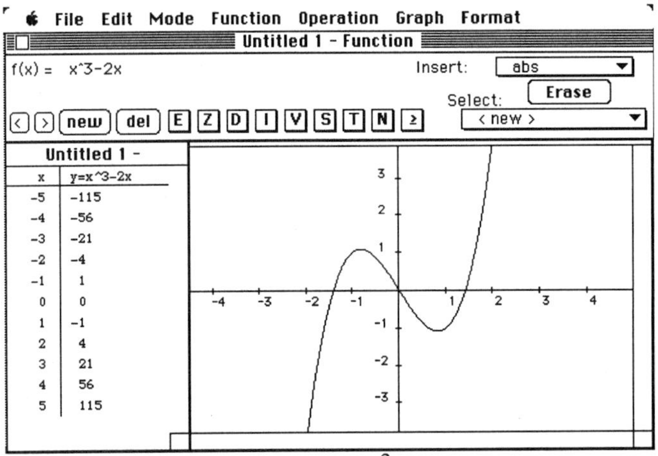

Graph of $f(x) = x^3 - 2x$

The bottom of the Function window contains a tool palette. The tools do various tasks such as [E]valuating, finding [Z]eros, [D]ifferentiating and so on.

- Click on the [Z] tool. The tool is highlighted and a dialog box appears that provides choices for the left endpoint a and the right endpoint b of the interval that contains the smallest real zero.

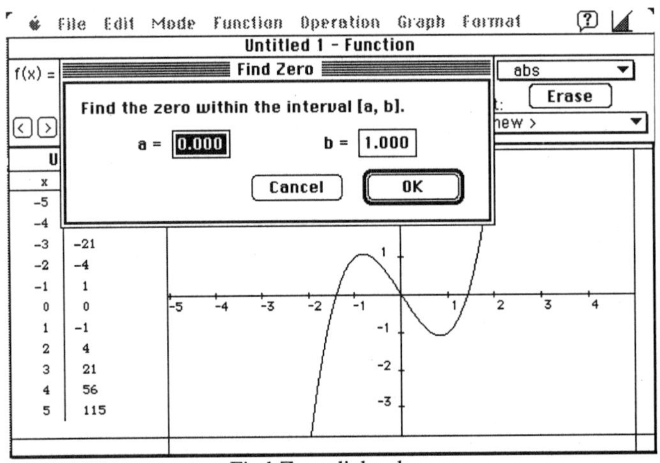

Find Zero dialog box

- Enter $a = 1$ and $b = 2$. Click the OK button and an approximation of the smallest real zero, f(1.41421356) = 0, will be displayed in the Data window.

Technology Tip: When some menu options are chosen a dialog box is displayed that contains various buttons and edit cells for entering information. You can click in any cell to make it active or use the Tab key to move from one cell to the next.

8.2.2 Entering Functions: Basically, BestGrapher is a function grapher and the first step in using the program is to enter a function. The format for entering a function is very similar to ordinary mathematics notation. Legal functions are, for example:

(x + 2)(x + 3), sin x, cos(2x), xln x and arctan(exp x)

All implied parentheses and multiplication are evaluated correctly. The * sign is not needed in BestGrapher but will be accepted if used.

- For division, use the slash symbol, / .
- If you type π (Option-p), BestGrapher will treat it as if you entered an approximation of π to 10 decimal places. For example, sin(πx) will graph as a sin curve with period 2.
- You may use any type of parentheses, (, [or { .
- To raise something to a power use the caret symbol ^ .
- When using BestGrapher you may type in upper or lower case letters.
- To edit a function rule, you can use the standard Macintosh text-processing techniques-- cutting, copying and pasting. Insert text by clicking at the insertion point and typing the text. Delete text by dragging over it to highlight it and pressing the Delete key.

Example: Sketch a graph of $\mathbf{f(x) = \pi cos^2(3x)}$. Evaluate the function f at x = 2.3.

- Click on the Function window to make it active.
- Type the expression π (cos(3x))^2 into the Function window.
- Click the Plot button (or press the Return key); the function will be graphed and a table of values will be displayed in the Data window.
- Click the E tool and a dialog box appears. Enter x = 2.3 and click the Evaluate button. The value 2.0904 is displayed in the Data window.

• Click the Close box in the upper left-hand corner of the dialog box to close it.

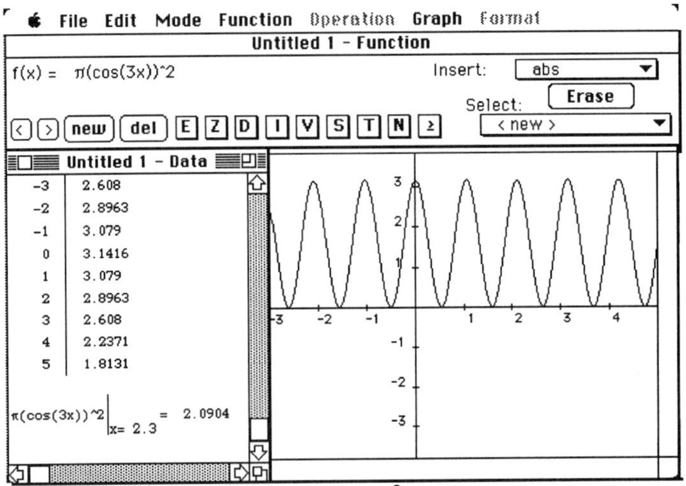

Evaluation of $f(x) = \pi^2\cos(3x)$ at $x = 2.3$

Technology Tip: Notice in the screen display above that the Data window has been enlarged. If you are unable to read all of the information in the Data window, the window may be 1) scrolled up or down, or 2) enlarged by resizing it.

8.2.3 Additional Features for Entering Functions: In addition to entering a function from the keyboard, it is possible to enter a previously defined function from one of two pop-up menus that are located in the Function window. A pop-up menu named Insert that lists all predefined functions in BestGrapher is located on the right side of the Function window. Clicking the Insert menu displays the list and the selected function is pasted into the text function box.

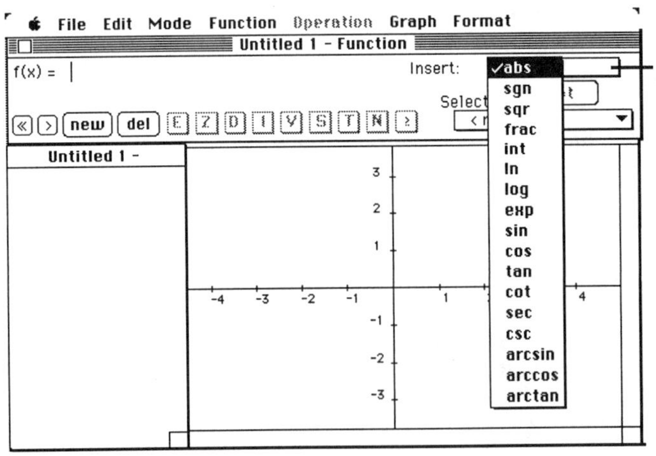

Clicking the Insert menu box displays the predefined functions and pastes the selected function into the text function box.

A second pop-up menu named Select is located in the lower right-hand corner of the Function window. Functions may be saved for future reference by storing them in the Select menu list. To put the current function into the Select list for future reference, click on the new button. The current function is then appended to the list of previously saved functions.

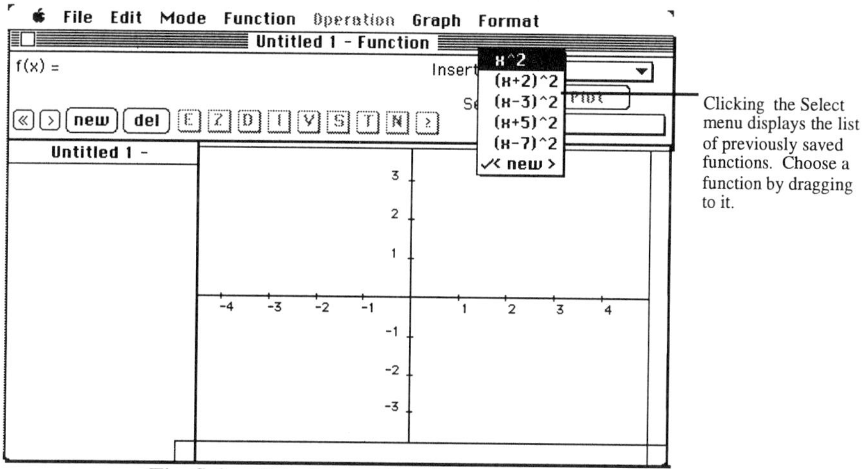

The Select list of saved functions

To recall a function from the Select list, click on the Select menu box, drag to the desired function and release the mouse.

The <, >, new and del buttons in the tool palette may be employed to manage the Select list of saved functions.

- < makes the previous function in the Select list the current function.
- > makes the next function in the Select list the current function.
- new appends the current function to the Select list.
- del deletes the current function from the Select list.

8.2.4 The Viewing Rectangle: The coordinate plane is infinite; with a graphing utility like BestGrapher you view one rectangle of the plane at a time. This viewing rectangle, called Plot in BestGrapher, is a lens through which you see a close-up or distant view of a graph by changing the dimensions of the viewing rectangle. The dimensions of the standard or default BestGrapher viewing rectangle are x minimum = -5.0, x maximum = 5.0, y minimum = -3.8 and y maximum = 3.8.

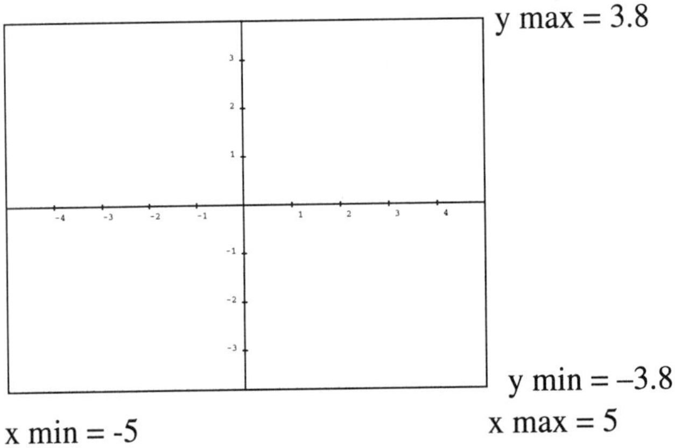

The standard viewing rectangle

If you wish to see or change the settings of the Plot window, choose the command Preferences under the Graph menu.

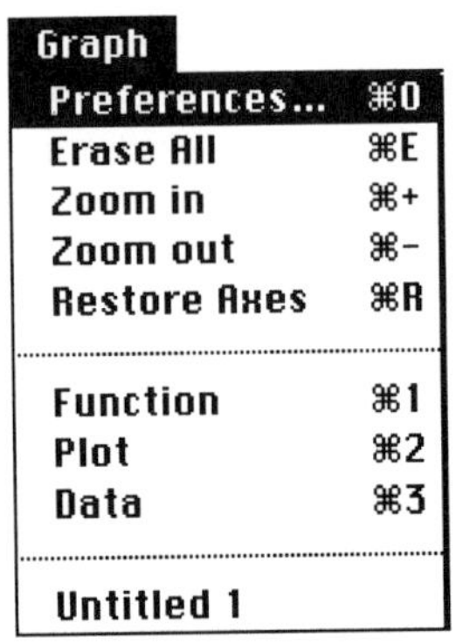

A dialog box appears in which the initial dimensions of the Plot viewing rectangle are displayed.

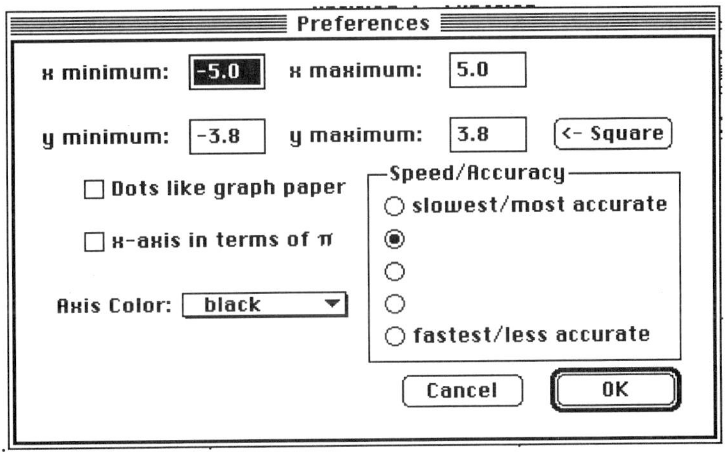

The Preference dialog box

To change the dimensions of the Plot window, use the Tab key to move from one cell to the next, or click in any cell to activate it.

By choosing different viewing rectangles of a graph it is possible to obtain different views of a graph's shape.

Example: Use BestGrapher to graph the function $\mathbf{f(x) = 0.1x^4 - x^3 + 2x^2}$ in the viewing rectangle a) [-5,5] x [-3.8,3.8] and b) [-15,15] x [-15,15].

a) Enter the rule 0.1x^4 – x^3 + 2x^2 and click on the Plot button.

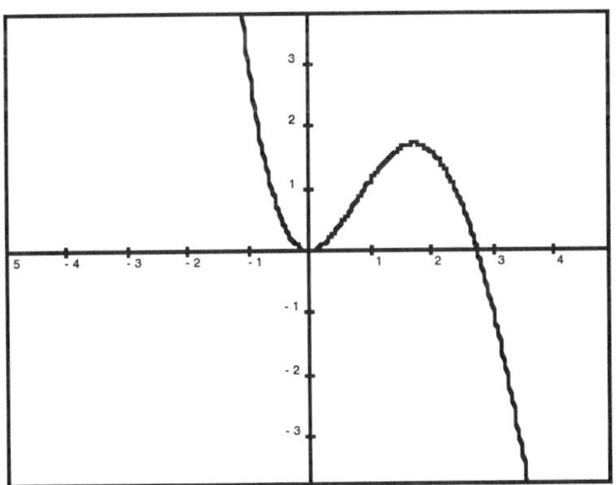

Graph of $f(x) = 0.1x^4 - x^3 + 2x^2$

b) To change the dimensions of the Plot window

• Choose Preferences under the Graph menu.

• A dialog box appears in which you can set
x minimum = -15
x maximum = 15
y minimum = -15
y maximum = 15

• Click the OK button and the following graph is sketched in the viewing rectangle [-15,15] x [-15,15].

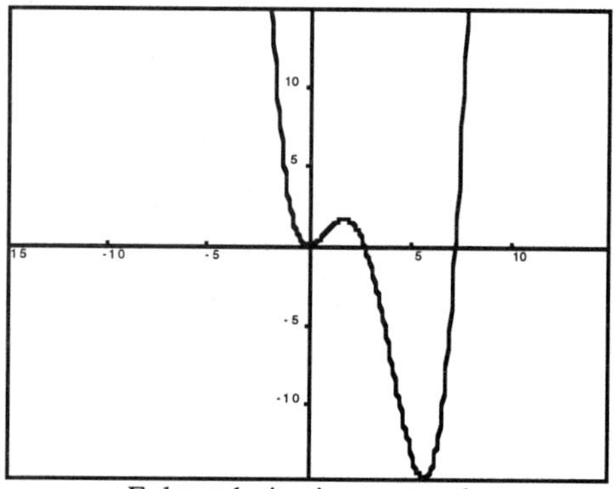

Enlarged viewing rectangle

8.2.5 Zooming: The BestGrapher viewing rectangle can be automatically modified. If all you want to do is zoom out or zoom in, without any interest in the particular x- and y-ranges, then choose the Zoom in or Zoom out commands under the Graph menu.

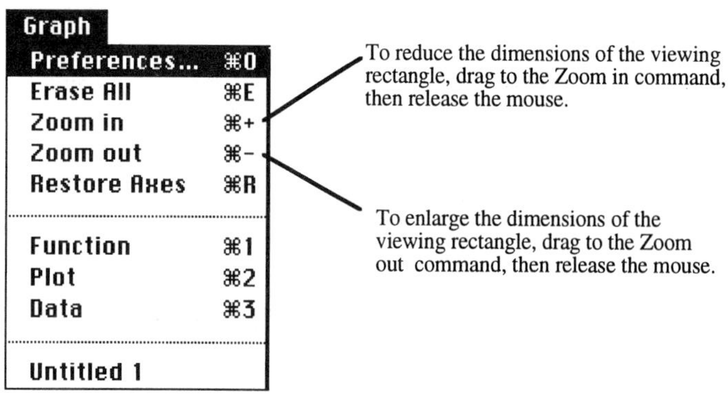

The following graphs illustrate the effect of zooming in and zooming out.

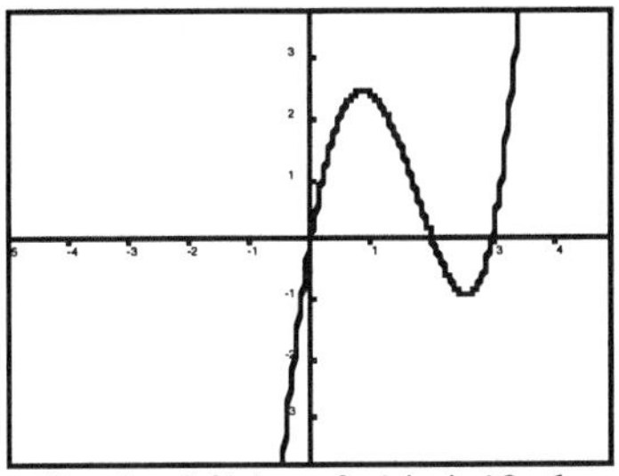

Graph of f(x) = .2x^4–4x^2+6x

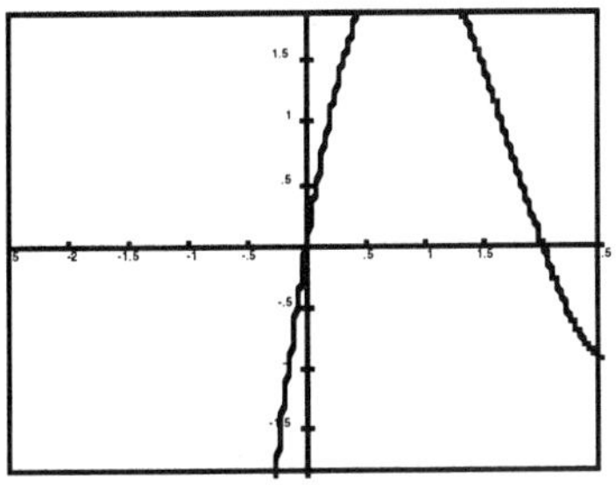

Zoom in

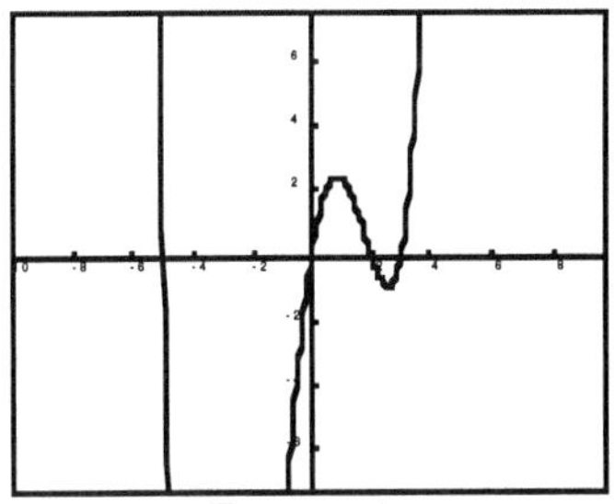

Zoom out

How far did we zoom in or zoom out in the graphs above? You can always choose Preferences under the Graph menu to see the new dimensions of the viewing rectangle.

Technology Tip: If you should zoom in or out too much and lose the curve, choose the Restore Axes command from the Graph menu to reset the standard viewing rectangle.

We now investigate one of the especially powerful features of BestGrapher - the ability to put a rectangular box around a piece of a curve and then have that part of the curve magnified to fill the viewing rectangle.

Example: Plot the functions $\mathbf{f(x) = 2cosx}$ and $\mathbf{g(x) = x^3 - 2x}$ on the same coordinate axes and determine the number of times that the graphs intersect.

- Choose Restore Axes under the Graph menu to reset the default viewing rectangle.
- Enter the function f(x) = 2cosx and click the Plot button.
- Click the New button to clear the text function box and store the function f in the Select list.

• Enter and plot the function $g(x) = x^3 - 2x$.

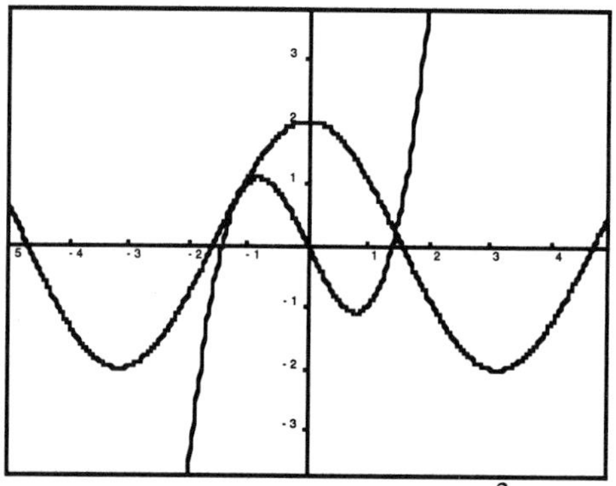

Graphs of $f(x) = 2\cos x$ and $g(x) = x^3 - 2x$

The graphs appear to intersect in two points; there is an intersection point in the first quadrant and a possible intersection point in the second quadrant. We would like to see more detail. Imagine a rectangular box surrounding the portion of the curves that we are interested in.

• Use the mouse to position the cursor into one corner of that rectangular box.

• Now click the mouse and drag it to the opposite corner of that box (you will see the rectangle change in shape as you drag the cursor).

• When you are satisfied with the second corner's position release the mouse.

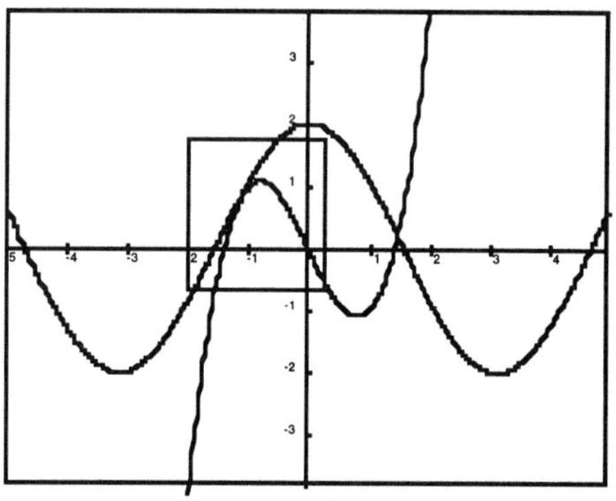

Box drawn

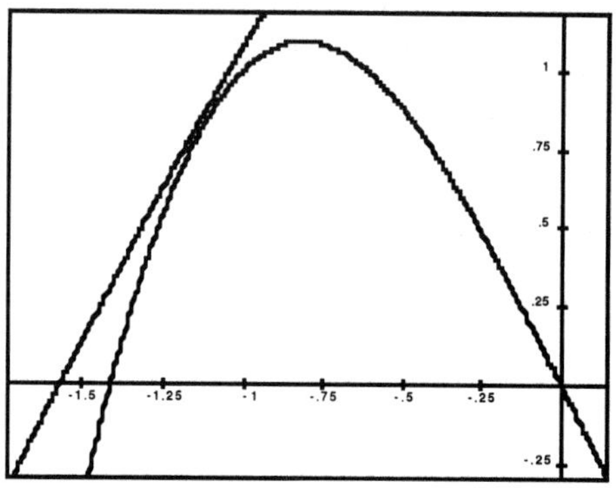

New viewing rectangle

It appears that the graphs intersect only once in the first quadrant.

*8.2.6 **Tracing:*** The Trace command under the Function menu allows you to move a cursor along a graph showing the x and y coordinates of the cursor position at the bottom of the Plot window. When in Trace mode, the left- and right-arrows move the cursor. Alternatively, clicking and holding the mouse down will move the cursor. The up- and down-arrows change the speed of the cursor. Pressing the [esc] key takes you out of Trace mode.

Example: Use the Trace feature to determine the approximate maximum value of the function $\mathbf{f(x) = x^3 sin(2x)}$ on the interval [0,2].

• Enter the function as x^3sin(2x) .

• Choose Preferences under the Graph menu and set the viewing rectangle so that $-1 \le x < 3$ and $-1 \le y \le 3$.

• Click the Plot button to graph the function.

• Choose the Trace command under the Function menu.

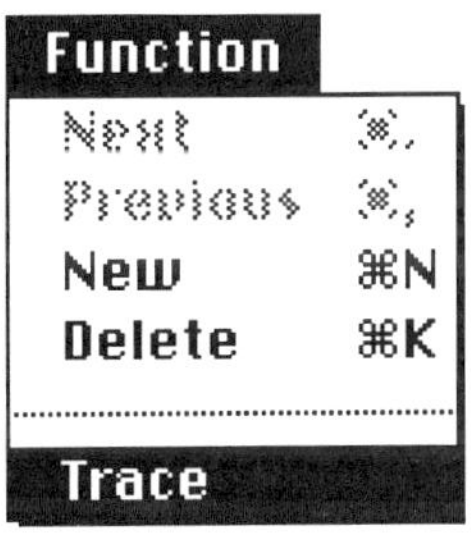

Drag down to the Trace command, and then release the mouse button

Notice that a cursor is placed at the middle of the most recently drawn graph.

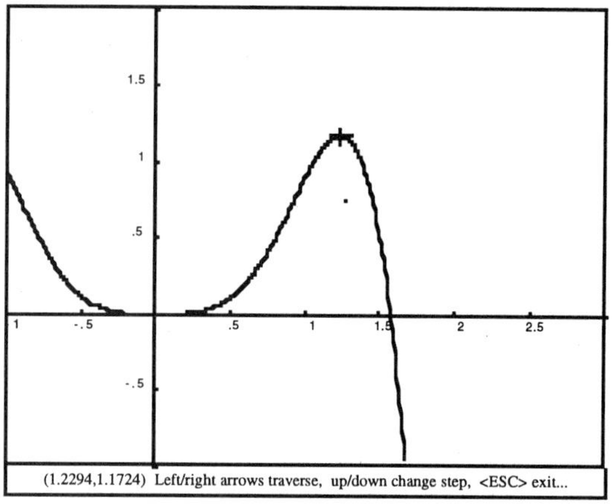

Trace on the graph of $f(x) = x^3\sin(2x)$

- Use the left- and right-arrow keys to move the cursor along the graph to see that the approximate maximum value is y = 1.1724 occurring at x = 1.2294.

- Press the [esc] key to exit Trace mode.

8.2.7 Differentiate a function: BestGrapher will differentiate a function symbolically and plot the graph of the derivative function.

Example: Graph the function **f(x) = sin(2x)** and its derivative on the same coordinate axes. Find the x-coordinate of a relative maximum point on the graph of f.

- Enter and plot the function **f(x) = sin(2x)**.

- Click the [D] tool and a dialog box appears that gives you the opportunity to change the color and style of the derivative graph. Click the [OK] button and BestGrapher plots the derivative function and displays its rule.

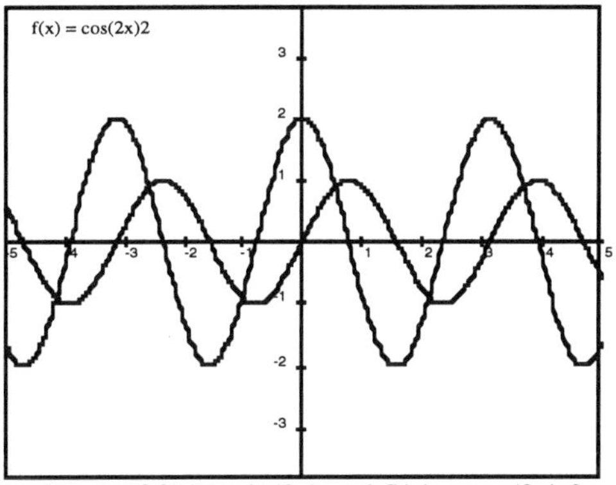

Graph of $f(x) = \sin(2x)$ and $f'(x) = \cos(2x)\,2$

Notice that the zeros of the derivative correspond to the relative maximum and minimum points on the graph of $f(x) = \sin(2x)$.

- Use the [Z] tool to approximate the zeros of $\mathbf{f'(x) = \cos(2x)2}$ in the interval [0, 1].
- A relative maximum of $\mathbf{f(x) = \sin(2x)}$ occurs at approximately x = 0.7854

8.2.8 Integrate a Function: BestGrapher will numerically approximate a definite integral using your choice of method and number of subintervals.

Example: Use the Trapezoid Rule with 10 subdivisions to approximate the $\int_{-1}^{2} (x - \sin x^2)\, dx$.

- Enter and graph the function $\mathbf{f(x) = x - \sin(x^2)}$.
- Choose the Integrate Command by clicking the [I] tool. A dialog box appears that offers four methods of approximating the definite integral.

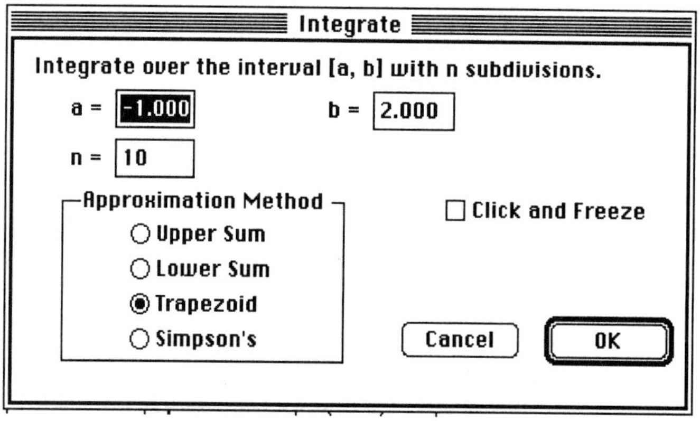

- Enter a = –1, b = 2 and n = 10; click on the button for the Trapezoid method and then click the OK button.

The Plot window is redrawn with the 10 trapezoids sketched and the trapezoid approximation displayed, $\int_{-1}^{2} (x - \sin x^2)\, dx. \approx .397007635$

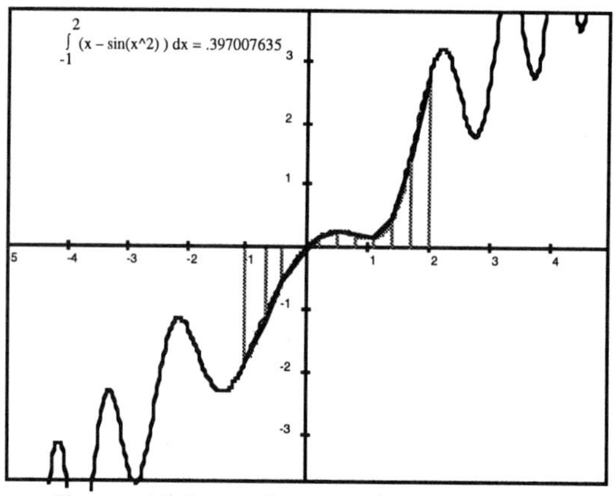

Trapezoid Approximation, 10 subdivisions

8.2.9 ***Volumes of Solids of Revolution:*** BestGrapher has a Find Volume option that makes it possible to approximate volumes of solids of revolution. If a function f is continuous and nonnegative on the interval [a, b] and R is the region bounded by the graph of f, the x-axis and the lines x = a and x = b, then the volume of the solid obtained by rotating R about

a) the x- axis is $V = \pi \int_a^b [f(x)]^2\,dx$, (disks) b) the y- axis is $V = 2\pi \int_a^b x\,f(x)\,dx$, (shells).

Example: Approximate the volume of the solid that is generated by rotating the first quadrant region bounded by the graph of **f(x) = x lnx** and the line **x = 2** about the y-axis.

- Enter and graph the function **f(x) = x lnx.**
- Choose the Find Volume command by clicking the [V] tool. A dialog box appears that offers a disk or shell method of approximating the volume of the solid of revolution.

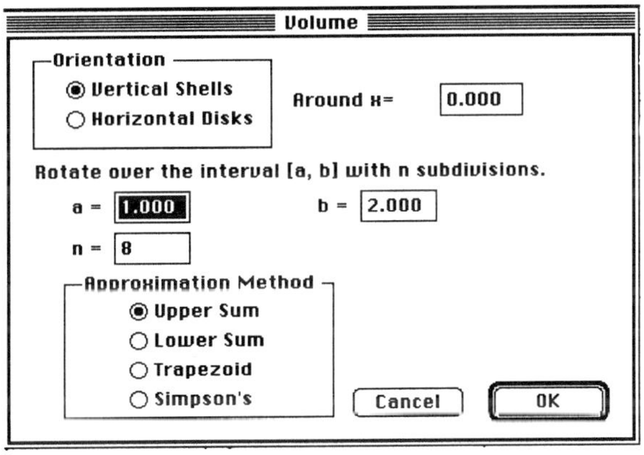

- Click the Vertical Shells button and enter x= 0 as the equation of the vertical line around which the region is to be rotated.
- Specify the interval and number of subdivisions by entering a = 1, b = 2 and n =8.
- Now click on the Upper Sum button to determine the method of approximating the definite integral.

Upon clicking on the OK button, 8 shells are sketched and an upper sum approximation of the volume is displayed

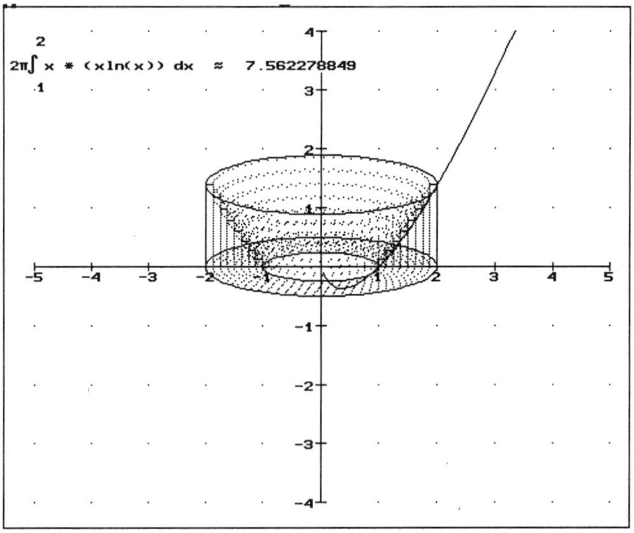

8.2.10 Parametric Mode: BestGrapher allows you to plot a curve that is expressed parametrically by functions x = f(t) and y = g(t) over the domain $a \le t \le b$. This makes it possible to plot several parametric curves and employ the zoom and trace features. The steps for defining a parametric graph are similar to those for defining a function.

Example: Graph the curve defined by the parametric equations

$$\mathbf{x = t + 1} \text{ and } \mathbf{y = 3 - t^2} \text{ for } -2 \le t \le 2.$$

Approximate the value of t that produces the largest y-coordinate.

- Enter parametric mode by selecting Parametric under the Mode menu.

Drag down to the Parametric command, and then release the Mouse botton.

- Enter the parametric equations: **x(t) = t + 1**

  y(t) = 3 – t^2

- Enter the domain $-2 \le t < 2$.

• Click the Plot button.

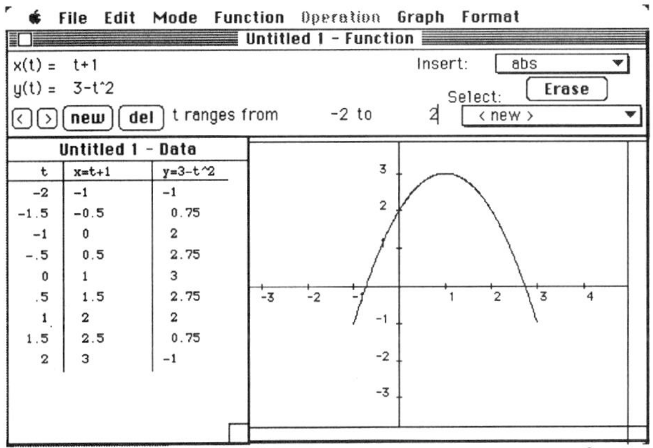

Graph of parametric equations x = t+1 and y = $3\text{-}t^2$

• Now select Trace under the Graph menu.

Note that as the cursor is moving along the curve the values of x, y and t are displayed along the bottom of the Plot window.

• Use the arrow keys to see that the approximate maximum is y = 3 at t = 0.

8.2.11 Polar Curves: If Polar in the Mode menu is checked, all subsequent graphs will be plotted in polar coordinates; that is, an angle coordinate ø and a radius coordinate r, (r, ø).

Example: Plot the polar equation **r = 3cos(2ø)** on the interval $0 \leq ø \leq \pi$.

• If Polar in the Mode menu is not checked, select Polar.

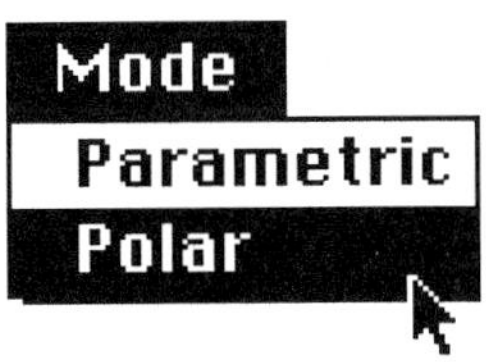

Drag down to the Polar command, and then release the mouse button.

• The Function window should contain default values of ø, $0 \leq ø \leq 2\pi$. If necessary enter the desired values for ø.

• Click the Plot button to graph the polar curve.

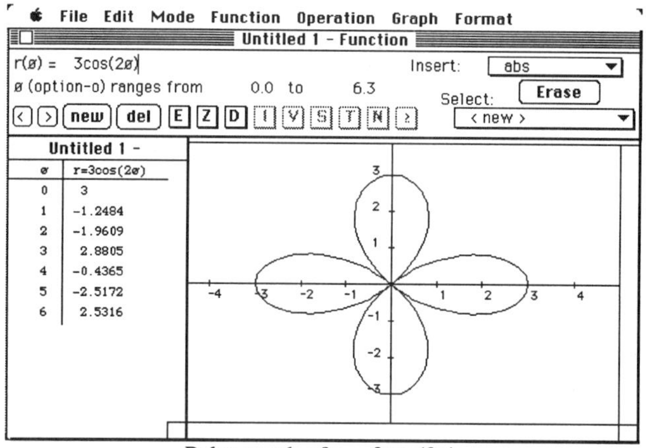

Polar graph of r = 3cos(2ø)

• Now the Trace or Zoom commands may be used to examine the curve.

8.2.12 Saving and Printing Your Work: While you are working in BestGrapher, functions may be saved to, or retrieved from the Select list; however, the Select list is lost when you exit the program. In order to make a list of functions available for a later session at the computer it is necessary to choose the Save command under the File menu; your work will be saved under the name Untitled-1. If you wish to give the file containing your work a different name, choose Save As... from the File menu and complete the list of choices you are given. In either case, BestGrapher will save your list of functions and the settings and display options that you have selected for each function.

BestGrapher allows you to print the contents of the Data window and the Plot window. Make sure that your printer is on and properly connected; click in the appropriate window to make it active and then choose Print under the File menu.

If you want to print the entire screen, make sure that the windows are arranged as you want them to appear; then use the screen dump command: Press Command-Shift-4.

8.3 Problem Solving with BestGrapher

This section contains a collection of problems from algebra, precalculus and calculus that demonstrate the problem solving capability of BestGrapher.

8.3.1 Domain and Range of a Function: A mathematical function is a rule, or set of instructions, that assigns an output to each input. The **domain** is the set of possible input values and the **range** is the set of possible output values. Here we will examine the domain and range of a function using BestGrapher.

Example: Plot the function defined by $\mathbf{f(x) = x + 3 + \sqrt{4 - x^2}}$
Use the graph to approximate the domain and range of f.

Solution:

- Enter the function as x + 3 + sqr(4 – x^2) and press the Plot button.

- Only a piece of the graph appears on the screen. This indicates that some points of the graph of f do not lie within the standard viewing rectangle. To expand the viewing rectangle, choose the Zoom out command from the Graph menu to obtain the graph below.

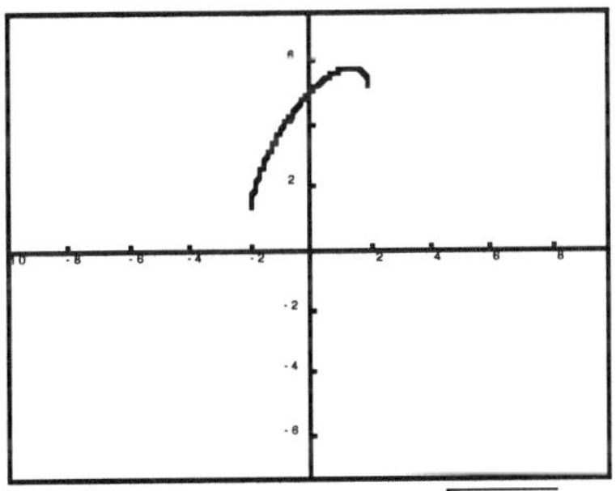

Graph of $f(x) = x + 3 + \sqrt{4 - x^2}$

- You can see from the graph that the domain is the set of real numbers x such that $-2 \leq x \leq 2$.

- The range appears to be between 1 and a value less than 6. To approximate the maximum range value of f, we trace along the graph to the maximum point and zoom in to get a closer and closer approximation. We estimate that the range of f is all values f(x) such that $1 \leq f(x) \leq 5.8284$.

Activities and Questions to Explore

1. Use BestGrapher to approximate the range of the following functions.

a) $f(x) = 5x - x^2 - 17$ b) $f(x) = x^3 + x - 15$

c) $f(x) = 3x^4 + 4x^3$ d) $f(x) = (x-2)\sqrt{3-x}$

8.3.2 Equation Solving: Remember that a zero (or root) of the function f refers to a number z in the domain of f such that f(z) = 0. Thus, finding function zeros means seeking the x coordinate of the points at which the graph intersects the x-axis. It is easy to convert any equation-solving problem into a zero-finding problem by simply moving everything nonzero to one side of the equation. For example, solving

$$\sin x = x^2 - x - 6$$

is equivalent to solving

$$\sin x - x^2 + x + 6 = 0.$$

which means seeking zeros for the function $f(x) = \sin x - x^2 + x + 6$. Thus the zero finding capabilities of BestGrapher can be employed to approximate the solutions of an equation.

Example: Use BestGrapher to approximate solutions of $\mathbf{x^2 = 3x + 1}$.

Solution: In standard form, this equation is $x^2 - 3x - 1 = 0$.
If we graph $f(x) = x^2 - 3x - 1$, then our task becomes equivalent to finding the zeros of the function f.

• Enter the function as x^2 – 3x – 1 and press the Plot button to obtain the graph below.

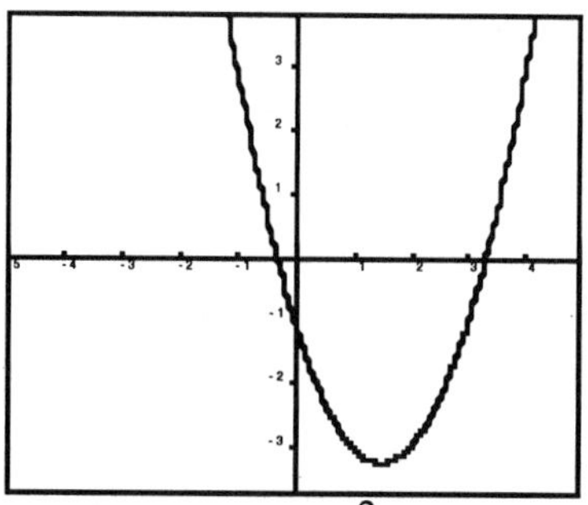

Graph of $f(x) = x^2 - 3x - 1$

- The function f has two zeros, one in the interval [-1, 0] and a second zero in the interval [3, 4]. Click on the Z tool and enter a = -1 and b = 0 into the dialog box in order to see that the approximate zero in the interval [-1, 0] is -0.30278

- Click on the Z tool and enter a = 3 and b = 4 into the dialog box in order to see that the approximate zero in the interval [3, 4] is 3.3028.

Thus the approximate solutions of the equation $x^2 = 3x + 1$ are {-0.30278, 3.3028} .

Activities and Questions to Explore

1. Use BestGrapher to approximate the solutions of the following inequalities. Give the answers in interval notation where the endpoints are accurate to two decimal places.

a) $2x - 1 < 4 - 3x$ b) $x^2 + x \leq 6$ c) $|3x - 8| \leq 4$

Technology Tip: BestGrapher employs the Bisection Method to approximate a continuous functions zeros. Briefly, given an initial interval [a,b], the program checks to see if f(a) and f(b) are opposite in sign. If so, the Intermediate Value Theorem guarantees that the continuous function must have a zero in [a,b]. The midpoint m = (a+b)/2 is calculated, and f(m) is compared to f(a) and f(b). If m happens to be a zero, the program displays this information; otherwise, by comparing signs, it learns which half of [a,b] contains the zero to be located. Now the mid-value check is repeated, using the new interval [a,m] or [m,b]. In this way smaller and smaller intervals are defined that contain a zero of f. This iteration process continues until an interval of suitable short length is found or the last midpoint is a zero. Unhappily, the Bisection Method will not always find a function zero. It requires that a function change sign at the zero sought. Thus it will not work with a function like $f(x) = (x - \sqrt{2})^2$.

8.3.3 Graphing Conic Sections: To graph an equation using BestGrapher, you must first write the equation as one or more functions. For example, to graph the circle $x^2 + y^2 = 9$ you can write the upper part of the circle as

$$f(x) = \sqrt{9 - x^2}$$

and the lower half of the circle as

$$f(x) = -\sqrt{9 - x^2}.$$

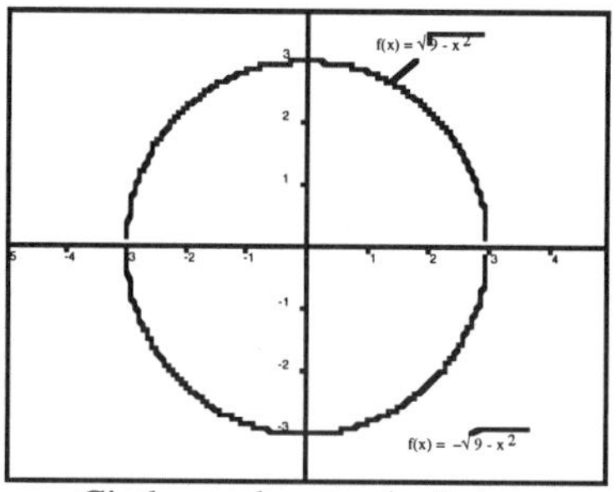

Circle graph - standard view

Example: Graph the parabola $\mathbf{y^2 = x + 4}$ and show that the normal lines to the parabola at the points (-3, 1) and (-3, -1) intersect on the axis of the parabola.

Solution: To graph the parabola $y^2 = x + 4$, we plot two functions $f(x) = \sqrt{4 + x}$ and $f(x) = -\sqrt{4 + x}$ on the same axes.

- Enter the upper half of the parabola as sqr(4 + x) and click the Plot button.
- Click the N button and enter the value -3 in the dialog box. Click the OK button to draw the normal line at the point (-3, 1) on the upper half of the parabola.
- Click the new button to clear the function $f(x) = \sqrt{4 + x}$ from the text box.
- Enter the lower half of the parabola as –sqr(4+x) and click the Plot button.
- Click the N button and enter the value -3 in the dialog box. Click the OK button to draw the normal line at the point (-3, -1) on the lower half of the parabola.

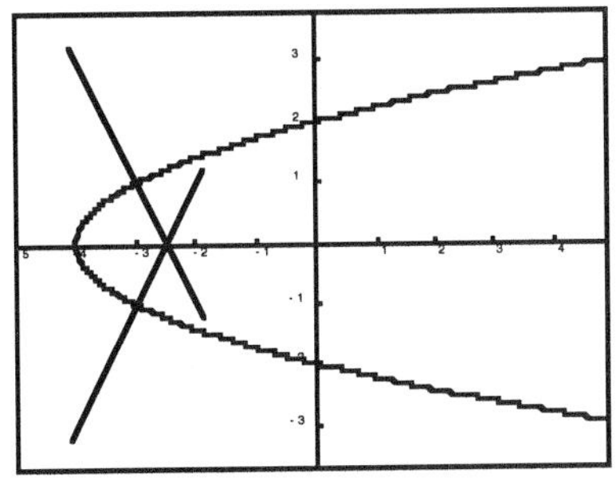

Intersection of normal lines

Activities and Questions to Explore

1. Use BestGrapher to plot and identify the following conic sections.

a) $x^2 + y^2 = 16$ b) $\frac{x^2}{9} + \frac{y^2}{16} = 1$ c) $\frac{x^2}{4} - \frac{y^2}{9} = 1$

8.3.4 Maximum and Minimum Values: Finding a maximum or minimum value is often an important part of problem solving. For example, manufacturers want to maximize their profits, contractors want to minimize their costs, and a physician would like to select the smallest dosage of a drug that will cure a disease. Determining the maximum or minimum value of some quantity can often be reduced to finding the largest and smallest value of a function on some interval.

Example: A hiker finds herself in a forest 2 miles from a straight road. She wants to walk to her car which is parked 10 miles down the road. If she can walk 4 mph along the road, but only 3 mph through the forest, toward what point on the road should she walk in order to reach her car in the least time?

Solution: From the figure, the distance to the point P on the road is $\sqrt{x^2 + 4}$ and the distance from P to the car is $10 - x$.

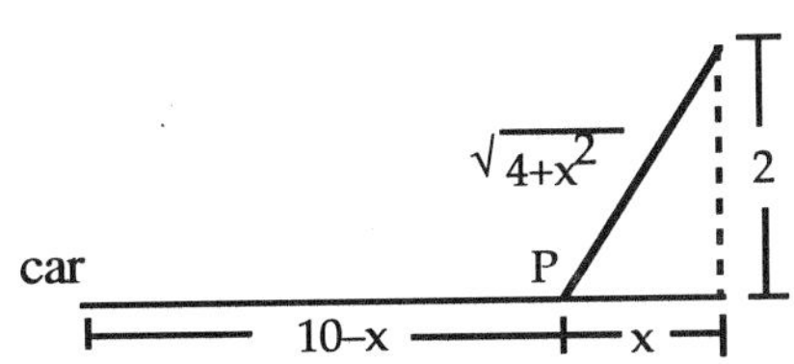

Since time = distance/rate, the total time f(x) to reach the car is

$$f(x) = \frac{\sqrt{4+x^2}}{3} + \frac{(10 - x)}{4} \quad \text{with } 0 \le x \le 10.$$

- Enter the function f as sqr(4+x^2)/3 + (10 – x)/4.
- Choose Preferences under the Graph menu and set the horizontal dimension of the viewing rectangle so that $-2 \le x \le 12$; click the Square button to produce a square viewing rectangle.
- Click the Plot button and see the following graph.

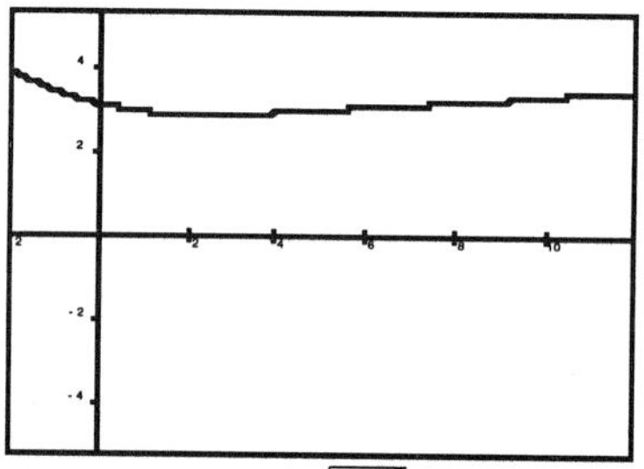

Graph of $f(x) = \frac{\sqrt{4+x^2}}{3} + \frac{(10-x)}{4}$

- To locate the minimum value we first graph the derivative of f(x) by clicking the [D] tool. Then to approximate the zero of the derivative that corresponds to the minimum value on the graph of f, click the [Z] tool and find that the approximate minimum time is 2.941 hours at x = 2.268 miles.

Activities and Questions to Explore

1. Find the maximum and minimum values of the function on the given interval.

   a) $f(x) = x - x^3$ on [0, 1]. b) $f(x) = 3x - x^2$ on [0, 3].

2. A weight oscillates on a spring; its height is given by $f(x) = \sin x + \cos x + 1$.

   a) What are the highest and lowest points?

   b) How large an interval do you need to use in order to determine the largest and smallest points?

*8.3.5 **Area of a Region Between Two Curves*** The definite integral has a wide variety of applications. For example, integrals can be used to measure the area between two curves.

Example: Approximate the area of the region R bounded above by the graph of $\mathbf{f(x) = 2 \sin x}$ and and below by the graph of $\mathbf{g(x) = x^2}$.

Solution: The picture below shows the region we are interested in.

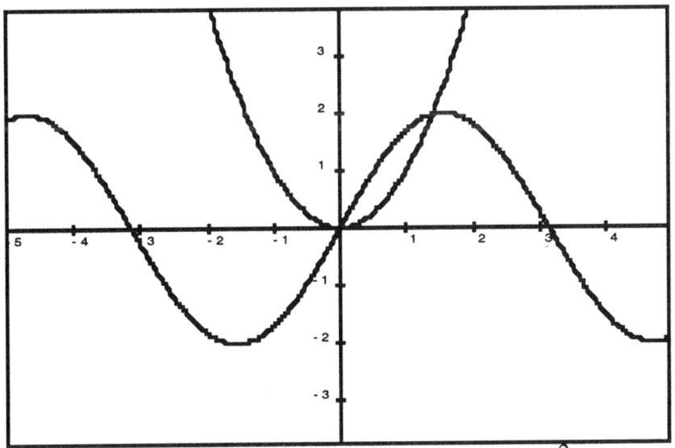

Graphs of $f(x) = 2 \sin x$ and $g(x) = x^2$

In this region, $2 \sin x \geq x^2$, so that Area = $\int_a^b (2 \sin x - x^2)\, dx$ where a and b are the x-values of the points of intersection of the curves. The graph of $y = 2 \sin x - x^2$ below indicates that a = 0 and b is a point to the right of the origin in the interval [1, 2].

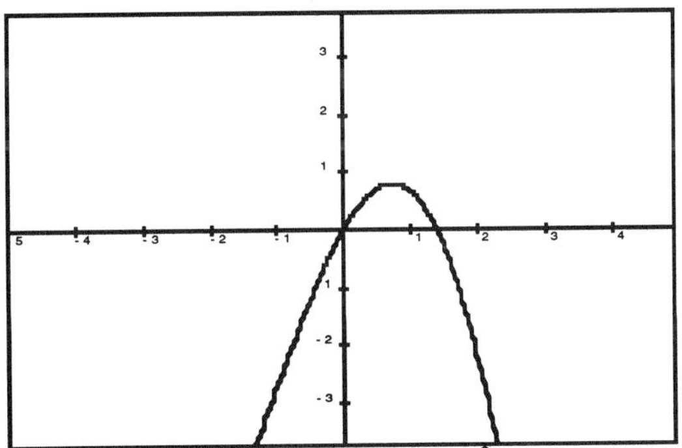

Graph of $y = 2 \sin x - x^2$

To estimate b we apply the zero finding capability of BestGrapher to the function $y = 2 \sin x - x^2$. You should verify that b = 1.4044

To approximate the integral $\int_{0}^{1.4044} (2\sin x - x^2)\, dx$

click the [I] tool and on the interval [0, 1.4044], use Simpson's rule with 20 subdivisions to obtain the approximate area = 0.74542

Note that the area between curves may also be fonund by integrating each function separately and taking the difference of the results, rather than integrating the difference function.

Activities and Questions to Explore

In Exercises 1–2, sketch the region bounded by the graphs of the given functions and find the area of the region.

1. $f(x) = x^2 + 2x + 1$ and $g(x) = 2x + 5$.

2. $f(x) = \arctan x$ and $g(x) = x^2 - 1$.

8.3.6 Simulating the Motion of a Particle: Combining parametric mode and the BestGrapher trace feature, it is possible to simulate the linear motion of a particle.

Example: Let the position (x-coordinate) of a moving particle on the line $y = 1$ be given by

$$\mathbf{x(t) = t^2 - 2t} \quad \text{for} \quad 0 \le t \le 3.$$

Using Parametric mode in BestGrapher, simulate the motion of the particle.

Solution: • Choose parametric mode by selecting Parametric under the Mode menu.

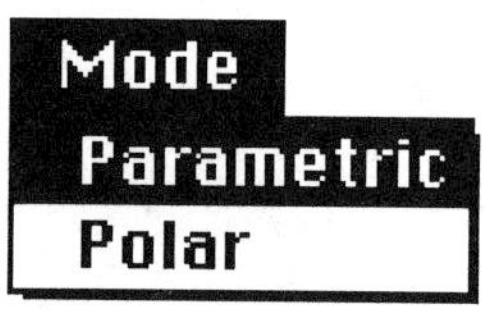

Drag down to the Parametric command, and then release the Mouse botton.

• Enter the parametric equations: $\mathbf{x(t) = t^2 - 2t}$

$\mathbf{y(t) = 1}$

- Enter the domain $0 \leq t \leq 3$
- Click the Plot button.

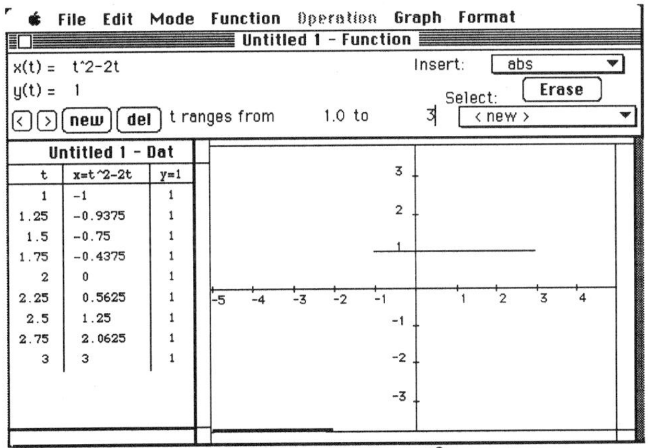

Graphs of parametric equations $x = t^2 - 2t$ and $y = 1$

- Choose Trace under the Function menu and use the arrow keys to position the cursor at the point where $t = 0$.
- Now hold down the right arrow key and watch the motion of the particle.

Activities and Questions to Explore

1. What is the coordinate of the particle at t = 0, 1, 2, and 3?
2. What is the total distance traveled by the particle for t = 0 to t = 3?
3. If the parameter t represents time in seconds, what is the average speed of the particle?
4. At what points and at what time is the particle at rest? moving to the right?
5. Does it appear that the particle is moving at a constant speed?

8.4 BestGrapher Menus and Shortcuts

8.4.1 Menus: Like menus in a restaurant, BestGrapher menus let you choose among the different actions that the program can perform.

The **FILE Menu -** allows you to create a **New** file; **Open**, **Close** or **Save** a file; **Print** the active window or **Quit** the program.

The **EDIT Menu -** allows you to **Copy** the contents of the Plot window to the clipboard or **Cut, Copy** and **Paste** in the Function and Data window.

The **MODE Menu** - allows you to select **Parametric** or **Polar** mode.

The **FUNCTION Menu -** allows you to select the **Next** or **Previous** function in the list of previously saved functions; save a **New** Function or **Delete** a function from the list of functions; **Trace** along a curve,showing the x- and y-coordinates of the cursor location.

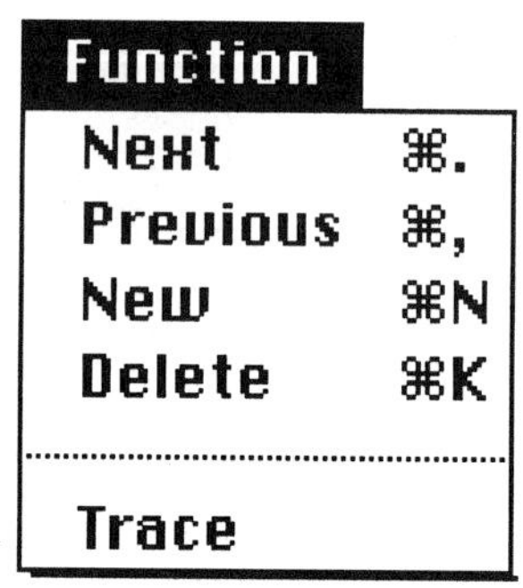

The **OPERATION Menu-** The nine items in this menu are tasks that will be performed on the last function graphed.

•Evaluate: Evaluates a function at an argument you specify.

•Find Zero: Searches for a function zero on an interval you supply.

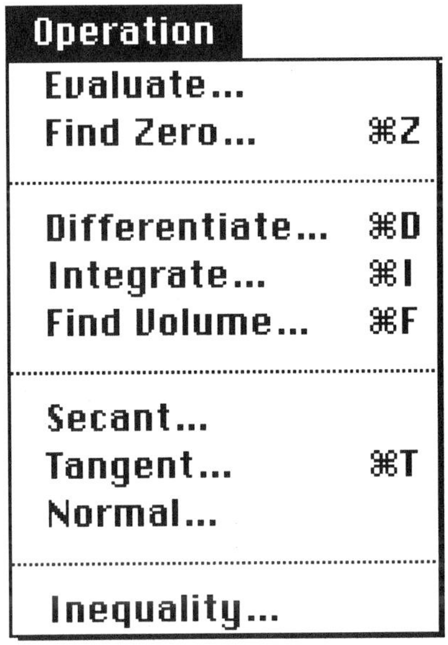

•Differentiate: Displays the graph and derivative rule of the current function.

•Integrate: Approximates the definite integral of the current function on a specified interval.

•Find Volume: Rotates a piece of a function graph around a specified line.

•Secant: Draws a secant to a curve.

•Tangent: Draws a tangent to a curve.

•Normal: Draws a normal line to a function graph.

•Inequality: Shades the region above or below a function graph.

The **GRAPH Menu** -

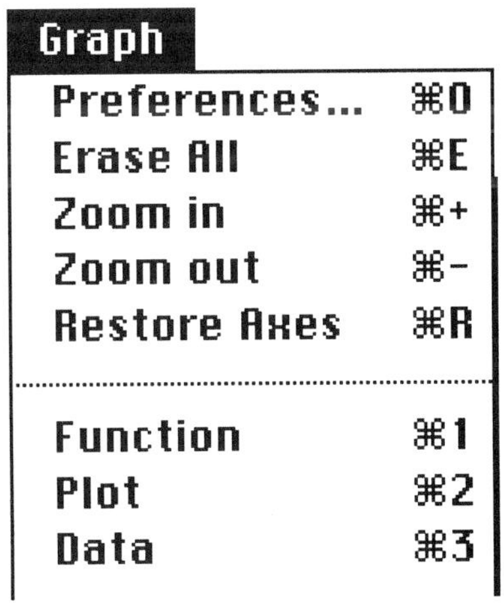

•Preferences: Brings up a dialog box that allows the dimensions of the viewing rectangle to be changed and the color of the axes or the plotting speed to be modified.

•Erase All: Clears the Plot and Data window.

•Zoom in(out): allows you to zoom in or out on the curves in the Plot window.

•Restore Axes: Redefines the default viewing rectangle, $-5 \leq x \leq 5$ and $-3.8 \leq y \leq 3.8$.

•Function(Plot or Data) will activate the chosen window.

The **FORMAT Menu** - Displays submenus for changing the color and thickness of the current function graph.

8.4.2 Shortcuts: Many of the menu commands in BestGrapher have keyboard equivalents listed at the right of the menu. In addition, BestGrapher offers some other shortcuts to facilitate operations and tasks.

The following list of keyboard shortcuts is divided into four subsections.

Category	Action	Shortcut
Function plotting	To pause or resume initial plotting of a function	pause/F15 or tab during function plotting
	To toggle faster plotting and the above pausing option on/off	⌘ tab before function plotting
	To cancel initial plotting of a function	⌘ period during function plotting
File maintenance	To close an entire file, instead of only the current window	option close
Function List maintenance	To plot the current function and add a new function	option plot
	To clear the only defined function	Delete menu item or Del button
Trace	To move left (right) along curve by current step size	← (→)
	To decrease (increase) step size	↓ (↑)
	To change step size to an absolute value	1 - 9
	To jump to left-most point of curve within **Plot window**	home
	To jump to right-most point of curve within **Plot window**	end
	To exit trace	esc
	To move continuously along curve	mouse button

Answers: The following are answers to the Activities and Questions to Explore in Section 7.3.

7.3.1	1. a) $(-\infty, -10.75)$	b) $(-\infty, \infty)$	c) $[-1, \infty)$	d) $(-\infty, 0.3849)$
7.3.2	1. a) $(-\infty, 1)$	b) $(-3, 2)$	c) $[1.33, 4]$	
7.3.3	1. a) circle	b) ellipse	c) hyperbola	
7.3.4	1. a) max = 0.3849, min = 0		b) max = 2.25, min = 0	
	2. a) largest = 2.4142, smallest = –0.4142			b) (0, 6.28)
7.3.5	1. 10.3333			
	2. 1.6335			
7.3.6	1. $x(0) = 0$, $x(1) = -1$, $x(2) = 0$, $x(3) = 3$;			
	2. 2 units			
	3. average speed = distance/time = 5/3 units per second			
	4. At rest at $t = 1$; moving to the right when $1 < t < 3$.			
	5. Particle is not moving at a constant rate..			

Answers: The following are answers to the Activities and Questions to Explore in Section 8.3.

8.3.1	1. a) $(-\infty, -10.75)$	b) $(-\infty, \infty)$	c) $[-1, \infty)$	d) $(-\infty, 0.3849x)$
8.3.2	1. a) $(-\infty, 1)$	b) $(-3, 2)$	c) $(1.33, 4)$	
8.3.3	1. a) circle	b) ellipse	c) hyperbola	
8.3.4	1. a) max = 0.3849, min = 0		b) max = 2.25, min = 0	
	2. a) largest = 2.4142, smallest = −0.4142		b) (0, 6.28)	
8.3.5	1. 10.3333			
	2. 1.6335			
8.3.6	1. $x(0) = 0$, $x(1) = -1$, $x(2) = 0$, $x(3) = 3$			
	2. 2 units			
	3. average speed = distance/time = 5/3 units per second			
	4. At rest at $t = 1$; moving to the right when $1 < t < 3$.			
	5. Particle is not moving at a constant rate.			